Effective Physical Security
Third Edition

Lawrence J. Fennelly, Editor
Crime Prevention Specialist

ELSEVIER
BUTTERWORTH
HEINEMANN

AMSTERDAM • BOSTON • HEIDELBERG • LONDON
NEW YORK • OXFORD • PARIS • SAN DIEGO
SAN FRANCISCO • SINGAPORE • SYDNEY • TOKYO

Elsevier Butterworth–Heinemann
200 Wheeler Road, Burlington, MA 01803, USA
Linacre House, Jordan Hill, Oxford OX2 8DP, UK

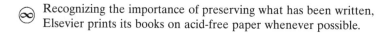 Recognizing the importance of preserving what has been written,
Elsevier prints its books on acid-free paper whenever possible.

Library of Congress Cataloging-in-Publication Data
Application submitted.

British Library Cataloguing-in-Publication Data
A catalogue record for this book is available from the British
Library.

ISBN: 0-7506-7767-8

For information on all Butterworth–Heinemann publications
visit our website at www.bh.com

05 06 07 08 09 10 9 8 7 6 5 4 3 2

Printed in the United States of America

*To those who are very dear in my life: My wife, Annmarie, and our four
children, Alison, Larry, Bill, and Stephen, and their spouses. Plus our very
beautiful grandchildren, William and Margaret Boyce; Claire, Megan and Brian
(twins) Fennelly; Abigail and Emma Fennelly; and Lawrence J. Fennelly V.*

Contents

Foreword

When Larry Fennelly started out on the Harvard University Police Department more than thirty years ago (now retired), he knew nothing about crime prevention per se and knew less about physical and procedural security and assets protection until he attended the National Crime Prevention Institute at the University of Louisville in Kentucky. What were his goals? First to be a good cop, a superior officer, and to protect the assets of the university to which he had been assigned.

But he was also a visionary. He was able to identify the state of the art of loss prevention in the early 1980s and edited his first book that is now in its fourth edition. Since the *Handbook of Loss Prevention and Crime Prevention*, he has written/edited 25 books read by thousands and internationally accepted.

In those intervening years of change and development he learned a lot. He progressed on the job and became a superior officer, a respected member in and out of his own campus enforcement environment, a proud parent and grandparent, and thankfully for all of us who have read his writings, a respected crime prevention practitioner. Much of what he learned and experienced over these past years is contained in his books.

This is not a conventional security book as much of his practical personal experiences have influence over the three sections found within this effort. He breaks *Effective Physical Security, Third Edition*, down into design, equipment, and operations. Contained in each section are the necessary specifics to insure that we practitioners who have a need can reference the particular and immediate dilemma and come up with a practical amount of knowledge to solve this moment's crisis.

Overall this book contains the knowledge and experience of more than a dozen practitioners who have dozens of years of experience in the field. This book, as well as others, will service as one of the stages of development for your assets protection program.

Since September 11, 2001, the world has changed, security demands have also changed. The level of security that we had on September 10, 2001, is no longer acceptable. You must advance with the times, think out of the box, and become a visionary as well. This text and others will assist you.

Louis A. Tyska, CPP

Chapter 1

The Influence of Physical Design*

NATIONAL CRIME PREVENTION
INSTITUTE (NCPI)

The relationship between physical design and informal social control of crime is a new idea only in the sense of its systematic application to the modern urban scene. Prior to the development of the modern city, most societies took some precautions to relate security in the physical environment to a responsibility for security actions by the inhabitants themselves.

In the rush of modern urban development, however, economic and political priorities seem to have far outweighed security priorities, with the result that many urban settings now seem deliberately designed to discourage informal social control. No colonial community would have done so, even when stockades were no longer needed for defense against Indians. New England towns continued to be constructed so that the homes and stores formed a hollow square around a central Common where social activities could take place and where livestock could be kept in relative security. In this kind of environment, everyone knew everyone else's business. While this meant less personal privacy than the modern city dweller may enjoy, it also meant a high degree of shared responsibility for controlling undesirable behavior and unwanted intrusion.

Only recently have students of modern urban society begun again to take serious note of the relationship between physical design and informal social control. Jane Jacobs first applied the concept to modern cities in 1961. In her book, *The Death and Life of Great American Cities*,[1] she theorized that multiple land uses along residential streets provided

an interaction between the physical design and the users (pedestrians and residents), which promoted natural and informal surveillance and, therefore, increased the safety of the streets.

Lee Rainwater, in an evaluation of a public housing project in St. Louis (1966), discussed the effect of physical design on the attitudes of public housing residents, pointing out that inappropriate architectural design was directly related to antisocial behavior.[2]

Elizabeth Wood, writing in 1961, suggested that current design patterns in public housing projects appeared to discourage informal social relationships and gatherings, thereby preventing the development of social interactions through which residents could create informal social controls and self-policing.[3]

Schlomo Angel, in 1968, found that variations in the level of pedestrian and vehicular traffic could either encourage or discourage crimes.[4] Too few users provided enough potential victims, but not enough potential witnesses.

Gerald Leudtke and E. Lystad found, as the result of studies in Detroit, that

> many of the features of urban form and structure . . . could tend to facilitate or decrease the probability of crime. Such physical features include the condition and maintenance of buildings, streets, and alleys; evidence of recent construction; mixtures of land use; rates of pedestrian traffic and pedestrian accumulation within various land uses; location of structures on an urban grid pattern; and distance to adjacent structures. Other examples are types of parking facilities; visibility into structures from roads, sidewalks and adjoining buildings; concealment by trees, shrubs, parked automobiles, fences, signs, and advertising; the visibility of entrance

*National Crime Prevention Institute (NCPI), *Understanding Crime Prevention*, pp. 120–131, Butterworth Heinemann, 2001

1

points; building setbacks; and, the number and arrangement of entrance points in a building.[5]

In 1969, Oscar Newman and George Rand[6] developed a theory of territoriality (now referred to as defensible space), which held that proper physical design of housing encourages residents to extend their social control from their homes and apartments out into the surrounding common areas. In this way, they change what previously had been perceived as semipublic or public territory into private territory. Upgrading the common areas in this way results in increased social control and an interaction between physical environment and its users that reduces crime.

As Newman himself defines it,

Defensible space is a surrogate term for the range of mechanisms—real and symbolic barriers, strongly defined areas of influence, improved opportunities for surveillance—that combine to bring an environment under the control of its residents. A defensible space is a living residential environment that can be employed by inhabitants for the enhancement of their lives, while providing security for their families, neighbors, and friends. The public areas of a multifamily residential environment devoid of defensible space can make the act of going from street to apartment equivalent to running the gauntlet. The fear and uncertainty generated by living in such an environment can slowly eat away and eventually destroy the security and sanctity of the apartment unit itself. On the other hand, by grouping dwelling units to reinforce association of mutual benefit, by delineating paths of movement, by defining areas of activity for particular users through their juxtaposition with internal living areas, and by providing for natural opportunities for visual surveillance, architects can create a clear understanding of the function of a space, who its users are and ought to be. This, in turn, can lead residents of all income levels to adopt extremely potent territorial attitudes and policing measures, which act as a strong deterrent to potential criminals.[7]

A study by Reppetto,[8] in Boston indicated the need to expand the crime prevention through environmental design (CPTED) process to include whole neighborhoods and provide for comprehensive data collection efforts, which would both define the nature of crime patterns and suggest appropriate countermeasures.

Reppetto was also able to show that closely-knit communities do tend to protect their members through informal social controls. This finding was further emphasized by John Conklin in *The Impact of Crime:*

A tightly knit community can minimize the problem of street crime. However, informal social control also poses a threat to the diversity of behavior that exists in a pluralistic society, even though it may curb violent crime. Still, street crime would decline if interaction among the residents of a community were more frequent, and if social bonds were stronger. A sense of responsibility for other citizens and for the community as a whole would increase individuals' willingness to report crime to the police and the likelihood of their intervention in a crime in progress. Greater willingness of community residents to report crime to the police might also obviate the need for civilian police patrols. More interaction in public places and human traffic on the sidewalks would increase surveillance of the places where people now fear to go. More intense social ties would reinforce surveillance with a willingness to take action against offenders.[9]

C. Ray Jeffrey, in his classic theoretical work *Crime Prevention Through Environmental Design* (1971),[10] written before Jeffrey became aware of the works of Newman and others, proposed a three-fold strategy involving not only physical design, but also increased citizen participation and the more effective use of police forces. He contended that the way to prevent crime is to design the total environment in such a manner that the opportunity for crime is reduced or eliminated.

Jeffrey contends that both the physical and social characteristics of an urban area affect crime patterns. Better physical planning is a key to unlocking the potential for improved physical security and the potential for development of informal social control. He also argues for high levels of precision in the analytical stages that precede physical planning for crime reduction.

One of the major methodological defects in ecological studies of crime rates has been the use of large units and census tract data as a basis for analysis. The usual units are rural–urban, intricacy, intercity, regional, and national differences . . . Such an approach is much too gross for finding the physical features associated with different types of crimes.

We must look at the physical environment in terms of each building, or each room of the building, or each floor of the building. Fine-grain resolution is required in place of the usual large-scale photographs . . . Whenever crime rates are surveyed at a micro level of analysis, it is revealed that a small area of the city is responsible for a majority of the crimes. This fact is glossed over by gross statistical correlation analysis of census tract data, which ignore house-by-house or block-by-block variations in crime rates. For purposes of crime prevention we need data that will tell us what aspects of the urban environment are responsible for crime, such as the concentration of homicide or robbery in a very small section of the city.[11]

Defensible Space

Oscar Newman and others have explored and further defined the defensible space concept in recent years through design studies and experiments involving existing and new public housing projects. The following summary of defensible space techniques will give the practitioner an initial understanding of this important application of physical design to the urban residential environment.

Design for defensible space involves attempts to strengthen two basic kinds of social behavior called *territoriality* and *natural surveillance.*

Territoriality

The classic example of territoriality is "a man's home is his castle" tradition of the American single-family home and its surroundings. In this tradition, the family lays claim to its own territory and acts to protect it. This image of the home as a castle reinforces itself "by the very act of its position on an integral piece of land buffered from neighbors and the public street by intervening grounds."[12]

As the urban setting has grown, the single family home has become, to developers, an economic liability. Family housing has moved into the row house (townhouse), apartment complex, high-rise apartment structure, and massive public housing project. Whatever the benefits of this transition, the idea of territoriality has been largely lost in the process. The result is that "most families living in an apartment building experience the space outside their apartment unit as distinctly public; in effect, they relegate responsibility for all activity outside the immediate confines of their apartment to the public authorities."[13]

As residents are forced by the physical design of their surroundings to abandon claim to any part of the outside world, the hallways, stairways, lobbies, grounds, parking lots, and streets become a kind of no-man's land in which criminals can operate almost at will. Public and private law enforcement agencies (formal controls) attempt to take up the slack, but without the essential informal social control that a well-developed social sense of territoriality brings, law enforcement can do little to reduce crime.

Natural Surveillance

The increased presence of human observers, which territoriality brings, can lead to higher levels of natural surveillance in all areas of residential space. However, the simple presence of increased numbers of potential observers is not enough, because natural surveillance, to be effective, must include an action component. The probability that an observer will act to report an observed crime or intervene in it depends on:

- The degree to which the observer feels that his personal or property rights are violated by the observed act;
- The extent to which the observer is able to identify with the victim or property under attack; and
- The level of the observer's belief that his action can help, on the one hand, and not subject him to reprisals on the other.

Obviously, the probability for both observation and action is greatly improved by physical conditions, which create the highest possible levels of visibility.

Design Guidelines

Defensible space offers a series of architectural guidelines, which can be used in the design of new urban residential complexes to promote both the residential group's territorial claim to its surroundings and its ability to conduct natural surveillance.[14]

- **Site design** can stress the clustering of small numbers of residential units around private hallways, courtyards, and recreation areas. In these restricted zones, children can play, adults can relax, and strangers can easily be identified and questioned. Such private spaces can be created by internal and external building walls and access arrangements, and by the use of perceptual barriers such as low fences, shrubbery, and other boundary markers.
- **Site interrelationships design** can be used to create semiprivate connecting and common spaces between and among the private family clusters. Walkways, vehicle access ways, parking areas, recreational facilities, lobbies, and laundry and shopping areas can be designed so that each cluster relates to them much like each resident of a cluster relates to his common private space. Physical design can be used to further extend the sense of territoriality and the possibility for informal social control.
- **Street design** and design of other public spaces can be engineered to make these spaces into semipublic extensions of the residential clusters

and their connectors. Closing streets to through traffic, installing benches and play areas near the streets, providing adequate lighting, and placing perceptual barriers to indicate the semipublic nature of the area can help to define these spaces as part of the shared residential group territory.

- **Surveillance-specific design** can be used in each of the above design areas to increase general visibility by providing adequate lighting, by reducing or eliminating physical barriers to visibility, and by the visibility-promoting location of key areas (for example, entrances, lobbies, elevator waiting areas, recreational and parking areas) so as to be directly visible from as many points of view as possible.

Modifying Existing Physical Design

Cost limitations prevent substantial reconstruction of most existing urban residential facilities. However, a number of relatively low-cost techniques can be used to modify existing facilities so as to promote territoriality and natural surveillance. These include:

- Installing adequate security devices (locks, doors, and windows) in each residential unit;
- Dividing common lawn areas (front or back) into private yards and patios through the use of shrubbery, low fences, and other perceptual barriers;
- Improving the attractiveness and semiprivacy of pathways and other common outside areas by use of decorative paving and lighting: installing benches and other seating arrangements at strategic intervals, careful landscaping, and tying play areas, parking and vehicle access ways to the overall design;
- Reducing the number of public access points and providing the remaining points with good lighting, visibility, and security; and
- Establishing audio and video surveillance (monitored by residents or by security staff) in strategic internal areas.

It should be emphasized, in summary, that creating defensible space is not the same as creating a hardened security system (as might be found, for example, in a high-rise luxury apartment). In fact, it is almost the opposite, defensible space operates on the premise that the living environment must be opened up and used by residents and others, not closed in. It is only in the open, used environment that people can be stimulated to establish the self-policing condition, which is informal social control. In this open living environment, opportunities for

crime may continue to exist, but the probability for criminal activity is reduced.

It should also be emphasized that the physical design component of defensible space should always be accompanied by efforts to develop and sustain active citizen participation and by strategies for improved interaction between citizens and law enforcement agencies.

Crime Prevention through Environmental Design

Crime prevention through environmental design (CPTED), is still a rapidly growing field of study and experimentation. CPTED attempts to apply physical design, citizen participation, and law enforcement strategies in a comprehensive, planned way to entire neighborhoods and major urban districts, as well as to specific urban subsystems, such as, public schools and transportation systems.

Cautions

Before summarizing the CPTED approach, we would suggest that the practitioner view CPTED developments with a healthy skepticism, at least for the present. There are several reasons why a sense of caution is in order:

- Although the effectiveness of some of the specific techniques used in CPTED experiments can be verified, the overall effectiveness of the CPTED approach has yet to be conclusively demonstrated.
- There is some disagreement among crime prevention theorists as to the correctness of the assumptions on which current CPTED programs are based.
- The magnitude of the typical CPTED project may be well beyond the practitioner's current ability to plan, implement, and manage.
- The cost of a typical CPTED project can represent a major financial investment, and unless the investment can be justified on a research and demonstration basis, there is no guarantee that it will be cost effective.

Despite these cautions, it is useful for the practitioner to be aware of the principles and current applications of the CPTED concept so that he or she can watch its developments and make appropriate use of the knowledge that it may produce.

Recent Projects

In a project combining the best of current community policing techniques with the principles of CPTED the city of Manchester, New Hampshire, proved the value of this integrated approach. In Manchester, the police department formed partnerships with community organizations and provided appropriate crime prevention training, including CPTED to all of the officers assigned to the project areas. By combining the concepts of community policing with the application of CPTED, and other related crime prevention strategies, the community realized remarkable reductions in several crime categories. The area encompasses three areas of public housing in which CPTED principles were applied. The changes in community perceptions about crime were measured through surveys and the crime statistics were updated frequently to give the police department the best possible data. In this Enterprise Community area drug activity was reduced 57%, robbery fell 54%, burglary was reduced 52%, and police calls for service dropped 20%. Additionally, the perceptions of the citizens of the area were markedly improved. This example demonstrates the levels of success possible when sound policing, crime prevention, and the concepts of CPTED are combined in the correct proportions. As a result of these levels of success the project was recognized by the Department of Housing and Urban Development (HUD) through the awarding of the John J. Gunther Award. This award recognizes the best practices and was awarded in this instance in the category of Suitable Living Environment.[15]

Territorial Defense Strategies

Territorial defense strategies emphasize prevention of property-related crimes such as breaking and entering, auto theft, and household larceny. Within this group there are five related strategy areas: land use planning, building grounds security, building perimeter security, building interior security, and construction standards.

- **Land use planning strategies** involve planning activities aimed at avoiding land use mixtures that have a negative impact on neighborhood security, through zoning ordinances and development plan reviews.
- **Building grounds security strategies** provide the first line of defense against unauthorized entry of sites and offer social control mechanisms to prevent dangerous and destructive behavior of visitors. The emphasis is on the access control and surveillance aspects of architectural design. The target environment might be a residential street, the side of a housing complex, or alleyways behind or between business establishments.
- **Building perimeter security strategies** provide a second line of defense for protecting site occupants and property by preventing unauthorized entries of buildings. They involve physical barriers, surveillance and intrusion detection systems, and social control mechanisms.
- **Building interior security strategies** provide the third line of defense for protecting site occupants and property by preventing unauthorized access to interior spaces and valuables through physical barriers, surveillance and intrusion detection systems, and social control mechanisms.
- **Construction standards strategies** involve building security codes that require construction techniques and materials that tend to reduce crime and safety hazards. These strategies deal both with code adoption and code enforcement.

Personal Defense Strategies

The second basic strategic approach focuses on the prevention of violent or street crimes such as robbery, assault, and rape, and the reduction of fear associated with these crimes. Specific strategies included safe-streets-for-people, transportation, cash-off-the-streets, and citizen intervention.

- **Safe-streets-for-people strategies** involve planning principles derived primarily from the CPTED concepts of surveillance and activity support. Surveillance operates to discourage potential offenders because of the apparent risk of being seen and can be improved through various design modifications of physical elements of the street environment (e.g., lighting, fencing, and landscaping). Pedestrian traffic areas can be channeled to increase their use and the number of observers through such measures as creating malls, eliminating onstreet parking, and providing centralized parking areas.
- **Transportation strategies** are aimed at reducing exposure to crime by improving public transportation. For example, transit waiting stations (bus, trolley) can be located near areas of safe activity and good surveillance, or the distance between stations can be reduced, which improves accessibility to specific residences, business establishments, and other traffic generating points.

- **Cash-off-the-streets strategies** reduce incentives for crime by urging people not to carry unnecessary cash and provide commercial services that minimize the need to carry cash.
- **Citizen intervention**, unlike the three previous activities, consists of strategies aimed at organizing and mobilizing residents to adopt proprietary interests and assume responsibility for the maintenance of security.

Law Enforcement Strategies

The third general approach involves police functions that support community-based prevention activities. There are two activities: police patrol and citizen/police support.

- **Police patrol strategies** focus on ways in which police deployment procedures can improve their efficiency and effectiveness in responding to calls and apprehending offenders.
- **Citizen/police support strategies** consist of police operational support activities that improve citizen/police relations and encourage citizens to cooperate with the police in preventing and reporting incidents.

Confidence Restoration Strategies

This fourth general strategy for commercial and residential environments involves activities that are aimed primarily at mobilizing neighborhood interest and support to implement needed CPTED changes. Without such interest and support, it is unlikely that programs of sufficient magnitude could possibly be successful, particularly in many high-crime-rate neighborhoods where people have lost hope. There are two specific strategy areas: investor confidence and neighborhood identities.

- **Investor confidence strategies** promote economic investment and, therefore, social and economic vitality.
- **Neighborhood identity strategies** build community pride and foster social cohesion.

Most of these specific strategies are discussed in this and other chapters (some under different names). As a whole, this list of strategies is well organized and provides a good framework with which to view the possible interaction of a variety of crime prevention efforts.

Demonstrations

To see how these strategies were applied, let us look briefly at the major changes described in the American Architecture Foundation's presentation, *Back from the Brink, Saving America's Cities by Design*.[16] This provides examples of CPTED applications, with very little mention of crime, as applied in Portland, Oregon, and some other locales. The principles applied are sound, workable redesign strategies, which accomplish the goals of CPTED, without over-reliance on their direct crime prevention intent. Indeed, they are not presented as crime prevention, but redevelopment efforts, which consider the quality of life above most other considerations.

The CPTED applications in the featured cities achieve the following:

- Reduce opportunities for crime and fear of crime by making streets and open areas more easily observable, and by increasing activity in the neighborhood;
- Provide ways in which neighborhood residents, business people, and police can work together more effectively to reduce opportunities and incentives for crime;
- Increase neighborhood identity, investor confidence, and social cohesion;
- Provide public information programs that help business people and residents protect themselves from crime;
- Make the area more accessible by improving transportation services;
- Improve the effectiveness and efficiency of governmental operations; and
- Encourage citizens to report crimes.

The steps taken to achieve these objectives included:

- Outdoor lighting, sidewalk, and landscaping improvements;
- Block watch, safe homes, and neighborhood cleanups;
- A campaign to discourage people from carrying cash;
- A major improvement and expansion of public transportation;
- Improved street lighting; and
- Public transportation hubs that are purpose built.

These improvements have enhanced the quality of life and provided an atmosphere of improvement in each of the communities featured.

The application of CPTED to school design has been promoted in a number of locations through the work of local practitioners, and in cooperation with school district personnel.

Additional CPTED case studies and information may be found in our text, written by Tim Crowe, *Crime Prevention through Environmental Design, Applications of Architectural Design and Space Management Concepts*.[17] This text offers CPTED as a specific topic and is widely used by students and practitioners.

The Future of CPTED

The most consistent finding in evaluations of CPTED and related projects is that the users of space must be involved in design decisions. Their involvement insures that the designs are realistic and that the users will comply with the behavioral objectives of the plans. Numerous applications of CPTED concepts have been tried successfully on a spot basis, which tends to support the idea that the more simplistic approaches are the most viable. That is, it seems reasonable to assume that the crime prevention practitioner may confidently use CPTED strategies in very specific, controlled environmental settings.

There are many hundreds of examples of CPTED strategies in practice today. It is unfortunate that most of the successful applications have not been publicized well, since they are usually part of ongoing field activities that do not come to the attention of evaluators or government agencies. However, it has been noted that most applications center on some mixture or interaction between the three basic CPTED processes of natural surveillance, natural access control, and territoriality. The most basic common thread is the primary emphasis on naturalness—simply doing things that you already have to do, a little better.

The most productive uses of CPTED, in the foreseeable future, will center on the following simplistic strategies:

- Provide clear border definition of controlled space;
- Provide clearly marked transitional zones, which indicate movement from public to semipublic to private space;
- Relocate gathering areas to locations with natural surveillance and access control, or to locations away from the view of would-be offenders;

- Place safe activities in unsafe locations to bring along the natural surveillance of these activities (to increase the perception of safety for normal users and risk for offenders);
- Place unsafe activities in safe spots to overcome the vulnerability of these activities with the natural surveillance and access control of the safe area;
- Redesignate the use of space to provide natural barriers to conflicting activities;
- Improve scheduling of space to allow for effective use, appropriate "critical intensity," and the temporal definition of accepted behaviors;
- Redesign or revamp space to increase the perception or reality of natural surveillance; and
- Overcome distance and isolation through improved communication and design efficiencies.

The future of CPTED rests with the persons who shape public and private policy. Crime prevention practitioners will have to communicate CPTED concepts in terms that relate to the overall priorities of their organizations or communities. Productivity, profitability, and quality of life are concerns that affect policy makers—not specifically security or crime prevention for its own sake. Accordingly, chief executives, builders, architects, planners, engineers, and developers will have to embrace CPTED design objectives. Elected officials and legislative bodies will have to be held accountable for assuring that CPTED is considered in capital improvement and development plans. Property owners and residents of neighborhoods and commercial areas need the opportunity to question planning, zoning, and traffic signalization decisions. Finally, strategic plans that encompass 20-year community development periods require an assessment of crime prevention needs and programs.

Conclusion

The application of environmental design concepts by the crime prevention practitioner can be as cost effective as the design of crime risk management systems for individual clients. Such application must be based, however, on sound analysis of particular crime patterns and the physical and social conditions that are related to those patterns. It should stress innovative solutions that are appropriate to the particular circumstances, that are cost effective and that will not create more problems than they solve. It should stress working with "things as they are" rather than with "things as they ought to be."

The practitioner needs, above all, to become well acquainted with the people and organizations responsible for physical development and redevelopment in his or her community. The best opportunities for applying crime prevention through environmental design occur when buildings, street layouts, street lighting programs, new subdivisions, shopping centers, and housing projects are still in the planning stages, and crime prevention principles can be incorporated before construction starts.

In keeping with the theory that the quality of the physical environment impacts human behavior, we think that crime prevention and community development go hand-in-hand. Physical design that enhances the environment from a balanced economic-social-political standpoint can also discourage criminal activity, and the concept of crime prevention through environmental design can be used in any situation—high-density urban areas, small cities and towns, and even rural areas. The essential role of the practitioner is to see the "whole picture" and to see to it that physical design, citizen participation, and police activities fit together.

In terms of physical design itself, the major task of the crime prevention practitioner is to analyze existing and planned physical design, determine how it relates to existing or potential crime patterns, and recommend physical design countermeasures to the proper person or organization.

References

1. Jane Jacobs. *The Death and Life of Great American Cities*, Vintage Books, New York, 1961.
2. Lee Rainwater. "Fear and the Home-as-Haven in the Lower Class," *Journal of the American Institute of Planners*, January 1966, pp. 23–37.
3. Elizabeth Wood. *Housing Design, a Social Theory*, Citizens' Housing and Planning Counsel of New York, Inc., New York, 1961.
4. Schlomo Angel. *Discouraging Crime Through City Planning*, University of California Press, Berkeley, 1968.
5. Gerald Leudtke and E. Lystad. *Crime in the Physical City*, Final Report, LEAA Grant No. NI 69–78, 1970.
6. Oscar Newman and George Rand study (1969), published by Oscar Newman, *Defensible Space*, Macmillan Publishing Co., New York, 1972.
7. National Institute of Law Enforcement and Criminal Justice. *Urban Design, Security, and Crime*, Proceedings of a seminar held April 12–13, 1972, published by the Law Enforcement Assistance Administration (LEAA), p. 15.
8. Thomas A. Reppetto. *Residential Crime*, Ballinger Publishing Co., Cambridge, MA, 1974.
9. John Conklin. *The Impact of Crime*, Macmillan Co., New York, 1975, p. 299.
10. C. Ray Jefferey. *Crime Prevention Through Environmental Design*, Sage Publications, Beverly Hills, CA, 1971.
11. C. Ray Jefferey. "Behavior Control Techniques and Criminology: 1975–2075," Ecology Youth Development Workshop, University of Hawaii School of Social Work, Honolulu, December 1975.
12. Op. cit., Newman, pp. 51–52.
13. Ibid.
14. Oscar Newman. *Design Guidelines for Creating Defensible Space*, LEAA, Washington, DC, 1976.
15. Ronald L. Robidas. "Reports on Activity in Project Area for the Manchester (NH) Police Department," 1996.
16. American Architecture Foundation. *Back from the Brink, Saving America's Cities by Design*, 56 mins. videocassette, American Architecture Foundation, 1996.
17. Timothy D. Crowe. *Crime Prevention through Environmental Design, Applications of Architectural Design, and Space Management Concepts*. Butterworth, Stoneham, MA, 1991.

Chapter 2
Risk Assessment and Management

MURRAY NEAL

Risk assessment and management can be defined as: A method to identify precisely, the risks and all the probable effects that those risks will have on the person(s) and/or organization being protected, to minimize that risk to an acceptable level, and the proper implementation of measures to deal with the remaining elements associated with that risk.

Risk cannot be eliminated, but it can be managed. Risk can be reduced to a manageable level through the proper risk analysis research and assimilation of data—then, a thorough implementation of measures designed to avoid, reduce, or eliminate remaining factors associated with that risk.

Good security and crisis management policies and procedures evolve from an accurate analysis of perceived risk. You need to know exactly what you are up against. You will not know which policies and procedures are necessary until you have properly assessed your risk. To perform a risk assessment, you must collect as much information, whether "dirty" or not, as possible about the company and its key personnel. This information needs to be evaluated and quantified to level of significance to ensure that it is not "bad" information. The information is then broken into subcategories to establish a linking pattern (trends and patterns), these trends and patterns allow you to establish the problem or associated risk(s). From this point, you may then start the risk analysis process.

This process first starts with a thorough understanding of the factors that greatly enhance the chances of risk occurring. These are predictability, probability, and convenience.

$$RISK <\text{_____}> PREDICTABILITY$$
$$100\% \quad 0\% \quad 100\%$$

The preceding shows the relation risk has to the predictability of risk. The predictability is the percentage of chance that one can predict that upcoming events are likely to cause great security risk to persons or organizations. The greater the risk, the less likely you can predict events leading to that risk. On the other hand, the more that you can foresee and predict upcoming events, the less risk there is or the more you can reduce that risk factor.

Predictability for security purposes is mainly an indicator of behavior. The behavior being an observable response based on stimuli. The stimuli are the actions or inactions incurred by the person or organization, so that

$$RISK <\text{_____}>PROBABILITY$$
$$100\% \quad 0\% \quad 100\%$$

This shows the relation risk has to the probability of risk. Probability reflects what is historically known and is directly related to risk. Probability takes into consideration the likelihood of an incident occurring by the number of actual occurrences of incidents in the past, which are supported by empirical evidence. Probability is considered more of a true indicator of events than predictability when discussing security, as it is based on actual history.

Terrorism, for example, has shown through history to continue its ideologies, strategies, and tactics over and over and with a high percentage of probability. When risk is high and incidents have occurred repeatedly, then there is a great probability that, when that risk is high again, like incidents may occur in the same manner.

As before, predictability for security purposes is mainly an indicator of behavior. For example, terrorist activity including kidnapping has occurred numerous times and the kidnapped individual provides for several needs or requirements of the terrorists: money from ransom, propaganda, supplies, release of sympathizers for hostages, and so forth. History also shows that the majority of kidnappings happen in a vehicle en route to or from a residence.

Therefore, the probability of risk is shown to be high, indicating that future kidnappings probably will be from a vehicle and are likely to be used to fulfill such needs or requirements. The predictability shows us that the terrorists always choose their targets based on their stimuli or reaction to their goals and beliefs. It is highly predictable that those who press close to an incursion with those goals and beliefs or those who provide immediate response to their goals have a higher risk of terrorist involvement.

Actually, probability and predictability work well for security, as one will fill in information where the other is lacking information. When there are no facts to support probability, then the security/protection detail can objectively base the predictability of an occurrence through their judgment guided by behavioral traits. If sufficient information is lacking to show any history or severity of incidence, then the probability is low and the predictability takes its place in the assessment of events or incidents.

Therefore, *risk assessment,* as we are concerned with, deals with the methods utilized to identify all the risks involved by determining the risk's probability and predictability as it relates to security. *Risk management,* as we are concerned with, deals with our ability to properly implement and maintain an effective security plan, or better yet, a definitive protection plan based on what is known, derived from our assessment.

Through this implemented protection plan, we manipulate the elements that are foreseeable by eliminating, avoiding, or controlling each to increase our predictability. Increasing our predictability reduces our risk factor.

Implementation of security measures or strategies designed to reduce these elements is accomplished only after thorough and proper security advance work, research, reconnaissance, or surveillance and analysis of such data.

The saying "proper planning prevents poor performance" or "an ounce of prevention is worth a pound of cure" too often is taken for granted. The first saying can be directly related to the integrity of the security or protection plan, in that, only if all elements are taken into consideration (personnel, equipment, scheduling, liaisons with outside agencies, training, proper advance work, research and intelligence, proper assimilation of data, and the proper implementation of measures) can one reasonably expect to have far better than average performance when needed. Too often, the advance information obtained that is crucial to a company's executive in travel is always days old or not even current at all.

Always expect the unexpected. Do not fall in along side those who have thought it could happen only to the other guy. *Do not be incident driven!* Just because something has not happened yet, does not make a good excuse not to enact preplanned, proactive, preventive measures.

Oftentimes, events such as involvement in other countries or sales of a specific product to new customers has a profound effect upon people directly or indirectly related to such events. Remember, we live in a politically, socially, and economically volatile world. These types of events probably have not occurred yet, but as most companies and people find out as they continue to grow and reach out, especially on an international scale, it happens all too soon.

Cost-consciousness is often looked at by "bean counters" in a cost effective/productive means at the present and usually counters any necessary security plans by justifying figures with such statements as, "It is not cost effective to implement at this time," all the while not foreseeing the immediate future. This type of decision making oftentimes does not weigh the risk factors enough to consider the maximum loss due to substantial interruption of corporate or individual activity, direct cost loss, indirect cost loss, replacement cost loss, and future loss due to events, whether implicated directly or not.

Oftentimes, companies spend a dollar to save a dime. It is always more prudent to prepare for a disaster and not need that preparation than to need it and not be prepared. Such words of wisdom have been handed down by those fortunate enough to have the foresight to try to keep others from falling into the same pitfalls. History need not continue to repeat itself.

Once you get behind the "eight ball," so to speak, you will never get ahead of it; you are always playing catch up. Dealing with life-and-death situations, one should *never* be anywhere but ahead of the game or "eight ball."

The elements of risk that the security or protection detail are assigned to avoid and eliminate should always be in arrears; ensure that those elements always have to chase and run to keep up. If you maintain and control your direction and objectives, then the risk factor or vulnerability is reduced substantially.

The implementation of such measures and strategies pose one other objective to overcome: being able to provide the necessary measures and strategies, while not inconveniencing the persons or the organization to an unacceptable degree.

RISK <_____> CONVENIENCE
100% 0% 100%

The more "hard line" is the security, the less convenient it is for the person(s) or organization. The more convenient it is, the less secure is the person(s) or organization. Convenience also guides or invites the chances of risk occurring. If the opportunity is offered, and it is convenient, then the risk is low to the "terrorist," who will accept the remaining minimal risk and attack. However, if you harden the target and increase the "terrorist's" risk during an attack, then your chances of a higher risk leading to an attack are minimized. Statistics have shown that terrorists choose the targets that provide at least an 80% chance of success. Therefore, it is necessary to have a specific sequence for risk analysis to follow. Risk management is maintained only through a complete and proper analysis and then only through the proper implementation of strictly adhered-to measures.

There is a price to implement an effective risk assessment and management program. However, the price of not having the program is far higher in the long term, as overconfidence arises due to the "threat" usually being underestimated, and when the minimal program becomes necessary, it usually only has a minimal impact on the actual risk. Any security specialist, whether in an executive position or field operative, should always be extremely prudent in his or her decision-making process. *Prudence* is defined as: "care, caution, good judgment, and wisdom in looking and planning ahead."

The process from risk analysis through risk management follows a very definitive sequence of 10 steps:

1. Define the problem
2. Define the objective(s)
3. Evaluate current measures and resources
4. Identify the risk
5. Evaluate the risk
6. Select risk reduction measures
7. Develop risk reduction measures
8. Implement risk reduction measures
9. Evaluate risk reduction measures
10. Redefine risk identification and restart risk analysis process

There are extensive relationships among all the respective elements within each category and subcategory. Simply outlining each makes the task easier. However, as programmers have learned, the most effective way to track and analyze all the interrelated information is to use a flowchart. Techniques in flowcharting are used where large amounts of information have to be either analyzed or a linking pattern of continuity established. Illustrations always provide a clearer view for such complex relationships. Flowcharts can have categories color-coded for use by those assigned to analyze all necessary information in their charge. Color-coding enhances areas that are affected or not affected or places emphasis on the severity or importance of specific events, incidents, and information. Using a flowchart is like using a road map instead of written directions, and it aids in the analysis process.

One of the most difficult and time-consuming processes that must be accomplished to establish a linking pattern between risk and the exposures leading to it is to ensure that all flowcharts have every conceivable risk listed for every activity. One of the best places to start is to locate trends and patterns consistent with the company or individual activities. When looking for trends and patterns (routines), whether new or changes in those previously established, it is often too easy to overlook specifics or details when such are included in your daily routines. To see changes, usually we look at broad-range statistical reports, charts, graphs, and the like.

When looking through such sources, take a close look at the "statistically significant" targets. Oftentimes, you might be assessing risk for a venue to which you will travel. However, do the statistics cover your traveled course en route? Probably not, just specific incidents relating to the venue location. There are many significant incidents of violence throughout the world. You need to ensure that chronology is designed to encompass your specific needs. Furthermore, many incidents are omitted due to the sensitive nature of the information associated with them.

Chapter 3

Designing Security with the Architects

LAWRENCE J. FENNELLY

Too often, when a building complex was built, the contractor turned over the keys to the owner and that was it. During the 1990s, management was saying: "Hold it, we want some say as to what type of locks, lighting, and alarms you install and exactly what kind of hardware to put on our exit doors."

Security was being neglected because the security personnel had no chance for input. Yes, it is a great building and the contractor can be proud; the cement, plumbing, and electrical work is perfect, but to cut costs, deadbolt locks, eye viewers in the doors, chains, and nonremovable hinges were omitted. Key-in knob locks were installed. A pipe wrench opens this type of door lock or expansion of the doorframe pops the door open.

The crime/loss prevention officer is not concerned just with locks. The concern is the overall vulnerability of the site. If you believe that most crimes can be prevented, then you must be involved in the early stages of designing security.

We have, from the 1990s, seen a new approach; namely building security codes (see Appendix 3.A, which follows). Buildings should be constructed with a level of security in mind. Law enforcement has the knowledge of crime trends and of burglary; therefore, they should be involved with state and local planning boards.

Designing Security with the Architects

Crime prevention and security officers throughout the country today are working with various architects for the sole purpose of improving the state of security within the community. Crime is not always predictable, because it is the work of human scheming. In our efforts to combat this threat, it is essential that we all attempt to reduce the opportunity so often given to the criminal to commit crime. Every building, large or small, creates a potential crime risk and planners and architects owe it to their clients to devise and implement effective security measures.

The subject of designing security with architects is another way of conducting a security survey, but in this case, it is before construction. It extends far beyond the protection of doors and windows. It even deals with the quality of one vendor's products versus another of a lesser quality. The following checklist is for use as an initial guide to assist you with the architects to obtain better security.

Anticipation of Crime Risk Checklist

1. As with any security survey, your first step is to consult with the occupants of the complex.
2. Identify areas that will house items of a sensitive nature or items of value, like safes or audiovisual equipment.
3. Identify the main crime targets.
4. Assess the level of protection required.
5. Examine the facilities that the company currently occupies. From that survey, the building characteristics and personality can tell you how the structure has been used or abused.
6. Is cash being handled within the building that has to get to a bank?
7. Is there a concentration or even distribution of valuables within the complex? Decide on the area most vulnerable to criminal attack and

make your recommendation to harden that target.

8. Reduce entrances to a minimum, thereby reducing movement of staff and visitors.
9. What crime risk is in the area?
10. What is the level of police patrol and police activity in the area?
11. What are the distances from the complex to the local police and fire stations?
12. Have the materials being used met state and national standards?
13. Who cleans and secures the complex day and night? Are these people dependable, intelligent, and reliable?
14. Make note of employee behavior.

Designing Security and Layout of Site

Designing security into a new complex should begin with interior security. Work your way to the exterior and then to the outer perimeter. Keep in mind these six points before you sit down with the architects:

1. Elimination of all but essential doors and windows
2. Specification of fire-resistant material throughout the interior
3. Installation of fire, intrusion, and environmental control systems
4. Separation of shipping and receiving areas
5. Provisions for the handicapped
6. Adequate lighting around the perimeter, before, after, and during construction.

Building Site Security and Contractors

It is safe to say that all contractors experience a theft of stocks or material before completion of the site. They should be made aware of this and be security conscious at the beginning of construction, before theft gets costly. Thefts that appear to be of an internal nature should be analyzed in relation to previous such thefts at other sites.

Site Security Checklist

1. The contractor should appoint security officers or a liaison staff person to work with police on matters of theft and vandalism.
2. Perimeter protection:
   a. Gate strength
   b. Hinges
   c. Locks and chains
   d. Lighting
   e. Crime rate in the neighborhood
   f. Construct a 10- or 12-foot fence topped with three rows of barbwire.
3. Location of contractor's building on site:
   a. Inspect security of this building.
   b. Review their security procedures and controls.
   c. Light building inside and out.
4. No employees should be permitted to park private cars on site.
5. Materials and tools on site should be protected in a secured yard area.
6. Facilities for storage and security of worker's tools and clothes should be kept in a locked area.
7. The subcontractor is responsible to the main contractor.
8. Security officers should patrol at night and on weekends.
9. Use a temporary alarm protection for the site.
10. Payment or wages to employees should be with checks.
11. Deliveries of valuable material to site and the storage of such items should be placed in a secured area.
12. Establish a method to check fraudulent deliveries using authorized persons only.
13. Check for proper posting of signs around the perimeter.
14. Identify transportable material and property. Operation Identification should be available.
15. Method used to report theft:
    a. Local police
    b. Office
    c. Insurance company
    d. Security company

If guards are needed to protect the site, determine:

1. Hours of coverage
2. Whether guards answer to the general contractor or the owner of the complex (they should answer to the general contractor)
3. Whether they are employed by the general contractor or a contract guard company
4. Their police powers
5. How they are supervised
6. What type of special training they receive
7. Whether local police have been advised of their presence on the site
8. The uniform of the guard on duty, flashlight (size), firearms, night sticks, or chemical agents

9. How promotions in the guard company are obtained
10. What keys to the complex the guard has
11. What the guard's exact duties are; whether guard has a fixed post or a roving patrol
12. Review the guard's patrol
13. Whether guards carry a time clock
14. Whether they write a report on each shift
15. Who reviews these reports
16. Whether each guard has sufficient responsibilities and is active during tour of duty
17. Whether the guard has an up-to-date list of who to call in case of emergency

Building Design: Interior Checklist

1. Locate the payroll office
2. Examine security as it pertains to cash and the storage of cash overnight
3. Be familiar with cars parking within the complex
4. Employ staff supervision of entryways
5. Avoid complex corridor systems
6. Visitors:
   a. Are they restricted as to how far they can maneuver?
   b. Are there special elevators?
   c. Is there limited access?
7. Determine the provisions and placement of the reception desk
8. Determine where vulnerable equipment and stock are housed
9. Custodial quarters:
   a. Where are they housed?
   b. Is there a phone?
   c. What other security devices are installed?
   d. Can this area be secured when the staff leaves at night?
10. Proper security of staff quarters
11. Industrial plants designed and laid out to combat internal vandalism
12. Electric, water, and gas meters should be built into the outside wall for service access
13. Department stores and other buildings accessible to public use, in addition to shape and layout, designed with deterrents to prevent crime:
    a. Access for handicapped and disabled persons—guard rails, telephones, toilets
    b. Provisions for one-way mirrors throughout the store
    c. Closed circuit television—Who monitors it? Is it hooked up to the alarm system with a recorder?
    d. Beeper or signal system

e. Zoned intrusion alarm panel on street floor for quick police response
f. Zoned fire alarm panel on street floor for quick fire department response
g. Lighting 24 hours a day
h. Display area vulnerable
i. Freight elevator access to the street

14. Apartments:
    a. Avoid overdensity
    b. Avoid neurosis, fire hazards, and floods
    c. Plan on reduction of vandalism
    d. Trash chutes and storage areas kept clear
    e. Basement access reduced
    f. Security in tenants' storage area
    g. Key security implemented
    h. Foyer also locked
    i. Vandal-proof mailboxes
    j. Who occupies complex—Upper, middle, or lower class people? All white, all nonwhite, or mixed families? Combination of classes and races? Senior citizens?

Building Design: Exterior Access Checklist

1. External doors:
   a. Choice of final exit door
   b. Design style and strength of door and frame
   c. Choice and strength of panels: glass and wood
   d. Ensure hinges cannot be removed from the outside
   e. Minimum number of entrances
   f. Secure fire doors
   g. Make tools and ladders accessible (garage doors)
   h. Provide lights over entrances
   i. Choice of locks and hardware
   j. Use only steel doors and frames
   k. Eliminate exterior hardware on egress doors wherever possible
2. Building line:
   a. Lines of vision
   b. Hidden entrances
3. Architectural defects affecting security
4. Roof:
   a. Access
   b. Skylights
   c. Pitch angle
5. External pipes—flush or concealed?
6. Podium blocks—access to upper windows
7. Basement:
   a. Access points inside and out
   b. Storage areas
   c. Lighting

    d. Fuel storage areas
    e. Number of entries to basement, stairs, and elevators
    f. Grills on windows
8. False ceilings—access to and through
9. Service entrances:
    a. Service hatches
    b. Ventilation ducts
    c. Air vent openings
    d. Service elevators
    e. Grills on all ducts, vents, and openings over 12 inches

Building Access: Windows and Glass

The purpose of the window, aside from aesthetics, is to let in sunlight, allow visibility, and provide ventilation. The following types of windows provide 100% ventilation: casement, pivoting, jalousie, awning, and hopper. The following provide 50–65% ventilation: double-hung and sliding.

Factors to consider in the selection of type and size of a window are

1. Requirements for light, ventilation, and view requirements
2. Material and desired finish—wood, metal, aluminum steel, stainless steel
3. Window hardware—durability, function
4. Type of glazing
5. Effectiveness of weather stripping
6. Appearance, unit size, and proportion
7. Method opening (hinge or slider), choice of line of hinges
8. Security lock fittings
9. Accessible louver windows
10. Ground floor—recommend lower windows, large fixed glazing and high windows, small openings
11. Size and shape to prevent access
12. Size because of cost due to vandalism
13. Use of bars or grilles on inside
14. Glass:
    a. Double glazing deterrent
    b. Type of glass
    c. Vision requirements
    d. Thickness
    e. Secure fixing to frame
    f. Laminated barrier glass—uses
    g. Use of plastic against vandalism
    h. Fixed, obscure glazing for dwelling house garages
    i. Shutters, grilles, and louvers for sun control and visual barriers as well as security barrier

Ironmongery

The Lock and Its Installation

By definition, a lock is a mechanical, electrical, hydraulic, or electronic device designed to prevent entry to a building, room, container, or hiding place to prevent the removal of items without the consent of the owner. A lock temporarily fastens two separate objects together, such as a door to its frame or lid to a container. The objects are held together until the position of the internal structure of the lock is altered—for example, by a key—so that the objects are released.

1. Perimeter entrance gates:
    a. Design
    b. Locking devices and hardware
    c. Aesthetics
2. Door ironmongery:
    a. Theft-resistant locks—choice of manufacturer, design
    b. Electrically operated
    c. Access control
    d. Mortise security locks
    e. Sliding bolts
    f. Flush bolts
    g. Dead bolts
    h. Hinge bolts
    i. Nonremovable hinges on all outside doors
    j. Key control system
    k. Door viewers
    l. Safety chains
    m. Choice of panic bolts
    n. Fire doors
    o. Sliding doors
    p. Additional locks and padlocks
    q. Quality of locks used
    r. Sheet metal lining protection of door
3. Window ironmongery:
    a. Security window locks built-in during manufacture
    b. Security window locks fitted after manufacture
    c. Transom window locks
    d. Locking casement stays
    e. Remote-controlled flexible locks
4. Additional ironmongery:
    a. Hardware of the highest quality
    b. Control of keys
    c. High-grade steel hasps
    d. Strong lock for strong door or window needs strong frame

Our objective is prevention of the defeat of locks through force. When stress is applied to a door in the form of bodily force, pry bars, or jacks, something has to give. Every mechanical device has its fatigue and breaking points, although no one, to our knowledge, has properly defined this point for doors, locks, and frames in terms of pounds of pressure or force.

Doors

There are four types of door operation: swinging, by-pass sliding, surface sliding, and slide-hinged folding.

Physical door types are wood, metal, aluminum, flush, paneled, French, glass, sash, jalousie, louvered, shutter, screen, Dutch, hollow-core doors, solid-core doors, batten doors, pressed wood doors, hollow metal-framed doors, and revolving doors.

Garage and overhead doors can be constructed in a panel type, flush, or webbed.

Each of these doors needs a specific type of security hardware. I am not going to go into these specifics, but I want to mention some additional factors to consider in the selection of hardware:

1. Function and ease of door operation
2. Material, form, surface texture, finish, and color
3. Durability in terms of anticipated frequency of use and exposure to weather and climatic conditions. Finish aluminum and stainless steel are recommended in humid climates and where corrosive conditions exist (e.g., sea air).

Finish door hardware should include

1. Locks, latches, bolts, cylinders, and stop works, operating trim
2. Nonremovable hinges
3. Panic hardware
4. Push and pull bars and plates
5. Kick plates
6. Stops, closers, and holders
7. Thresholds
8. Weather stripping
9. Door tracks and hangers

Standards have yet to be adjusted to determine the minimum lock requirements necessary for security, but various considerations are evident from the variety of provisions that currently exist. A deadbolt, or dead latch, or both is essential. The standard latch, which functions primarily to keep the door in a closed position, can easily be pushed back with such instruments as a credit card or thin metal objects.

The door should be of solid construction. If wood is used, the door should have a solid wood core. Doors should be installed so that hinges are located on the inside. If this is not possible, hinges should be installed in a manner which will prohibit their being removed or the pins being tampered with.

Rolling overhead doors not controlled or locked by electric power can be protected by slide bolts on the bottom bar. With crank-operated doors, the operating shaft should be secured. Chain-operated doors can be secured in a manner that allows a steel or cast iron keeper and pin to be attached to the hand chain.

Intrusion Alarm Systems Checklist

1. Quality of products being used—Are they listed in Underwriters' Laboratories?
2. Vulnerable materials in protected areas
3. Smallest area to be protected
4. Audible alarm termination type of horn
5. Instant or delayed audible warning
6. Silent alarms, connected to police or central station
7. Choice of detection equipment—motion, infrared magnetic contacts, or the like
8. Degree of protection—building perimeter, site perimeter, target protection, internal traps, overall construction
9. Sufficient alarm zones (plus extras) to fit the lifestyle of the complex
10. If a union contractor, then the alarm company must be a union company or obtain permission for a nonunion alarm vendor
11. Influence of environmental aspect in architects' selection of alarm components
12. Electric outlets for areas where power is needed
13. Methods of monitoring a supervised line
14. Service provider in the event of breakdown

Closed Circuit Television (CCTV) Checklist

1. Quality of products to be used—analog or digital
2. Type and style of lens and monitors used
3. Monitoring the monitors
4. Electric outlets at each camera location
5. Service provider in the event of breakdown
6. Size of control room to determine the amount of controls and panel that can be monitored
7. Installation and repair system provider
8. Time lapse recorder and tape quality or digital recorder.

Card Access Control Checklist

1. Credit card size, private post office box number printed on it, so lost cards can be returned

2. Card type—magnetic, electric circuit continuity, magnetic stripe, passive electronic, IR optical, differential optics—and capacities.
3. Site location will determine:
   a. Number of entry control points
   b. Number of badges needed
   c. Rate at which persons must be passed through entry-control points
   d. The number of levels of access accommodated
   e. Procedures used to issue badges
4. Equipment:
   a. Tamper alarm to detect tampering with the electrical circuits
   b. Battery backup supply
   c. Capability to detect tampering with line circuits
5. Card access control over lifestyle of building
6. Applications, aside from security:
   a. Controlled access to buildings and parking areas
   b. Alarms
   c. CCTV
   d. Watch guard tours
   e. Heating system
   f. Smoke and fire detection
   g. Temperature and humidity controls
   h. Refrigeration and air conditioning controls
   i. Time and attendance
   j. Elevator control
   k. Gas pump control
   l. Xerox copy control

Storage Rooms, Safes, and Vaults Checklist

Storage Rooms

1. Considerations:
   a. Vulnerabilities
   b. Contents
   c. Risk management principles
   d. Type of storage area
   e. Period of complex occupancy
   f. Underwriters' Laboratory listing
2. Placement—Can it be seen from outside?
3. Construction and type of material
4. Restrictions on open area around storage room
5. Installation factors in design stage
6. Intrusion protection
7. Fire protection
8. Ventilation of storage room
9. Water- and fireproofing
10. Emergency exit

Safes

1. Correct type of safe required for needs; money versus document type safe
2. Wheels removed and bolted down
3. Placement of safe—visibility
4. Weight factor and floor weight capacity
5. Security of safe to fabric of building
6. Provisions of area in concrete for installation of floor safe

Vaults

1. A U.S. Government Class 5 security vault door, which has been tested and approved by the government under Fed. Spec. AA-D-600B (GSA-FSS) and affords the following security protection, which applies only to the door and not to the vault proper:
   a. 30 worker-minutes against surreptitious entry
   b. 10 worker-minutes against forced entry
   c. 20 worker-hours against lock manipulation
   d. 20 worker-hours against radiology techniques
2. Door options:
   a. Right- or left-hand door swing
   b. Hand or key change combination lock
   c. Optical device
   d. Time-delay lock
3. Weight of vault versus floor strength
4. Wall thickness
5. That which is protected determines the degree of protection

Exterior Lighting Checklist

1. Lighting adequate to illuminate critical areas (alleys, fire escapes, ground-level windows)
2. Foot-candles on horizontal at ground level (a minimum of 5 foot-candles)
3. Sufficient illumination over entrances
4. Perimeter areas lighted to assist police surveillance of the area
5. Protective lighting system and the working lighting system on the same line
6. Auxiliary system designed to go into operation automatically when needed
7. Auxiliary power source for protective lighting
8. Frequency of auxiliary system tested
9. Protective lights controlled by automatic timer or photocells or manually operated
10. Hour this lighting is used
11. Switch box(es) and automatic timer secured

12. Ease of compromising protective lights (e.g., unscrewing of bulbs)
13. Type of lights installed around the property
14. Cost-effectiveness
15. Vandal-proofing of fixtures
16. Glare factor
17. Even distribution of light
18. Lights mounted on the building versus pole fixtures

Crime Prevention Awareness Points

1. Has the general contractor made arrangements to secure the perimeter and provide adequate lighting of the complex before starting work?
2. Has the general contractor been advised to secure equipment and work area from internal theft and so advise all subcontractors? Be sure to inspect the area and make immediate recommendations.
3. How good is entrance gate security?
4. Can vehicles park close to the construction site?
5. Is the building too close to adjoining property?
6. Is the site subject to vandalism or attack before completion?
7. Will cars be parking around the complex after completion?
8. Could landscape coverage pose a crime risk?
9. Are external lights on the building or on the grounds?
10. What security is given to main utilities, transformers, and the like, preferably underground?
11. Are temporary construction locks installed throughout the building during the construction process and later replaced with the permanent hardware after all exterior and interior work has been completed and the site is ready for occupancy?
12. Times when site is most vulnerable, between the time construction has ended and when the new occupants have completely moved in, there tends to be confusion. Are movers and decorators allowed uncontrolled access to the site? While something can be carried in, something else can be carried out. Identification badges should be used during this period.
13. Do the size of the complex and the amount of occupancy give you an idea of the complex's potential crime rate?
14. Does the period our society is going through have an effect on the conditions the architects are working under in planning a building for construction.

Appendix 3.A
Model Residential and Commercial Building Security Ordinance

Any builder, contractor, or owner desiring to have a decal awarded to any single- or multifamily dwelling currently existing, under construction, or to be constructed may voluntarily meet the following specifications dealing with building security.

Residential Buildings

Exterior Doors

1. All exterior doors, except sliding glass doors or metal doors, with or without decorative moldings, shall be either solid-core wood doors or stave or solid wood flake doors and shall be a minimum of

$1\frac{3}{8}$ inches in thickness. No hollow-core doors or hollow-core door filled with a second composition material, other than just mentioned, is considered a solid-core door.

2. All exterior door hinges shall be mounted with the hinge on the interior of the building, except where a nonremovable pin hinge or stud bolt is used (such hinges may be installed with the hinge facing the exterior of the building).

3. The shim space between the door buck and door frame shall have a solid wood filler 12 inches above and below the strike plate area to resist spreading by force applied to the door frame. Screws securing the strike plate area shall pass through the strike plate and door frame and enter the solid wood filler a minimum of $\frac{1}{4}$ inch.

4. No glazing may be used on any exterior door or window within 40 inches of any lock, except
   a. That glass shall be replaced with the same thickness of polycarbonate sheeting of an approved type. (Plexiglass shall not be used to replace glass.)
   b. That door locks shall be a double cylinder keyed lock with mortised deadbolt that extends into the strike plate a minimum of 1 inch.
   c. *French doors* shall have a concealed header and threshold bolt in the stationary, or first/closed door, on the door edge facing.
   d. *Dutch doors* shall have a concealed header type securing device interlocking the upper and lower portions of the door in the door edge on the door strike side provided that a double cylinder lock with a 1-inch deadbolt be provided on the upper and lower sections of the door and the header device be omitted.
   e. *Sliding glass doors:*
      (1) Sliding glass doors shall be installed so as to prevent the lifting and removal of either glass door from the frame from the exterior of the building.
      (2) Fixed panel glass door (nonsliding) shall be installed so that the securing hardware cannot be removed or circumvented from the exterior of the building.
      (3) Each sliding panel shall have a secondary locking or securing device in addition to the original lock built into the panel. The second device shall consist of a Charley bar type device, a track lock, wooden or metal dowel, or inside removable pins or locks securing the panel to the frame.
      (4) All "glass" used in exterior sliding glass doors and fixed glass panels is laminated safety glass or polycarbonate sheeting. Plexiglass or single strength glass will not qualify for this program.

5. Locks and keying requirements:
   a. Except as provided in Section A.4.b (glass in exterior doors), all exterior doors where the lock is not within 40 inches of breakable glass shall incorporate a single cylinder mortised or bored locking device with a 1-inch deadbolt.
   b. Locking materials:
      (1) No locking device on an exterior door shall be used that depends on extruded plastics for security or strength feature of the locking or securing mounts. Plastics and nylon materials may be used to a minimum degree in lubricant or wear-resistant features.
      (2) Cylinders used in locking devices must resist pulling from the exterior of the building.
      (3) Cylinder rings shall be compression resistant and may or may not be free turning to resist circumvention from the exterior.
      (4) Deadbolts shall be case-hardened steel or contain a case-hardened steel rod, fixed or movable, inside the deadbolt feature. The deadbolt is to be dead locked against reasonable end pressure.
   c. During construction each contractor or party building a home or apartment for occupancy by another shall, during the construction period, use a keying system that satisfies either
      (1) The original cylinders used during the construction period may be repinned and new keys furnished to the owner or occupant.
      (2) Reasonable key control shall be exercised and all full cut keys fitting the exterior doors upon occupancy shall be given to the renter or owner. In cases of rental property, master keys and grant master keys shall be kept under security.

Windows

Double Hung Wood

1. All locking devices to be secured with $\frac{3}{4}$-inch full-threader screws.
2. All window latches must have a key lock or a manual (nonspring-loaded or flip type) window latch. When a nonkey-locked latch is used, a sec-

ondary securing device must be installed. Such secondary securing device may consist of

a. Each window drilled with holes at two intersecting points of inner and outer windows and appropriate-sized dowels inserted in the holes. Dowels to be cut to provide minimum grasp from inside the window.
b. A metal sash security hardware device of approved type may be installed in lieu of doweling.

Note: Doweling is less costly and of a higher security value than more expensive hardware.

Sliding Glass Windows

The same requirements apply as for sliding glass doors.

Awning-Type Wood and Metal Windows

1. No secondary device is required on awning type windows but crank handle may be removed by owner as security feature after residence establishment.
2. Double hung metal windows are secured similarly to the double hung wood window, using metal dowels.

Miscellaneous

All front entrance doors without other means of external visibility shall be equipped with a door viewer that shall cover at least 160° of viewing. Such viewer shall be installed with the securing portion on the inside and be nonremovable from the outside.

Commercial Buildings

Doors

1. All exterior doors shall meet the requirements as set forth for residential buildings. Should glazed doors be installed, they shall be of laminated safety glass or polycarbonated sheeting.

2. Doors not controlled or locked by electric power operation, such as rolling overhead or cargo doors, shall be equipped with locking bars that pass through guide rails on each side. The locking bars shall have holes drilled in each end and a padlock placed in each end once the bar is in the locked position. The padlock shall have a case-hardened shackle with locking lugs on the heel and toe of the shackle and a minimum of four-pin tumbler operation.

Other Exterior Openings

1. Fixed glass panels, sliding glass and double hung windows, awning type and metal windows must meet or exceed the requirements set forth for residential buildings.
2. Skylights and other roof openings shall be constructed of laminated safety glass or polycarbonated sheeting.
3. Hatchways shall be of metal construction or wood with a minimum of 16-gauge sheet metal attached with screws. Unless prohibited by local fire ordinances, the hatchways shall be secured by case-hardened steel hasps and padlocks meeting the requirements set forth in cargo doors.
4. Air ducts or air vent openings exceeding 8×12 inches shall be secured by installing a steel grille of at least $\frac{1}{8}$-inch material of 2-inch mesh or iron bars of at least $\frac{1}{2}$ inch round or $1 \times \frac{1}{4}$-inch flat steel material spaced no more than 5 inches apart and securely fastened with round-headed flush bolts or welded.
5. Single unit air conditioners mounted in windows or through the wall shall be secured by flat steel material $2 \times \frac{1}{4}$ inch formed to fit snugly over the air conditioning case on the outside and secured with round-headed flush bolts through the walls.
6. All commercial establishments maintaining an inventory and assets of $5000 or more, or having a high incident rate of housebreaking in the past, shall have an intrusion detection system installed. The system shall cover all possible points of entry to include entry through the walls and roof. The system shall be a silent type with a hookup to the servicing police agency and shall have a backup energizing source.

Appendix 3.B
Standards

I do not have enough time and space in this chapter to address the subject of standards. The following is a list of organizations who have implemented or produced and supported standards:

International Code Council (ICC).
International Building Code (IBC)
American Institute of Architects
BOMA, International and the Associated General Contractors
Building Officials and Code Administrators International
Southern Building Code Congress International, Birmingham, AL
International Conference of Building Officials, Whittier, CA
U.S. Occupational Safety and Health Administration (OSHA)
American National Standards Institute (ANSI)
National Fire Protection Agency (NFPA) 5000 Building Construction and Safety Code
American Society of Chemical Engineers (ASCE)
U.S. Federal Emergency Management Agency (FEMA)
American Society for Industrial Security (ASIS)
National Lighting Bureau
Illuminating Engineering Society of North America
International Association of Lighting Management Companies

Standards for Doors

Standards that apply to doors have been implemented or produced and supported by the Architec-
tural Manufacturers Association (AAMA), ANSI, American Society for Testing and Materials (ASTM), National Association of Architectural Metal Manufacturers (NAA), NFPA, Steel Door Institute (SDI), Underwriters' Laboratory (UL), and International Standards Organization (ISO).

Standards for Windows

Standards that apply to windows have been implemented or produced and supported by the AAMA, ANSI, UL, ASTM, Consumer Product Safety Commission, ISO, ASTM F1233 (8), UL 752, UL 972, NSA 65–8.

Standards for Alarms

Standards that apply to alarms have been implemented or produced and supported by the UL, Institute of Electrical and Electronic Engineers (IEEE), ISO, NFPA, and National Burglar and Fire Alarm Association (NBFAA).

Conclusion

Have you met the required standard for the project you are working on?

Chapter 4
Security Surveys

LAWRENCE J. FENNELLY

A security survey is a critical on-site examination and analysis of an industrial plant, business, home, or public or private institution to ascertain the present security status, identify deficiencies or excesses, determine the protection needed, and make recommendations to improve the overall security.[1]

It is interesting to note that a definition of *crime prevention* as outlined by the British Home Office Crime Prevention Program—"the anticipation, recognition, and appraisal of a crime risk and the initiation of action to remove or reduce it"—could, in fact, be an excellent definition of a security survey. The only difference, of course, is that a survey generally does not become the "action" as such but rather a basis for recommendations for action.

This definition can be divided into five components and analyzed so that its implications can be applied to the development of a working foundation for the security surveyor:

1. *Anticipation.* How does the anticipation of a crime risk become important to the security or crime prevention surveyor? Obviously, a primary objective of a survey is the anticipation or prevention aspects of a given situation—the pre- or before-concept. Thus, an individual who keeps anticipation in the proper perspective maintains a proper balance in the total spectrum of security surveying. In other words, the anticipatory stage could be considered a prognosis of further action.

2. *Recognition.* What does an individual need to conduct a survey of the relationships between anticipation and appraisal? Primarily, the ability to recognize and interpret what seems to be a crime risk becomes an important skill a security surveyor acquires and develops.

3. *Appraisal.* The responsibility to develop, suggest, and communicate recommendations is certainly a hallmark of any security survey.

4. *Crime risk.* As defined in this text, a crime risk is the opportunity gained from crime. The total elimination of opportunity is most difficult, if not improbable. Therefore, the cost of protection is measured in (1) protection of depth and (2) delay time. Obviously, the implementation of the recommendation should not exceed the total (original or replacement) cost of the item(s) to be protected. An exception to this rule would be human life.

5. *The initiation of action to remove or reduce a crime risk.* This section indicates the phase of a survey in which the recipient of the recommendations decides whether to act, based on the suggestions (recommendations) set forth by the surveyor. In some cases, the identification of security risk is made early in a survey and it is advisable to act on the recommendation prior to the completion of the survey.

The responsibility to initiate action based on recommendations is the sole duty of the recipient of the survey. This is to suggest that the individual who receives the final evaluation and survey is the individual who has commensurate responsibility and authority to act.[2]

There are basically three types of surveys:

1. *A building inspection* is used to advise a tenant in a large complex of his or her vulnerabilities as

they pertain to the physical characteristics of the dwelling.

2. *A security survey,* on the other hand, would be conducted on the whole complex in contrast to only a portion of the site.

3. *A security analysis* is a more in-depth study, including risk management, analysis of risk factors, environmental and physiological security measures, analysis of crime patterns, and fraud and internal theft.

The Best Time to Conduct the Survey

Most crime prevention officers and security directors agree that a survey is most effective after a crisis within the corporation, after a breaking and entering or major larceny, or on request. There are times when a merchant, hoping to get something for nothing, calls the crime prevention officer in the town to conduct such a survey, when in reality there is no intention of spending a dime for improvement. A close friend of mine conducted a detailed security survey on a factory warehouse and office building. The recipient of the survey followed only one of his recommendations, which was to leave a light on over the safe in the back room of his warehouse. The owner had completely disregarded other recommendations such as hardware improvements on doors, windows, and skylights. Unfortunately, thieves returned and almost put him out of business.

Classification of Survey Recommendations

The various classifications of recommendations can be best explained through an example. The classifications are maximum, medium, and minimum. The example selected is a museum that contains $25 million in various art treasures; the complex has no security.

Maximum Security

Obviously, the museum needs an alarm system; therefore, our maximum security classification recommendation should read:

> Alarm the perimeter (all exterior and interior doors, all windows and skylights). Four panic alarms to be installed at various locations, and six paintings, which are worth $12 million should be alarmed—each on a separate 24-hour zone.

I specifically did not mention ultramaximum security because this term applies to an armed camp— machine guns, guards in full battle dress armed with semiautomatic rifles, grenades, flamethrowers, mines, and locking devices equipped with dynamite, which will blow up when the intruder attempts picking the lock. It is dramatic and it is ultramaximum. It is not ridiculous for Fort Knox to provide ultramaximum security to protect its billions in gold bullion.

Medium Security

A medium security classification recommendation would read:

> Alarm all basement windows and all ground floor windows that are at the rear of the building. Install one panic alarm by the main entrance. Alarm the six paintings worth $12 million, each alarm on a separate 24-hour zone.

Minimum Security

Finally, a minimum security classification recommendation would read:

> From a risk management point of view, alarm the six paintings which are worth $12 million, each painting to be alarmed on a separate 24-hour zone.

First Step

These three examples clearly show the degree of security one can obtain by trying to plan a security package. I have stated these examples because your first step in conducting a security survey is an interview with the individual to whom you turn over your report. During this interview, you form an appraisal on the degree of protection required.

Sometimes, you may have to state all three recommendations in a report. Other times, you must be conscious that you may force the receiver of your report to accept less security than suggested because you did not thoroughly and clearly explain your security points.

Developing Security Points

Like most professionals, we need tools to do an effective job. The following are suggested to assist you when conducting your surveys: tape measure, floor plans, magnifying glass, flashlight, camera with flash, small tape recorder, screwdriver, penknife, pencil, and paper.

Your survey is to be conducted systematically so that the recipient can follow your recommendations in some kind of order. Start with the perimeter of the building. Once inside the building, start at the basement and work your way to the attic. Do not be afraid to be critical of the area that you are in. This is what the recipient wants.

After you have done several surveys you will develop a style of putting them together and they become easy.

Dos and Don'ts in Developing a Report

Dos

1. Be honest in your recommendations. You are the expert.
2. Call the shots as you see it.
3. Be critical—physically tear the property apart in your mind as part of the process.

Don'ts

1. Don't over exaggerate your reports. They are too important.
2. Don't inflate the report with maps and floor plans.
3. Don't repeat your statements.

The written report should include the following:

Page One: Introduction or sample covering letter
Page Two:
    A. Identification of building
    B. Specific statement of the major problem.
    C. Alternative recommendations to the problems
    D. List of your further recommendations.

General statements such as the following can be included in the report:

1. Physically inventory all property at least once a year. Your inventory should list the name of the item, the manufacturer, model, serial number, value, color, and date purchased.
2. Engrave all property in accordance with the established Operation Identification program.
3. All typewriters should be bolted down and all files, cabinets, and rooms containing valuable information or equipment should be locked when not in use.

Other Keys to Being an Effective Surveyor

Only when you have developed the ability to visualize the potential for criminal activity will you become an effective crime scene surveyor. This ability is the part of the process referred to as an art. Nonetheless, it is important that, when you arrive on a survey site, you are prepared to give a property owner sound advice on the type of security precautions to consider.

In summary, to be a good crime prevention surveyor, you have to be a good investigator. You must understand criminal methods of operation and the limitations of standard security devices. In addition, you must be knowledgeable about the type of security hardware necessary to provide various degrees of protection.[3]

Nine Points of Security Concern

1. *General purpose of the building* (i.e., residence, classroom, office). Consider the hours of use, people who use the building, people who have access, key control, and maintenance schedule. Who is responsible for maintenance? Is the building used for public events? If so, what type and how often? Is the building normally opened to the public? Identify the significant factors and make recommendations.
2. *Hazards involving the building or its occupants.* List and prioritize (e.g., theft of office equipment, wallet theft, theft from stockrooms). Identify potential hazards that might exist in the future.
3. *Police or guard security applications.* What can these guards do to improve the response to the building and occupants from a patrol, investigation, or crime prevention standpoint? Would the application of guards be operationally effective or cost-effective?
4. *Physical recommendations.* Inspect doors, windows, lighting, and access points. Recommend physical changes that would make the building more secure, such as pinning hinges on doors and fences.
5. *Locks, equipment to be bolted down, potential application of card control and key control.* Make specific recommendations.
6. *Alarms.* Would an alarm system be cost effective? Would the use of the building preclude the use of an alarm? Are the potential benefits of an alarm such that the building use should be changed to facilitate it? Consider all types of alarms, buildingwide or in specific offices. Consider closed

circuit television and portable or temporary alarm devices.

7. *Storage.* Does the building have specific storage problems, such as expensive items that should be given special attention, petty cash, stamps, calculators, microscopes? Make specific recommendations.

8. *Trespassing.* Are there adequate "No Trespassing" signs posted? Are other signs needed?

9. *Custodians.* Can custodians be used in a manner that would be better from a security standpoint?

Personality of the Complex

Each complex that you survey will have a distinctive personality. Let us take an average building, which is opened from 9 A.M. to 5 P.M. The traffic flow is heaviest during this period. During the span from 5 P.M. to 1 A.M., the building is closed to the public. Some staff member's may work late. Who secures the building? At 1 A.M., the cleaning crew arrives and prepares the building for another day. The whole personality of the complex must be taken into consideration before your report is completed.

Let us take a further example of building personality. The complex is 100 × 100 feet and it has two solid-core doors, one large window at the front of the building, and is air-conditioned.

Case 1. The complex is a credit union on the main street next door to the local police department versus the same credit union on the edge of town.

Case 2. This is a large doctor's office. The doctor is an art buff and has half a million dollars in art in the office versus a doctor who has no art but has a small safe with about $200 worth of Class A narcotics inside.

Case 3. This building houses a variety store that closes at 6 P.M. versus a liquor store that is open until 2 A.M.

In these cases, I have given six examples of the personality of a complex. As I stated, your recommendations must be tailored to fit the lifestyle and vulnerabilities of these buildings.

Positive and Negative Aspects of Making Recommendations

In making your recommendations for security improvements, you must consider the consequences of your suggestion in the event the property owner implements it. Negative as well as positive aspects are involved. Take, for example, a housing complex that has a high crime rate from outsiders and within. Your recommendation is, "Build a 10-foot high fence around the complex."

Positive Aspects

Crime is reduced—the environment can be designed so that the individual considering the criminal act feels that there is a good chance to be seen by someone who will take action and call the police.

Vandalism is less—the target of attack can be made to appear so formidable that the person does not feel able to reach the target. It adds to the physical aesthetics of the area through environmental design.

The visual impact is negative—this insures the property of the residents, adding to their secure environment. Limiting the number of points of entry and establishing access control primarily decreases crime opportunities and keeps out unauthorized persons.

Negative Aspect

A fortress environment may create more of a psychological barrier than a physical one. It is socially undesirable and yet is being replicated throughout our country at an increasing rate.

Community Reaction

This cannot be disregarded. Furthermore, vandalism at the time of early installation should be considered.

Consciousness of fear may develop by those tenants whose apartments face the fence; but as the tenants come and go it will eventually be accepted.

All fences are subject to being painted by groups with a cause.

Crime Analysis

It is not necessary for you to be a statistician, but the more you know about and understand the local crime problems, the better equipped you are to analyze the potential crime risk loss in surveying a business or a home.

Crime analysis collection is simply the gathering of raw data concerning reported crimes and known offenders. Generally, such information comes from crime reports, arrest reports, and police contact cards. This is not to say that these are the only sources available for collecting crime data.

The analysis process as applied to criminal activity is a specific step-by-step sequence of five interconnected functions: crime data collection, crime data collation, data analysis, dissemination of analysis reports, and feedback and evaluation of crime data.

Crime analysis of the site you survey supplies you with specific information to enable you to further harden the target in specific areas where losses have occurred. It is a means of responding "after the fact," when a crime has been committed.

Key Control

Key control is a very important factor in conducting a survey. Check whether the clients are in the habit of picking up keys from employees at their termination and if they have an accurate record of who has which keys. Within a few short minutes, you should realize whether or not the recipient of your survey has a problem.

Almost every company has some sort of master key system, because many people must have access to the building without the inconvenience of carrying two dozen keys around every day. Master keys are required for company executives, middle managers, security department, as well as the maintenance department.

Guidelines for Key Control

- Purchase a large key cabinet to store and control the many keys in your possession.
- Two sets of key tags should be furnished or obtained with the new key cabinet: one tag should read "file-key, must not be loaned out," and the second tag should read "Duplicate." The key cabinet should be equipped with *loan tags,* which identify the person to whom a key is loaned. This tag is to be hung in the numbered peg corresponding to the key that was used.
- Establish accurate records and files, listing the key codes, date key was issued, and who received it.
- Have each employee sign a receipt when he or she receives a key.
- All alarm keys should be marked and coded.
- A check should be made of what keys are in the possession of guards and staff.
- Do not issue keys to any employee unless absolutely necessary.

- Only one person should order and issue keys for the complex.
- Change the key cylinder when an authorized key holder is discharged for cause. Furthermore, discharged or retired employees should produce keys previously issued at the time of termination.
- Periodic inspections should be made to ensure that possession of keys conforms to the record of issuance. These periodic inspections should be utilized to remind key holders that they should immediately notify you of any key loss.
- The original issue of keys and subsequent fabrication and reissuance of keys should ensure that their identity is coded on the keys so the lock for which they were manufactured cannot be identified in plain language.

Closed Circuit Television

Closed circuit television (CCTV) is a valuable asset to any security package and an even more valuable tool if hooked up to a recorder. CCTV is a surveillance tool that provides an added set of eyes. If this equipment is on the site you are surveying, it is your job to evaluate its operation and effectiveness:

1. Is it working properly?
2. How is it being monitored?
3. Is it placed where it will be most beneficial?
4. What are the type and quality of the lens and components?

Intrusion Alarms

If the site, which you are surveying, already has an alarm system, check it out completely. Physically walk through every motion detector unit. Evaluate the quality of the existing alarm products versus what is available to meet the needs of the client.

I surveyed a warehouse recently that was only 5 years old. It was interesting to note that the warehouse had a two-zone alarm system. The control panel was to the right of the front door, which was about 15 feet from the receptionist. Both alarm keys were in the key cylinders, and, according to the president of the company, "The keys have been there since the system was installed." My point is, for a dollar, another key could be duplicated and then the area is vulnerable to attack.

Another time, while doing a survey of an art gallery in New York, the security director stated that he had not had a service call on his alarm system in

2 years. We then proceeded to physically check every motion detection unit and magnetic contact. You can imagine his reaction when he found out that 12 out of the 18 motion detection units were not working.

In conclusion, intrusion alarms come in all shapes and sizes, using a variety of electronic equipment. It is advisable to be familiar with the state of art of electronics so that you can produce an effective report.

Lighting and Security

What would happen if we shut off all the lights at night? Think about it. Such a foolish act would create an unsafe environment. Senior citizens would never go out and communities would have an immediate outbreak of thefts and vandalism. Commercial areas would be burglarized at an uncontrollable rate. Therefore, lighting and security go hand in hand. This example may seem far-fetched, but in fact, installation of improved lighting in a number of cities has resulted in the following: decreased vandalism, decreased street crimes, decrease in suspicious persons, decrease in commercial burglaries, and in general, a reduction in crime.

Streetlights

Streetlights have received widespread notoriety for their value in reducing crime. Generally, streetlights are rated by the size of the lamp and the characteristics of the light dispersed. More specifically, four types of lighting units that are utilized in streetlighting. The most common, and oldest, is the incandescent lamp. It is the least expensive in terms of energy consumed and the number needed. As such, incandescent lighting is generally recognized as the least efficient and economical type of street lighting for use today.

The second type of lighting unit that, as a recently developed system, has been acclaimed by some police officials as "the best source available," is the high-intensity sodium vapor lamp. This lamp produces more lumens per watt than most other types. It is brighter, cheaper to maintain, and the color rendition is close to that of natural daylight.

The third and fourth types of devices commonly used for streetlighting are the mercury vapor and metal halide lamps. Both are bright and produce good color rendition. However, the trend now is to use metal halide because it is more efficient than mercury vapor.

Other Security Aspects

Depending on the type of facility that you are surveying, the following should be reviewed:

1. Communications network, walkie-talkies, and locations of interior and exterior phones.
2. Guard force and security personnel, their training, police powers, uniforms, use of badges, and method of operation.

Your objectives are to identify vulnerabilities, evaluate the site, and provide critical assessment. Methodology and style are purely those of the surveyor, but do not forget they also represent a document from you and your department.

Security Survey Follow-Up

The follow-up to your security survey takes many forms, from actually sitting down with the recipient to going by the site and seeing if any changes have actually taken place. Some police departments produce five to seven surveys a day. They do not evaluate their performance because of the time and personnel involved. In this way, they fail to examine their own effectiveness. The reason for the follow-up is to encourage increased compliance and ensure that recommendations are understood. Without this step you will not know if the recipient has taken any action.

The basic security survey framework consists of five steps:

1. Generating the survey request
2. Conducting the physical inspection
3. Delivering survey recommendations
4. Following up after the report is completed
5. Evaluating the program

For every crime that is committed, there is a crime prevention or loss reduction defense or procedure that, if followed, could delay or prevent a criminal from committing that act.

Physical security involves implementing those measures that could delay or deny unauthorized entry, larceny, sabotage, fire, and vandalism. This chapter of security surveys is geared to assist both private security and public law enforcement to harden a target and assist the community to further reduce losses.

To further assist your security survey, several checklists are included at the end of this chapter.

Residential Security

A large percentage of home burglars enter by a door or window. In most cases the front, rear, bulkhead, or garage door is unlocked. Front and rear doors often have inadequate locks or are built in such a way that breaking the glass to the side of the door or on the door itself allows the burglar to simply reach inside and unlock the door. Windows on the first-floor level are the crook's next choice for entry. Basement windows are the least desirable because they may require the burglar to get dirty and, like executives, this person is concerned about appearance.

Defensive Measures

Doors (Front, Rear, Basement, and Garage)

The first important item is to install deadbolts on all entry doors. A cylinder deadbolt with a 1-inch projecting bolt, made of hardened steel should be utilized. This lock should be used in conjunction with a standard entry knob lock. Viewing devices with a wide-angle lens on entry doors is also standard to prevent unwanted intrusions into the home.

1. *Doors with glass in them.* The backdoor is one of the burglar's favorite entryways. Most rear doors are made partly of glass, and this is an open invitation to a burglar. This type of door must have a double cylinder deadbolt for protection. This type of lock requires a key to open it from the inside as well as the outside, because most burglars break the glass and try to gain entry by opening the locked door from inside.
2. *Sliding glass doors.* These entries should be secured so they cannot be pried out of their track. Also, you can prevent jimmying of your door by putting a "Charley bar" made from wood and cut to size and placed in the track when closed (see Figure 4-1).

Bulkheads should also be included as part of your overall security package, and secured with square bolt or deadbolt locks.

Windows

Windows come in a variety of shapes, sizes, and types, each of which presents a different type of security problem. Windows provide an inviting entryway for a burglar, who does not like to break glass because the noise may alert someone. On double-hung sash-type windows, drill a hole through the top corner of

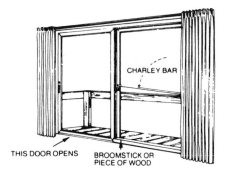

Figure 4-1 To prevent forced sliding of aluminum sliding doors, you can mount a Charley bar, which folds down from the side.

the bottom window into the bottom of the top window. Place a solid pin into the hole to prevent the window from being opened (see Figure 4-2). Keyed window latches may also be installed to prevent the window from being opened. In addition, grilles and grates may be installed over extremely vulnerable accesses.

Entrances

Any opening through which a human body can pass is an entrance. Front doors, basements, patio doors, garages that have access to the house, and windows on the second floor are all entryways to burglars. No one way is more important to protect than another.

Setting up Inner Defenses

Even with the precautions already mentioned, a burglar may still get into the home. Once there, you should try to slow down this spree, as time is the one element working against the criminal. One successful method is to convert a closet into a vault, by installing a deadbolt lock to the door. You have now considerably strengthened your inner defenses. Restricting access from one part of the home to another via deadbolts and the like gives the burglar yet another obstacle to overcome.

Having a burglar alarm stand watch for you is like an insurance policy. The homeowner may never need it, but it is comforting to know it's there. The very best system is a perimeter system that stops an intruder before entering the dwelling, but it is also costly. Less expensive methods involve using pads under rugs and motion detectors.

Remember, no home can be made 100% burglar proof, but in most instances, by making it extremely

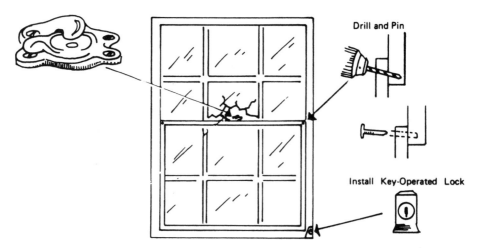

Figure 4-2 A double-hung window can be easily jimmied open with a screwdriver. Glass can be broken adjacent to the crescent latch or by prying against hardware, and the screws can be popped out. To prevent this, drill a hole through the top corner of the bottom window and place a solid pin in the hole. You can also install a key-operated lock.

difficult for the burglar to enter your home, you discourage crime. The burglar will move on to a home where the pickings are easier.

Residential security is more important than we realize. Just ask the victim of a home that has been burglarized. The mother and wife responds, "I felt personally threatened and upset over the losses but more upset over the fact that our home was violated." The father and husband responds "I'm happy my wife and daughter weren't home or they could have been hurt. Now I've got to call the police, my insurance agent, the repairman, and maybe an alarm company."

Too often people say, "It won't happen to me," "Our neighborhood never had a theft," "I sleep with a small gun by my bed," "I have a dog for protection," or "I don't need an alarm system." These are before-the-incident excuses. The cause of residential crime can be found in the individual's environment and lifestyle. Crime can be controlled and losses reduced by corrective human behavior. Physical security measures play an important role in preventing many crimes, but these measures are effective only if they are installed and used properly.

Alarms

Residential intrusion alarms are becoming more popular and installed more frequently. The control panel (Underwriters' Laboratories listed) also bandies the fire alarm system. An audible horn distinguishes which system has gone off. The control panel should have an entrance/exit delay feature, which aids in the overall reduction of false alarms. Depending on the style of the home, any number of components can be used. However, keep in mind that only a total coverage system should be recommended and installed.

Lighting

Improved lighting provides another residential security measure. Although some studies documented crime reduction after improved lighting systems were installed; these studies typically have not accounted for displacement effects. Even if individuals living in a residence reduce the likelihood of a burglary by better lighting, they may only be displacing the burglary to another, less lit area.

Home Security Checklist

Massachusetts Crime Watch[4] put together the following home security checklist, which deals with 35 security checkpoints.

Entrances

1. Are the doors of metal or solid wood construction?
2. Are door hinges protected from removal from outside?

3. Are there windows in the door or within 40 inches of the lock?
4. Are there auxiliary locks on the doors?
5. Are strikes and strike plates securely fastened?
6. If there are no windows in the door, is there a wide-angle viewer or voice intercommunications device?
7. Can the lock mechanism be reached through a mail slot, delivery port, or pet entrance at the doorway?
8. Is there a screen or storm door with an adequate lock?
9. Are all exterior entrances lighted?
10. Can entrances be observed from the street or public areas?
11. Does the porch or landscaping offer concealment from view from the street or public area?
12. If the door is a sliding glass door, is the sliding panel secured from being lifted out of the track?
13. Is a Charley bar or key-operated auxiliary lock used on the sliding glass door?
14. Is the sliding door mounted on the inside of the stationary panel?

Entrances from Garage and Basement

15. Are all entrances to living quarters from garage and basement of metal or solid wood construction?
16. Does the door from garage to living quarters have auxiliary locks for exterior entrance?
17. Does the door from basement to living quarters have an auxiliary lock operated from living quarters side?

Ground Floor Windows

18. Do all windows have key-operated locks or a method of pinning in addition to regular lock?
19. Do all windows have screens or storm windows that lock from inside?
20. Do any windows open onto areas that may be hazardous or offer special risk of burglary?
21. Are exterior areas of windows free from concealing structure or landscaping?

Upper Floor and Windows

22. Do any upper floor windows open onto porch or garage roofs or roofs of adjoining buildings?
23. If so, are they secured as adequately as if they were at ground level?
24. Are trees and shrubbery kept trimmed back from upper floor windows?

25. Are ladders kept outside the house where they are accessible?

Basement Doors and Windows

26. Is there a door from the outside to the basement?
27. If so, is that door adequately secure for an exterior door?
28. Is the outside basement entrance lighted by exterior light?
29. Is the basement door concealed from the street or neighbors?
30. Are all basement windows secured against entry?

Garage Doors and Windows

31. Is the automobile entrance door to the garage equipped with a locking device?
32. Is garage door kept closed and locked at all times?
33. Are garage windows secured adequately for ground floor windows?
34. Is the outside utility entrance to garage as secure as required for any ground floor entrance?
35. Are all garage doors lighted on the outside?

Protecting Personal Property

A number of programs have been developed throughout the country that are geared to aid the citizen to reduce losses in the community. A number of these programs follow:

1. *Operation Identification* is a program that started in 1963 in Monterey Park, California. This program encourages citizens to engrave their personal property with a state driver's license number.
2. *Bicycle registration and antitheft program.* Some communities have started a mandatory registration of bicycles as well as an educational program. The educational program identifies poor-quality locks used to secure bikes as well as providing instructions for properly securing a bike.
3. *Auto theft prevention* is another educational program, which is generally implemented by the distribution of printed material and is covered at community meetings. How many times have you seen a person keep the engine running while going into the store to buy milk? This is an example of giving the criminal an opportunity to commit a crime.

4. *Neighborhood watch.* This program, initiated in 1971, encourages people to report suspicious circumstances in their neighborhoods to the police, as well as familiarizing the citizens with crime prevention techniques to reduce criminal opportunity. Be alert for these suspicious signs:[5]
   - A stranger entering a neighbor's house when the neighbor is not home.
   - Unusual noises, like a scream, breaking glass, or an explosion.
   - People, male or female, in your neighborhood that do not live there.
   - Someone going door-to-door in your neighborhood, if he or she tries to open the doors or goes into the backyard, especially if a companion waits out front or a car follows close behind.
   - Someone trying to force entry into a home, even if wearing a uniform.
   - A person running, especially if carrying something of value.

   The person who sees anything suspicious is to call the police immediately. Give the responding officers a physical description of the person and license plate number of the car. Even if nothing is wrong, such alertness is appreciated.

5. *Security surveys.* Many police departments today have trained crime prevention officers who can provide security survey assistance to residents, enabling the citizen to better protect the family, home, and environment.

6. *Citizen patrols.* The citizen patrol can be viewed as part of the long historical tradition of vigilantism in this country, with all the ambivalence present in that term. Presently, where their numbers are reported to be increasing in a number of suburban communities and cities across the country, citizen patrols are seen ideally as performing a relatively simple and narrowly defined role—to deter criminal activity by their presence. Their function should be that of a passive guard—to watch for criminal or suspicious activity and alert the police when they see it. Drawing on information that exists about current citizen groups, what are the advantages over other protective measures?
   - Patrols are relatively inexpensive.
   - Patrols can perform a surveillance function effectively.
   - Patrols take advantage of existing behavior patterns.
   - Patrols can improve an individual's ability to deal with crime.
   - Patrols contribute to other desirable social goals related to neighborhood cohesiveness

and the provision of a desirable alternative to less acceptable activity.

In practice, however, patrols exhibit serious shortcomings:

- The typical patrol is formed in response to a serious incident or heightened level of fear about crime. The ensuing pattern is cyclic: increased membership, success in reducing criminal activity at least in a specific area, boredom, decreasing membership, dissolution. As a result, patrols tend to be short-lived.
- The passive role of a patrol is difficult to maintain.
- The police are reluctant to cooperate with a patrol and may even oppose it.
- The patrol may aggravate community tensions.

The principal problems of patrols relate to their inability to sustain the narrow, anticrime role they initially stress. They may be an effective temporary measure to deal with criminal contagion in a particular area. Over the longer term, however, the inherent risks may outweigh the continued benefits. The proliferation of patrols in recent years is evidence that they fill a need, but it should be recognized that patrols are no substitute for adequate police protection.

In conclusion, residential security can best be obtained by getting the facts on what you can do to secure your home, analyzing these facts, and arriving at a decision and implementing security measures.

Conclusion

In January 2003, the American Society for Industrial Security International came out with a set of "General Security Risk Assessment Guidelines." In these guidelines it is recommended that, when conducting a security survey or risk assessment of a complex, you consider the following seven points from their report:

1. Assets are people, property, intangible property, and information; identify the risks attached to each.
2. Conduct a cost/benefit analysis and explore the value of all benefits to be a accrued. Are the recommendations that are made affordable, feasible, available, practical, and state of the art?
3. Consider the risk, risk analysis, risk assessment, probability, and vulnerability to incidences.
4. Gathering statistical data: material obtained from in house, material obtained from local and state police agencies, material from the FBI, Uniform

Crime Report database, and the type of incidents in similar complexes as well as rating of current Homeland Security color code.

5. Examine the frequency of events and what can be done to reduce and remove the overall threat.

6. Identify the assets; for example, a warehouse with a million dollar inventory—30 people have access, maybe more—alarm system control panel is a dialer non-UL, 22 years old; or a museum worth a $52-million dollar inventory, four people have total access, and 5-year-old fire and intrusion alarm all points are tested monthly.

7. Reassessment of your complex annually.

References

1. Raymond M. Momboisse. *Industrial Security for Strikes, Riots and Disasters* (Springfield, IL: Charles C. Thomas, 1968), p. 13.
2. Arthur A. Kingsbury. *Introduction to Security and Crime Prevention Surveys* (Springfield, IL: Charles C. Thomas, 1973), pp. 6, 7.
3. Washington Crime Watch. *Crime Prevention Training Manual,* Security Survey Section, p. 8.
4. Massachusetts Crime Watch. *Home Security Test Booklet*, LEAA, 1980.
5. Dick LaFaver. *The Home Security Book,* #16. Shell Oil Company, p. 6.

Appendix 4.A
Site Survey and Risk Assessment*

VICTOR HAROLD

Crime prevention, or lessening the potential for crime, begins with a major in-depth security analysis of the business or facility. A survey of the interior and exterior will point out security deficiencies and potential for intrusion or the probability that a crime will occur at that spot.

After the survey, an appraisal and recommendation for action should be immediately undertaken. A timetable for implementing the recommendations should be originated and strictly followed.

It is possible the site survey is beyond the ability of most business management. If it is, you are advised to obtain the services of a qualified security professional.

You are also urged to have this service performed immediately. Consider the vulnerability of your business to imminent criminal intrusion. Many burglarized companies as well as those, which were victimized by white-collar crime, have suffered irreversible losses, slowdown, and even shutdown.

This appendix broadly points out the external and internal geographical areas that may require immediate and long-term consideration to help prevent criminal breach of the premises.

1. Can you obtain a neighborhood crime statistics report from the local police?
2. Can you determine if there has been any labor unrest in the area?
3. Can you obtain a report that details the extent of damage a labor unrest may have had on a firm in the area?
4. What is the prevalent type of damage done to companies during a labor unrest in the area?
5. Has your company ever been victimized by the labor unrest of other companies in the area?
6. Have prior tenants or owners of your facility ever reported a criminal incident?
7. What types of crimes are the most prevalent in the area? List by percentage and frequency.
8. Is your facility very visible from the local roads?
9. Is there easy access by emergency vehicles to your building from the local roads?

*Reprinted with permission of Victor Harold from *How to Stop Theft in Your Business*.

10. Have you a chart showing the frequency of police patrols in the area?
11. Do you know how long it would take an emergency or police vehicle to reach your facility?
12. Have you an evaluation of your building's roof and doors which details the length of time it will take for a break-in to be successful?
13. Have you an evaluation of the safes, locks, and other devices to ascertain how long they can delay being opened?
14. If you require separate storage of high-risk or valuable items, are they placed in a high security area that discourages intrusion?
15. Is personnel movement within the building controlled?
16. Have the door and window hardware been evaluated for ease of entry?
17. Have window openings been secured? (Check with local fire department codes.)
18. Are important files and computer operations secured in an area that prohibits unauthorized entry?
19. Is the lighting sufficient throughout all work areas?
20. Are vent and roof access panels and doors wired and latched to prevent intrusion?
21. Have you prevented external access to the locker rooms, vending and lounge areas?
22. Are the financial handling areas separate and secure?
23. Do you keep confidential your safe's contents; the combinations and the controls needed to maintain security?
24. Are the removable panels and grates in which a person or inventory may be concealed periodically removed and checked?
25. Can these panels and grates be more securely fastened without compromising the item to which they are installed?
26. Will you require police, fire department, or building department approval to more securely fasten those panels and grates?
27. Are the incoming electrical lines well secured and vandal free?
28. Are the panels on all electrical items fastened?
29. Are the electrical power grids, panels, backup, power supplies, etc., kept in a separate locked area?
30. Have you conducted a walk around the property to see if trees, hedges, walls, and fences can hide a person or goods?
31. Have you considered immediate action to correct?
32. If some visibility obstructions exist, are you taking steps to correct?
33. To prevent inventory from going out with the trash, are you keeping a secure trash collection area?
34. To prevent roof access, are trees and their branches next to buildings removed?
35. Are ladders kept secure?
36. Are you aware that noisy equipment can mask unauthorized entry?
37. Are all exterior building entry points alarmed?
38. Are you aware that certain internal and external conditions may affect the alarm?
39. Is there a log of alarm malfunctions and their causes?
40. Have all the causes of alarm malfunction been remedied?
41. Is there an alarm listing and maintenance schedule?
42. Has the police or security company's response to an alarm been tested?
43. Are key management personnel frequently tested on alarm use?
44. Have key personnel been given specific alarm control assignments, to include alarm opening, closing, checkout procedures, and accountability?
45. Are there clearly established money handling procedures to follow for safeguarding cash deposits, etc.?
46. Do you have a policy for reporting thefts other than security breaches? (Anonymously, if you think it is best.)
47. Are office machines, shop equipment, and other easily movable items marked for identification purposes?
48. Are vendors, sales people, and repairpersons logged in and out and, when necessary, given visitor's passes?
49. Are the employees frequently updated on security procedures?
50. Are you keeping a file of security deficiencies and a schedule for correction?

Appendix 4.B
Physical Security Survey*

VICTOR HAROLD

Exterior Physical Characteristics: Perimeter

Grounds

1. Is the fence strong and in good repair?
2. Is the fence height designed so that an intruder cannot climb over it?
3. Is the distance of the fence from the building designed so that an intruder cannot crawl under it?
4. Are boxes or other materials placed at a safe distance from the fence?
5. Are there weeds or trash adjoining the building, which should be removed?
6. Are stock, crates, or merchandise allowed to be piled near the building?
7. Is there a clear area on both sides of the fence?
8. Are unsecured overpasses or subterranean passageways near the fence?
9. Are fence gates solid and in good condition?
10. Are fence gates properly locked?
11. Are fence gates' hinges secure and non-removable?
12. What types of lock and chain are used to secure gate?
13. Have unnecessary gates been eliminated?
14. Do you check regularly those gates that are locked?
15. Are blind alleys near buildings protected?
16. Are fire escapes and exits designed for quick exit but difficult entry?

17. Is the perimeter reinforced by protective lighting?
18. Has shrubbery near windows, doors, gates, garage, and access roads been kept to a minimum?
19. What are the physical boundaries of the residence's grounds?
20. Does lighting illuminate all roads?
21. Is there a procedure to identify vendors, subcontractors, and visitors before entrance to the gate?

Exterior Doors

1. Are all doors strong and formidable?
2. Are all door hinge pins located on the inside?
3. Are all door hinges installed so that it would be impossible to remove the closed door(s) without seriously damaging the door or jamb?
4. Are all door frames well constructed and in good condition?
5. Are the exterior locks double cylinder, deadbolts, or jimmy-proof?
6. Can the breaking of glass or a door panel then allow the person to open the door?
7. Are all locks working properly?
8. Are all doors properly secured or reinforced?
9. Are all unused doors secured?
10. Are the keys in possession of authorized personnel?
11. Are keys issued only to personnel who actually need them?

*Reprinted with permission of Victor Harold.

12. Are the padlocks, chains, and hasps heavy enough?
13. Are the hasps installed so that the screws cannot be removed?
14. Are all hasps, padlocks, and chains case-hardened?

Exterior Windows

1. Are nonessential windows either bricked up or protected with steel mesh or iron bars?
2. Are all windows within 14 feet of the ground equipped with protective coverings?
3. Are the bars or screens mounted securely?
4. Do those windows with locks have locks that are designed and located so they cannot be reached or opened by breaking the glass?
5. Are small or expensive items left in windows overnight?
6. Is security glass used in any of these windows?
7. Are windows located under loading docks or similar structures protected?
8. Can windows be removed without breaking them?
9. Are all vents and similar openings having a gross area of 1 square foot or more secured with protective coverings?
10. Are windows connected to an alarm system adequately protected?
11. Are windows not secured by bars or alarms kept locked or otherwise protected?
12. Have windows (doors) been reinforced with Lexan?
13. Are all windows properly equipped with locks, reinforced glass, or decorative protective bars or sturdy shutters?
14. Are unused windows permanently closed?

Other Openings

1. Do you have a lock on manholes that give direct access to your building or to a door that a burglar could easily open?
2. Have you permanently closed manholes or similar openings that are no longer used?
3. Are your sidewalk doors or grates locked properly and secured?
4. Are your sidewalk doors or grates securely in place so that the entire frame cannot be pried open?

5. Are your accessible skylights protected with bars or an intrusion alarm?
6. Did you eliminate unused skylights, which are an invitation to burglary?
7. Are exposed roof hatches properly secured?
8. Are fan openings or ventilator shafts protected?
9. Does a service tunnel or sewer connect to the building?
10. Do fire escapes comply with city and state fire regulations?
11. Are your fire exits or escapes designed so that a person can leave easily but would have difficulty in entering?
12. Do fire exit doors have a portable alarm mounted, to communicate if the door is opened, or is it hooked up to the intrusion alarm?
13. Can entrance be gained from an adjoining building?

Exterior Lighting

1. Is the lighting adequate to illuminate critical areas (alleys, fire escapes, and ground level windows)?
2. How many foot-candles is the lighting on horizontal at ground level (estimation, Underwriters' Laboratories [UL])?
3. Is there sufficient illumination over entrances?
4. Are the perimeter areas lighted to assist police surveillance of the area?
5. Are the protective lighting system and the working lighting system on the same line?
6. Is there an auxiliary system that has been tested?
7. Is there an auxiliary power source for protective lighting?
8. Is the auxiliary system designed to go into operation automatically when needed?
9. Are the protective lights controlled automatically by a timer or photocells or is it manually operated?
10. What hours is this lighting used?
11. Does it use switch box(es) or is it automatically time secured?
12. Can protective lights be compromised easily (e.g., unscrewing of bulbs)?
13. What type of lights are installed around the property?
14. Are they cost effective?
15. Are the fixtures vandal proof?
16. Is there a glare factor?
17. Is there an even distribution of light?

Interior Physical Characteristics

1. Name of the site
2. Address
3. Full name and exact title of the administrative officer
4. Telephone number
5. Name of the surveying officer
6. Full name and exact title of the security liaison
7. Describe the security problem at this site
8. What is the general purpose of the site?
9. What is the range of hours in use?
10. Which hours and days represent high activity use?
11. How many people have access to the site?
12. Is the site normally open to the public?
13. List the number of rooms occupied by the various departments and offices
14. Who does maintenance?
15. On what schedule does maintenance operate?
16. List the estimated dollar value of equipment and property in each department or office
17. What area has the highest dollar value?
18. What area contains the most sensitive material?

Interior Lighting

1. Is there a backup system for emergency lights?
2. Is the lighting provided during the day adequate for security purposes?
3. Is the lighting at night adequate for security purposes?
4. Is the night lighting sufficient for surveillance by the local police department?

Doors

1. Are doors constructed of a sturdy and solid material?
2. Are doors limited to the essential minimum?
3. Are outside door hinge pins spot-welded or bradded to prevent removal?
4. Are those hinges installed on the inward side of the door?
5. Is there at least one lock on each outer door?
6. Is each door equipped with a locking device?

Offices

1. Can entrances be reduced without loss of efficiency?
2. Are office doors locked when unattended for long periods?
3. Does the receptionist have a clear view of the entrance, stairs, and elevators?
4. Are maintenance people, visitors, and the like required to show identification to the receptionist?
5. Are desks and files locked when the office is left unattended?
6. Are items of value left on desks or in an unsecure manner?
7. Are all typewriters bolted down?
8. Are floors free of projections, cracks, and debris?
9. During normal working hours, is the storage facility kept locked when not in use?
10. How many people have keys to this door?

Keys

1. How many keys are issued? How many master keys?
2. Is there a key control system?
3. What is the basis of issuance of keys?
4. Is an adequate log maintained of all keys issued?
5. Are key holders ever allowed to duplicate keys?
6. Are keys marked "Do Not Duplicate"?
7. If master key(s) are used, are they devoid of markings identifying them as such?
8. Are losses or thefts of key(s) promptly reported to security officer or police?
9. Who (name and title) is responsible for issuing and replacement keys?
10. When was the last visual key audit made (to ensure they had not been loaned, lost, or stolen)?
11. Were all the keys accounted for? (If not, how many were missing? How often do you conduct visual audits?)
12. Are duplicate keys stored in a secure place? Where?
13. Are keys returned when an employee resigns, is discharged, or is suspended? (If not, why not?)

Locks

1. Are all entrances equipped with secure locking devices?
2. Are they always locked when not in active use? (If not, why not?)
3. Is the lock designed or the frame built so that the door cannot be forced by spreading the frame?

4. Are all locks in working order?
5. Are the screws holding the locks firmly in place?
6. Is the bolt protected or constructed so that it cannot be cut?
7. Are locks' combinations changed or rotated immediately upon resignation, discharge, or suspension of an employee having possession of a master key(s)? If not, why not?
8. Are your locks changed once a year regardless of transfers or known violations of security? If not, why not?
9. When was the last time the locks were changed?

Petty Cash

1. How much petty cash is kept?
2. Are funds kept to a minimum?
3. Where is petty cash secured?
4. Are blank checks also stored there?
5. Are checks presigned?
6. Is the accounting system adequate to prevent loss or pilfering of funds accessible to unauthorized persons at any time?
7. Are funds kept overnight in a safe, locked desk, or file cabinet?
8. Is this storage area secure?
9. Are locks in the storage area replaced when keys are lost, missing, or stolen?
10. How many people handle petty cash?

Safes

1. What methods do you use to protect the safe combination?
2. Are combinations changed or rotated immediately upon resignation, discharge, or suspension of an employee having possession of the combination? If not, why not?
3. Is your safe approved by Underwriters' Laboratories?
4. Is your safe designed for burglary protection as well as fire protection?
5. Where is (are) safe(s) located?
6. Is it well lit at night?
7. Can it be seen from outside?
8. Do you keep money in your safe?
9. Do you keep cash at a minimum by banking regularly?
10. Do you use care in working the combination so that it is not observed?
11. Do you spin the dial rather than leaving it on "day lock"?
12. Do you have a policy of making certain that the safe is properly secured and the room, door(s), and windows are locked, night light(s) are on, and no one is hidden inside?
13. Is your safe secured to the floor or wall?
14. Are combinations changed at least every 6 months? If not, when was the last time?
15. Do you have a protective theft alarm? If yes, is it local or central?
16. When was the system last tested?

Inventory Control

1. When was the last time an inventory of business equipment was made, listing serial numbers and descriptions?
2. Were any items missing or unaccounted for?
3. Are all typewriters and the like bolted down or otherwise secured?
4. Has the site marked all of their business equipment?
5. Is all expensive business equipment stored in a security cabinet or room?

Appendix 4.C
Plant Security Checklist*

VICTOR HAROLD

1. Have you obtained a list of certified protection professionals from the American Society for Industrial Security (Arlington, Virginia)?
2. Have you assigned a senior executive to act as liaison with the security consultant?
3. Have you assessed overall plant vulnerability to a variety of risks?
4. Have you checked with local police agencies about the incidence of vandalism, damage, reported internal losses, burglaries, and other crimes in the vicinity?
5. Have you checked with fire officials about the local incidence and type of fires and extent of losses?
6. Do you do periodic reviews of the plant security system, especially with a view toward effectiveness?
7. Do you periodically review the efficiency and willingness of the assigned security executive to carry out the function?
8. In many situations, the cost of security is far greater than actual or expected loss. Have your circumstances been analyzed for cost effectiveness?
9. Do you maintain a list of security regulations? Is it properly posted? Is it periodically reviewed?
10. Are you certain that there has been no negligence in the guard force?
11. How often do you review the methods used to screen new employees, and are you certain screening is done?
12. Is there a policy to prevent laxity and indiscriminate use of badges and passes?

13. On termination of employment of a senior executive, are locks, codes, and passwords changed?
14. Have you trained line supervisors to check daily the plant's physical condition, both interior and exterior?
15. Do you tell your plant engineers to check daily critical utility areas for damage; that is, sewers, telephone, water, and electricity?
16. If security equipment is to be installed, has the installation plan been approved by a qualified group; that is, fire department, architect, police department, or engineer?
17. Has there been a recent security evaluation of hardware, containers, fire control equipment, safety items, locks, and bars?
18. Do you have a daily inspection of interior and exterior intrusion detection systems, fire systems, and sprinkler systems?
19. Do you daily test and examine your alarm system for jumpers and proper operation?
20. Is your alarm system of the divided type; that is, can small segments be disconnected from the still operational main system?
21. Do you have a security communication network? Are all parts operating?
22. If you use closed circuit television and cameras, are all stations functioning well?
23. When purchasing new equipment, is the suitability and reliability of the items checked out by a dependable group?
24. Have you a study showing that your security measures can generate a return on investment because losses are avoided and assets are recovered?

* Reprinted with permission of Victor Harold.

25. Has a thorough security survey identified various probable events, such as pilferage or white-collar crime, to which the company is vulnerable?
26. Can an approximate dollar amount be placed on each factor?
27. Will the survey estimate the cost versus benefit ratio of attempting to correct any security infringement?
28. Does the security survey answer the following:
    a. What is the possibility of a specific occurrence?
    b. What is the probability of a specific occurrence?
    c. What set of circumstances has to be in place for a situation to happen?
    d. If a problem occurs, how much will it cost to correct and restore?
    e. Is there any personal risk to my people?
    f. If we do not install a security system, can we handle most situations on our own?
    g. What is the correct security level required to accomplish the mission?
29. Do you minimize contact between employees and nonemployees (as much as possible)?
30. Do you keep a record of which employee has keys to specific areas?
31. Are locks changed regularly?
32. Are doors double or triple locked?
33. Are external signs posted stating that alarm systems are in operation?
34. Because the roof is a weak spot, has it been properly protected from intrusion, such as with sensitive sonic alarms or microwave?
35. Have perimeter entrances been minimized to prevent accessibility by key?
36. Have you determined whether you need a badge or employee pass identification system?
37. Are your employees trained to challenge an unrecognized visitor or nonpass-wearing person?
38. Are outside service vendors escorted to the job site? Periodically checked or stayed with? Escorted out?
39. Do you retain a security consultant to annually review physical security needs and update security devices?
40. Do your employees know you will prosecute theft offenders?
41. Have you requested that your alarm agency notify you if the premises have been visited during unusual hours by an employee with a key?
42. Are office keys given only to those who need access?
43. Have you a record of which key was given to whom?
44. Do you collect keys immediately from discharged employees?
45. Do you change the locks of areas in which discharged employees had access?
46. Are keys marked with "Do Not Duplicate" logos?
47. Are serial numbers ground off keys to prevent duplication by number?
48. Is a responsible executive in charge of key distribution?
49. Are spare keys kept in a secure cabinet?
50. Are duplicate records kept, indicating key distribution, date and time issued?
51. Can your telephones be locked to prevent unauthorized after-hours use?
52. Have you a locksmith who periodically checks all lock operations?
53. Can personal items be secured in a locked desk drawer?
54. Are important papers kept in a double-locked and fireproofed file?
55. When filing cabinets are unlocked for use, are keys removed and secured?
56. Are office machines bolted down and locked?
57. Are your office machines and plant equipment marked for identification?
58. Are the serial numbers of office and plant equipment recorded, duplicated, and secured?
59. Are briefcases with important documents left in a locked cabinet?
60. Are important papers removed from desks and locked when the area is not staffed?
61. When the building shuts down for the evening or weekend, are doors and windows checked by a manager?
62. Do service personnel from outside vendors have proper identification?
63. When shutting down for the evening, are potential hiding places checked?
64. Are the police and fire department numbers posted near each telephone?
65. Are safe combinations changed very frequently?
66. Are the guards' watch-clock tapes checked every evening?
67. Have you determined if a shredder is necessary?
68. Do you avoid keeping large sums of cash overnight?
69. Do visitors sign in?
70. If the employees wear passes, do your security people check them even if the wearers are familiar?
71. If you have a facility that requires constant security, do you escort your visitors?

72. Is a vigil kept on outside maintenance people, especially communications workers?
73. If you have a sensitive security area, is access to it kept limited?
74. Is the security area marked with signs and color-coded?
75. Do you need an area where sensitive talks take place?
76. Do you periodically check offices for signs of tampering, such as moved desks, paint marks, putty and other fillers used to seal holes, dust and scratch marks, and more?
77. Do you avoid discussing on the phone what you are going to do about your security situation?
78. Do you avoid ordering security sweeps and changes in security structure over the phone?
79. Do you test the integrity of the security service by ascertaining if they will plant a device?
80. Do your security officers observe the counter-surveillance people at work?
81. Are the items prone to tapping or targets for security intrusion sealed? Are the seals checked regularly?
82. If a bug is found, do you continue to search for more?
83. Are all entry places alarmed?
84. Do you have a locker area for employees' personal use? Is the facility kept secure?
85. Are your security guards routinely given polygraphs?

Appendix 4.D
Guard Security Checklist*

VICTOR HAROLD

1. Have you determined whether or not you have limited security requirements?
2. If you have determined that your security needs are complex, have you talked about your needs to a select group of trustworthy agencies?
3. If your security needs are simple, are you aware that it is time consuming and a waste of productivity to obtain a wide variety of competitive bids?
4. Have you checked with a local law enforcement official for recommendations?
5. Have you checked with colleagues who are using security services for recommendations?
6. If you are analyzing a security agency, have you requested information on the amount, type, and stipulations of their insurance coverage?
7. Have you requested information on the security agency's clients, the names of current customers, and the length of time the account has been with the agency?
8. Have you requested information on the agency's financial status?
9. Is the agency willing to reveal guard training techniques?
10. Does the agency have guard incentive programs?
11. Does the agency have a career program for its guards?
12. Do the guards meet educational and medical checks?
13. Has the agency a set of standards to which guards are held? What are they?
14. Have you reviewed the credentials of the senior executives of the guard company?
15. Will your account have a representative assigned who is from the highest level of management?
16. Will the agency you select have the capabilities to offer other services, such as investigations, dis-

*Reprinted with permission of Victor Harold.

aster planning, executive protection, employee screening, and polygraph testing?

17. Have you determined if the agency you are selecting has a union affiliation? Which one?
18. Will there be a union conflict if your employees go on strike?
19. Have you visited the agency's local office?
20. Have you discussed prior clients and why they no longer are clients?
21. Have you visited current accounts and talked to management?
22. In the contractual arrangement with the guard company, have you avoided too much control over their employees?
23. Have you double-checked the insurance liability of the agency?
24. Does the contract with the guard company assure that it is an independent contractor, relieving your firm of joint employer liability?
25. Have you reviewed the contract's provisions for replacing unsatisfactory guards and terminating the contract?
26. Does the contract guarantee costs?
27. Does the contract contain penalties for nonperformance or poor performance?
28. Is there an agreement by the guard company to refrain from doing business with a competitive company?
29. Have you assigned a senior person to monitor security services to determine that standards are being met and the agency's contractual obligations are being fulfilled?
30. If your plant is paying for guard services, have you discussed wages and job-related expenses, such as travel, holidays, and supervisors?
31. Have you discussed any special training required to accomplish the assignment, such as firearms, CPR, fire safety, and first aid?
32. If your situation requires a formal presentation and contract, have the documents been reviewed by your legal counsel and insurance company?
33. Have you reviewed provisions for contract terminations?

Appendix 4.E
Office Security Checklist

The UCLA Campus Police Department put together the following office security checklist, which deals with 30 security points pertaining to operational procedures, as well as physical characteristics.

1. Do you restrict office keys to those who actually need them?
2. Do you keep complete, up-to-date records of the disposition of all office keys?
3. Do you have adequate procedures for collecting keys from former employees?
4. Do you secure all typewriters, adding machines, calculators, photocopiers, and the like with maximum-security locks?
5. Do you restrict duplication of office keys, except for those specifically ordered by you in writing?
6. Do you require that all keys be marked "Do Not Duplicate" to prevent legitimate locksmiths from making copies without your knowledge?
7. Have you established a rule that keys must not be left unguarded on desks or cabinets, and do you enforce that rule?
8. Do you require that filing cabinet keys be removed from locks and placed in a secure location after opening cabinets in the morning?
9. Do you have procedures that prevent unauthorized personnel from reporting a "lost key" and receiving a "replacement"?
10. Is a responsible person in charge of issuing all keys?
11. Are all keys systematically stored in a secured wall cabinet either of your own design or from a commercial key control system?
12. Do you keep a record showing issuance and return of every key, including name of person, date, and time?
13. Do you use telephone locks to prevent unauthorized calls when the office is unattended?

14. Do you provide at least one lockable drawer in every secretary's desk to protect purses and other personal effects?
15. Do you have at least one filing cabinet secured with an auxiliary locking bar so that you can keep business secrets under better protection?
16. Do you record all equipment serial numbers and file them in a safe place to maintain correct identification in the event of theft or destruction by fire?
17. Do you shred all important papers before discarding in wastebaskets?
18. Do you lock briefcases and attaché cases containing important papers in closets or lockers when not in use?
19. Do you insist on identification from repair personnel who come to do work in your office?
20. Do you deposit incoming checks and cash each day so that you do not keep large sums in the office overnight?
21. Do you clear all desks of important papers every night and place them in locked, fireproof safes or cabinets?

22. Do you frequently change the combination of your safe to prevent anyone from memorizing it or passing it on to a confederate?
23. When working alone in the office at night, do you set the front door lock to prevent anyone else from getting in?
24. Do you have the police and fire department telephone numbers posted and handy?
25. Do you check to see that no one remains behind hiding at night if you are the last to leave the office?
26. Are all windows, transoms, and ventilators properly protected?
27. Do you double-check to see that all windows and doors are securely locked before you leave?
28. Are all doors leading to the office secured by heavy-duty, double-cylinder deadbolt locks?
29. If your office is equipped with a burglar alarm system or protected by a guard service, do you make sure the alarm equipment is set properly each night?
30. Do you have a periodic security review made by a qualified security expert or locksmith?

Appendix 4.F
Home Security Checklist

VICTOR HAROLD

Exterior

1. Do you have a burglar alarm?
2. Are there stickers on your windows and doors, stating that the property is under surveillance?
3. Are bicycles, garden equipment, and other items kept indoors and locked?
4. Is your mailbox locked?
5. Are front and back doors kept lighted in the evening?
6. Are shrubs and trees trimmed low, below window level?
7. Do you arrange for mail and newspaper pickup or stop deliveries, if you are not at home?

8. Is your grass kept mowed while you are away?
9. Is there a neighborhood watch program?
10. Do you place lights on timers or photocells if you go away?
11. Are police notified of your extended absence?

Doors

1. Do all doors, especially the garage, close tightly?
2. Are all doors double locked?
3. Are overhead doors locked when not in use? Is there a track lock?
4. If padlocks are used, are they of high quality?

5. If hinges and hasps show, are the screws and hinge pins of the type that cannot easily be removed?
6. If your car is in the garage, are the doors locked and the keys removed?
7. Are the entrance doors solid core?
8. Is there a security plate in the lock area to prevent jimmying?
9. Are there peepholes in the entrance doors?
10. If the entry doors have glass, is the glass 40 or more inches from the lock?
11. Are sliding doors locked and has an antislide bar on the lower track, as well as bars on top of the doors, been installed to prevent lifting door off the track?

Windows

1. Are the window air conditioners bolted to prevent removal from the outside?
2. Can the basement windows be locked?
3. Do you use auxiliary pins and other locks on all windows?
4. If windows are kept open for ventilation, can they be locked in the open position?

General Home Security

1. Can all exterior doors be locked from the inside?
2. Are the locks on all exterior doors of the dead-bolt type?
3. If a door or window is opened while you are home, will there be a warning sound or light?
4. When you retire or leave, do you check doors and windows to be certain they are locked?
5. When repair people and utility company representatives come to your door, do you request identification?
6. Can your basement door be locked to prevent entry into the house?
7. Are extra house keys kept isolated or hidden?
8. Do you avoid indiscriminate handing out of duplicate keys?

9. If you park your car in a public lot, do you separate the car keys from the house keys?
10. Have you an outside light that remains on all night?
11. Are all low level windows that are easily accessible kept doubly secure with latches and bolts?
12. Have you installed window and door devices that audibly and visually indicate that a break-in is in progress or has occurred?
13. Are your skylights well secured; that is, not easily removed from the roof?
14. Are window air conditioners well installed and not removable from the outside?
15. Are your portable fire extinguishers kept in good condition?
16. Are they kept in easily accessible areas?
17. Are smoke and heat detectors installed near sleeping areas and on every level of the house?
18. Are the detectors tested frequently?
19. Are fire drills a regular routine with your family?
20. Do you have an emergency notification system to enable other households to know that a situation (medical, panic, and robbery) is occurring?
21. If a suspicious vehicle is in the area, is a description and the license number noted?
22. If you go away, can you get a neighbor to park a spare car in your driveway?
23. Do you have a home safe for valuable items?
24. Should you have an alarm system survey to help determine your security and safety needs?

Miscellaneous

1. Is valuable property inventoried, periodically updated, and the list secured?
2. Is the list of serial numbers of those items that have been recorded kept off the premises?
3. Are valuable items marked with a scriber and an identifying number?
4. Are emergency telephone numbers memorized and prominently displayed near the telephone?
5. Do you avoid keeping cash in the house?
6. If you have weapons, are they secured?

Appendix 4.G
Fire Safety Inspection

MICHAEL SROBERGER, CPP, CPO, and CSS

The following inspection is designed to be the basis of a revised and property-specific inspection program. Some of the entries refer to functions performed with a "reasonable frequency." In reviewing your specific property or location, care should be taken to consider the nature of the structure, geographic location, intended use, and actual use. In many cases, functions that are best performed on a daily basis, in one environment, can be reasonably performed on a weekly or possibly monthly basis, in a different environment.

In addition, note that every application is unique, in some manner. As such, what might be prudent for one location, however seemingly similar, might be insufficient at another location. While benchmarking of a similar program is highly recommended, this also should be seen as simply a basic guideline, in the creation of a customized, location-specific program.

Some sections pose inspection inquiries that reference a large number of possible locations or items to be reviewed. One example would be the inspection of sprinkler heads. In designing the actual checklist for such an inspection, it is often desirable to break down the physical layout of the facility into reasonable and manageable zones. Identifying sets of sprinkler heads by the room in which they are installed allows the person performing the inspection to review them as a set and make comments in reference to that area of coverage. In cases such as fire doors, it might be reasonable to identify them with a location number, which could be included not only on the inspection form, but a numbered tag, on the hinge-side edge of the door, for later identification.

Administrative and Planning Phase

- Are copies of all locally enforced codes maintained on site, for reference?
- Does the facility meet requirements of locally enforced Building Code?
- Does the facility meet requirements of locally enforced Fire Prevention Code?
- Does the facility meet requirements of locally enforced Life Safety Code?
- Does the facility have a written and appropriately distributed Fire Prevention and Response Plan? Is this plan known to all employees? Is training provided to those with defined responsibilities? Is all training documented and securely filed? Is the plan reviewed annually, updated as required, and redistributed?
- Does the facility maintain a fire brigade? Is the fire brigade training documented and securely filed? Is the fire brigade training conducted in conjunction with the local fire department? Is the fire brigade comprised of persons, or positions, that are present or represented at all times?
- Are all inspection reports retained for a reasonable number of years, as defined by local codes, insurance requirements, or industry standards? Are inspection reports filed in a secure location?
- Are all employees trained in basic fire prevention concepts and fire event response procedures? Is the content of this training consistent and reasonably inclusive?

Is this training documented and securely filed?
Is annual refresher training conducted?
Is annual refresher training documented and securely filed?

General Physical Inspection Phase

- Are all fire exit routes clearly marked?
Are all exit routes unobstructed at all times?
Are all exit routes and egress hardware items in compliance with Americans with Disabilities Act (ADA) requirements?
- Are all fire doors and egress hardware items in proper working order?
- Are service areas secured against unauthorized entry when not in use?
- Are all areas free of loose or disorganized combustible items (such as rags or empty boxes)?
- Are all storage areas well organized, to allow ease of access in emergency situations?
- Are flammable or combustible items properly stored to protect against accidental ignition?
- Are flammable or combustible items properly stored to protect against unauthorized usage or tampering?
- Are all fire lanes clearly marked? Are fire lanes maintained in an unobstructed condition, at all times?
- Are master keys available for fire department use at all times?
- Are all electrical panels accessible at all times? Are all panels clearly marked, to facilitate emergency power disconnection?
- Are gas line shutoff valves accessible at all times?
- Are all gas-operated pieces of equipment inspected for wear and damage with reasonable frequency? Are inspections documented and filed in a secure location?
- Are all heat-generating devices (such as boilers, furnaces, and dryers) provided a reasonable clear zone, based on levels of heat output, where storage of any kind is prohibited?
- Are all ducts inspected regularly and cleaned as required?
- Is the use of extension cords discouraged in all areas?
- Are all electrical cords and electrically operated items inspected for wear or damage with reasonable frequency? Are such inspections documented?
- Are designated smoking areas clearly defined and at a proper minimum safe distance from any common or identified ignition threats? Are appro-

priate ash and cigarette receptacles available for use in these areas?

Extinguisher Inspection Phase

- Have all extinguishers been inspected and serviced as required by a licensed vendor or trained technician within the past 12 months?
- Are all extinguishers of a type appropriate for most probable types of fires in the immediate area?
- Are specialty extinguishers available in those areas that would require them?
- Are persons trained in the use of the extinguishers available in the areas where they are typically present? Is this training documented and filed in a secure location?
- Are extinguishers inspected with reasonable frequency (daily, in most cases), to ensure that they are present and have not been tempered with or discharged? Is each extinguisher inspection fully documented, and securely filed?

Stand Pipe, Fire Hose, and Control Valve Inspection Phase

- Do tamper switches, linked to an alarm system, monitor all control valves?
- Are all control valves inspected and tested annually by a licensed vendor or trained technician?
- Are all stand pipes, control valves, and fire hoses accessible at all times?
- Are fire hoses inspected, per manufacturer recommendations, for wear and decay?

Sprinkler System Inspection Phase

- Are all flow switches inspected and tested annually by a licensed vendor or trained technician?
- Are all sprinkler heads of a type appropriate for the location in which it is installed?
- Are all sprinkler heads installed and maintained within the manufacturers recommendations?
- Are all sprinkler heads provided with a clear area of operation, in compliance with local Fire Codes?
- Does the sprinkler system have a pressure maintenance pump? If so, is this pump inspected and tested with reasonable frequency (weekly, in most cases) by a licensed vendor or trained technician?

- Are all areas requiring sprinkler system coverage, per the local fire code, provided with such coverage?

Hazardous Materials Inspection Phase

- Are proper warning placards utilized in areas of chemical storage and usage?
- Is proper personal protective equipment (PPE) provided for initial response to fire and emergency situations related to any hazardous materials that are maintained or utilized on site?
  Is training provided in the use of this PPE?
  Is such training documented and filed in a secure location?
- Is the fire department made aware of storage areas, use areas, and large arriving or departing shipments of hazardous materials?
- Are all appropriate containment, standoff distance, and warning signals utilized in storage areas?

Alarm System Inspection Phase

- Is the system monitored by a licensed, off-site monitoring service?
- Is the system inspected and tested annually by a licensed vendor or trained technician?

- Is this inspection documented and filed in a secure location?
- Is the area of coverage broken down into identified zones?
- When activated, does the alarm system clearly identify the location of the potential fire?
- Are audible alarms heard in all areas of a zone, when activated? Is the system designed to warn adjacent zones, inclusive of floors above or below?
- Are strobes visible in all areas of a zone, when activated? Is the system designed to warn adjacent zones, inclusive of floors above or below?
- Does the alarm system record activation and use history? For what length of time is this history retained?
- Does the system audible signal include a prerecorded advisory message?
  If so, does this message recommend a route or method of egress?
  If so, does this message advise against the use of elevators, if any are present?
- Does the system automatically recall or drop elevators, on activation? Are override keys available for fire department use?
- Are detector types installed, as appropriate for the specific location of installation? If the intended use of a given area is altered, is the type of detector also reviewed and changed to match the updated intended use of that area?

Chapter 5

Crime Prevention through Environmental Design Strategies and Applications

TIMOTHY CROWE

Crime Prevention through Environmental Design Strategies

Crime prevention through environmental design (CPTED) strategies have emerged from history and contemporary crime prevention experiments. Most of the strategies are self-evident. That is, the reader will probably think, "I knew that." The strategies and examples contained in this chapter are basic. Their applications are unlimited.

CPTED concepts have been and are being used in public housing projects. School and university properties are using CPTED applications that were initially pioneered in the Broward County, Florida, school CPTED program that was funded by the federal government. The list of potential CPTED applications is endless.

It would be difficult to find any human function that is not amenable to the use of CPTED concepts. It is merely a matter of looking at the environment from a different perspective, questioning everything, and learning the language of the various professions involved in making decisions about our communities. Learning the language means being able to communicate with others and understand their objectives. This is the principal reason why CPTED planners are trained to share concepts and ask questions that no one would have thought to ask.

CPTED planners are trained to reprogram their thinking from focusing solely on security and crime prevention to emphasizing the objectives of the agency or organization they are trying to help. It is important to remember a CPTED motto, "What are you trying to do here, and how can we help you do it better?" If you are meeting your objectives, the potential for crime and loss will be reduced. It is an axiom that human functions that achieve their objectives experience fewer crimes and losses. Crime and loss are a by-product of human functions that are not working.

The following nine major CPTED strategies may be used in any number of combinations:

1. *Provide clear border definition of controlled space.* It is common law requirement that space must be defined to preserve property rights. Boundaries may be identified physically or symbolically. Fences, shrubbery, or signs are acceptable border definition. The underlying principle is that a "reasonable individual" must be able to recognize that he or she is passing from public to private space. The arrangements of furniture and color definition are means of identifying interior spaces. Plaques and pictures on walls in hallways help to define ownership and are powerful environmental cues that affect the behavior and predispositions of owners, normal users, and abnormal users alike.

2. *Provide clearly marked transitional zones.* It is important to provide clearly marked transitional zones on moving from public, to semipublic, to semiprivate, to private space. As transitional definition increases, the range of excuses for improper behavior is reduced. The user must be

made to acknowledge movement into controlled space.

3. *Relocation of gathering areas.* It is appropriate to formally designate gathering or congregating areas in locations with good natural surveillance and access control. Gathering areas on campuses may be placed in positions that are out of the view of undesired users to decrease the magnetic effect or attraction.

4. *Place safe activities in unsafe locations.* Within reason, this strategy may be used to overcome problems on school campuses, parks, offices, or institutional settings. Safe activities serve as magnets for normal users, who exhibit challenging or controlling behaviors (e.g., staring) that tell other normal users that they are safe and tell abnormal users that they are at greater risk of scrutiny or intervention. Some caution must be used to insure that a safe activity is not being placed in an unreasonable position it cannot define.

5. *Place unsafe activities in safe locations.* Positioning of vulnerable activities near windows of an occupied space or within tightly controlled areas help overcome risk and make the users of these areas feel safer.

6. *Redesignate the use of space to provide natural barriers.* Conflicting activities may be separated by distance, natural terrain, or other functions to avoid fear-producing conflict. For instance, the sounds emanating from a basketball court may be disruptive and fear-producing for a senior citizen or toddler gathering or play area. The threat need not be real to create the perception of risk for the normal or desired user.

7. *Improve the scheduling of space.* It has been found, generally, that the effective and productive use of spaces reduces risk and the perception of risk for normal users. Conversely, abnormal users feel at greater risk of surveillance and intervention in their activities. Well-thought-out temporal and spatial relationships improve profit and productivity, while increasing the control of behavior.

8. *Redesign or revamp space to increase the perception of natural surveillance.* The perception of surveillance is more powerful than its reality. Hidden cameras do little to make normal users feel safer and, therefore, act safer when they are unaware of the presence of these devices. Likewise, abnormal users do not feel at greater risk of detection when they are oblivious to surveillance potentials. Windows, clear lines of sight, and other natural techniques are often as effective as the use of mechanical or organized (e.g., guards) methods.

9. *Overcome distance and isolation.* Improved communications and design efficiencies increase the perception of natural surveillance and control. School administrators have learned to carry portable radios to improve their productivity, as well as create the perception of immediate access to help. Restroom locations and entry designs may be planned to increase convenience and reduce the cost of construction and maintenance.

CPTED Applications

There are many examples of CPTED applications. Those that follow are intended to stimulate readers to think of adaptations to their own environmental setting. Each situation is unique, requiring its own individual application of CPTED concepts. No two environmental settings are exactly the same, even though they serve the same function. Accordingly, the reader, now ideally a CPTED user, must use the strategies that make the most sense within each different location.

Objectives for the Commercial Environment

1. *Access controls.* Provide secure barriers to prevent unauthorized access to building grounds, or restricted interior areas.

2. *Surveillance through physical design.* Improve opportunities for surveillance by physical design mechanisms that increase the risk of detection for offenders, enable evasive actions by potential victims, and facilitate intervention by police.

3. *Mechanical surveillance devices.* Provide businesses with security devices to detect and signal illegal entry attempts.

4. *Design and construction.* Design, build, or repair buildings and building sites to enhance security and improve quality.

5. *Land use.* Establish policies to prevent ill-advised land and building uses that have negative impact.

6. *Owner and management action.* Encourage owners and management to implement safeguards to make businesses and commercial property less vulnerable to crime.

7. *User protection.* Implement safeguards to make shoppers less vulnerable to crime.

8. *Social interaction.* Encourage interaction among business people, users, and residents of commercial neighborhoods to foster social cohesion and control.

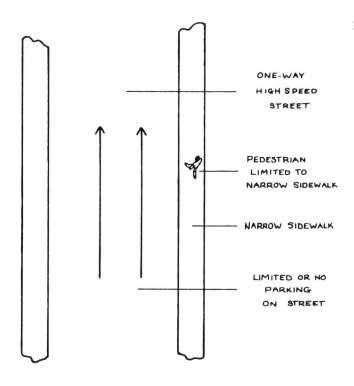

Figure 5-1.

ONE-WAY
HIGH SPEED
STREET

PEDESTRIAN
LIMITED TO
NARROW SIDEWALK

NARROW SIDEWALK

LIMITED OR NO
PARKING
ON STREET

9. *Private security services*. Determine necessary and appropriate services to enhance commercial security.
10. *Police services*. Improve police services to efficiently and effectively respond to crime problems and enhance citizen cooperation in reporting crime.
11. *Police and community relations*. Improve police and community relations to involve citizens in cooperative efforts with police to prevent and report crime.
12. *Community awareness*. Create community crime prevention awareness to aid in combating crime in commercial areas.
13. *Territorial identity*. Differentiate private areas from public spaces to discourage trespass by potential offenders.
14. *Neighborhood image*. Develop a positive image of the commercial area to encourage user and investor confidence and increase the economic vitality of the area.

Downtown Streets and Pedestrian Areas

Downtown Streets

Poor design and use (see Figures 5-1 and 5-2):

1. The growing dominance of the vehicle over pedestrians resulted in off-street parking, one-way streets, synchronized traffic signals, and shrunken sidewalks to accommodate the auto.
2. Pedestrian-oriented businesses have failed or enticed the buyer to the shopping centers and malls. As businesses moved, there was less pedestrian activity, which forced more businesses out.
3. Narrow pedestrian footpaths increased conflict and fear between vagrants and other abnormal users of space. Normal users avoided these streets, thereby reinforcing the decline of business and normal downtown activities.
4. Downtown streets became "no man's" land at nights and on weekends.
5. Pedestrian malls were created to replace the vehicle with people, but most failed because the designers lost track of their three Ds (detect, deter, deny). Aesthetics outweigh function, resulting in the replacement of the vehicle with cement objects, in the place of people.
6. Many of the cement objects—amenities and landscaping—attracted abnormal users. Liter and bird droppings made outdoor sitting areas undesirable for normal users.
7. Normal users feel threatened and unsafe in these areas. Abnormal users feel safe and at low risk of intervention. Authorities are obliged to surrender

Figure 5-2.

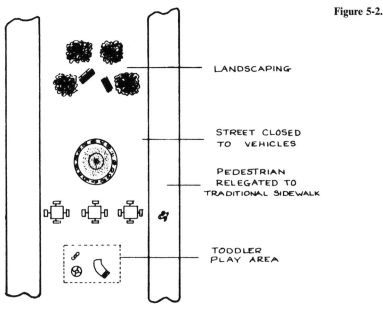

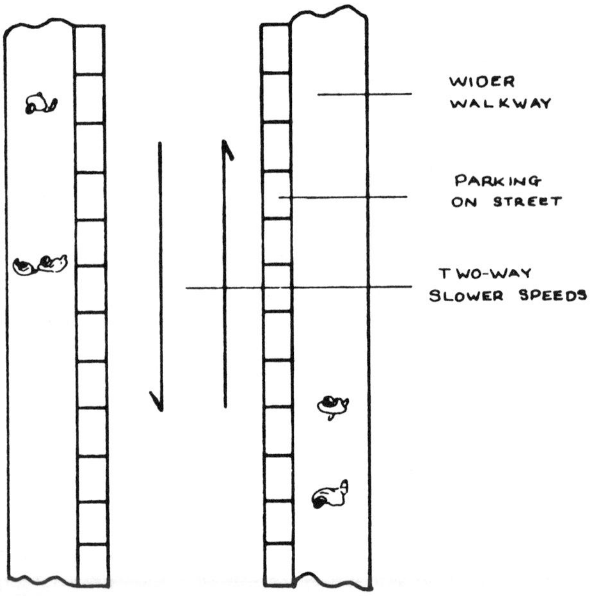

LANDSCAPING

STREET CLOSED
TO   VEHICLES

PEDESTRIAN
RELEGATED TO
TRADITIONAL SIDEWALK

TOODLER
PLAY AREA

Figure 5-3.

WIDER
WALKWAY

PARKING
ON STREET

TWO-WAY
SLOWER SPEEDS

these areas to vagrants because of special interest group pressure and the lack of any consistent normal use of the area.

For good design and use (see Figures 5-3 and 5-4):

1. One option is to purposely decrease the vehicle capacity of the street by reestablishing on-street parking, wide sidewalks, two-way streets, and non-synchronous traffic signals. This should reroute commuter and other through traffic.

2. Higher pedestrian capacity limits vehicular access to those with terminal objectives on the block (e.g., residents or purposeful shoppers).

3. Another option is to schedule the street for tem-

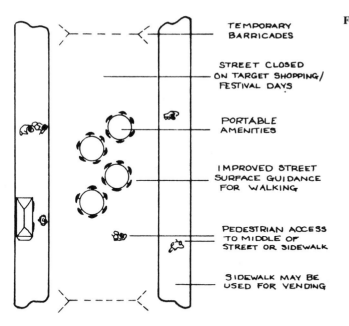

Figure 5-4.

TEMPORARY
BARRICADES

STREET CLOSED
ON TARGET SHOPPING/
FESTIVAL DAYS

PORTABLE
AMENITIES

IMPROVED STREET
SURFACE GUIDANCE
FOR WALKING

PEDESTRIAN ACCESS
TO MIDDLE OF
STREET OR SIDEWALK

SIDEWALK MAY BE
USED FOR VENDING

porary closings on target shopping days and festival times. Portable amenities may be used that can be stored when not in use. Businesses may be granted variances of local codes to use vendor carts and other forms of extended business activities in the street.
4. The planned increase of normal users makes them feel safer and exhibit controlling and challenging behaviors much as they do in indoor shopping malls.
5. Abnormal users feel at greater risk.

Barriers to Conflict

For poor design (see Figure 5-5):

1. A toddler or senior recreation is immediately contiguous to a conflicting activity of basketball.
2. Basketball involves aggressive behavior and noise, which is annoying and threatening to senior citizens and parents with small children.
3. The athletic activity may serve as a magnet for abnormal users of space.
4. The designated athletic activity may legitimize certain offensive behaviors, such as swearing and physical abuse, which threatens normal users and passersby.

For good design (see Figure 5-6):

1. A natural barrier of distance, elevation, or the parking lot may be used to avoid conflict.
2. Any natural barrier reduces the propensity for the undesirable or abnormal users to preempt the contiguous spaces.
3. Abnormal users feel at greater risk when they have to pass through a clear barrier.

Outdoor Sitting Areas

For poor design and use (see Figure 5-7):

1. Sitting walls have replaced the traditional benches and picnic tables in open spaces, but they are easy to hide behind and serve as a barrier to effective surveillance.
2. Elevation drops and terraced sitting areas reduce perceived opportunities for natural surveillance, which makes abnormal users feel safer in colonizing or preempting these spaces.
3. Tourists and office workers who may desire to eat lunch in these areas or take an evening stroll are afraid to go there if vagrants are already there or have left signs of their regular use (e.g., liter, graffiti, human waste).
4. Liter and waste present odor problems and may attract scavengers. If it looks and smells bad, it must be bad, which defeats the purpose.

For good design and use (see Figure 5-8):

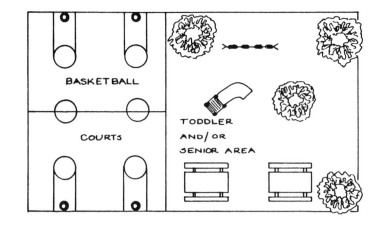

Figure 5-5.

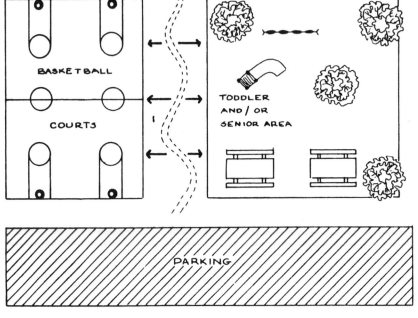

Figure 5-6.

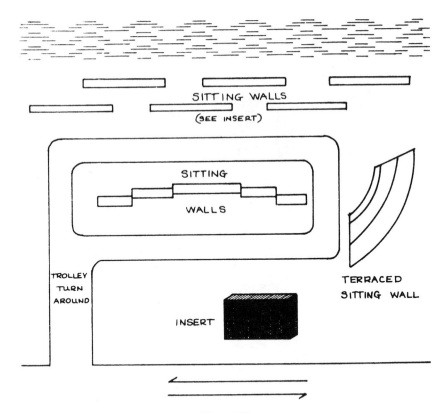

Figure 5-7.

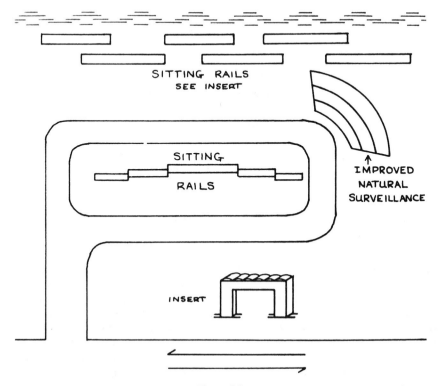

Figure 5-8.

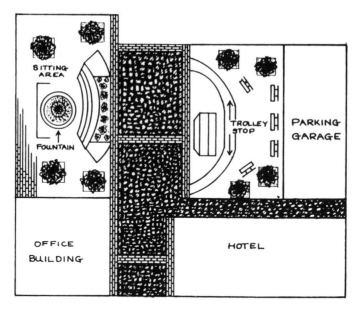

Figure 5-9.

1. Sitting rails may be used in the place of the more expensive walls. These increase natural surveillance and prevent improper use while still meeting the functional and aesthetic demands of the open space.
2. Terraced sitting or staging areas should be oriented so they are clearly visible from the street.
3. Open spaces can be made to work with CPTED concepts while reducing overall construction costs. Normal users will feel better about coming to these areas and displace abnormal users.

Plazas

For poor design and use (see Figure 5-9):

1. A typical plaza in a rehabilitated business area meets all the local code requirements for landscaping and aesthetics but at the cost of reducing the usable square footage.
2. Aesthetics or form outweighed function in the selection of cobblestones to use in replacing the street paving. These stones are difficult to walk on, especially for women in high-heeled shoes and the elderly.
3. Benches, tables, and the fountain area may easily be colonized by vagrants or serve as targets for pigeons.

4. Normal users feel at risk and abnormal users feel safe.

For good design and use (see Figure 5-10):

1. Compromises must be made between form and function. Paving tiles may be used in the place of cobblestones to make it easier for walking.
2. Portable amenities and landscaping may be substituted for permanent furnishings to increase flexibility in planning outdoor events.
3. Vehicles may be allowed limited and restricted access to facilitate a wide range of uses and to allow police patrols.
4. A well and constantly used plaza will attract normal users and make people feel safe.

Pedestrian Mall

For poor design and use (see Figure 5-11):

1. The present design and traffic flow pattern reduces the parking opportunities.
2. The pedestrian area and upgraded median are excellent, but is all of this space needed everyday? Will it be used regularly or mostly on holidays and weekend shopping days?
3. This design plan is a problem for senior citizen shoppers who may have to park some distance away. Parallel parking is also a problem for the senior citizen shopper.

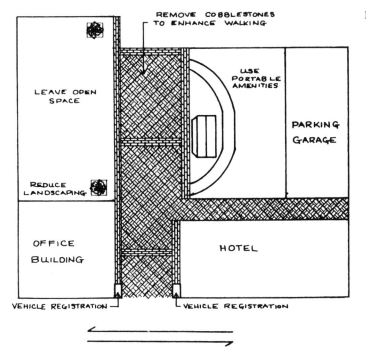

Figure 5-10.

PEDESTRIAN MALL

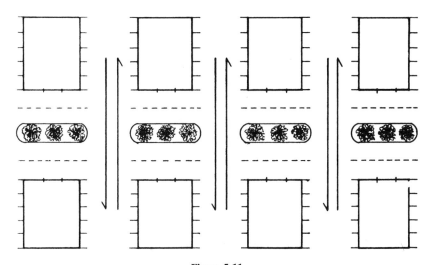

Figure 5-11.

For good design and use (see Figures 5-12 and 5-13):

1. Traffic flows may be controlled to allow for angle parking to recover needed parking close to shops.
2. Vehicular speed may be radically controlled to reduce pedestrian conflict.
3. Barricades may be used to close off vehicular access during certain periods of high pedestrian activity or low use. The design is flexible, allowing a variety of use patterns based on commercial and promotional planning.
4. Barricades in Figure 5-13 may be used permanently or temporarily to control through access of vehicles.

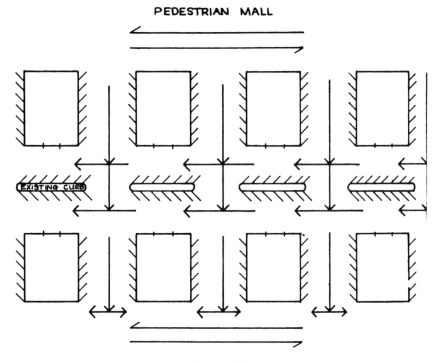

Figure 5-12.

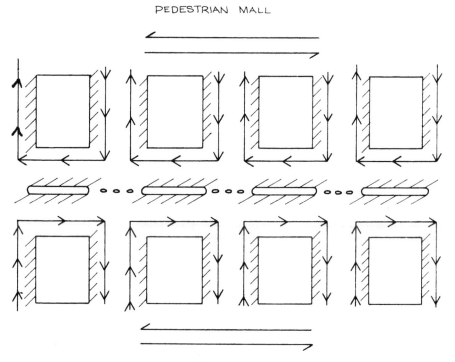

Figure 5-13.

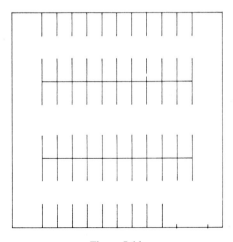

Figure 5-14.

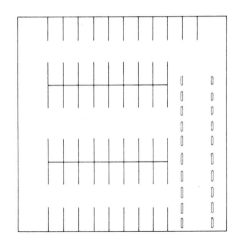

Figure 5-15.

Parking Lots and Structures

Parking Lots

For poor design and use (see Figure 5-14):

1. A typical lot layout on the ground level or each level of an off-street garage. Late arrivals get the less desirable spots, which are generally located in unobserved places. Early arrivals take the best, safest spots, but they are the first to leave—at the safest times when an attendant may still be there.
2. The last in are the last out, generally when the lot is deserted.
3. This situation has been overlooked for years, with the assumption that the early arriver should naturally get the advantage. This is not a valid assumption where customers or employees are legitimately shopping later hours or scheduled for late shifts. Fear, higher victimization, and liability problems arise.

For good design and use (see Figure 5-15):

1. Barriers are used to divert parking activity to create safe locations for the late arrival.
2. A variety of plans may be used, depending on a parking needs assessment. Floors may be alternately closed. Aisles may be partially opened.
3. Some balance between the legitimate needs of the early arrival and late arrivals should be met.
4. Physical barriers (e.g., cones or barricades) are less upsetting to users than attendants or guards directing flow past what are perceived as choice spots. However, guards or attendants are useful in a rule enforcement or reinforcement function.

Parking Lot Access

For poor design and use (see Figure 5-16):

1. The parking attendant's location prevents this person from providing natural surveillance over the employee parking area.
2. Landscaping may serve as additional barriers to natural surveillance.
3. Employees feel less safe and abnormal users will perceive a low risk of detection.
4. A guard has to be employed to protect employees and their vehicles.

For good design and use (see Figure 5-17):

1. The parking attendant's location is naturally in a position to control all parking areas.
2. Employees feel safer and abnormal users know they will risk detection.
3. This design frees the guard for patrolling activities elsewhere.

Parking Structures

For poor design and use (see Figure 5-18):

1. Ground levels of parking garages are underused and create a fortress effect on the pedestrian, as well as on contiguous land uses.
2. Reinforced concrete retaining walls are used commonly and reduce surveillance opportunities. This creates the perception of lack of safety for the normal user and low risk for abnormal users.

Figure 5-16.

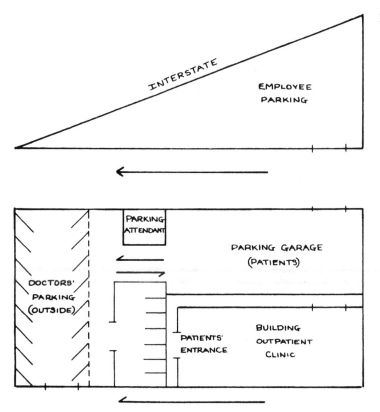

Figure 5-17.

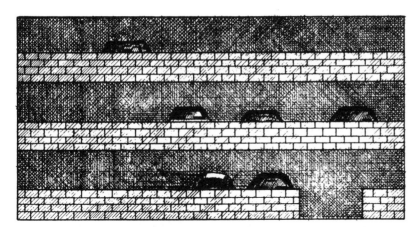

Figure 5-18.

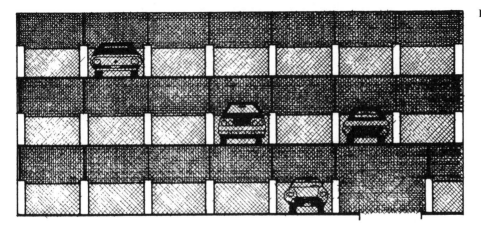

Figure 5-19.

3. Retaining walls do more to hide the automobile than assure safety. Designers and local planners are often confused regarding the purpose of the walls.
4. Lighting inside is located generally over the driving lanes, instead of illuminating the parking spots where people are outside of their cars, and most vulnerable. Cars have their own lights; people do not.

For good design and use (see Figure 5-19):

1. Ground spaces should be dedicated to pedestrian-oriented businesses and activities, leaving the airspace for the car. This increases business revenue and enhances the perception of natural surveillance and access control for the garage and adjoining street space.
2. Retaining walls should be replaced with stretched cable or railings that allow for maximum surveillance and illumination. This produces a considerable cost saving and improves the perception of

safety for normal users. Designers may even improve on the aesthetics over the concrete walls.
3. Reflective paint or materials should be used inside, and all pedestrian areas should be illuminated to increase feelings of safety.

Office and Industrial Systems

Office Access

For poor design and use (see Figure 5-20):

1. Elevators from below ground to working floors so that people have access to all floors.
2. Main entrance from which people could go directly to elevators without registering.
3. Side entrance that allows no surveillance by receptionist or guard and access to the elevators.
4. Guard or receptionist booth that is not centrally located but positioned so the person stationed there cannot see who enters or exists.

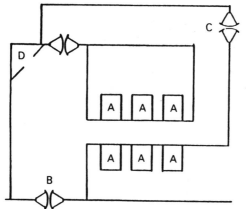

A. Through elevators from below ground to working floors
B. Main entrance
C. Side entrance
D. Guard booth

Figure 5-20.

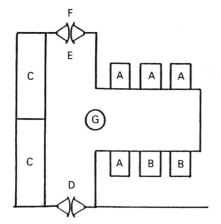

A. Elevators serving lobby and specified floors above
B. Elevators serving lobby and floors below
C. Rest rooms
D. Building main entrance
E. Main floor corridor
F. Controlled access/egress door
G. Receptionist/Security Guard station

Figure 5-21.

For good design and use (see Figure 5-21):

1. Elevators serving lobby and floors above.
2. Elevators serving lobby and floor below.
3. Restrooms which are visible from the entrances.
4. Main entrance.
5. Main floor corridor visible from main entrance.
6. Controlled access/egress door.
7. Security or receptionist station to screen entrances.

Office Building Site Plan and Parking

For poor design and use (see Figure 5-22):

1. Parking is undifferentiated by time of day and day of week.
2. Through access and nighttime use are poorly defined and unclear.

3. Cars parked anywhere are not subject to scrutiny by security, law enforcement officials, or building management.

For good design and use (see Figure 5-23):

1. Parking is zoned and clearly identified by allowable spatial and temporal uses.
2. Improper parking is more subject to notice and scrutiny by local law enforcement officials and security officers.
3. Zones may be closed, depending on need.

Shipping and Receiving and Vehicle Access

For poor design (see Figure 5-24):

1. Confused and deep internal access for external vehicles.

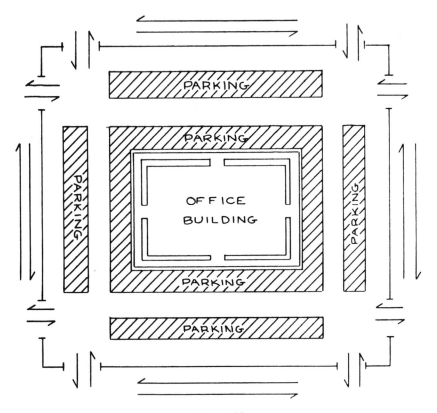

Figure 5-22.

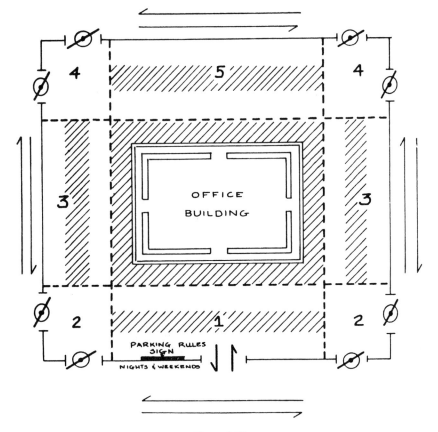

Figure 5-23.

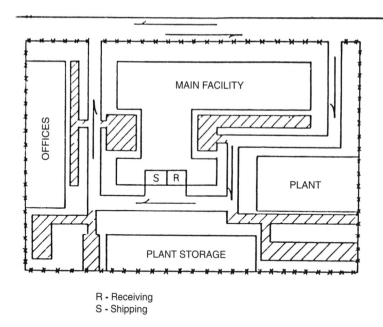

Figure 5-24.

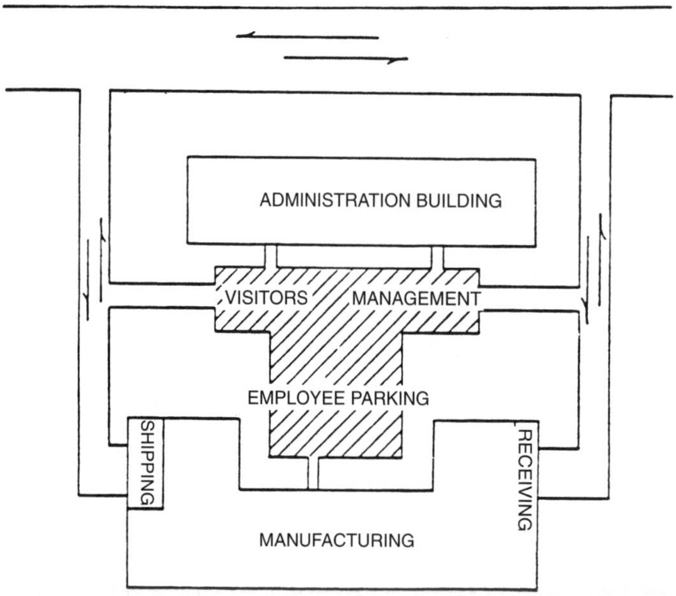

R - Receiving
S - Shipping

Figure 5-25.

2. Easy mix of external vehicles with those of employees.
3. Multiple access from facilities to employees' vehicles.
4. Shipping and receiving in same location legitimizes people coming and going with boxes.
5. Guard or full-time monitor required to screen access and packages.

6. Wide range of excuses for improper behavior, thus increasing pressure on guards or shipping and receiving clerks.

For good design (see Figure 5-25):

1. Parking segregated from external delivery on vendor vehicle access to property.

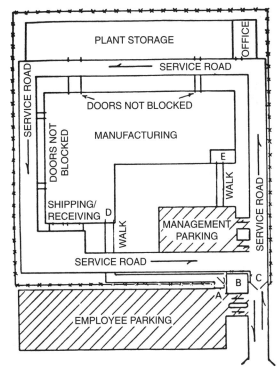

A. Pedestrian gate
B. Guard station
C. Vehicular gate
D. Employee entrance
E. Receptionist

Figure 5-26.

3. Shipping and receiving located in same site, which may encourage abuse.
4. Extended locations of employee parking and strict access control through security negatively affects morale and subsequent labor negotiations.
5. Receptionist position provides little natural access control and surveillance.
6. Perimeter security fencing encloses a large area, which increases cost and vulnerability.

For good design (see Figure 5-27):

1. Campus site plan, which emphasizes openness and natural distance to increase an intruder's perception of risk of surveillance.
2. Convenient employee parking in front of building increases perception of surveillance of the employee from the building, while decreasing the negative effect of isolated parking on morale.
3. Segregated shipping and receiving may reduce opportunity for theft.
4. Guard post may be partially staffed or eliminated altogether, by replacing it with a receptionist or other natural (nonorganized) function to provide the perception of natural access control and surveillance.
5. Reduced magnitude and cost of perimeter security.
6. Employee parking is protected by distance from public street access and direct line of sight from the reception areas.
7. Site development and building costs should be reduced. Internal space footage requirements also are reduced.

2. All employee and visitor parking clearly visible from buildings.
3. Shipping and receiving separated by distance, which reduces range of excuses.
4. Legitimate behavior narrowly defined by location.
5. Transitional definition of movement is clear from opportunities for signs and rule enhancement in purchase and shipping orders and policies.

Plant Design

For poor design (see Figure 5-26):

1. Confusing vehicular internal access.
2. Too much access for external vehicles to building entrances, which may easily promote collusion between employees and vendors or subcontractors.

Hallways and Restrooms

Hallways

For poor design and use (see Figure 5-28):

1. Most hallways in schools, hospitals, and offices are left undifferentiated. They do not identify what is on the other side of the wall nor who owns it.
2. Hallway uses become confused by the placement of lockers and furniture. Hallways are for movement, not for gathering.
3. Tenants or persons assigned internal spaces or work areas actively control their space, but will assume little proprietary regard for the adjoining hallways or corridors.
4. Hallways usually carry the definition of extremely public space, even though extremely private space is only inches away.

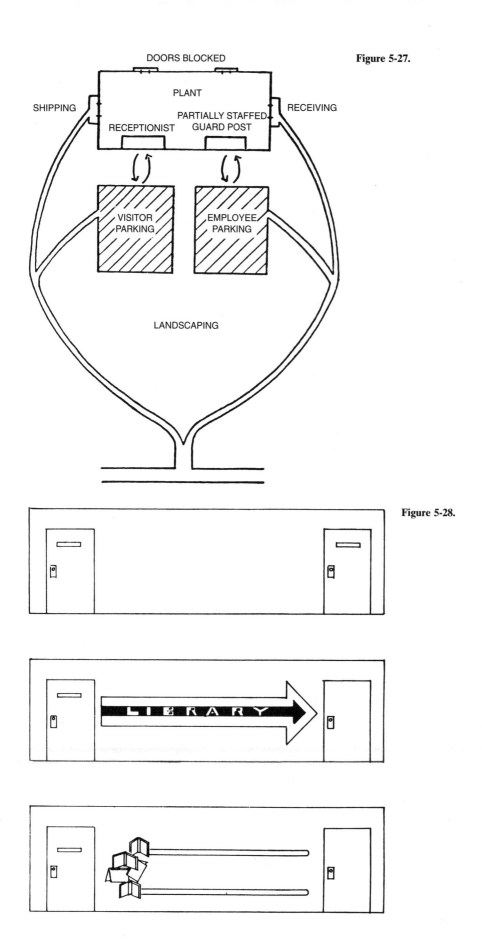

Figure 5-27.

Figure 5-28.

5. Some new buildings prohibit any decoration or encroachment by tenants into hallway systems, as part of an interior decorating plan.
6. Multiple-purpose classrooms or meeting spaces suffer from lack of ownership.
7. Normal users demonstrate avoidance behavior in these undifferentiated spaces, which makes abnormal users feel safer and in control.

For good design and use:

1. Hallways may be assigned to the tenant of the adjoining internal space. Users should be influenced to mark their turf to identify their boundaries.
2. Boundaries and turf cues should be extended to consume unassigned or undifferentiated spaces.
3. The legitimate uses of hallways and corridors need to be reinforced through policies and signs.
4. Graphics may be used to promote movement and indicate direction.
5. Floor coverings and colors may be used to identify public versus private spaces.
6. Normal users recognize and honor others' turf or ownership cues. Normal users feel safer in these areas and exhibit challenging and controlling behaviors. Abnormal users respond to these cues by avoiding these areas or with avoidance when they are in the vicinity.

Restroom Location and Entrance Design

For poor design and use (see Figure 5-29):

1. Restrooms are traditionally isolated by location, as a cultural sensitivity and for economic reasons.
2. Public restrooms are common sites for illegal and illicit activity.
3. Many children are afraid to use the restroom at school.
4. Malls and shopping centers have tended to hide the restroom, as a means of reducing demand for this nonrevenue-bearing activity.
5. The lack of convenient and clean restrooms clearly reduces the average time per visit to most stores and businesses, thereby reducing sales.
6. Isolated locations and double-door entry systems present unsafe cues to normal users and safe cues to abnormal users.
7. Double-door entry systems produce a warning sound and transitional time that is an advantage to abnormal users.
8. A normal user or guard must move inside the second door swing to figure out what is going on in a restroom.

For good design and use (see Figure 5-30):

1. Restrooms should be located in the most convenient and accessible location to increase use, which increases the perception of safety.
2. A maze type entry system or doors placed in a locked open position increases convenience and safety.
3. Normal users may determine who is in the restroom by glancing around the privacy screen or wall.
4. Abnormal users feel at greater risk of detection.
5. Customer (or student) convenience and safety should contribute to attaining the objectives of the space.

Informal Gathering Areas

For poor design (see Figure 5-31):

1. Hallways and corners in schools, office buildings, malls, and apartments attract small groups of abnormal users who preempt this space and promote conflict.
2. Normal users avoid these areas, which reinforces the perception of risk.
3. Congestion is often created elsewhere because of the avoidance by normal users.
4. The avoidance reinforces the perception of safety and turf ownership of the abnormal users.

For good design (see Figure 5-32):

1. A safe activity may be located in the poorly used space to displace the unsafe use.
2. A safe activity serves as a magnet for normal users, who are attracted to the area.
3. The safe activity and normal user behavior creates and intensifies the perception of risk for the abnormal user.
4. Space utilization and productivity will go up in most cases.

Malls and Shopping Centers

Shopping Mall Parking

For poor design (see Figure 5-33):

1. Parking is 360° and undifferentiated.
2. Safety hazards persist because of uncontrolled access to all lanes.
3. Undesirable nighttime activities can occur.
4. Transition from public to private space is not defined.

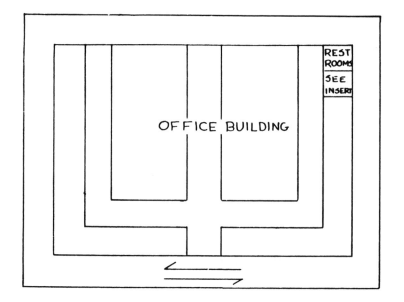

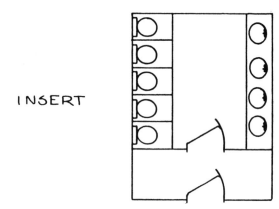

INSERT

Figure 5-29.

For good design (see Figure 5-34):

1. Parking is in enclaves in relation to business entrances.
2. Lateral access by vehicles is severely restricted.
3. Aesthetic design opportunities are enhanced to screen ugly parking lots.
4. Extreme transitional definition exists, thereby reducing escape opportunities.
5. Parking areas may be closed with barricades at different times of the day.

Mall Design

For poor design and use (see Figure 5-35):

1. Malls have traditionally been designed in a fortress style, which turns it back on the parking areas.
2. Many dead walls on the last used sides, or back-sides, of malls prevent opportunities for advertising, and limit natural surveillance.
3. Designers tend to reflect their perceptions of areas in their designs. Buildings in isolated areas will end up fortresslike in form. The dead walls serve as a barrier to surveillance from or to the building, even though that many people are inside the building, separated by a 16-inch wall from the parking area.

For good design and use (see Figure 5-36):

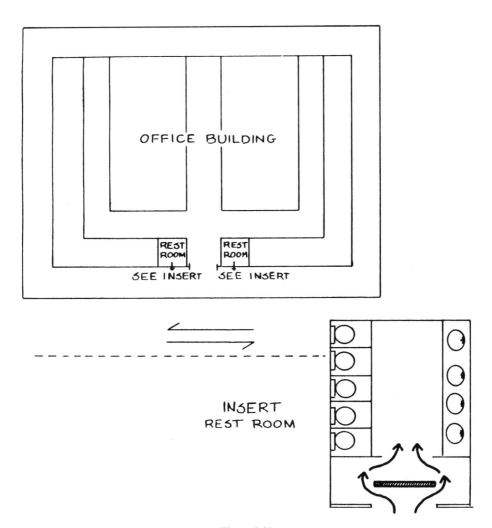

Figure 5-30.

1. Display cases may be attached to dead walls to market products and reduce the negative effect of the fortress designs.
2. Active displays with lighting and mannequins will attract attention and create the impression of natural surveillance.
3. False windows and lighting panels may also break up the monotony of the fortress design and reinforce the impression of natural surveillance.

Barriers to Conflict

For poor design (see Figure 5-37):

1. Shopping center parking is contiguous to a major conflicting activity, a play area.

2. The location of the basketball hoops legitimizes the presence of young persons in and near the parking area, to chase balls and for informal gathering.
3. Normal users feel that their property and their persons are at greater risk.
4. Abnormal users feel safer.
5. Even legitimate use of the play area is perceived negatively by others.

For good design (see Figure 5-38):

1. Distance may be used as a natural barrier to conflicting activities.
2. The natural barrier of distance reduces the range of excuses for being in the wrong place.
3. Abnormal users feel at greater risk of scrutiny and detection.

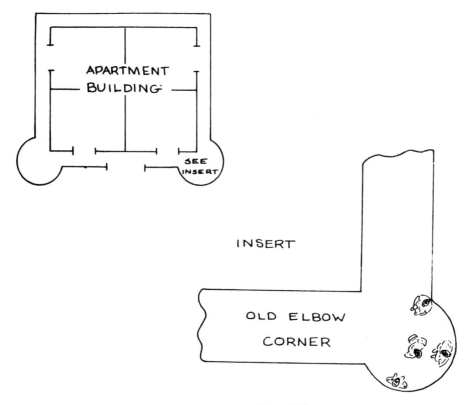

Figure 5-31.

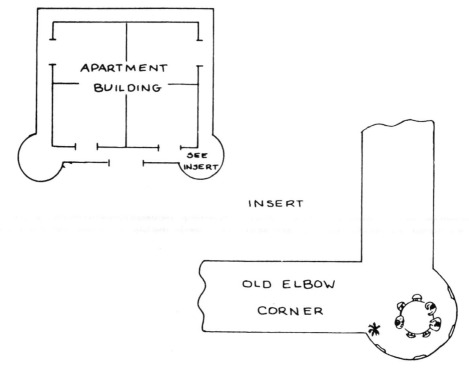

Figure 5-32.

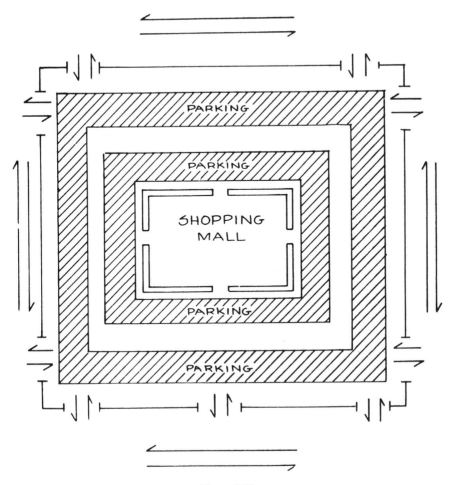

Figure 5-33.

Convenience Stores and Branch Banks

Convenience Stores: Traditional Design

For poor design and use (see Figure 5-39):

1. Gas pumps were installed after original site planning, so most were placed wherever there was an open area. This often resulted in a site placement difficult to watch from the cashier location in the building. Some stores installed windows that affect the location and surveillance of the cashier.
2. Parking is traditionally in front, but walkways are generally too narrow for customers to avoid close contact with young people or construction workers who legitimately hang out in these areas.
3. Telephones are often placed too close to the store entrance. Young people, as well as some undesir-

ables, hang out in these areas, which turns off normal adult customers. Robbers like to stand at a pay phone as a cover for casing the store.

4. Although the research is conflicting, the centrally located cashier station results in the cashier having his or her back to customers when only one clerk is on duty. A frontal or rear location of a central cashier station would be preferable.
5. It is common for stores to obscure the front windows with signs and orient gondolas and shelves perpendicular to the front of the store. Signs prevent customers and police from looking into or out of the store. Improper gondola and shelf orientation prevents clerks from observing customers. Likewise, abnormal users feel safer in stores where gondolas and shelf systems eliminate natural surveillance.

For good design and use (see Figure 5-40):

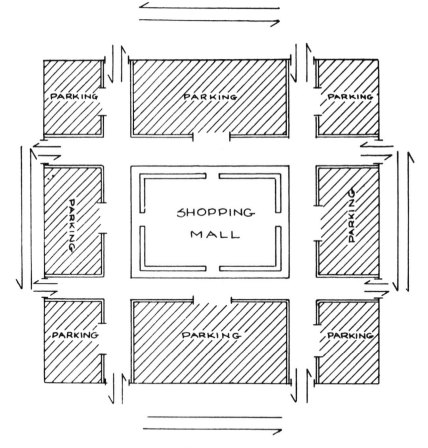

Figure 5-34.

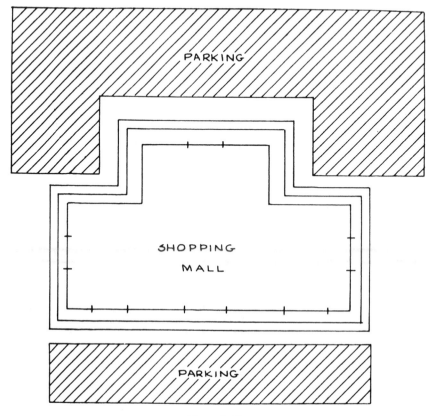

Figure 5-35.

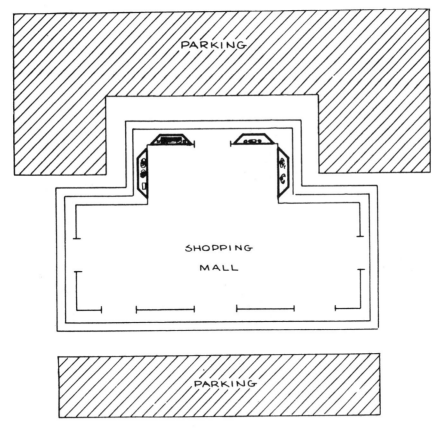

Figure 5-36

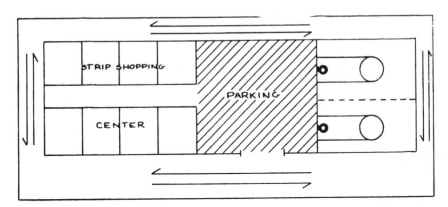

Figure 5-37.

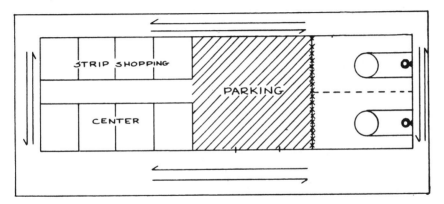

Figure 5-38.

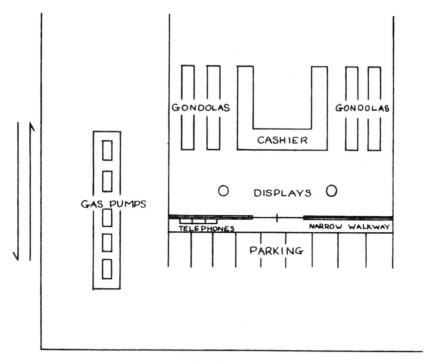

Figure 5-39.

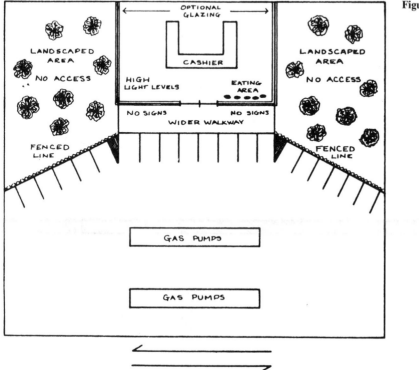

Figure 5-40.

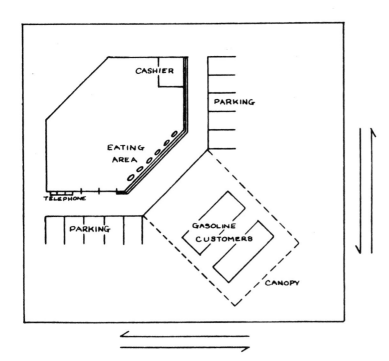

Figure 5-41.

1. Parking in front is always more convenient and safer.
2. Most stores use ample amounts of glass in the front, which improves both natural and perceived surveillance.

Convenience Stores in Locations near Dense Commercial or Housing Sites

1. Convenience stores located in these sites experience robberies associated with access from the rear of the store to the front. Escape is easy around the back of the store into dense commercial building or housing sites.
2. Customers are afraid to use these stores because of hanging-out by local residents and undesirable users, such as drug dealers and unruly young people.
3. The standard modus operandi is for the perpetrator to come from behind the building to the front and rob the cashier. Escape is so easy that stakeout teams of police may not catch the robber they observe committing the offense, because the person may easily melt into the buildings that are contiguous to and behind the convenience store.
4. A fenced line that takes the corner of the building diagonally to the property line reduces or eliminates the robberies that come from behind

the store. The fence increases the offender's perception of exposure, even though it does not provide a continuous enclosure of the property.

Convenience Stores: Hexagon Shaped

Elements of poor design and use include:

1. Double entry systems make customer control difficult.
2. Eating areas that attract people who hang out.
3. The design that works only on corner lots.

For good design and use (see Figure 5-41):

1. Telephone location and interior management may reduce customer conflict between juveniles and construction workers and adult buyers.
2. Well-lighted gasoline areas serve as a sea of light, attracting customers.
3. Eating areas in the front of the store attract adult customers, who may find it inconvenient to eat hot foods in their automobiles. Small seat and table designs will keep people from lingering or hanging out.
4. Marketing studies have demonstrated that impulse customers prefer a store that has other customers, which means that they have to see them to be attracted.

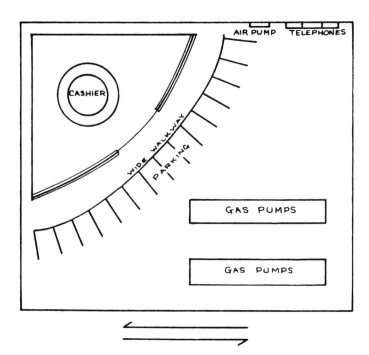

AIR PUMP   TELEPHONES

CASHIER

WIDE WALKWAY

PARKING

GAS PUMPS

GAS PUMPS

Figure 5-42.

5. Segregation of customer groups is achieved by the hexagonal design, which makes these groups less threatening to each other.

Convenience Stores: Fan Shaped

Some examples of poor design and use include:

1. Some stores do not have continuous glass across the front.
2. Fan designs, which are ineffective in midblock locations.

For good design and use (see Figure 5-42):

1. Clear view for cashier of all parking and gas pump areas.
2. Corner locations allow for effective vehicle access and excellent surveillance and control.
3. Elevated store and cashier locations increase control and customer confidence in safety.
4. Site efficiency, in terms of cost/benefit.

Convenience Stores: Kiosk Shaped
(Figure 5-43)

1. Store oriented to gas sales.
2. 300° surveillance for cashier.
3. Late night robbery control through use of a bank teller window.

4. Welcoming environment includes high light levels and bright colors.
5. Newer site plans place the car wash to the side instead of the back of the property.
6. Employee compliance with security procedures makes the kiosk store one of the most safe and defensible.

Branch Banks

For poor design and use (see Figure 5-44):

1. Most branch banks were designed as mini-fortresses, reflecting the architect's perception that people have more confidence that their money is safe.
2. Corner lots are the most desired to allow for drive-through on the side and back. Engineers desired this to reduce the hazard of vehicles slowing down on the public street to enter a parking area that was visible from the street. Planners desired parking on the side or in back to hide the vehicles. Planners concluded by the middle to late 1950s that cars were ugly and asphalt parking lots were uglier, so they promoted local codes requiring that buildings be placed on the front lot line, so that parking could be hidden behind the structure.
3. Automatic teller machines (ATMs) were originally located adjacent to the secure teller area so

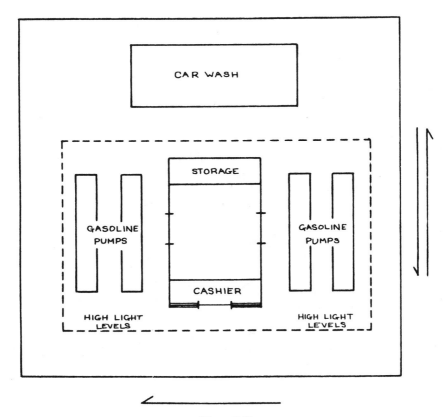

Figure 5-43.

that they could be serviced easily. The traditional design and flow plan caused the secure teller areas to be in the back of the bank, so ATMs ended up being placed in areas with little or no natural surveillance.
4. Customers have to park on the side or in the back of the bank and then come around on foot to the front or side doors. This is inconvenient and increases their perceived exposure to robbers.
5. Studies have shown that robbers prefer the fortress-type branch bank, because they feel that they are less exposed to surveillance from the outside. The fortress design is based on an assumption that went unchallenged for over 30 years.

For good design and use (see Figure 5-45):

1. Bank placed on the rear lot line, allowing customer parking and access from the front.
2. ATM located in area with the greatest natural surveillance and independent from the building. Customers prefer to drive up to the ATM and remain in or close to their vehicle for safety and convenience.

3. Parking should be in front where it is most visible. A curb lane should be used to bring the vehicle deep into the property prior to allowing it to disperse into the parking area. This will reduce the concern about traffic hazards by increasing the exit speed of the vehicle.
4. The curb lane for vehicle access serves as a transitional process that forces the user to acknowledge movement from public to semipublic to private space.
5. The building design should emphasize a maximum of glass to increase the perception of natural surveillance and openness from and to the structure.
6. Abnormal users feel a greater risk because of the improved natural surveillance and access.

Objectives for the Residential Environment

1. *Access control.* Provide secure barriers to prevent unauthorized access to building grounds, buildings, and restricted building interior areas.

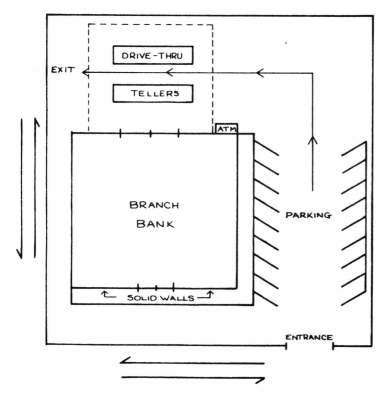

Figure 5-44.

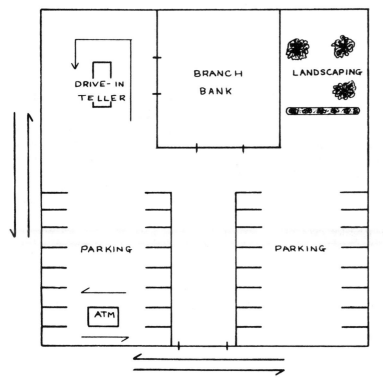

Figure 5-45.

2. *Surveillance through physical design.* Improve opportunities for surveillance by physical design mechanisms that increase the risk of detection for offenders, enable evasive actions by potential victims, and facilitate intervention by police.
3. *Mechanical surveillance devices.* Provide residences with security devices to detect and signal illegal entry attempts.
4. *Design and construction.* Design, build, or repair residences and residential sites to enhance security and improve quality.
5. *Land use.* Establish policies to prevent ill-advised land and building uses that have a negative impact.
6. *Resident action.* Encourage residents to implement safeguards on their own to make homes less vulnerable to crime.
7. *Social interaction.* Encourage interaction by residents to foster social cohesion and control.
8. *Private security services.* Determine appropriate paid professional or volunteer citizen services to enhance residential security needs.
9. *Police services.* Improve police service to provide efficient and effective policing.
10. *Police/community relations.* Improve police/community relations to involve citizens in cooperative efforts with police to prevent and report crime.
11. *Community awareness.* Create neighborhood/community crime prevention awareness to aid in combating crime in residential areas.
12. *Territorial identity.* Differentiate private areas from public spaces to discourage trespass by potential offenders.
13. *Neighborhood image.* Develop positive neighborhood image to encourage resident and investor confidence and increase the economic vitality of the area.

Residential Streets

In Figure 5-46,

1. Street is quiet with a small amount of through traffic.
2. Residents recognize neighbors' cars and stare at nonresidents, who may be passing through or stopping.
3. Gutters are clean and front yards are well maintained, which indicates extended territorial concern. Front porches have furniture and other signs of use.

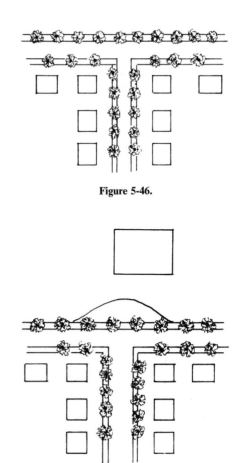

Figure 5-46.

Figure 5-47.

In Figure 5-47,

1. A proposed land use change involves building a new neighborhood school, which is generally socially desirable.
2. The school generates increased pedestrian and vehicular activity. Nonresident cars park in front of homes, taking up what previously was viewed as the proprietary space of residents.
3. Property value growth and retention falls. Residents subconsciously turn their backs to the street and alter their patterns of property use.
4. The controlling or challenging behaviors of residents (e.g., staring and verbal challenges) diminishes.

In Figure 5-48,

1. The neighborhood school is changed to an expanded school that loses its neighborhood identity. Users have very little attachment or concern for the neighborhood.

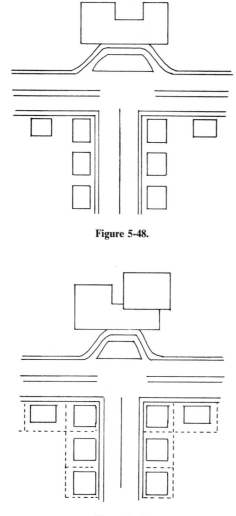

Figure 5-48.

Figure 5-49.

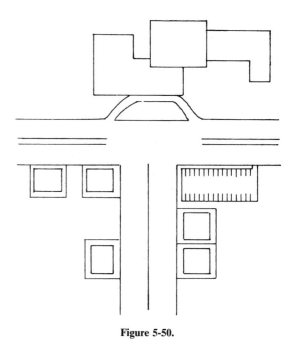

Figure 5-50.

2. Traffic increases and more parking activity occurs in the neighborhood. Property values drop and long-term or original residents move out.
3. New residents accept the changed conditions and exhibit few signs of extended territorial identity and concern.

In Figure 5-49,

1. The expanded school is further developed to regional status.
2. Streets already are upgraded from residential and subcollector status to the next higher level of traffic flow. Street capacity improvements result in the increase of on-street parking and the removal of the trees. Sidewalks and front yards are pushed closer to the dwelling units.

3. The neighborhood is already susceptible to zoning change request and the possibility of the development of transient housing, which may be disguised as low-income or scattered-site publicly supported housing.
4. Any major land use change contributes to higher demand for public services, increased housing turnover, and a growing crime rate.

In Figure 5-50,

1. The encroachment of marginal business or transient housing ultimately is replaced by high-density commercial or industrial activities, which are the only viable land uses once the original site has deteriorated.
2. Vacant or abandoned lots are used in the interim for overflow parking and unauthorized drug dealing or recreational use. The area is perceived as dangerous or undesirable for residential uses. Normal users avoid the area and abnormal users feel that they have lower risk of detection or intervention.
3. Some unscrupulous developers use this process as a means of controlling large parcels of land for long-term development, while capitalizing the long-term plans through the short-term investment in transient housing or marginal commercial activities, both of which help progressively reduce the property value.

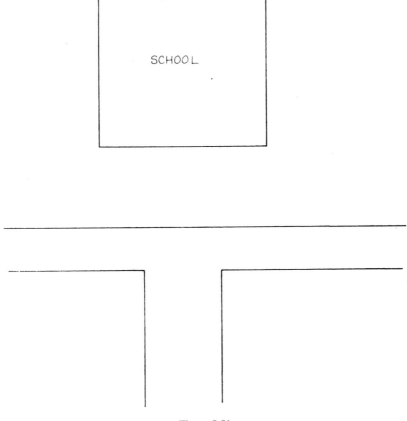

Figure 5-51.

In Figure 5-51,

1. Access to the new school is isolated from the contiguous residential streets, school property vehicular access is planned for an alternative location connected to an existing high-capacity commercially or industrially oriented street.
2. Pedestrian flow through the residential area still increases, but vehicular and parking activity are diverted.

In Figure 5-52,

1. An alternative strategy to the conflict created by the new school is to create a major setback to allow for a transition lane and temporary waiting lane for buses and parents picking up students.
2. Traffic control devices or procedures are used to direct and divert vehicles from the residential area.

In Figure 5-53, a partial choker is used to divert right turn traffic from the affected neighborhood. In Figure 5-54,

1. The street affected by the traffic associated with the school may be permanently diverted by closing the street with a cul-de-sac or turnaround T.
2. Emergency vehicle access may be enhanced through the use of drive-over plantings or knock-down gates. Malleable steel pins or links may be used in latching devices or chains to make it easy for emergency vehicles to push open the barriers.

In Figure 5-55, the street affected by the traffic associated with the school is closed in the middle, creating a dead end. The middle street closure uses a turnaround ball or T to facilitate emergency and public service vehicle access.

In Figure 5-56,

1. The street affected by the traffic associated with the school is choked off by the installation of entrance narrowing devices, walls, and columns.
2. The entrance definition is physical or symbolic. Columns and entrance definition may be installed

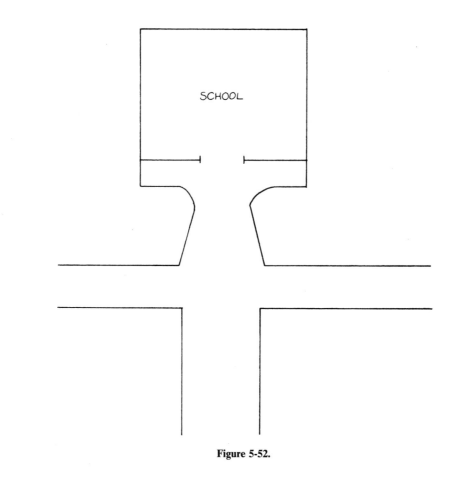

Figure 5-52.

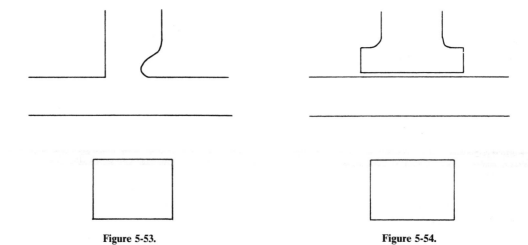

Figure 5-53.   **Figure 5-54.**

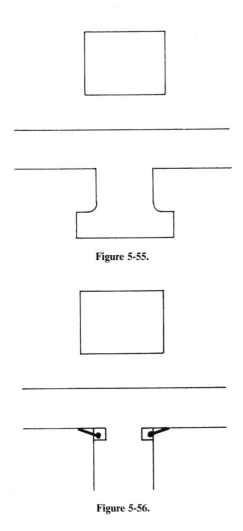

Figure 5-55.

Figure 5-56.

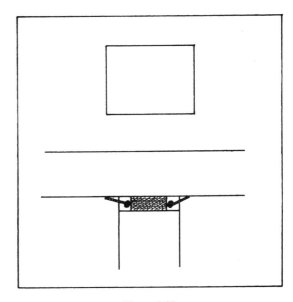

Figure 5-57.

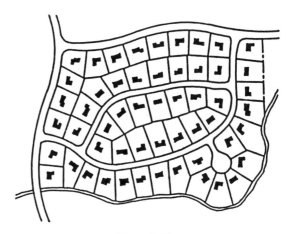

Figure 5-58.

without encroaching on the roadway in situations where the street entrance is too dangerous for a choking effort or other factors are involved, such as the preferences of residents.

In Figure 5-57,

1. The street affected by the traffic associated with the school is choked off with entrance definition devices.
2. The pedestrian walkway is upgraded through the installation of paver tiles or by raising the cross-walk by 3 inches to serve as a modified speed hump that warns drivers that they are entering a private area.

Residential Development: Curvilinear Streets

In Figure 5-58,

1. Conventional curvilinear plans minimize unas-signed space, which extends territorial concern.
2. Children are more likely to be observed and con-trolled by residents.
3. Some bleed-through traffic may occur if drivers become aware that they may avoid the northwest major intersection.

In Figure 5-59,

1. Cluster curvilinear streets are presently more appealing because of amenities and green areas, which are marked heavily by developers. Many local planning regulations require these features in planned unit developments.

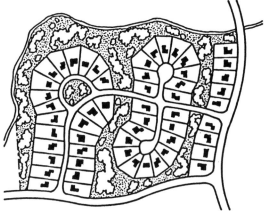

Figure 5-59.

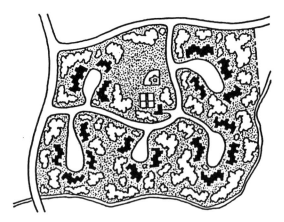

Figure 5-60.

2. The increase in unassigned areas may result in reduced proprietary concern of residents. Unassigned areas may be aesthetically appealing, but residents feel little attachment and may psychologically turn their backs on activities occurring there.
3. Deed restrictions or covenants are often very strict in terms of what residents may do in the open areas. This further reduces territorial concern.
4. Young people often go unsupervised in the open or green areas. There is some evidence in public housing, as well as in planned developments (cluster concept), that children growing up in undifferentiated environments fail to learn respect for property rights, which negatively affects their values and behavior.
5. CPTED planners may recommend that open areas be assigned to contiguous cluster of homes. Landscaping or other physical changes may be used to establish border definition.
6. Residents may be provided with financial and other inducements to participate in the maintenance of the open or green areas. This participation increases their proprietary concern for the previously unassigned space.

In Figure 5-60,

1. A townhouse cluster design is economically viable. Open spaces and amenities are important attractions to buyers.
2. This townhouse development creates an excessive amount of unassigned space, which is often protected by strict deed restrictions or covenants.
3. Territorial concern is reduced and abnormal users feel safer in accessing the open areas. Young

people are less likely to be scrutinized in these areas.
4. The ball field and tennis courts serve as a magnet to nonresidents. This could produce conflict and reduce the likelihood of controlling behavior by residents. Use by nonresidents legitimizes their presence in the development, which increases the abnormal users' perception of safety (low risk of detection or intervention). The normal user feels threatened and therefore exhibits avoidance, which affects other normal users. Abnormal users are reinforced by these cues, which say that no one owns this space or is willing to challenge its improper use. Normal users stop using these areas altogether, which has been a problem in public housing and parks.
5. CPTED planners may recommend the assignment of open areas to clusters of buildings. Landscape and other physical changes may be made to enhance border definition.
6. Residents may be induced to participate in maintenance of these areas through financial or other inducements. This extends proprietary concern for these areas.
7. CPTED planners may recommend the addition of one or two buildings on the north side of the development to provide a natural barrier to potentially conflicting activities. This appeals to the developer as a profitable move that produces the added benefits of increased perception of safety. CPTED planners may recommend the closure of the internal street in the middle, or at one end, to eliminate through traffic. This helps eliminate or reduce the probability of drive-by drug sales.

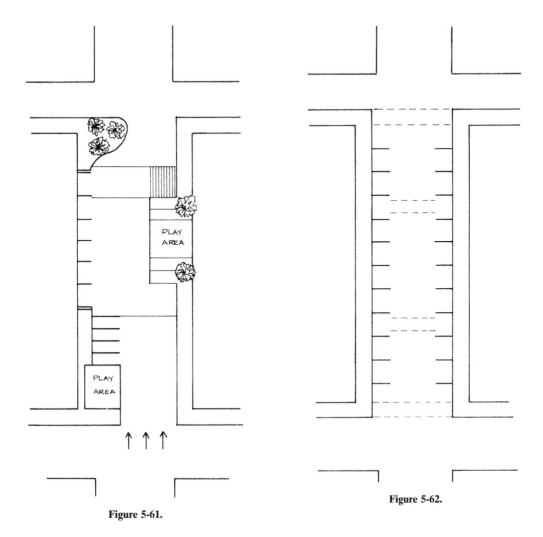

Figure 5-61.

Figure 5-62.

Residential Streets: Options for Private Use

In Figure 5-61,

1. Each end of the block is choked off. One end uses a closure of the incoming lane (ingress). The other end closes the outgoing lane (egress).
2. Play areas are installed to thrust activities more into previously public areas to increase visual and physical attention.
3. A combination of straight-in parallel parking is used.

In Figure 5-62,

1. Additional crosswalks are added to break the street into four areas. This increases the definition of the pedestrian space in the street.

2. Crosswalks should be legally designated under local ordinances to create pedestrian right of way.
3. Crosswalks may be raised 2–3 inches to reinforce the driver's perception of transition.

In Figure 5-63,

1. A combination of parking, parallel and straight-in, may be introduced to create space for more landscaping. This combination of landscaping and parking narrows the entrance (ingress and egress).
2. Crosswalks are upgraded to enhance transitional definitions.
3. A middle block or central area is defined with texture change, to be used for occasional block activities. Entrances are choked off or closed with

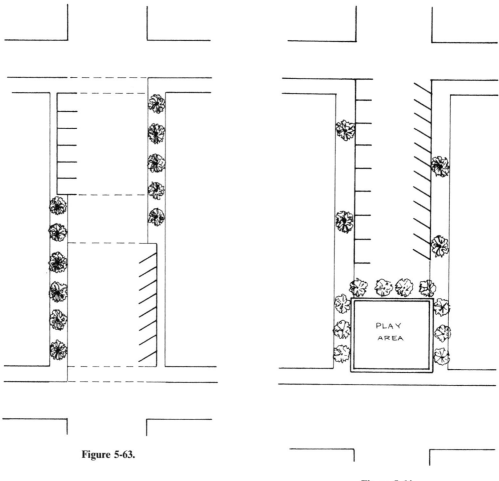

Figure 5-63.

Figure 5-64.

barricades during planned block parties or functions.

In Figure 5-64,

1. One end of the street is closed by installing a play area with safety barriers.
2. Parking arrangements are alternated between angle and parallel to create more parking and narrow the street.

In Figure 5-65,

1. Entrances are choked to slow traffic.
2. A block gathering area is installed to create a place for parties and other functions. These areas also further the perception of the block as private.

In Figure 5-66,

1. A simple closure creates a cul-de-sac effect that eliminates through traffic.

2. A drive-over (for emergency vehicles) area is created by reducing the elevation of the center of the planter. Replaceable flowers or bushes are used to increase the perception of closure in the drive-over area. Another option is to use knock-down bollards.

In Figure 5-67,

1. Landscaping improvements are installed to make the street more appealing for pedestrian activity.
2. An additional crosswalk is installed in the middle of the block to enhance pedestrian convenience and slow traffic.
3. Crosswalks should be legally designated under city ordinance. They may also be raised 2–3 inches to reinforce the driver's perception of transition.

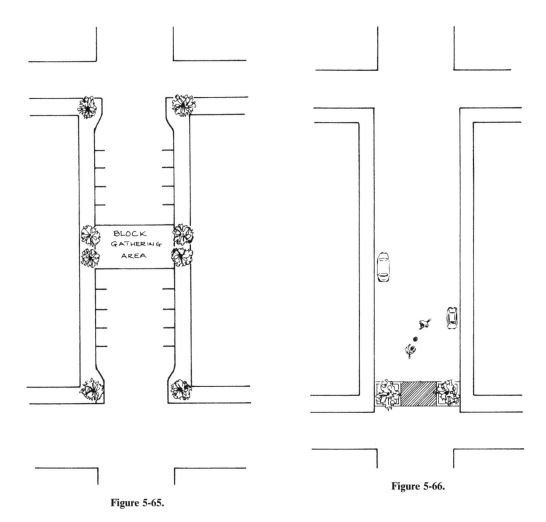

Figure 5-65.

Figure 5-66.

Residential Streets: Recovery of Grid Systems

In Figure 5-68,

1. Boundary control is established by creating cul-de-sacs in the middle of most access streets.
2. Access is limited to two points that connect with internal streets.

In Figure 5-69,

1. Internal controls are established by installing a system of diagonal diverters to loop traffic in and out.
2. Through traffic is denied. The diverter angles should be based on resident input and an analysis of access needs.

In Figure 5-70,

1. One-way traffic flows are established to reduce through access.

2. Speed controls are used to reduce pedestrian and vehicle conflict that result from higher speeds on the one-way system.
3. Parking plans may be altered to include alternating combinations of angle parking and street landscaping.

In Figure 5-71,

1. An ad-hoc plan of cul-de-sacs, diagonal diverters, and one-way flows make the streets more private.
2. This approach provides some flexibility for long-term planning.

Objectives for the School Environment

1. *Access control.* Provide secure barriers to prevent unauthorized access to school grounds, schools, or restricted interior areas.

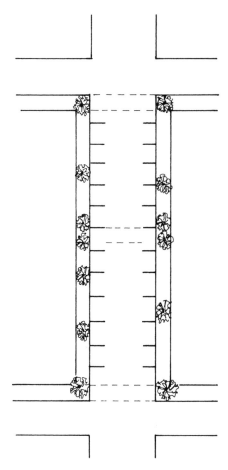

Figure 5-67.

BOUNDARY CONTROL

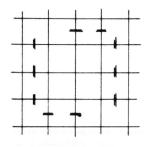

Figure 5-68.

INTERNAL CONTROL

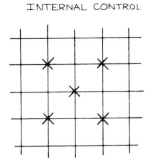

Figure 5-69.

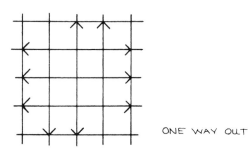

ONE WAY OUT

Figure 5-70.

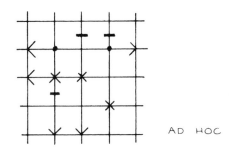

AD HOC

Figure 5-71.

2. *Surveillance through physical design.* Improve opportunities for surveillance by physical design mechanisms that increase that risk of detection for offenders.
3. *Mechanical surveillance devices.* Provide schools with security devices to detect and signal unauthorized entry attempts.
4. *Congestion control.* Reduce or eliminate causes of congestion that contribute to student confrontations.
5. *Psychological deterrents.* Provide psychological deterrents to theft and vandalism.
6. *User monitoring.* Implement staff and student security measures at vulnerable areas.
7. *Emergency procedures.* Provide teachers with means to handle emergency situations.
8. *User awareness.* Initiate programs to promote student awareness of security risks and countermeasures.
9. *User motivation.* Encourage social interaction, social cohesion, and school pride by promoting extracurricular activities, providing amenities, and upgrading the visual quality of the school.

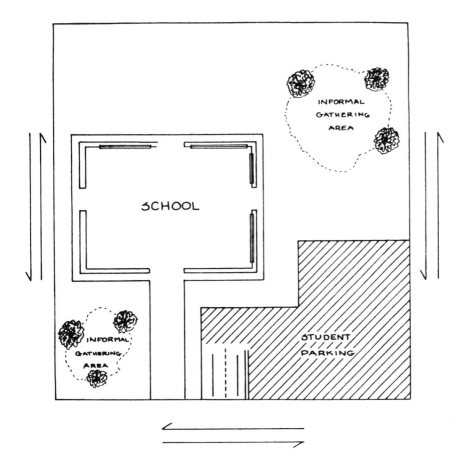

Figure 5-72.

10. *Territorial identity*. Highlight the functional identities of different areas throughout the school to increase territorial identity and reduce confusion.
11. *Community involvement*. Promote public awareness and involvement with school faculty and student achievements and activities.

School Campus Control

For poor design (see Figure 5-72):

1. Informal gathering areas are preempted by groups of students, who often promote conflict.
2. Isolated areas are used by students who wish to smoke or engage in unauthorized or illicit behavior.
3. Interlopers or trespassers seek out out-of-sight areas to contact students for drug sales or other improper activities.
4. Areas are very difficult to monitor and control.

5. Most authorities attempt to maintain surveillance of these areas in an attempt to control behavior.

For good design (see Figure 5-73):

1. By designating formal gathering areas, all other areas become off limits.
2. Anyone observed in spaces not designated as formal gathering areas is automatically subject to scrutiny.
3. Abnormal users feel at greater risk and have fewer excuses for being in the wrong places.
4. Teachers and administrators assume greater challenging powers by the clear spatial definition.

High School Parking Lots

For poor design (see Figure 5-74):

1. Multiple access points increase the perception that the parking area is public and provide many escape routes for potential offenders.

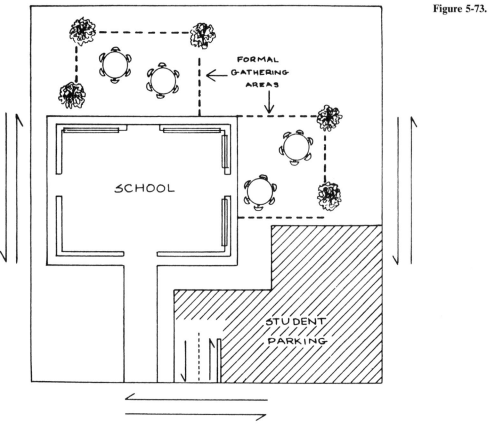

Figure 5-73.

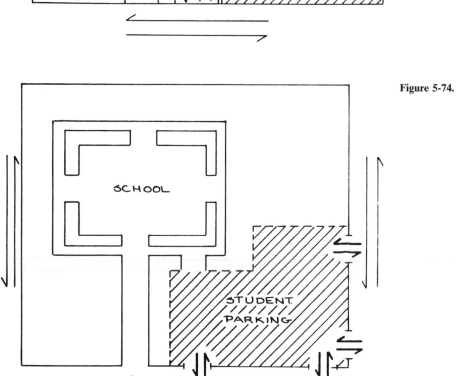

Figure 5-74.

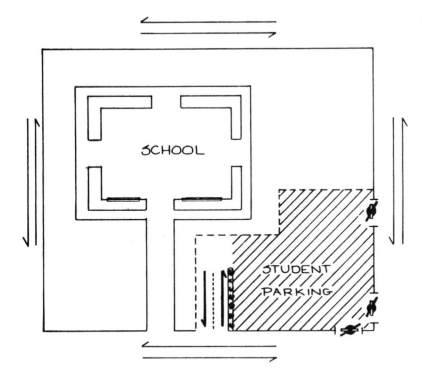

Figure 5-75.

2. The location on the periphery of the site reduces any clear transitional definition of movement from public to private space, allowing an abnormal user to feel safe or at low risk of confrontation.
3. The openness of the lot increases the range of excuses for improper use.

For good design (see Figure 5-75):

1. Use of barricades to close off unsupervised entrances during low-use times controls access and reinforces the perception that the parking area is private.
2. The curb lane in the open entrance forces the user to make a transition from public to semipublic to private space, with a radical turn into the parking area.
3. The symbolic isolation creates the perception that escape is easily blocked.
4. Violation of the barricade and traffic control devices draws attention to the abnormal user and establishes probable causes sufficient to stop the individual for questioning.

Student Parking and Driver Education Relationships

For poor design (see Figure 5-76):

1. Student parking is an unsafe activity.
2. Student parking on the periphery of the campus is in an unsafe location.
3. The isolated location has few opportunities for natural surveillance.
4. Poor transitional definition creates the perception of safety for abnormal users and risk for normal users.

For good design (see Figure 5-77):

1. Driver education is safe activity, monitored by responsible teachers and students.
2. The switch of driver education with student parking in an existing location provides a natural opportunity to put a safe activity in an unsafe location and an unsafe activity in a safe location.
3. The new location for student parking (in this hypothetical example) is in the direct line of sight from office windows.

Courtyards and Corridors

For poor design and use (see Figure 5-78):

1. Many site planners or users of space fail to adequately define the intended purpose and uses of courtyards.

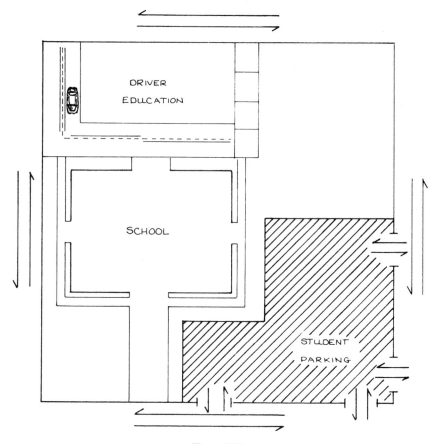

Figure 5-76.

2. Uses could be aesthetics, thermal support of the building, or as gathering areas. Each use presents different requirements and space management plans and policies.
3. Corridor and courtyard confusion is exacerbated by the installation of benches and other furnishings along the corridors.
4. Benches are sometimes used as barriers to access to courtyards, with the mistaken idea of protecting the grass from encroachment by students or pedestrians.
5. Corridor and courtyard conflict often leads to congestion, noise, and personal conflict.
6. Groups of students or others often colonize or preempt spaces, creating further conflict and fear.
7. Normal users will avoid using these areas. Abnormal users feel safer and at low risk of detection or intervention.

For good design and use (see Figure 5-79):

1. The intended purpose and uses of the courtyards and adjoining corridors are clearly defined both in policy and physical design.

2. Furnishings for courtyards intended for gathering are designed to break up group size or to provide only minimal comfort to shorten the staying time.
3. Portable amenities may be used more effectively than permanent ones, depending on intended use patterns. Accordingly, physical support is provided only when the specific behavior is desired.
4. Normal users feel safer in moving through these areas. Abnormal users are more subject to control and find it more difficult to preempt these spaces.

School Lunchtime Hallway Use

For poor design and use (see Figure 5-80):

1. The same hallway is used for coming and going.
2. Conflict occurs as some groups attempt to go to the cafeteria while others attempt to return to class.
3. The arrival of the first group and the departure of the second are the most controlled because no other group moves at the same time. All persons

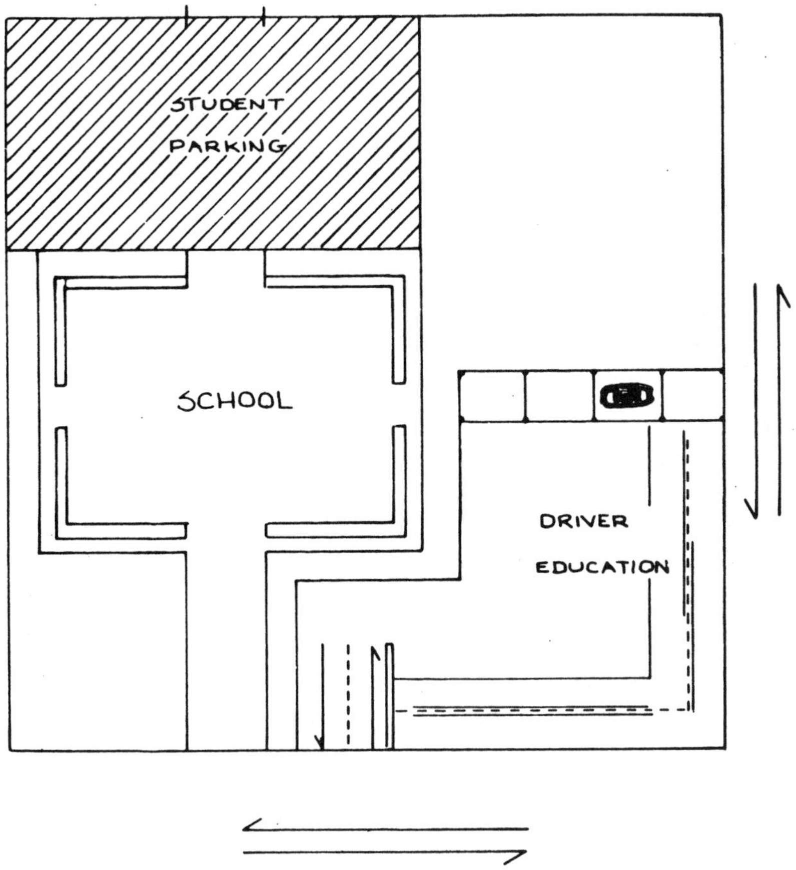

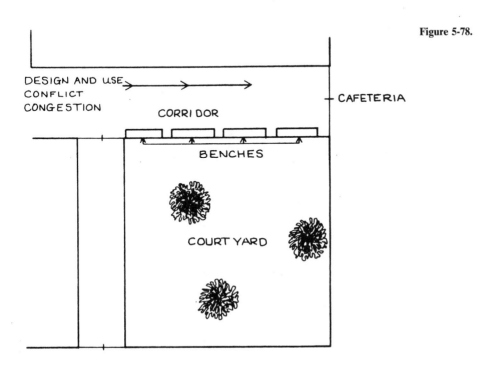

Figure 5-77.

STUDENT PARKING

SCHOOL

DRIVER EDUCATION

Figure 5-78.

DESIGN AND USE
CONFLICT
CONGESTION

CAFETERIA

CORRIDOR

BENCHES

COURT YARD

MAIN BUILDING

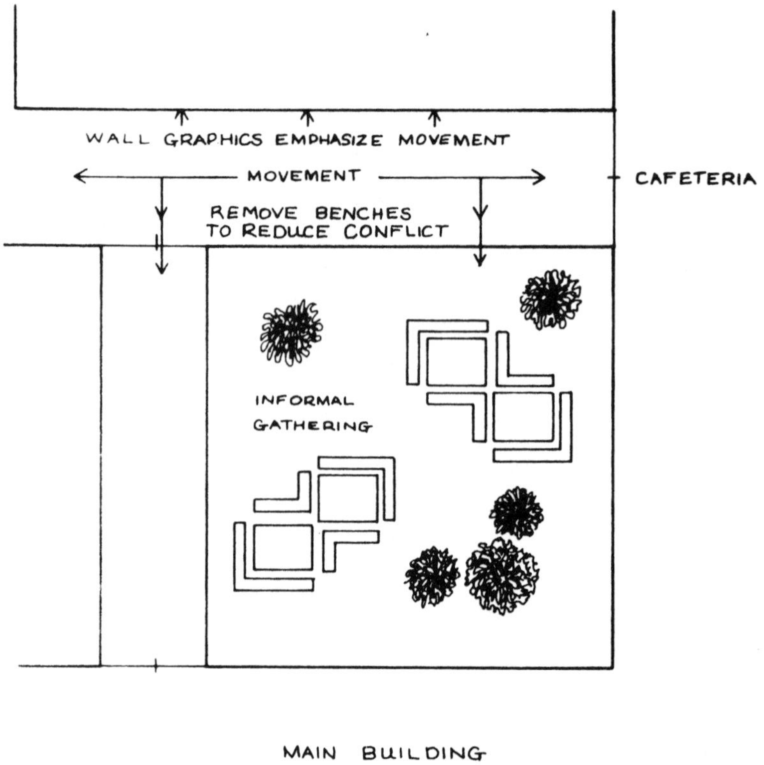

Figure 5-79.

WALL GRAPHICS EMPHASIZE MOVEMENT

MOVEMENT

CAFETERIA

REMOVE BENCHES
TO REDUCE CONFLICT

INFORMAL
GATHERING

MAIN BUILDING

Figure 5-80.

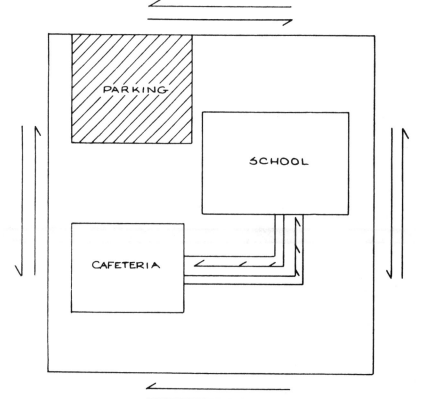

PARKING

SCHOOL

CAFETERIA

Figure 5-81.

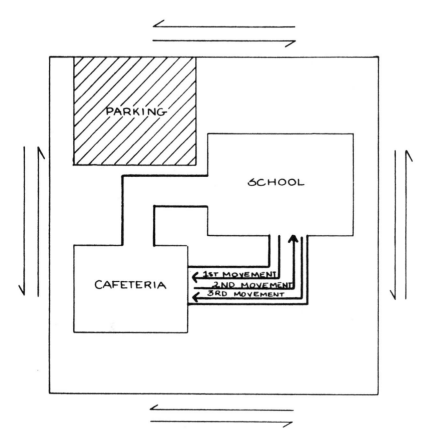

are supposed to be going in the same direction, so the hall monitors and administrators are perceived to be more powerful. There is a limited range of excuses for improper behavior.

4. Hall monitors lose control because of the coming and going after the first group eats.
5. Getting groups, after the first, through the lunch line takes longer because of the conflict and congestion.
6. Most classroom and locker thefts in school systems occur during the lunch period.

For good design and use (see Figure 5-81):

1. Ingress and egress to the cafeteria may be separated spatially and temporally to define movement relationships.
2. Each group arrives faster, with fewer stragglers.
3. Abnormal users of space feel at greater risk of detection.
4. A time, or temporal, separation of movements to and from the classroom area requires the addition of at least 5 minutes for each shift. This time may

be taken from that allotted for eating, since each group will arrive faster and, therefore, is fed faster.

Safe Activities in Unsafe Locations

For poor design (see Figure 5-82):

1. Many noncurricular activities at schools (e.g., military recruiting, college orientation, picture and ring sales, and club functions) are assigned to locations in the office, cafeteria, or gymnasium.
2. Office, cafeteria, and gymnasium areas provide poor design support for these noncurricular activities.
3. These noncurricular activities often impede the normal operations of the functions of the existing space.

For good design (see Figure 5-83):

1. Problem areas on school campuses are well known and easy to map.

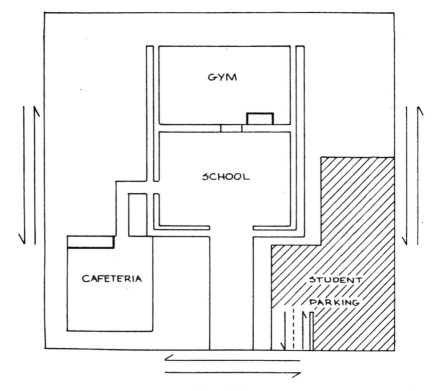

Figure 5-82.

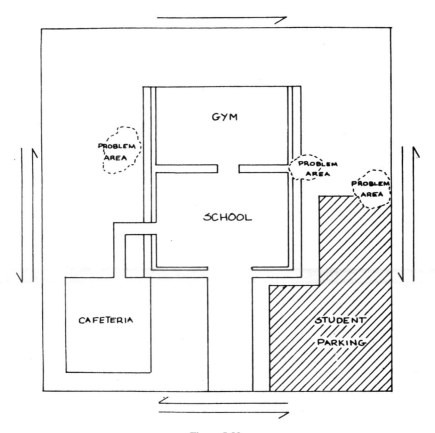

Figure 5-83.

2. Problem areas shift with changing groups and trends of supervision.
3. Safe activities may be placed reasonably in many problem areas to attract normal users and displace abnormal or undesirable activity.
4. Normal users feel safer and abnormal users fell at greater risk or unsafe.

Convention Centers and Stadiums

Convention Center

For poor design and use (see Figure 5-84):

1. Many convention centers are purposely placed in deteriorated areas to stimulate renewal. They are financed largely by public tax dollars or publicly backed bonds, since normal investors will not take the risk.
2. Convention centers suffer from fortress designs, which must reflect the designer's negative perception of the location, as well as the unique logistic requirements of convention activities.
3. Parking and pedestrian access are impeded by the fortress designs and by the deteriorated condition of surrounding areas.
4. Local codes often require parking to be placed behind structures and obscured by landscaping.
5. Local codes generally require the creation of plazas and open sitting areas. Developers are influenced to install fountains to enhance the aesthetics of an open area, but experience has shown that fountains and amenities in open areas attract vagrants, especially if they have already become established as the indigenous population.
6. Convention centers and their related parking structures usually are not designed to contain a variety of pedestrian-oriented businesses at the ground level, which would attract people all day and on weekends.

For good design and use (see Figures 5-85 and 5-86):

1. Change local codes to allow parking in front of convention centers, where it is safer.
2. Delay installation of permanent amenities and fountains until the intended user population has clearly taken control of the site.
3. Thrust the convention center and parking structures into the airspace above, and place businesses and nightclubs at the ground level to increase year round and evening activity. This will improve business and increase the number of normal users, who feel and act safer.
4. Consider altering the exterior and use patterns of existing sites by adding galleries to offset fortress efforts and increase both real and perceived surveillance opportunities. Galleries may be used to increase outdoor activities for exhibits and vendors, thus putting safe activities in what had been perceived to be unsafe locations.

INTERSTATE HIGHWAY   **Figure 5-84.**

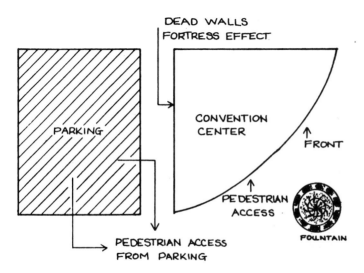

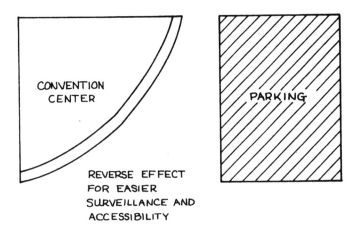

Figure 5-85.

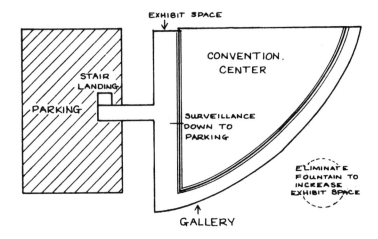

Figure 5-86.

Stadium Entrance and Ticket Control

For poor design and use (see Figure 5-87):

1. Traditional designs provide no transition from undifferentiated parking and informal gathering areas to the entrance and ticket control functions.
2. Groups of students and others tend to congregate in front of entrance locations, which produces fear and concern for adults and young people who wish to enter the stadium.
3. Ticket booth personnel and gate attendants cannot see over the groups of bystanders.
4. Normal users feel the lack of control and avoid these areas or pass through them quickly, reinforcing the control by abnormal users.

For good design and use (see Figure 5-88):

1. A funnel design forces informal gathering farther out into the parking area.

STADIUM   **Figure 5-87.**

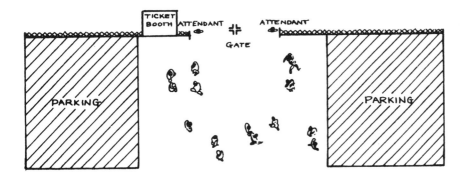

STADIUM   **Figure 5-88.**

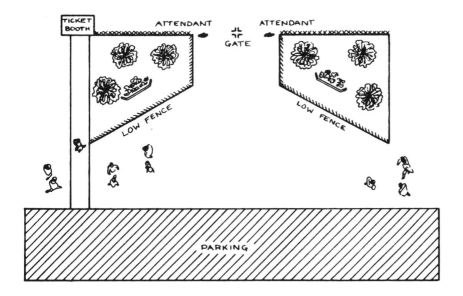

2. Gathering is more difficult deeper into the parking area because of the perceived pedestrian/vehicular conflict.
3. Gate attendants have greater line-of-sight control of the parking lot and pedestrian areas.
4. The range of excuses for different behaviors narrows with the width of the funnel as one approaches the gate. Attendants have more power to exert their influence over persons seeking entry as they are channeled into the funnel.
5. Normal users feel safer as they approach the entrance because of the narrow definition of behavior deep into the funnel—movement only.

Chapter 6
Physical Security*

DR. GERALD L. KOVACICH and
EDWARD P. HALIBOZEK

Paradise is now shut and locked, barred by angels, so now we must go forward, around the world and see if somehow, somewhere, there is a back way in.
—Heinrich von Kleist

This chapter introduces the fundamental principles of physical security. The concept of security in physical layers is introduced and addresses external barriers (such as, fences, walls, gates, buildings, and lobbies) and internal barriers (such as, access control systems). Internal controls and intrusion detection systems are also addressed, as is the use of current technology, such as biometrics.

Definition of Physical Security

No business is without security problems and assets protection risks. These risks and problems take many forms. Effectively mitigating them is not a happenstance occurrence. Problem elimination and risk mitigation require planning and an understanding of security needs, conditions, threats, and vulnerabilities. Assessing security conditions and planning for appropriate levels of assets protection begins with the basics: risk management.

Physical security is the most fundamental aspect of protection. It is the use of physical controls to protect the premises, site, facility, building, or other physical assets belonging to IWC. The application of physical security is the process of using layers of physical protective measures to prevent unautho-

rized access, harm, or destruction of property. In essence, physical security protects a property, plant, facility, building, office, and any or all of their contents from loss or harm.

Physical security contributes to protection of people and information. Sophisticated protection measures, other than physical, are employed to protect people and information. Nevertheless, physical security measures are part of the overall protective package. They are the baseline security measure, or foundation, on which all other security measures and functions are built.

For IWC, physical security measures are used to ensure that only authorized persons have access to IWC facilities and property. The measures employed must be appropriate for each separate operating environment. The IWC manufacturing facility requires physical security measures and functions and controls that may differ from those used at one of the IWC sales offices. Manufacturing facilities in different parts of a country or in different countries generally require differing physical security measures—one size does not fit all. In any event, physical security measures are the baseline of protection for IWC. All other security measures will be integrated with physical security measures, developing a protection profile of assets protection within layers.

It is the responsibility of the IWC corporate security manager (CSM) to determine what physical security controls are necessary to provide an adequate level of protection. To do this, the CSM must know the facility or site layout. The CSM must understand the operating requirements and operation of the enterprise, conduct an initial physical security survey, and periodically conduct supplemental surveys as part of the CSM's risk management survey program. This will allow for a thorough

*Kovacich and Halibozek, *The Manager's Handbook for Corporate Security*, pp. 186–206, Butterworth Heinemann, 2003

understanding of threats and vulnerabilities and enable the development and implementation of sufficient controls.

Security in Layers

What physical security measures are used to protect IWC assets depends greatly on what assets need to be protected, where they are located, and what threats, vulnerabilities, and risks pertain to them. Applying an appropriate level of protection for each environment requires a specific understanding of that environment. To best accomplish this, you should start at the beginning.

> Physical security measures should be designed into a facility during the facility design phase and built into the facility during the construction phase.

Ideally, architects and security professionals would work together taking into consideration all aspects of assets protection requirements applicable to the proposed operating environment. This type of planning helps create optimum security at the lowest possible cost. If done properly, security problems created by so many buildings being designed without any consideration given to security controls would no longer be the issue that it usually is these days.

As the IWC CSM, if you are not working with new construction and are occupying an existing building, designing in architectural security may not be possible. If retrofitting or renovation of the site or facility is necessary to accommodate the new business operating environment, then security may still be considered as part of the design. If not, physical security issues should at least be addressed prior to occupancy or operation. Security problems resulting from a failure to make security part of the design and construction phase will probably be of a structural nature and too expensive to undo or fix. The only solution in this case is the application of protective measures that otherwise might not have been needed, thus adding costs. Since the CSM knows that the foreign IWC facilities will be moved, it is important that the CSM coordinate the move to facilities that meet the IWC assets protection physical security criteria, or arrange to locate to another facility, or modify the existing facility before the IWC move takes place.

The application of physical security controls should be approached in layers. There is no single physical control that will fulfill all of IWC's security needs. Layering controls from the outer boundaries of each of the IWC facilities to the inner boundaries

will allow you to build a security profile to meet IWC's specific security needs.

Outer Layers of Protection

The outer layers of protection for a facility depend on the type of facility and its location (see Figure 6-1). For example, an office building located within a city may only have as its outer layer, or perimeter, the walls of the building, whereas a manufacturing facility located in an industrial district may be on a large parcel of land with parking lots, storage areas, and grounds surrounding the building or buildings. On a facility of the second type, the perimeter is usually a barrier, such as a wall or fence, located at or near the edge of the property line.

The perimeter of a facility takes many forms. For an office building it may be the building walls. For a factory it may be a fence line or a wall at the property edge. The outermost layer of protection could also be a highway; a natural physical barrier, such as a river, lake, or other body of water; or other man-made barriers. Whatever the barrier, it is the first layer of physical security. It may be at the perimeter's edge or inside the perimeter. Regardless of where it is situated, it is the layer of first control. Inside the outer layer, the use of other layers of physical security may be necessary.

Grounds

Not all facilities have grounds. Grounds serve many purposes. They may be purely decorative to create a pleasant environment for customers and employees. They may be functional and serve as a place to locate storage areas and warehousing facilities. They may also serve as a buffer or barrier between the perimeter of the facility and the buildings where work is done and people, physical assets, and information are housed. If kept clear, grounds serve as a clear zone, allowing for unobstructed observation of the area. If used for storage or other purposes, they should be kept organized and maintained. In this way, disruptions are easier to identify and the risk of hazards is reduced.

Roads

Roads are both necessary and problematic. They allow employees and customers to have easy access to the facility. However, they also allow unauthorized

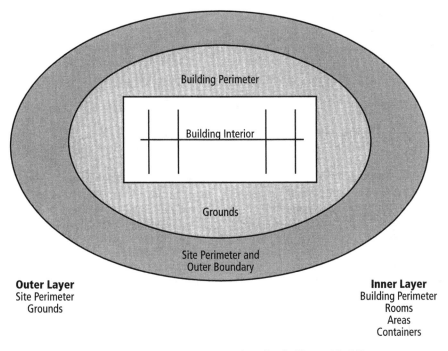

Figure 6-1. Illustration of layers within a site, facility, and building.

personnel to have easy access to the facility. The degree of control necessary on all roads leading to your facility will vary. Any controls used will depend on the type of road and its use. Is it a public road or a private road? Public roads do not allow for additional controls. They belong to the municipality, city, or state and exist to facilitate movement of vehicles and people. If a facility is adjacent to a public road, controls can begin only where the road ends and your property begins. Private roads allow for much greater control. Owners of private roads can install controls that allow for restricted passage. Owners of private roads can make the determination as to who has access and under what conditions. Ideally, controls on any road should begin as close to the outer perimeter as possible.

In an office-building environment, public roads generally lead to parking lots that are often adjacent to the buildings. This means perimeter controls begin at the parking area or at the walls of the buildings.

Fences, Walls, Gates, and Other Barriers

There are two types of barriers used for perimeter protection: natural barriers and structural barriers.

- Examples of natural barriers include rivers, lakes, and other bodies of water; cliffs and other types of terrain that are difficult to traverse; and areas dense with certain types of plant life (e.g., blackberry bushes that are very thorny and dense).
- Examples of structural barriers include highways, fences, walls, gates, or other types of construction that prohibit or inhibit access.

None of these barriers completely prevent access. They do, however, make it more difficult for unauthorized persons to gain access. When used with other layers of physical control, they can be very effective.

Fences

The most commonly used form of barrier, other than the walls of a building, is the fence. Fences vary in type, size, use, and effectiveness. They are erected quickly for a reasonably low cost, as is the case with the basic chain link fence. They are made more complicated and effective by adding barbed wire or concertina wire, alarm systems, or double fencing with alarmed clear zones between. The type of fence selected and used is determined by the specific needs. Again, balance the costs versus the risks.

At IWC's U.S. factory, the perimeter does not have the advantage of a natural barrier, so fencing was necessary. The fencing used is very typical in that it is 7 feet high, made with 9-gauge wire. It rests no more than 2 inches above the ground and in areas where the soil is loose. A concrete trough/border lies at the base to prevent gaps from erosion or human intrusion. At the top of the fence is a "guard" of 4 strands of barbed wire placed at a 45° overhang that faces away from the property. This actually extends the height of the fence by 1 foot and provides added difficulty for anyone attempting to scale the fence. Naturally, buildings, structures, and trees are sufficiently far away from the fence line as to not offer assistance to those who would attempt unauthorized entry. When looking at enhancing physical security at one of the IWC properties, the physical security project leader advised the CSM to consider IWC's "good neighbor" policy. This policy states that the local city planning and beautification commission must also approve any changes made by IWC that affect the beauty of the surrounding area.

Walls

Walls serve the same purpose as fences. They are man-made barriers but generally are more expensive to install than fences. Common types of walls are block, masonry, brick, and stone. Walls tend to have a greater aesthetic value, appealing to those who prefer a more gentle and subtle look. Regardless of the type of wall used, its purpose as a barrier is the same as a fence's. To be most effective, walls ought to be 7 feet high with 3 to 4 strands of barbed wire on top. This will help prevent scaling. For aesthetic reasons, management may resist the use of barbed wire. Nevertheless, it should be seriously considered.

Walls also present a disadvantage in that they obstruct the view of an area. Chain link and wire fences allow for visual access on both sides, walls do not. This obstacle is overcome by keeping clear zones for several feet on each side of the wall and by using video cameras for observation. Use of roving patrols also increases visibility. When the walls of a building serve as a perimeter barrier in lieu of fencing, the issues are different. Scaling the wall to get to the other side is not an issue, but access to the roof is. Furthermore, controlling access to other openings in the building becomes more critical when the walls to the building are the only outer barrier separating the outside world from the assets requiring protection.

Gates

Gates exist to both facilitate and control access. The most secure perimeter allows no one through. However, that is not practical or desirable; people must come and go. Employees, customers, and other visitors need to have easy access to your facility. Gates allow for this.

Gates need to be controlled to ensure that only authorized persons and vehicles pass through. A variety of controls are used. Guards; electronic interactive access control systems, such as, card key or password access; or remote control access with video camera observation can all be useful. What you select depends on your specific needs and conditions (e.g., acceptable levels of risk). The number of gates to a facility should be kept to the minimum necessary, not the minimum desired. Controlling gates requires using resources. The more gates used the more resources it will take and the more potential problems are created, because any opening is always a potential vulnerability.

Gates when not in use should be locked or eliminated. Having the flexibility to open an additional gate when traffic demands are high is useful. Eliminating a potential vulnerability is more useful. If a periodic need for an additional gate does exist, when the gate is not in use it must be closed, locked, and monitored. Monitoring is done by video camera, roving patrols, or through the use of an alarm system.

Periodically, even monitored gates require physical inspection to ensure they are operable and secure.

Natural Barriers

The effectiveness of a natural barrier will depend on the barrier itself and how it is used. A body of water may be very effective in keeping pedestrian traffic away from your property but not very effective at keeping boat traffic from your property. In this case, a natural barrier needs to be augmented with a man-made barrier. In any case, natural barriers, as with man-made barriers, need to be monitored. Cliff sides can be scaled, water can be crossed, and difficult terrain can be overcome.

Other Openings

Openings not designed for personnel or vehicle traffic are also a concern and must be secured. Needing control are sewage pipes, drains, utility tunnels, large conduits, and heating, ventilation, and air conditioning ducts. Where it is appropriate to lock them, they should be locked. Those that cannot be locked should be monitored. Monitoring is in the form of an alarm system or physical inspection. Any opening larger than 96 square inches should have doors, bars, or grill work in place to prevent human access. These are installed as permanent or removable, with locking devices. For example, to prevent access through heating, ventilating, and air conditioning ducts, man bars can be installed inside the ducting. This is not practical for openings requiring access by maintenance personnel, where the use of removable grills or doors may be more practical. In any configuration, all openings must be assessed for vulnerabilities and appropriate protective measures implemented. Regular inspections or monitoring to ensure tampering has not occurred is essential.

Buildings and Doors

For many facilities, buildings and doors define where the outer layers of security end and the inner layers of security begin. Within a site, buildings are the separation point between the outer and inner layers of security controls. In the area between buildings and the outer perimeter (usually a fence line) of the facility lie a variety of security controls that make up the entire outer layer of security. In this configuration, it is best to keep the areas adjacent to building and door exteriors clear. In essence, create a clear zone of 10 to 15 feet where no storage, parking, or regular activity is authorized. Maintaining a clear zone allows for unobstructed observation by surveillance cameras and guards. Visual access to the clear zone becomes the first line of defense for the inner perimeter.

Parking

Providing parking space for employees, customers, and visitors is necessary. Unless the business is small and located on a street with public parking access, parking needs to be provided. Parking should not be allowed within the outer perimeter. Vehicles inside the perimeter make it easier for theft to occur. Employees with immediate access to vehicles inside the perimeter have a ready place to conceal stolen items. Furthermore, unless all vehicles are inspected, it will not be known what items of contraband or weapons are brought into the facility. If, for lack of space, parking must be permitted within the outer perimeter, additional fencing should be erected to separate the parking area from the remainder of the facility.

Parking can be a very sensitive subject. Where people park is often linked with their status within the company. City and state laws require sufficient parking to be set aside for disabled persons. Visitors like to park close to the areas they visit. Parking is difficult to manage and police. It is recommended that parking rules be established by senior IWC management or the human resources department with the CSM's input. Parking enforcement should be handled by security.

Company-owned vehicles are the only exception to parking within the perimeter. As an asset of IWC, these vehicles require protection. Protection is particularly important if the vehicles are loaded with merchandise, supplies, or raw materials. They should be parked in a secure, well-lighted area, and locked. However, they should not be parked in the same area as privately owned vehicles.

Lighting

Lighting serves several purposes. Adequate lighting reduces the possibility of accidents and injury. It also serves as a deterrent to would-be intruders. With adequate lighting, the IWC grounds, fences, walls, and buildings can be clearly observed. Guidance for specific levels of illumination are obtained through federal sources or from any company that sells or installs exterior and parking lot lighting. The best determination for assessing adequate lighting is conducting an actual test. Is the existing lighting sufficient as assessed under controlled and practical conditions? If not, you need more lighting.

Adequate lighting serves as a deterrent. Intruders are less likely to enter well-illuminated areas, fearing they will be observed. Lighting should be sufficiently protected to prevent tampering and destruction. It should be kept within the perimeter to reduce the possibility of damage. Lights should be placed high enough to ensure that tampering must be deliberate and difficult. When used as a deterrent, lighting should have a backup power supply in the event of a power disruption. Lighting requires little attention in that it can be programmed to turn on and off at specific times. It can be light-, movement-, or heat-sensitive. It can be linked to alarm systems and supports CCTV. After installation, it does require frequent inspection to ensure all systems are operational.

Specific lighting needs varies with each site or facility. As part of a site physical security survey,

Table 6-1. Strengths and Weaknesses of CCTV and Guards When Used in the Surveillance Process

	Strengths	Weaknesses
CCTV	Serves as a deterrent	Cannot respond to incident
	Flexibility of recording	Cost of initial installation
Camera with	Permanent record	Maintenance cost
Recording Capability	Reduced insurance rates	Employee perception of being watched
	Deterrent for crime	
	Multiple angles of view	
	Night view, works in low light	
Guards	Can act on observation	Cannot watch everything
or Security	Deterrent	Human error
Professionals	Mobility	No permanent record of observation
	Apply immediate judgment	Limited angles of observation

lighting should be considered. Areas that require direct protection should have lighting that not only illuminates the area but also does not interfere with security's ability to effectively monitor. Too much lighting can create a problem by producing bright spots that blind people and cameras. Doors, gates, and other entrances should be well illuminated. This allows for safe passage and for better observation by guards and cameras. Areas with heavy personnel and vehicle traffic also require good lighting, it reduces hazards and increases visibility. Large open areas with little traffic can use less lighting, but lighting must be sufficient to allow for general security observation and a safe environment.

This is sometimes a political issue in that executive management wants to lower utility costs, among other costs. Management sees security lights on in the daytime and complains to the CSM. All of a sudden the CSM has a directed task to see how much utility (e.g., electricity) costs are due to security. Management also wants to know how the costs can be reduced. If the CSM had thought about such a possibility early on, the return on investment for solar-powered lighting could have been considered. If solar-powered lights were installed they could be left on indefinitely with no electrical power costs involved. Of course, some executive managers still might not be satisfied. They might say, "Yes, but it gives a bad impression to those who don't know they are solar powered," or, "Ah yes, but we can save money on the light bulbs because they will burn out quicker if left continuously on." Sometimes a CSM can't win.

Surveillance

Surveillance is an important tool for security in its effort to protect assets. Generally, surveillance is accomplished by using security guards or surveillance cameras. Frequently a combination of both is used to achieve maximum observation and effectiveness for any facility. As part of a site physical security survey, the need for surveillance should be identified. This need should be assessed against the existing practice and capability. With this information, a plan for site or facility surveillance can be developed. The plan considerations are:

- Purpose of surveillance—deterrence or observation
- Identify critical or high-risk areas
- Camera and guard mix
- Location of cameras
- Recording capability needed
- Need for hidden cameras
- Type of cameras needed—wide or narrow angle of view, low or high level of light, availability of solar-powered cameras

Each choice has its strengths and limitations (Table 6-1).

The CSM, lacking in some resources, looks for alternative ways of providing assets protection in areas where there was no budget available for cameras. The CSM discusses the matter with the supplier of IWC surveillance cameras. The CSM is able to obtain free outdated and broken cameras. These are installed, with the LED powered by several batteries, indicating that the camera power is on and working. Appropriate signs advising of the surveillance cameras are posted in the area. To those passing through the area, it appears as if active surveillance cameras are installed and used. Such techniques have the same effect as active cameras; however, be advised that this is not a cure-all for expensive surveillance cameras. The cameras do not see miscreants' activities in that area, and therefore there is no patrol guard response. However, it is something to consider when short of surveillance camera budget.

Alarms

Alarms are one of the layers used in the many layers of protection for a facility. How they are used and to what extent should be determined in the planning process. The site physical security survey should identify vulnerabilities, current and potential, and the layers of protection in use. When assessed against known or suspected threats, the need for alarms to augment physical protections should be apparent.

Alarms augment barriers and guards. They call attention to problems not stopped or prevented by barriers and not observed by guards. In essence, they enhance the detection process. However, they also serve a deterrent function. Since most physical security controls include the use of alarm systems, intruders can assume they are part of the protection profile.

Alarm systems are used to call attention to an immediate problem. Unlike physical barriers (such as, walls, fences, or gates), they are not a physical obstacle in and of themselves used to slow down or stop an intruder. They are an alert mechanism used to call attention to an intruder or problem. Audible alarm systems may serve as an obstacle much more than silent alarm systems, since they let everyone in the general area know when there is an alarm activation.

There are many types of alarm systems. Within the physical security profile, intrusion detection and fire detection are used the most. As part of the outer barrier, intrusion detection is used to indicate penetrations in or between the various layers of protection. Different types of alarm systems are available for fences, gates, and walls, and all provide an alert if they are compromised.

Alarm systems are used as part of the protection profile for both inner and outer layers of physical security. When used as part of the outer layer of protection, they serve as an advanced warning notice that an outer layer has been compromised, thereby making the inner layers more vulnerable. They serve to protect property and assets stored within the outer layer by providing an indicator that an intruder is tampering with, or in the area of, the property being protected.

In any case, alarms are only effective if there is a response. Someone must react to an alarm. An alarm system without timely response is not effective. Responding to an alarm is essential, or the alarm becomes nothing more than an expensive annoyance (e.g., car alarms in public areas are generally ignored). Perpetrators often test alarm systems by causing their activation and watching for a response. No response lets perpetrators know that they have plenty of time to work with. Responses to alarms by security guards or others must be periodically tested and the response of the security guards or others timed. These must be no-notice tests—it is ridiculous to test security guard responses if they know a test is to be conducted.

Alarm systems provide balance for the overall physical security profile in both protection capabilities and costs. Alarms can reduce the need for a large, stationary guard force. They allow for a configuration of alarm monitors, respondents, and some form of patrol. They reduce or even eliminate the need for a stationary force. If alarm systems are not used, the function they serve must be fulfilled by using a larger guard force, or through the use of greater surveillance capability, or you can just assume a greater level of risk. Remember that it is not up to you to assume a greater level of risk by choosing not to install alarms in an effort to save money. Actually, alarms save money by replacing people in many instances. Before assuming additional risk caused by the lack of alarms, you must consult with executive management and have them accept that additional level of risk.

Alarm systems cost more to install than to maintain. The cost of alarm systems is greatest in the acquisition and installation phase. Once installed, maintenance and monitoring costs are generally much less than people costs. A return on investment can be calculated and used as a selling point on the value of alarm systems. Using alarm systems offsets the need for some guards. The savings in recurring guard costs can be compared to the cost for acquisition and installation of alarm systems. Over several years, it is usually more cost-effective to use alarm systems to augment security than to rely on a larger guard force.

If you were the IWC CSM, would you want a silent alarm that was only audible in the manned security command center or an alarm audible in the area that is alarmed and also at the security guard's console? The correct answer is, "It all depends." It depends on the area alarmed, the value of the assets located therein, the risks to those assets, and so forth. The key is to base your choice on a risk assessment or physical security survey of each particular environment.

Inner Layers

In the previous section we discussed elements that are generally considered to be part of the outer perimeter. They are the outer layers of physical security. For the most part they are layers of physical protection that lead up to the building walls. We also indicated that, depending on the environment of the outer perimeter, you as the CSM might actually begin security at the building walls. In this situation, the first layer of security is made up of the walls, doors, and windows of a building. Office buildings in urban environments represent a good example of this situation. Outside these buildings are conditions that are not controlled by the building occupants. There is a single layer of outer physical security controls protecting the inner layers, which doesn't leave much room for error. In this case, penetration of a single layer allows access to the inner layers of IWC. This condition should lead to a greater emphasis on the types of inner controls applied.

Buildings, Doors, Windows, and Glass

Buildings serve as perimeters. In urban areas, the walls, doors, and windows of office buildings may be the outermost perimeter and the only outer layer of security control for the entire facility. In other settings, buildings may serve as part of the outer perimeter or as the first layer of the inner perimeter. This will depend on the individual facility configuration. Whatever layer of protection it provides, full consideration must be given to all aspects of building protection. All openings must be addressed, and buildings generally have many of them. Doors, windows, and passageways for ducting and conduits all need to be controlled. Power, communications, and heating, ventilating, and air conditioning systems require entry points from the exterior of the building into the interior of the building. To ensure they are not used for unauthorized purposes, controls should be in place. Any openings that serve no useful function should be permanently closed.

Functional openings larger than 96 square inches should be modified to prevent human access. Windows should be locked and alarmed. Alarms should detect entry or tampering. In some cases, man bars or screening are necessary. Screens and man bars allow for the passage of air and visual inspection but do not allow for human access.

The type of glass used in windows will vary depending on the location or use of the window. Windows at ground level on a perimeter wall clearly require a stronger glass than those windows located on higher floors or inside the outer perimeter. In some areas they may need to be bulletproof. Furthermore, special glass may be required, for example, in earthquake areas. Should such glass be shatterproof or shatter inwardly or outwardly? The answer is that it all depends. Using a risk assessment approach that includes personnel safety factors (e.g., flying glass) will assist the CSM in making a cost-effective decision.

Doors should be locked when not in use and controlled when in use. Controls range from guards at the door controlling entry and exit to mechanical or electronic access control systems requiring cards and card readers or access codes. Exterior or perimeter doors must be hardened, and are generally built to be stronger than interior doors. It may be necessary to have interior doors of a similar strength and quality as exterior doors if those interior doors are part of an area used to provide specific protection to high value assets. All associated materials for doors must be consistent with the strength of the doors themselves. For example, a high-security door is of little use if weak latching devices or cheap locks are used to hold it in place. High-security doors should have high-security locks. Also look at the hinges. Are the hinges facing in or out; are they welded or is the pin removable? A locked door with hinges facing the direction of the potential penetrator does little good if the pins or hinges can be removed.

Locks, Keys, and Combinations

Locks are an essential part of physical security protection. They are a cost effective and simple means of denying access to unauthorized persons. The largest expenses for locks are the initial purchase, installation, and control of their use. Depending on usage, little maintenance is required. Although any lock can be overcome, the higher the quality of the lock the longer it will take. Simple locks can be picked or easily damaged. More sophisticated locks will buy more time against any attempt to bypass them. Locks vary in quality and type and a wide variety are available. Determining the appropriate lock for any door, window, or other opening is based on planned usage, specific needs, and the assets requiring protection.

Perhaps the most vulnerable aspect of locks is the failure to properly protect locks, keys, and combinations and control is critical. Poor key control can render any locking device useless. Issuance of master keys must be severely limited, particularly the issuance of grand master keys. All locks, keys, and combinations should be accounted for. Keys and combinations should be issued in accordance with employees' need to perform their job. If there is no specific need, locks, keys, and combinations should not be issued. A permanent record of personnel issued or assigned keys or lock combinations must be kept. When keys are lost or stolen, the locks should be rekeyed. When a master key is lost, all affected locks should be rekeyed. There may be times when this is not necessary, such as if a key were inadvertently destroyed and its recovery or use poses no risk.

Keys should never be issued on a permanent basis. An annual assessment of locks, keys, and combinations needs and requirements should be made. This assessment will also assist in identifying lost or stolen keys or combinations that were not reported to security.

Locks, keys, and combinations should be issued to individuals rather than groups if individual accountability is a requirement. Sharing is a risk in that a theft or misappropriation of an asset protected by the lock cannot then easily be attributed to a specific individual. It is no different from sharing computer passwords.

Roofs

It is important to remember that roofs may be part of the outer or inner perimeter. Roofs generally have openings for maintenance, power, heating, ventilation, air conditioning, and other conduits. The same principles applicable to barriers and walls are applicable to roofs. Openings must be controlled. Since routine access to roofs is generally not an issue, locking devices and barriers such as screens and bars are used. Ladders or stairs leading to roofs should be controlled. Access to the roof should be made difficult for unauthorized personnel.

Areas, Rooms, Containers, and Safes

Inside buildings there are open work areas, individual offices and rooms, storage containers, and safes. How they are protected depends on how they are used and on the value of the assets in them. Open work areas such as large bullpen areas, where many employees sit at workstations performing their daily duties, may not require additional controls. Once inside the building, employees and visitors may need to move freely in these areas. Since access authori-

zation is verified at either the outermost layer of security control (outer perimeter gate leading into the facility) or the first control of the inner perimeter (door or lobby allowing entry into the building), additional checks for general access are not necessary—again, based on risk management. Moreover, access to general office areas and rooms such as conference rooms, cafeterias, or rooms housing other employee services may not need additional controls. Employees in these areas must understand that they also have a responsibility for controlling access in that all individuals not known to them, or not wearing a current, corporate badge, should be challenged as to their need to be in the area.

Areas or rooms where more sensitive work is done or sensitive information and materials are located require additional controls. The simplest means for applying these controls is through the use of locking devices or access control systems on each entryway. From simple locking devices on doors to the use of electronic card readers or electronic personal recognition systems, varying degrees of physical controls can, and should, be used to limit access to sensitive work areas. The methods used depend on the application of a cost-risk philosophy.

Safes can be used for the most sensitive information or material. Safes are available in various sizes and strengths. Depending on the sensitivity of the information or material protected, simple combination lock or key lock safes may be sufficient. These safes can be obtained from a variety of manufacturers. For the most sensitive information and material, high-security safes and vaults may be necessary. For example, working with government classified material requires the use of government approved storage containers. The higher the classification of government material, the more stringent the requirement for storage containers becomes. The same philosophy should be applied for protecting sensitive IWC information.

Access Controls

Controlling access is a critical component of security in layers to protect corporate assets. Ensuring that only authorized personnel and vehicles enter and exit IWC facilities reduces the risk of loss or damage to all assets. Effective access controls require the integration of different security functions that serve as individual layers of protection. Used as part of an integrated system, the following are useful access control tools:

- Guards
- Locks—combination, code, or key
- Card reader systems—magnetic stripe, optical bar code, proximity cards, biometric systems (fingerprints, signatures, face or hand geometry, voice recognition, and retina recognition)

Part of the site physical security survey should focus on identifying access control vulnerabilities and existing access control practices. When vulnerabilities and existing practices are compared with what is actually needed, an access control profile that best fits your site can be developed and implemented. The access control profile must address who should have authorized access to the facility and under what conditions (e.g., weekdays but not weekends, normal business hours but not after business hours). It should also identify the individual security processes and tools needed to effectively design and implement proper access controls.

What Should Be Controlled?

Vehicles

All vehicles entering and exiting the facility must be controlled. Only authorized vehicles should be allowed on site. Procedures establishing traffic flow and parking need to be written and communicated. Violations of these procedures must be enforced. Not enforcing traffic and parking rules and regulations will quickly lead to a breakdown and abuse of controls. At the very least, consideration should be given to random inbound and outbound searches of vehicles to ensure that anything entering or leaving the facility has proper authorization.

Employees

Employees need easy access to their work areas, and access control procedures should be designed to facilitate their prompt and efficient movement in and out of the facility. Access control procedures should be the same for all employees, thereby creating a culture of respect and adherence to the process and practice. Requiring employees to use some form of identification to have authorized access to a site is a standard practice. Badges, access identification cards, and other forms of physical controls can be used to validate that a person is actually an employee and quickly allows him or her entry into or exit from the facility. If the site employee population is large (e.g., exceeds 50 people), do not rely only on personal

recognition for access authorization. Personnel changes take place regularly, and keeping up with employee changes and turnover is better accomplished with automated systems than with the memories of security personnel. Furthermore, all employees should be subject to random entry and exit searches as determined necessary by the degree of assets protection required. To this practice there should be no exceptions.

Often, the CEO and executive management set the tone. Their support or lack thereof is quickly seen and adopted by the employees. That is why the CEO and executive management must also wear IWC badges, even if "everyone knows who they are." As with all asset protection requirements, they must set the example.

Vendors, Suppliers, Customers, and Visitors

Very few people who are not employees should be allowed free and complete access to the facilities. If vendors or suppliers are assigned to an IWC site on a full-time basis and do require unrestricted site access to perform their work, they are to be provided with identification that indicates that they are not employees. Moreover, this status should be subjected to scheduled periodic review to revalidate the need. Any identification provided to allow access should have an established expiration date. As with employees, all must be subject to random entry and exit searches. For contract employees, the expiration date of the badge should not exceed their contract expiration date.

How Do You Control Them?

Vehicle and Personnel Gates

The first line of protection for access to a facility is at the vehicle and pedestrian gates. Through these gates employees and visitors enter the facility, so control must begin there. Processes should be in place to allow employees through and to properly process all visitors according to established procedures or parameters. The use of employee identification badges coupled with an electronic card identification system is one of the most common tools used for this purpose.

Building Lobbies and Doors

The same controls used for gates are generally effective for lobbies and doors. Some lobbies have guards who are also receptionists, or receptionists who double as guards. In either case, it is important that these people understand that their priority is access control and being a guard rather than a receptionist. If there is a conflict in that dual role, the CSM should ensure the separation of those functions by having two individuals perform the separate functions (for example, a receptionist as part of the human resources budget and a guard as part of the CSM budget). Executive management's idea is to have the lobby personnel appear very friendly and helpful. However, in some lobbies or access control areas they may want to provide the appearance of a no-nonsense security presence.

Interior Areas and Rooms

Inside a building, access is generally controlled by three effective mechanisms, two of which were discussed earlier. They are:

- Lock and key devices
- Card key access systems
- Other employees

Employees play an important role in controlling access to internal areas and rooms. When they encounter an unauthorized person inside an area or room, they should be trained to challenge that person and report the incident to security. This conditioning does not occur naturally, and will require employee awareness training to be conducted for all employees. Moreover, this type of behavior is best encouraged through positive recognition and reward.

Badges

The primary use of badges is employee identification. Badges can also be coupled with access control systems, expanding their use and effectiveness. Magnetic codes, bar codes, and proximity cards, which activate electronic locking devices, can be linked to the identification badge, making it a multifunctional identification and access tool. This tool can contain information pertaining to the specific characteristics of an employee. Identifying each individual by name and other specific personal information, such as photographs, encoded access authorizations, and pin numbers, is easily accomplished and makes the badge a very reliable authentication device. Sophisticated badge and access control systems are available from a variety of manufacturers. Computer technology and technology advancements in general have made the process of making badges more efficient, effective, and reliable.

To ensure reliability and effectiveness, the process of using a badge for employee identification must be controlled. Specific parameters for use must be established and maintained for the badge process to maintain its integrity. Rules governing the following aspects of a badge process will help ensure a very reliable system:

- Determine who is authorized to have a badge
- Identify what data is needed on each badge
- Security controls production, issuance, and accountability of badges
- Badges must be recovered from employees who leave the company
- Lost or stolen badges are reported and removed from the system
- Worn or damaged badges are exchanged for new badges
- A tracking system is used to ensure internal accountability of unused badge stock
- A periodic review of the badge issuing process is conducted
- Badges made but not in use must be controlled or destroyed
- Tamper-resistant features such as holography should be used to make counterfeiting more difficult
- Employees must understand the need for the badge process and adhere to proper usage

At small facilities such as IWC satellite offices, personal recognition is usually the best form of identification—as long as the process is in place to also identify those who have left the corporation. For larger facilities, generally with 50 or more employees, personal recognition is no longer practical and use of a more reliable employee identification system is needed. Badge systems generally fulfill this need. Again, the CSM must consider the risks of each option.

It is also necessary to control the access and movement of visitors, suppliers, and customers. For this, a badge process for nonemployees is used. It is similar to that of the employee badge process but more restrictive in the sense that it clearly identifies the visitor as someone who is not an employee and has obvious indicators on the badge calling out appropriate restrictions. Escort requirements, badge expiration dates, and specific areas authorized to visit are some of the useful data necessary for the visitor badge.

Employees must be familiar with the badge process. They should receive guidance and training as to how the process for employees and nonemployees works. Employees should be able to recognize authorized badges and react to unauthorized badges. Persons not wearing an appropriate badge or violating the parameters of the badge process should be challenged. Without the active participation of all employees, any badge process will be rendered ineffective.

Guards

Guards or plant protection officers are an integral part of a physical security profile. Depending on specific needs and the type of facility, their use will vary.

Guards add a human element to the physical security profile. They are used in situations where observation, training, and judgment are required to apply effective asset protection controls. For example, guards are often used for vehicle access control functions. They not only check proper identification of the vehicle and driver, but they also provide greater flexibility for vehicle inspection on a variety of cars and trucks that may have a need to enter the site. When an irregularity is observed, they possess the ability to react instantly to the situation by reporting or challenging those with questionable identification. Moreover, they make an assessment of a situation and determine if additional assistance is needed (e.g., responding to an alarm and determining whether an intrusion occurred or if the alarm was false).

Guards also provide the capability of patrolling a site or facility, making observations and taking note of changes or irregularities, all of which can be further investigated. The mobility of guards makes them particularly valuable, because their services are quickly applied to a particular need or situation.

One of the most common security functions outsourced is the guard force, since it obviously is human intensive and one of the more costly aspects of an assets protection program. Furthermore, high technology devices are replacing some of the security guard posts. At IWC, the guard force is a proprietary guard force. The CSM has decided that this function is the first security function that is evaluated for outsourcing as soon as the initial assets protection baseline is established for IWC, and that includes the initial implementation of the CAPP.

Another factor that must be considered is the use of armed guards. Executive management usually does not want an armed guard presence, and some laws may prohibit their use. However, if you want to create a presence of serious security, there is nothing like an armed guard at the corporate lobby to give that impression. There are many pros and cons of the use of armed guards. Because of the high value of some corporate assets, it may be deemed appropriate to have armed guards at some locations but not others. That presents the problem of who is placed in what guard positions and decreases the effective and efficient use of guards to fill any guard job within the corporation. In addition, the armed guards are more highly trained and may also press for higher pay for being armed. Their reasoning is that if they are armed, they are more trusted than those who are not armed, their job is more dangerous, and they are more highly skilled.

The use of armed guards is a serious issue that each CSM must address. At IWC, none of the guards are armed and an armed response from the local police has been deemed sufficient for IWC assets protection needs. This was based on a meeting between the CSM and local law enforcement personnel, where the response needs of IWC and the response time that the CSM could generally expect from patrol car officers and a SWAT team were discussed.

Alarms and Surveillance within the Inner Layer

The application of alarms and surveillance within the inner layer of security requires the same considerations as the application to the outer layer. The extent to which they are used or not used depends on threats, vulnerabilities, risks, and the criticality of assets within.

Physical Security Costs

The cost of physical security is always a concern. Reaching an appropriate balance between adequate levels of protection and the cost of that physical protection is difficult. Too little security leaves vulnerabilities in place, increasing risks. Too much security mitigates threats and vulnerabilities and reduces risks but leads to unnecessary expenditures. Inefficient application of security controls (spending more than you need to for a physical security service or product) uses scarce resources that otherwise are available for additional protective measures. Objectively demonstrating to management the effectiveness of security controls is problematic. It is difficult to quantify the value of deterrence achieved through the application of physical protective measures.

A common security axiom is: The more doors and openings a building has, the more difficult it will be to control access. There is a trade-off here: the

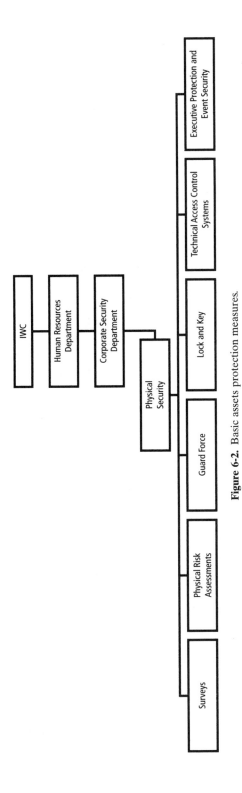

Figure 6-2. Basic assets protection measures.

cost of security weighed against the convenience of employees and others. It all comes down to costs and what executive management considers acceptable levels of risk.

Physical Risk Assessments

At IWC, the CSM knows that fundamental to developing an effective physical security profile as part of the CAPP is understanding the various threats to assets and the likelihood of an actual occurrence. Recognizing threats allows for cost-effective implementation of security measures. Implementing security measures that have little or no relationship to the type of threat associated with IWC may be an inefficient use of resources. Moreover, implementing redundant protective measures may not improve assets protection but will certainly consume resources better spent elsewhere.

Assessing the physical threats after identifying vulnerabilities is not easy. It requires an understanding of the business environment. One way to better assist the CSM in the effort to understand physical threats is through benchmarking. Identify businesses similar to yours and talk to them about their perceived threats. Try to find out what protective measures they implement to mitigate physical threats. There are other means of threat assessment:

- Consult experts in your line of business
- Seek the guidance of security professionals in similar situations
- Consult with your insurance provider
- Talk to risk managers
- Talk to the local police about crime in your area

Risk assessment is the product of determining the threats and understanding their consequences. If the consequences are significant, protective measures should be implemented. If the consequences are not significant, implementing additional protective measures may be an inefficient use of resources, and not adding value. Implementing physical security measures to the extent that all threats are eliminated is an action of risk avoidance. For some business, risk avoidance is appropriate. For most businesses it is not.

Physical Security for Classified Government Contracts

All of the physical controls mentioned in this chapter have applicability in some way to the physical security requirements of government contracts. However, for specific guidance, applicable government security publications and requirements documents (e.g., contracts) must be consulted.

In the United States, *The National Industrial Security Program Operating Manual*[1] is the basic document providing guidance for physical security. Special access programs and sensitive compartmentalized information activities generally have additional, very specific physical requirements addressing everything from construction specifications to locking devices. The applicable documentation must be consulted prior to planning construction for any area supporting these activities. The appropriate government-cognizant security officer must be consulted, since formal approval is generally required prior to use.

Summary

The physical security function through the CSM's physical security organization is the foundation for basic assets protection measures (see Figure 6-2). To this foundation, or baseline, additional controls for protection of assets are added, creating a complete protection profile. No single physical security control can satisfy all of the assets protection needs.

Physical security is built in layers. Each layer of security control serves a specific purpose by providing specific protections. Many controls used in conjunction with each other help to create a secure environment.

Conducting a site physical security survey should enable the gathering of all information necessary to make an intelligent and informed risk assessment of the sites or facilities and create a physical security profile. From this point, additional controls can be developed and implemented to provide the most cost-effective security profile tailored to the specific needs of the enterprise.

References

1. See http://www.dss.mil/isec/nispom.htm. *The National Industrial Security Program Operating Manual* (DoD 5220.22-M), dated January 1995, is published by the United States Department of Defense. It was issued in accordance with the National Industrial Security Program as authorized by Executive Order 12829.

Chapter 7

Barriers*

JOEL KONICEK and KAREN LITTLE

Doors, Gates, Turnstiles, and Electric Locks

It is easy to design passages that are difficult to enter. We can, for example, install heavy barriers, multiple locks and bolts, obstacles, and hidden traps. Fortunately, where the general public is concerned, safety rules require that no matter how difficult it may be to get in, people must be able to leave easily.

Barriers, doors, and locks used in public buildings are regulated by extensive legislation and local building codes. Engineers, architects, builders, consultants, locksmiths, police, fire, and regulatory agencies are all involved with designing, selecting, and installing the barriers used to control access. If any of these professionals fail to do the right thing, lawyers, insurance companies, and the courts have the ultimate say.

Security professionals, especially those in highly secure situations, specialize in pinpointing, then eliminating, weaknesses in facilities. Many electronic access control (EAC) managers, however, must accept physical weaknesses in their facilities (such as glass windows and doors). They counter this by increasing their watchfulness.

This chapter provides an overview of the complex subject of barriers, including electric locks, but it is not exhaustive. For further information about these devices, check the Web sites of associations, magazines, and testing laboratories. Two magazines in particular worth investigating are:

- *Locksmith Ledger International*, The Locksmith Publishing Corp., 708-692-5940; Monthly. Illus-

trates concepts related to locks, doors, and related security equipment.
- *SDM Field Guide*, Security Distributing and Marketing, 800-662-7776; Quarterly. Illustrates security-related planning concepts including wiring guides, EAC, CCTV, and sensor placement. Includes highly informative, well-illustrated "tests of knowledge and skill."

To get more out of this chapter, observe the barriers and locks you see in your daily life. Especially notice doors in shopping centers and medical complexes, fences around industrial areas, turnstiles, revolving doors, gates in parking lots, and so forth.

Exterior Barriers

In ancient times, thick stone walls secured the perimeters of villages and forts. Stone walls were surrounded by clear viewing areas (glacis), walkways providing guard patrol areas, and galleries serving as lookout points.

With the reduction of clan wars and the increase of peace, today the majority of our buildings feature minimum barriers, thin walls, and many glass windows. Even buildings at risk are relatively open and inviting. In general, we have replaced brute force and heavy barriers with *surveillance equipment*, and more important, intelligent friendliness.

Electronic access control is associated with some barriers because it serves to open gates, regulate traffic, and, with the aid of strategically located sensing devices, report problems. Sensors, woven through fencing barriers, for example, report problems when that fencing is stressed.

*Konicek, *Security, ID Systems and Locks: the Book on Electronic Access Control*, Butterworth Heinemann, 1997

To be regarded as a barrier, a structure or natural area must perform at least three functions:

1. **Define:** provide clear boundary markings of the area to be protected.
2. **Delay:** delay unwanted traffic, but not necessarily stop it.
3. **Direct:** direct traffic to proper entrances.

All barriers are designed to discourage three types of penetration. The first is penetration by *accident*. It is just about impossible, for example, for someone to walk through a securely locked door, but easy if the door is left open. Consequently, warning signs are usually posted by barriers to reduce accidental access. The last two types of penetration are by *force* and *stealth*.

The problem with penetration by force is that it ruins property. On the other hand, forced entry can quickly alert the authorities, plus leave evidence that helps to track the intruders. Penetration by stealth is very serious because the authorities may never know that a crime was committed.

Security designers are sometimes more concerned about combating penetration by the use of force and stealth than they are accidental penetration. The design of Super Max, an ultrahigh security United States prison, located in Denver, Colorado, is an example:

> There are seven layers of steel and poured cement between the outside walls and the cells. The yard is bounded by 12-foot fences, topped with razor wire, and overseen by six towers manned with armed guards. Guy wires are strung across the yard to prevent helicopter escapes and the entire facility is wired with state-of-the-art sensor technology.

Defeating penetration is often difficult.

Nature can nullify the purpose of exterior barriers, especially when these barriers are not rigorously monitored. Here are some examples:

- Drifting snow makes barriers easy-to-mount by piling up along the sides.
- Deep snow is easy to trench, which lets invaders sneak around unseen.
- Bushes, trees, and other vegetation that grow next to barriers provide natural ladders, hiding places, and areas to burn.
- Rain makes it easy to tunnel into the ground beneath the barriers.
- Heavy fog or driving rain hides unauthorized access attempts from view.

Structural barriers are also a problem:

It takes as little as 45 seconds for a man to batter a hole through an 8-inch mortar-filled concrete block wall with a 10-pound sledge hammer. Add another minute to that time to punch through a 5-inch mortar-filled concrete block wall containing $\frac{1}{2}$-inch steel reinforcing rods.

It takes a split second to break glass and between 1 and 2.25 minutes to punch through $\frac{9}{16}$-inch security glass. Common doors can be breached in under a minute.

Even though unauthorized penetration is always a concern, the majority of electronic access control (EAC) managers work in areas where the public has great accessibility. In these situations, more attention is given to watchfulness and traffic control than to building and guarding thick barricades.

As you can see from the statistics above, it does not take much for a willful person to break through walls and doors. Unattended and neglected property is always most at risk. The lack of physical might, however, does not mean that access control is not taken seriously.

Vehicle Barriers

Vehicle barriers delay unauthorized access, but do not necessarily prevent it. Many gates, in fact, are quite flimsy and, unless attended by guards, let pedestrians easily walk around.

Making sure the flow of traffic goes in the right direction, however, is important. Borrowing on ancient ideas for castle defense, some "wrong way" vehicle entrances hide spikes or other objects underground. When someone drives over them in the wrong direction, the spikes pop up and their tires are destroyed.

Another type of pop-up barrier is elevated after-hours and then lowered during normal traffic. These can appear in the middle of driveways or in conjunction with lowered gates.

Lightweight gates stop cars from plowing through but are not meant as a threat to the driver. In northern climates, where ice-slicks can impose a hazard, you would not want a gate so strong that it would kill the driver if his or her vehicle slipped out of control. Likewise, you would not want to decapitate a driver if his or her vehicle was hit from behind.

Heavy motorized gates are often left open during peak traffic periods in order to reduce wear on their mechanisms or to simply save time. In more secure areas, guards posted in nearby stations observe vehicle traffic.

Vehicle surveillance devices include closed circuit television (CCTV), lighting, two-way speaker systems, and a variety of sensing devices. Some of those sensing devices detect the presence of vehicles, while others sense when pressure has been applied to the fencing material itself.

Card and Proximity Vehicle Control

Card readers used at many EAC vehicle gates require every motorist to stop, roll down a window, insert a card, and then roll up the window again. All this can be irritating to drivers who pass the same checkpoint daily and the slowdown often causes traffic backups.

The railroad and trucking industries combated this problem by pioneering continuous-motion vehicular access control. Before employing this technology, freight haulers were required to stop, process forms by hand, wait for authorization, and then move on. With this technology, the haulers are now able to roll through checkpoints without stopping, wasting time, or energy. It works as follows:

> Each authorized vehicle contains a proximity token or bar code. These vehicles can be granted access by driving through an EAC checkpoint at speeds of up to 30 MPH without having to stop.
>
> The proximity or bar code reader, located on a tower, bridge, or on the side of a building, can sense tokens or bar codes within 30 feet and grant access in less than 1/10th of a second. Nonconforming vehicles, of course, trip alarms, or are directed to more secure gates for standard check-through procedures.

This technology has been adapted to automobiles and eliminates stopping at checkpoints. It now controls commuter traffic at international border crossings, toll roads, and large parking lots.

Doors

Function, governmental regulations, appearance needs, and cost all determine a door's style and materials. Beyond these factors, doors controlled by EAC have the following in common:

- A door closing mechanism
- An electronically or magnetically activated lock
- Sensors (switches) that determine whether or not the door is properly closed
- Computerized control either in the locking device itself, or in a nearby, hidden control panel

These points are discussed in the remaining portions of this chapter.

EAC requires that doorways, walls, and ceilings have a power source nearby and, in most cases, have adequate conduit and ducts in the walls or ceilings to hold electrical wiring. In areas where placing wire is difficult or prohibitively expensive, such as in an old elevator shaft, wireless EAC is substituted.

EAC systems also require wall or ceiling cavities large enough to contain control panels or wiring closets.

Door Closers

Mechanical door closers are as important to an EAC system as the electronics that power the locks. Door closers are spring-activated with tension strong enough to pull doors completely shut after use, yet not so strong that it makes opening the door a struggle, or warps the door during normal use. The mechanism attached to the spring that guides the door shut is called the arm.

Door closers fall into two main categories: concealed and surface mounted, a sample of which is seen in Figure 7-1.

Concealed closers are usually used on doors designed for a clean, "no-hardware" look because the arm is hidden from view. They can be difficult to adjust and service, however, because they are embedded into the top or bottom of the frame and door itself, requiring the door and frame to be perfectly balanced. Hardware replacement is usually manufacturer-specific and requires exacting specifications.

Surface mounted door closers are the most popular and fall into three main categories:

1. Regular-arm mounted
2. Top-jamb mounted
3. Parallel mounted

The most popular are the regular-arm and top-jamb styles, the latter of which is simply the regular-arm style installed upside down.

The *regular-arm* and *top jamb* door closers can stand the greatest deviation in door play. They are usually installed on the interior-side to reduce tampering, reduce weather damage such as rusting, and enhance the exterior appearance of the door.

The *parallel style* is less popular. The arm on this closer slides parallel to the door, rather than perpendicular to it. Unfortunately, it is difficult to service because it requires a well balanced door. This type of closer is usually used when a jamb mounted closer must be installed on the weather-side of a door. It is thought to be more weather-resistant

Door closers.

Figure 7-1. Door closers.

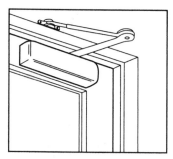

Surface Mount
Regular-Arm

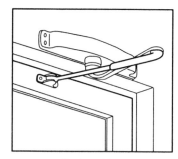

Surface Mount
Top-Jamb

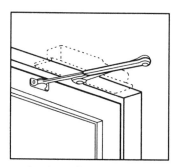

Overhead Concealed Mount
Exposed Arms

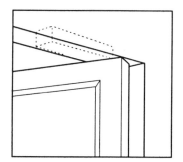

Overhead Concealed Mount
Pivoted Door

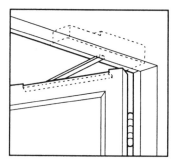

Overhead Concealed Mount
Hinged Door

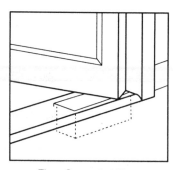

Floor Concealed Mount
Pivoted Door

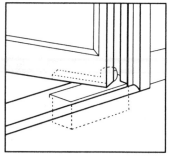

Floor Concealed Mount
Offset Pivoted Door

because its arm does not stick out and a roof of some sort can shield it.

The series of illustrations in Figure 7-1 show where door closers are commonly positioned on doors. Your understanding of these mechanisms can be greatly enhanced by observing the doors in public and private buildings.

Electronic and Electromagnetic Locks

The four most common types of locks used in EAC systems are the magnetic lock, electric strike lock, electric lockset, and electric deadbolt.

The strength of any lock is determined by the way in which it can stop unauthorized entry that uses cleverness or force. Electronic or electromagnetic locks, therefore, must be strong enough to guard against:

- Picking (where parts are manipulated)
- Drilling (which destroys the device)
- Electronic or magnetic trickery (which includes the use of unauthorized credentials and the manipulation of the power supply)

EAC electronic and electromagnetic locks are regarded as being either fail-safe or fail-secure and both have an important role in overall security:

- Fail-safe: The lock is *unlocked* when the power is off. This type of lock is usually used on a fire door. In the event of a fire, the locks can be released through the fire system or, if the power system fails, they unlock automatically.
- Fail-secure: The lock *remains locked* when the power is off. Power is required to unlock this type of lock and is usually used for normal locking situations.

Magnetic Locks

Magnetic locks secure doors through magnetic force and are *always* fail-safe devices. They are ideal for high-frequency access control usage because they are totally free of moving parts, which reduces wear and tear. Every magnetic lock consists of two components:

- Electromagnet
- Strike plate

The electromagnet is installed on the door frame and the strike plate on the door itself. When energized, the electromagnet attracts the strike plate with

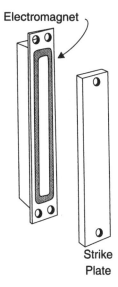

Figure 7-2. Electromagnet and strike plate of a magnetic lock.

a holding force ranging between 500 to 3000 lbs. (Figure 7-2).

All EAC systems require that some form of sensor reports whether a door is open or closed. Conveniently, many magnetic locks have that sensor built in, eliminating the necessity for a secondary sensor or switch. The two basic magnetic lock styles are called:

- Direct hold, which is surface mounted on the secure-side of the door frame and door.
- Shear (also called *concealed*), which is completely embedded within the door frame and the door itself.

The large, *direct hold* magnetic lock is ideal for use on poorly fitted doors and unframed glass doors because the two lock parts can be installed in rough proximity to each other. When energized, the electromagnet positioned on the frame attracts the strike plate on the door flush to its surface. This strong attraction does not require perfect horizontal or vertical alignment between the parts (Figure 7-3A).

Smaller *shear* magnetic locks, which are less than door thickness wide, are totally invisible to the eye when the door is closed. They are used when design and aesthetic considerations dictate that the lock be completely hidden. Concealing reduces the potential for tampering because the electrical wiring is completely enclosed within the door frame (Figure 7-3B).

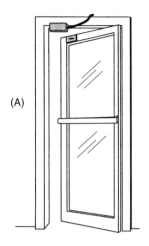

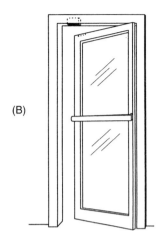

Figure 7-3. (A) Direct hold magnetic lock with power cord exposed. (B) Shear (hidden) magnetic lock.

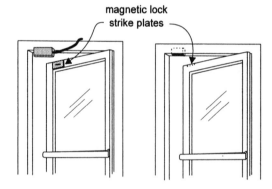

Figure 7-4. Alignment of magnetic lock strike plates.

The narrow surfaces on the shear electromagnet and the strike plate require precise alignment. A small bracket is often used on the frame to stop door travel so that these surfaces line up (Figure 7-4).

American National Standards Institute (ANSI) standards have defined three grades of magnetic locks. Grade one, which holds 1500 pounds, is designed for medium security. Grade two, at 1000 pounds, is for light security. Grade three, 500 pounds, simply holds a door shut. Most 180 pound men can force open a door equipped with an 850 pound magnetic lock.

As the holding attraction increases to 2000 or more pounds, a magnetic lock will stay joined even when the force of a blow is strong enough to shatter the door it secures. Consequently, in addition to the strength of the lock itself, the material strength of the

door, frame, and wall must also be considered when planning a high security door.

Electric Strike Lock

The electric strike lock is the most popular EAC locking device on the market and can be set up as either fail-safe or fail-secure. Its popularity stems from the fact that it comes in a wide variety of sizes and can replace existing mechanical locks without a great deal of difficulty. The strike, which is the electrically controlled portion of the lock mechanism, is mounted in a door frame (jamb) and does not require wiring through the door itself.

The electronic strike contains a bolt pocket, which is the indent that holds the protruding latch bolt or deadbolt secure in the frame. To open, the strike rotates away from the pocket, providing a path for the bolt to escape. This rotating side is called a *pivoting lip* or *keeper*. The latch bolt or deadbolt housing itself is mortised (embedded) in the door.

- *Latch Bolt:* The latch is a spring-loaded, beveled bolt. When the door closes, the beveled-side of the bolt slides over the strike, allowing the bolt to retract and then expand again in the bolt pocket once the door is fully shut.
- *Deadbolt:* The deadbolt is a solid metal rod or rectangularly-shaped bolt that has only two possible positions: protruding or retracted. The protruding bolt enters or escapes the bolt pocket in the frame only when the pivoting lip of the electric strike is rotated away from the frame.

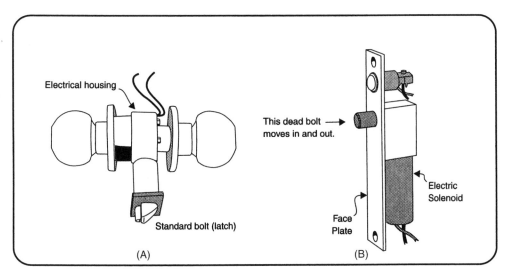

Figure 7-5. (A) Cylindrical-style electric lock. (B) Mortise-style electric lock.

The solenoid (magnetic coil) that activates the strike receives low AC or DC current through a power cord hidden in the frame. A soft buzzing noise can often be heard when AC current is used. This is caused by the vibrations of the alternating current pushing and pulling the solenoid 60 times per second.

Electric strikes and their related latch bolts come in a variety of styles suitable for installation on wood and metal frames. Each frame type, however, poses its own demands. A few of the many things to consider include:

- Wood frames can be weakened from the hollowing out required for installation of the electric strike and need additional anchors or brackets to protect the lock itself against forced-entry attempts.
- Tubular aluminum frames might be too shallow to accept an electric strike assembly.
- Hollow metal frames might be too weak to resist a forced entry, or else where filled with cement or plaster when installed, prohibiting the installation of the electric strike at a later date.

Electric Lockset

The electric lockset is very similar to a mechanical lockset and is available in cylindrical and mortise styles. The difference is that an electric solenoid (magnetic coil) replaces the mechanical action provided by a standard key. In addition, only the electric lock has fail-safe or fail-secure operational modes.

- *Cylindrical Lockset:* These are characterized by a doorknob or handle on each side of the door that are joined by a cylinder that controls the locking mechanism (Figure 7-5A).
- *Mortise-Style Lockset:* These are characterized by a lock, which is housed in a rectangular metal container, that is embedded at the edge of the door and is often enclosed within the door's thickness (Figure 7-5B).

Electric power is brought to the lock by threading wire from the frame through the door. Electric hinges (or pivots) completely conceal the wiring path when aesthetics are a consideration. Flexible cable loops are used when a seamless appearance is not necessary and must only be exposed on the secure side of the door.

Electric Deadbolt Lock

The electric deadbolt refers to the bolt *design* and is used as an alternative to a magnetic shear lock for doors that swing in two directions and double-doors. The electrically powered deadbolt is fitted into either the jamb or the door itself and when activated, it protrudes (as shown in Figure 7-5B) or swings into a mortised strike plate on the adjoining surface.

The deadbolt does not give way with a spring action. Once it is clicked in place, it stays in place until unlocked.

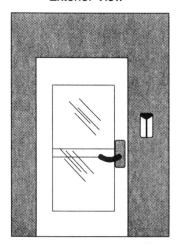

- Exterior View -   *- Interior View -*

Figure 7-6. Exterior and interior view of door with shear magnetic lock, door closed sensor, card reader, and control panel.

To increase holding strength, more than one set of electric deadbolts can be installed per door. Dual sets are common on large doors, as well as on both double-hung doors that swing away from each other from a center point. By installing electric deadbolts in the door header (top) and at the base, each door is secured and resistant to force.

Although electric deadbolts can be set in fail-safe or fail-secure modes, the majority of building and safety codes prohibit them for egress path use in high-rise buildings. Manufacturers have developed standard-compliant locks, but they are not in common use for these applications.

Fire Exits and Americans with Disability Act (ADA) Rules

The rules surrounding fire exits sometimes conflict with the purpose of electronic access control (EAC).

No one wants to be trapped inside a building during an emergency. This means that specific exits—doors leading to and from stairwells, between firewalls (and adjoining buildings), and directly outside—must be:

- Easy to see
- Easy to open in one single motion
- Designed with minimal hardware (that is, a smooth surface with only one opening device)

- Latched in a fail-safe mode (that is, "not locked" from the inside)
- Closed immediately when released (have automatic door closers)
- Constructed out of fire rated materials

Here is how fire codes effect EAC: In this simple example, the door is secured by a magnetic lock that can sense when the door is closed. To enter, a card is swiped through a card reader that sends the information found on the card to a control panel. If the card is valid, the control panel sends the instructions to unlatch the lock.

After the door is opened, the "door closed" sensor tells the control panel whether or not the door returned to the closed position. If the door does not close within a predetermined amount of time, the control panel triggers an alarm (see Figure 7-6).

Whether or not the door closes as scheduled, the EAC database saves the passcode user's name as well as date and time of his or her access. This creates an important trail of information.

Exiting, however, creates a different set of circumstances.

The exit bar in this example sends a signal to the control panel. The control panel then releases the magnetic lock. Unfortunately, this action leaves no record of the person who pushed the door open, because exiting bypasses the EAC recording system.

The Americans with Disability Act (ADA) imposes additional restrictions on door design, lighting, and usage. ADA requires that:

- Blind and sight impaired people must be able to touch specific types of door hardware and understand what to do next.
- Hearing and sight impaired people must be able to easily see exits. Consequently, there are rules regarding the size and color of exit signage, including the use of strobe lights.
- Physically weak people as well as those confined to wheelchairs must be able to push a latched door open with little or no trouble, eliminating knobs and multiple latches.
- Wheelchair confined people require doorways with clearings of at least 32 inches, which is enough room for a wheelchair to pass.

Exiting, obviously, opens previously secured passageways. To alert guards that someone is leaving, an egress button is sometimes found on the opposite side of a door protected by EAC. When pushed, this button disarms an alarm and tells the control panel that door usage is in compliance with the system. Egress buttons, unlike card readers, are subject to fire code regulations that forbid them to control locks. Egress buttons, therefore, can be bypassed without hampering travel, although doing so will trigger an alarm.

A "delayed egress" device on a fire exit door, however, postpones unlocking for up to 15 seconds. Pressing this device sends an alarm to a guard station and informs the guard that an exit attempt is being made. At this point, the guard can see the exit event on CCTV, talk to the person leaving through an intercom, or simply run to the scene if neither of those devices are there.

Obviously, a 15-second decay in exit can be frightening in an emergency situation, especially if the person attempting egress does not know what is happening. Extreme care must go into designing this type of exit system, which includes posting bold warning signs. A single push bar egress system is required even when delayed action is used.

It is very common to see fire code violations and when you do, it is our strong recommendation that you immediately report them to the fire department. The National Fire Protection Association (NFPA) code clearly states that only one action can be used to unlock a door with exit or fire exit hardware. Many companies, unfortunately, install additional locks. If the lights fail during an emergency, the extra burden of finding those locks could cause confusion, panic, and death.

Double-exit doors, where one door must be opened before the other is released, are forbidden. In the case where the doors have an overlapping astragal (center strip), which normally requires one door to open before the other, hardware must be installed that allows either door to open quickly. Locking arrangements on double-exit doors are tricky and mistakes are often made during installation. Always check to see that each door can be opened quickly, regardless of the other's position. If one doesn't open, the setup is in violation of fire code.

Heavy double exit doors are commonly seen in shipping and receiving areas. The temptation is to install additional handles to better distribute the weight of the door in order to make opening easier. This solution, however, would be in violation of fire codes. In the event of an emergency, it might not be obvious which handle is associated with the latch, which could, in turn, cause confusion and panic.

Stairwells pose additional security concerns. Fire codes require that people in stairwells be able to exit freely at any floor. Unfortunately, in some high rise buildings, these exits open into unrelated businesses. The temptation is to bar the exits to stairwell doors so that uninvited guests don't get in, which, of course, is in violation of fire code.

Internal Gates and Turnstiles

No matter how complex an EAC system is, "piggy-backing" or "tailgating" may be a problem. This happens when one authorized person uses his EAC credential to open a door and then bypasses further access control procedures by admitting additional people before the door is shut.

Gates and turnstiles decrease casual piggybacking by forcing people to enter one-by-one. This enforcement is greater when a gate or turnstile is positioned at the beginning of a narrow lane (also called an *alley*) which is designed to hold only one person at a time. Sensors strategically embedded in lane walls are programmed with a *delay feature* based on the time it takes an average person to travel through the enclosed area. If the lane is violated by nonstandard use, such as someone stopping in the lane, or more than one person at a time, an alarm is triggered.

Unfortunately, poorly planned gates, turnstiles, and lanes can slow traffic. To increase processing, multiple units are often installed to move high traffic and, to save energy, are selectively closed during low volume periods. Access to the Metro (subway) system in Washington DC, for example, uses an efficient multilane system. It requires that each passenger insert a magnetic striped fare card at a gate positioned at the beginning of a lane. Once the card is validated, the gate retracts and the passenger walks along the lane's area. Upon exiting the lane, the passenger retrieves his or her fare card and then, the process repeats itself for the next person in line. The whole thing takes place within seconds.

Mantraps (Secure Vestibules and Turnstiles)

Tight access control is obviously very desirable in high crime areas. Financial institutions, hit hard by increased robberies, are exploring ways to quickly screen visitors. Many European and South American banks, for example, are using glassed-in mantraps, called "double vestibule (hall) portals." These are used to unobtrusively examine visitors prior to admission, keep nonconforming people out, and make sure that two people do not enter at one time (piggybacking) as described in the following procedure:

- *Entering a building*—With the exterior (outside) door unlocked and the interior door locked, sensors and a metal detector determine whether *one per*son is present in the "enter hall" and is *free of weapons*. When access is granted, the exterior door locks and simultaneously, the interior door unlocks. This allows the occupant to enter into the building while at the same time preventing piggybacking. The system resets itself when the interior door is shut, allowing the next person to enter from the outside.
- *Leaving a building*—The person exits through the "exit hall," which reverses the door locking and unlocking process as reported above; however, does not include a weapon detection sensor.

David C. Smart, CPP, in the October 1994 issue of *Security Technology & Design*, reports that the Marshall Field Garden Apartment Homes, a low-income housing project in a high crime area in Chicago, has further refined this system. In order to pass through the mantrap, authorized people must also use a personal identification number (PIN) and biometric handprint scan that is associated with their apartment number. Temporary visitors use a time-limited version of this same identification process.

According to Smart, strict access control in this housing project has greatly reduced the number of people freely roaming the halls and has increased the tenants' feelings of security. In one case where a rape did occur, EAC records were checked and a visitor was quickly identified, found, and hauled off to jail.

One concern is that biometric scanning might interfere with American civil liberties. Smart indicates that the palm prints used by this system are not used in the judicial system. Care must be taken when installing a mantrap, however, to make sure that it meets all fire and safety regulations and it does not interfere with the public's civil rights.

Revolving Doors

Revolving doors can also be used to reduce piggybacking and pose as mantraps. Used with or without an EAC passcode, one section of the area can be set up to sense for metal detection and other conditions. If all conditions are met, a person can pass through the system. If conditions are not met, the interior doors remain locked and the person is directed back to the outside. As revolving doors are confining and have been known to cause feelings of panic, extreme care must be taken when using this type of system to meet all fire and ADA regulations.

Chapter 8

The Use of Locks in Physical Crime Prevention*

JAMES M. EDGAR and
WILLIAM D. MCINERNEY

Lock Terminology and Components

The effectiveness of any locking system depends on a combination of interrelated factors involved in the design, manufacture, installation, and maintenance of the system. A prevention specialist needs to understand the weaknesses and strengths of the various systems, and know how each must be used to achieve maximum benefit from its application. This requires a thorough understanding of the inner workings of the various types of locks. It is not sufficient to know what in someone's opinion is a good lock. A good lock today may not be as good tomorrow as technology improves and manufactures alter their designs and production techniques. A lock that is excellent in some applications may be undesirable in others. Knowledge of the basic principles of locking systems will enable a prevention specialist to evaluate any lock and determine its quality and its effectiveness in a particular application.

Key-Operated Mechanisms

A key-operated mechanical lock uses some sort of arrangement of internal physical barriers (wards, tumblers) which prevent the lock from operating unless they are properly aligned. The key is the device used to align these internal barriers so that the lock may be operated. The lock itself is ordinar-

ily permanently installed. The key is a separate piece, which is designed for removal from the lock to prevent unauthorized use.

Three types of key-operated locks will be introduced in this section: disc or wafer tumbler, pin tumbler, and lever.

Tumbler Mechanisms

A tumbler mechanism is any lock mechanism having movable, variable elements (the *tumblers*) which depend on the proper key (or keys) to arrange these tumblers into a straight line, permitting the lock to operate. The tumbler, which may be a disc, a lever or a pin, is the lock barrier element that provides security against improper keys or manipulation. The specific key that operates the mechanism (which is called the change key) has a particular combination of cuts, or bittings, which match the arrangement of the tumblers in the lock. The combination of tumblers usually can be changed periodically by inserting a new tumbler arrangement in the lock and cutting a new key to fit this changed combination. This capability provides additional security by protecting against lost or stolen keys.

Tumbler mechanisms and the keys that operate them are produced to specifications, which vary with each manufacturer, and among the different models produced by each manufacturer. These specifications are known as the *code* of the lock mechanism. The coding for each mechanism provides specifications

*Permission obtained from National Crime Prevention Institute, School of Justice Administration, University of Louisville.

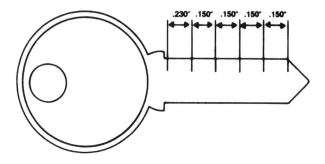

Figure 8-1. The spacing or position of each cut on the key is a fixed dimension corresponding to the position of each tumbler in the lock.

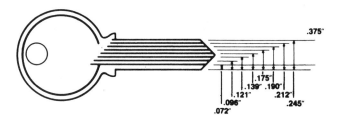

Figure 8-2. The depth interval (increment) of the steps of each cut or bitting is a fixed dimension.

for both the fixed and variable elements of the lock assembly. Fixed specifications include:

- The dimensions of each of the component parts of the lock and the established clearance between each part (e.g., the size and length of the key must match the size and depth of the keyway)
- The spacing of each tumbler position and their relation to each other (Figure 8-1)
- The depth intervals or increments in the steps of each cut or bitting (Figure 8-2)

The relationship between the dimensions of the tumblers and the bitting on the key is shown for a typical pin tumbler mechanism in Figure 8-3. These codes provide a locksmith with dimensions and specifications to produce a specific key to operate a particular lock or to key additional locks to the combination of a particular key.

The different arrangements of the tumblers permitted in a lock series are its *combinations*. The theoretical or mathematical number of possible combinations available in a specific model or type of lock depends on the number of tumblers used and the number of depth intervals or steps possible for each tumbler. If the lock had only one tumbler that could be any of 10 lengths, the lock would have a total of 10 combinations. If it had two tumblers, it would have a possible total of 100 (10×10) combinations. With three tumblers, 1000 ($10 \times 10 \times 10$) combinations are possible. If all five tumblers were used, the lock would have a possible 100,000 combi-

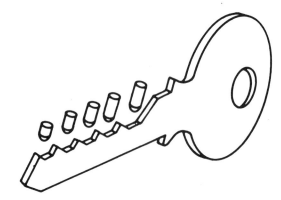

Figure 8-3. The depth of each cut corresponds to the length of each tumbler in the lock.

nations. The number of mathematically possible combinations for any lock can be determined by this method.

Due to a number of mechanical and design factors, however, not all of these theoretically possible (implied) combinations can actually be used. Some combinations allow the key to be removed from the lock before the tumblers are properly aligned (shedding combinations)—something that should not be possible with a properly combinated tumbler lock. Others, such as equal depth combinations, are avoided by the manufacturers. Some combinations result in a weakened key that is prone to

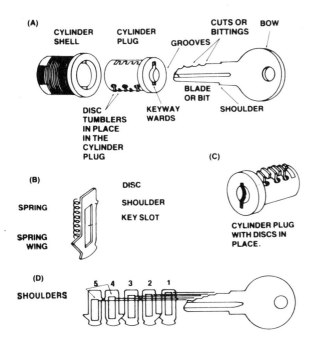

Figure 8-4. The key slots in the discs correspond to the cuts, or bittings, cut in the key. Note how each cut in the key will align its corresponding disc in a straight line with the others.

break off in the lock. Others are excluded because the space from one cut in the key erodes the space or positioning of adjacent cuts. The combinations that remain after all of these possibilities have been removed are called *useful combinations*. The useful combinations, which are actually employed in the manufacture of the lock series, are the basis for the *bitting chart* that lists the total combinations used in a particular type of model or lock. When other factors are equal, the more combinations that can actually be used in a lock, the greater its security. Total useful combinations range from one for certain types of warded locks to millions for a few high-security tumbler key mechanisms.

Disc or Wafer Tumbler Mechanisms

Disc tumbler mechanisms consist of three separate parts: keys, cylinder plug, and cylinder shell (or housing) (Figure 8-4). The plug contains the tumblers, which are usually spring-loaded flat plates that move up and down in slots cut through the diameter of the plug. Variably dimensioned key slots are cut into each tumbler. When no key is inserted or an improper key is used, one or more tumblers will extend through the sides of the plug into either the top or bottom locking grooves cut into the cylinder shell, firmly locking the plug to the shell. This prevents the plug from rotating in the shell to operate the lock. The proper change key has cuts or bittings

to match the variations of the tumblers. When inserted, the key aligns all of the tumblers in a straight line at the edge of the cylinder plug (the *shear line*) so that no tumbler extends into the shell. This permits the plug to rotate.

Disc mechanisms generally provide only moderate security with limited key changes or combinations. Depth intervals commonly used are from 0.015 to 0.030 inches, which permit no more than four or five depths for each tumbler position. Some models used as many as six tumblers. The more commonly found five-tumbler mechanism, which allows five depth increments for each tumbler position, would have a maximum of 3125 implied combinations. The number of useful combinations would, of course, be considerably fewer for the reasons indicated earlier. Some added security is provided by the common, although not universal, use of warded and paracentric keyways that help protect against incorrect keys and manipulation. Nevertheless, most of these locks may be manipulated or picked fairly easily by a person with limited skills. In addition, the variations cut into the tumblers can be *sight read* with some practice which the lock is installed. Sight reading involves manipulating the tumblers with a thin wire and noting the relative positions of each tumbler in the keyway. Since each lock has only a limited number of possible tumbler increments, the correct arrangement of these increments can be estimated with fair accuracy, permitting a

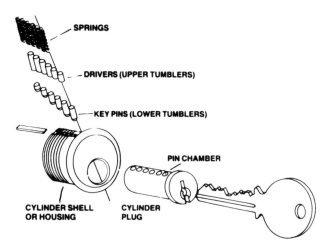

Figure 8-5. Basic pin tumbler cylinder lock mechanism.

key to be filed or cut on the spot to operate the lock.

Pin Tumbler Mechanisms

The pin tumbler mechanism is the most common type of key-operated mechanism used in architectural or builders' (door) hardware in the United States. The security afforded by this mechanism ranges from fair in certain inexpensive cylinders with wide tolerances and a minimum of tumblers to excellent with several makes of high-security cylinders, including those that are listed by Underwriters' Laboratories as manipulation- and pick-resistant.

The lock operates very much like disc tumbler mechanisms (see Figure 8-5). The locking system itself consists of a key, cylinder plug, and cylinder shell or housing. Rather than using discs, the mechanism uses pins as the basis interior barrier. Each lock contains an equal number of upper tumbler pins (*drivers*) and lower tumbler pins (*key pins*). The proper key has cuts or bittings to match the length of the lower pins. When it is inserted, the tops of the key pins are aligned flush with the top of the cylinder plug at the shear line. The plug may then rotate to lock or unlock the mechanism. When the key is withdrawn, the drivers are pushed by springs into the cylinder plus, pushing the key pins ahead of them until the key pins are seated at the bottom of the pin chamber. The drivers extending into the plug prevent it from rotating (Figure 8-6).

If an improper key is inserted, at least one key pin will be pushed into the shell, or one driver will extend into the plug. In either case, the pin extending past the shear line binds the plug to the shell. One

or more key pins may be aligned at the shear line by an incorrect key, but all will be aligned only when the proper key is used.

Depth intervals commonly used for pin tumbler cylinders vary from 0.0125 to 0.020 inches. These intervals allow between 5 and 10 depths for each tumbler position. The number of pins used ranges from three to eight—five or six being the most common number. Maximum useful combinations for most standard pin tumbler cylinders (assuming eight tumbler depth increments) are as follows:

3 pin tumblers approximately	130 combinations
4 pin tumblers approximately	1025 combinations
5 pin tumblers approximately	8200 combinations
6 pin tumblers approximately	65,500 combinations

These estimates assume that the useful combinations amount to no more than 23% of the mathematically possible combinations. Many common pin tumbler locks use fewer than eight increments, so the number of useful combinations for a specific lock may be much lower than the figures given above. Master keying greatly reduces the number of useful combinations.

Pin tumbler mechanisms vary greatly in their resistance to manipulation. Poorly constructed, inexpensive cylinders with wide tolerances, a minimum number of pins, and poor pin chamber alignment may be manipulated quickly by persons of limited ability. Precision-made cylinders with close tolerances, a maximum number of pins, and accurate pin

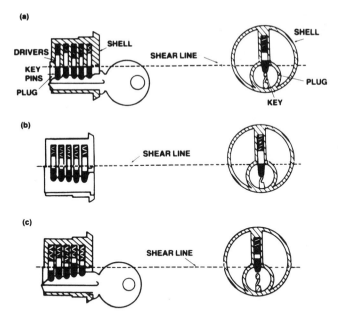

Figure 8-6. Operation of a pin tumbler cylinder mechanism. (a) When the correct key is inserted, the bittings in the key align the tops of the lower tumblers (key pins) with the top of the cylinder plug at the shear line. The plug may then be rotated in the shell to operate the lock. (b) When the key is withdrawn, the springs push the upper tumblers (drivers) into the cylinder plug. With the pins in this position, the plug obviously cannot be turned. (c) When an incorrect key is used, the bittings will not match the length of the key pins. The key will allow some of the drivers to extend into the plug, and some of the key pins will be pushed into the shell by high cuts. In either case, the plug cannot be rotated. With an improper key, some of the pins may align at the shear line, but only with the proper key will all five align so that the plug can turn.

chamber alignment may resist picking attempts even by experts for a considerable time.

Most pin tumbler lock mechanisms use warded keyways for additional security against incorrect keys and manipulation. The wards projecting into the keyway must correspond to grooves cut into the side of the key, or the key cannot enter the lock. When the wards on one side of the keyway extend past the centerline of the key, and wards on the other side also extend past the centerline, this is known as a *paracentric* keyway (Figure 8-7). While warded keyways are commonly used on most pin tumbler mechanisms, paracentric keyways are usually restricted to the better locks. They severely hinder the insertion of lockpicks into the mechanisms and the ability of the manipulator to maneuver the pick once it is inserted.

Modifications have been made to the drives in better locks to provide increased security against picking (see Figure 8-8). The usual modified shapes are the *mushroom* and the *spool*. Both of these shapes have a tendency to bind in the pin chamber when picking is attempted, making it more difficult to maneuver them to the shear line. To be consistently successful in picking pin tumbler cylinders with either type of modified driver, special techniques must be used.

There are a number of variations of the pin tumbler cylinder on the market. One that is seeing increasingly widespread use is the *removable core*

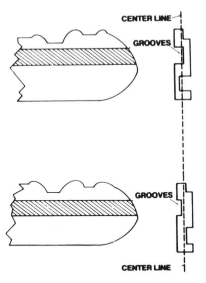

Figure 8-7. Milled, warded, and paracentric keys.

cylinder (Figure 8-9). These were originally produced by the Best Universal Lock Company whose initial patents have now expired. Most major architectural hardware manufacturers now have them available in their commercial lock lines. The type of cylinder uses a special key called the *control key* to remove the entire pin tumbler mechanism (called the *core*) from the shell. This makes it possible to quickly replace one core with another having a different combination and requiring a different key to operate. Because of this feature, removable core cylinders are becoming increasingly popular for institutional use, and use in large commercial enterprises where locks must be changed often.

Removable core cylinders do not provide more than moderate security. Most systems operate on a common control key, and possession of this key will allow entry through any lock in the system. It is not difficult to have an unauthorized duplicate of the control key made. If this is not possible, any lock, particularly a padlock, of the series may be borrowed and an unauthorized control key made. Once the core is removed from a lock, a screwdriver or other flat tool is all that is necessary to operate the mechanism. Additionally, the added control pins increase the number of shear points in each chamber, increasing the mechanism's vulnerability to manipulation.

Another variation that has been in widespread use for many years is *master keying*. Almost any pin tumbler cylinder can easily be master-keyed. This involves merely the insertion of additional tumblers called *master pins* between the drivers and key pins. These master pins enable a second key, the *master key*, to operate the same lock (see Figure 8-10). Generally, an entire series of locks is combinated to be operated by the same master key. There may also be levels of master keys, including submasters which open a portion, but not all, of a series; master keys

Figure 8-8. Pin tumbler modification.

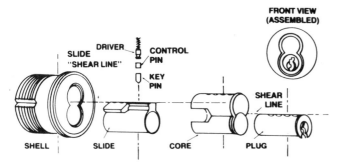

Figure 8-9. Removable core, pin tumbler, cylinder mechanism.

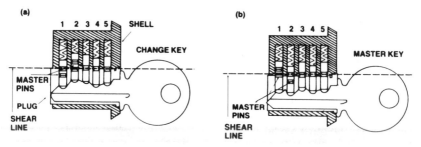

Figure 8-10. Master-keyed pin tumbler cylinder mechanism. (a) This is a simple master-keyed system using master pins in the first and second tumbler positions. When the change key is inserted, note that the top of the first master pin aligns with the top of the cylinder plug. The remaining positions show the key pins aligned with the top of the plug. This arrangement permits the plug to turn. (b) With the master key inserted, the first position aligns the top of the key pin with the cylinder plug. The master pin is pushed further up the pin cylinder. The second position shows the master pin aligning at the top of the plug. The master pin has dropped further down the pin hole in the plug. The remaining three positions are unchanged. This arrangement also allows the plug to rotate.

which open a larger part; and grand masters which open the entire series. In very involved installations, there may even be a fourth level (great grand master key).

There are a number of security problems with master keys. The most obvious one is that an unauthorized master key will permit access through any lock of the series. Less obvious is the fact that master keying reduces the number of useful combinations that can be employed since any combination used must not only be compatible with the change key, but with the second, master key. If a submaster is used in the series, the number of combinations is further reduced to those that are compatible with all three keys. If four levels of master keys are used, it should be obvious that the number of useful combinations becomes extremely small. If a large number of locks are involved, the number of locks may exceed the number of available combinations. When this occurs, it may be necessary to use the same combination in several locks, which permits one change key to operate more than one lock (*cross keying*). This creates an additional security hazard.

One way of increasing the number of usable combinations and decreasing the risk of cross keying is to use a *master sleeve* or ring. This sleeve fits around the plug, providing an additional shear line similar to the slide shear line in a removable core system. Some of the keys can be cut to lift tumblers to sleeve shear line, and some to the plug shear line. This system, however, requires the use of more master pins. Any increase in master pins raises the susceptibility of the lock to manipulation, since the master pins create more than one shear point in each pin chamber, increasing the facility that the lock can be picked.

While master-keyed and removable-core systems are necessary for a number of very practical reasons, you should be aware that they create additional security problems of their own.

The basic pin tumbler mechanism has been extensively modified by a number of manufacturers to improve its security. The common features of high-security pin tumbler cylinder mechanisms are that they are produced with extremely close tolerances and that they provide a very high number of usable combinations. Additional security features include the use of very hard metals in their construction to frustrate attacks by drilling and punching.

Lever Tumbler Mechanisms

Although the lever lock operates on the same principles as the pin or disc tumbler mechanism, its appearance is very different. Figure 8-11 illustrates a

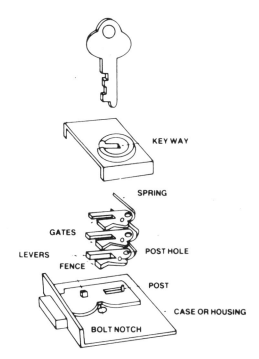

Figure 8-11. Lever tumbler mechanism.

typical lever mechanism. Unlike pin or disc tumbler devices, the lever lock does not use a rotating core or plug, and the bolt is usually an integral part of the basic mechanism thrown directly by the key. The only other type of mechanism in which the key directly engages the bolt is the warded mechanism. You will recall that the bolt in pin or disc tumbler systems is usually directly operated by the *cylinder plug*, not the key. The key is used to rotate the plug, but never comes into direct contact with the bolt.

Despite these somewhat deceptive appearances, the lever lock operates much like the other tumbler mechanisms. Each *lever* is hinged on one side by the *post*, which is a fixed part of the *case*. The *leaf springs* attached to the levers hold them down in a position, which overlaps the *bolt notch* as shown in Figure 8-12. In this position, the *bolt* is prevented from moving back into a retracted position by its *fence*, which is trapped by the front edges (*shoulder*) of the levers. When the key is inserted and slightly rotated, the bittings on the key engage the *saddle* of the lever, raising it to a position where the fence aligns with the slot in the lever (called the *gate*). In this position, the fence no longer obstructs the movement of the bolt to the rear, and the bolt can be retracted.

The retraction is accomplished by the key engaging the shoulder of the bolt notch. While the bittings

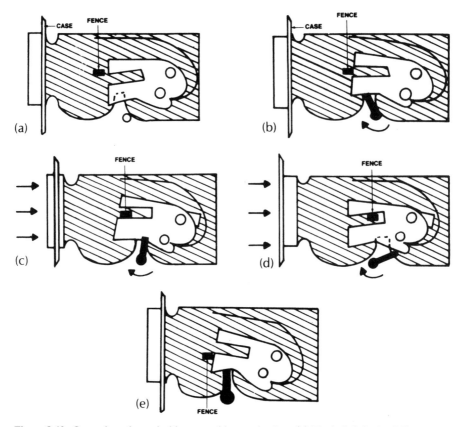

Figure 8-12. Operation of a typical lever tumbler mechanism. (a) The bolt is in the fully extended *locked* position and the key has been withdrawn from the keyway. In this position, the spring forces the lever down toward the bolt notch, trapping the fence against the forward edge (shoulder) of the lever. This prevents the bolt from being forced back. (b) The key has been inserted and the bitting on the key has lifted the lever against the spring tension, aligning the gate with the fence. The bolt can now be moved back into the retracted position. (c) The key has begun to force the bolt back into a retracted position by engaging a shoulder of the bolt notch at the same time it is keeping the lever suspended at the correct height to allow the fence to pass into the gate. (d) The bolt is now fully retracted and the key can be withdrawn. (e) If an improper key is inserted the bitting either will not lift the lever high enough for the fence to pass through the gate or the lever will be raised too high and the fence will be trapped in front of the lower forward shoulder of the lever. From this position, the bolt cannot be forced back into the retracted position.

of the key are still holding the levers in an aligned position, the key contacts the rear shoulder of the bolt notch, forcing the bolt to retract as the key is rotated. As the bolt is retracted, the fence moves along the gate until the bolt is fully withdrawn. When the key has rotated fully, completely retracting the bolt, it can be withdrawn.

If an improperly cut key is inserted and rotated in the lock, either the levers will not be raised far enough to align all of the gates with the fence, or one or more levers will be raised too high, so that the bottom edge of the lever obstructs the fence (as in Figure 8-12). In either case, the bolt is prevented from being forced to the rear, thus opening the lock.

Figure 8-13(a) shows one version of the basic lever. A number of variations are on the market. Some levers are made with projections built into the gate designed to trap the fence in various positions [Figure 8-13(b)]. The front and rear traps prevent the fence from being forced through the gate when the bolt is in either the fully extended or fully retracted position. Figure 8-13(c) shows another variation: serrated (saw-tooth) front edges. These serrations are designed to bind against the fence when an attempt

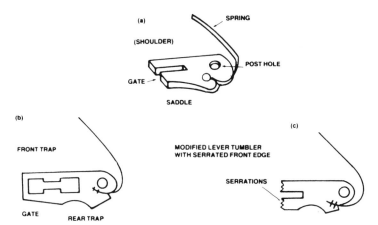

Figure 8-13. Lever tumblers. To operate the lock, the key contacts the lever at the saddle, lifting it until the fence is aligned with the gate. The saddles on the various tumblers are milled to different depths to correspond to different cuts on the key.

is made to pick the lock. They are commonly found on high-security lever tumbler mechanisms.

Lever mechanisms provide moderate to high security depending on the number of levers used, their configuration, and the degree of care used in the construction of the lock mechanism. Any mechanisms using six or more tumblers can safely be considered a high security lock. Some mechanisms use a double set of levers, requiring a double-bitted key. The levers are located on both sides of the keyway. This configuration makes the lock very difficult to pick or manipulate.

Lever locks are commonly found in applications where moderate to high security is a requirement, including safe deposit boxes, strong boxes, post office boxes, and lockers. The lever mechanisms available in the United States, because of the integrated, short-throw bolt are not ordinarily used as builders' hardware. But they are commonly used in that application in Europe and some of these locks have found their way into the United States.

Combination Locks

In principle, a combination lock works in much the same way as a lever mechanism. When the tumblers are aligned, the slots in the tumblers permit a fence to retract, which releases the bolt so that the bolt can be opened. The difference is where the lever mechanism uses a key to align the tumblers, the combination mechanism uses numbers, letters, or other symbols as reference points which enable an operator to align them manually. Figure 8-14 shows a simplified view of a typical three-tumbler combination lock mechanism. The tumblers are usually called *wheels*. Each wheel has a slot milled into its edge,

which is designed to engage the *fence* when the slot has been properly aligned. This slot is called a *gate*. The fence is part of the lever that retracts the bolt. The gates are aligned with the fence by referring to letters, numbers, or other symbols on the dial. The sequence of symbols, which permits the lock to operate, is its *combination*. A typical combination sequence using numbers is 10–35–75. The fact that three numbers are used in the combination indicates that the lock contains three tumblers. The number of tumblers in a lock always corresponds to the number of symbols used in its combination. Few modern combination locks use more than four tumblers because combinations of five or more symbols are unwieldy and hard to remember. Older models, however, use as many as six.

Both *drive cam* and dial are fixed to the *spindle* so that as the dial is rotated, the drive cam will also rotate in an identical fashion. The drive cam has two functions. It is the means by which motion of the dial is transferred to the wheels, and when all wheels are properly aligned and the fence retracted, it is the mechanism by which the bolt lever is pulled to retract the bolt.

The wheels are not fixed to the spindle, but ride on a *wheel post* that fits over the spindle. These wheels are free-floating and will not rotate when the dial is turned unless the *flies* are engaged. The flies are designed to engage pins on the wheels at predetermined points (determined by the combination of that particular lock). When the flies engage these pins, the wheels pick up the rotating motion of the dial. When the flies are not engaged, the wheels will remain in place when the dial is rotated.

To operate a typical three-wheel combination lock, the dial is first turned four times in one direction to allow all of the flies to engage their respec-

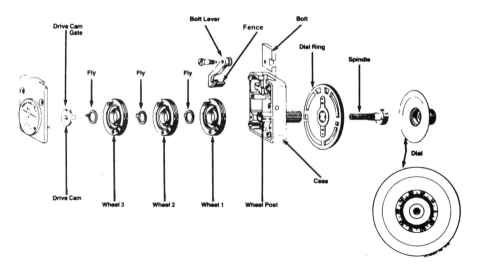

Figure 8-14. Three-tumbler combination.

tive wheels so that as the dial is being turned, all of the wheels are rotating with it. At this point the wheels are said to be *nested*. The object is to disengage each wheel at the spot where its gate will be aligned with the fence. To do this, the operator stops the dial when the first number of the combination reaches the index mark on the dial ring. This first stop aligns the gate of wheel 1 with the fence.

The operator then reverses direction to disengage wheel 1, which remains stationary, and rotates the dial three turns to the second number in the combination. When this number is under the index mark, wheel 2 is aligned. Again reversing direction to disengage wheel 2, the operator makes two turns to the last number of the combination. This aligns wheel 3. At this point all of the gates are aligned with the fence. The operator then reverses direction once again and turns the dial until it stops.

This last operation has two functions. It aligns the gate on the drive cam with the fence, which permits the fence to retract into the space provided, by the three gates in the wheels and the fourth gate in the drive cam. The bolt lever is now engaged with the wheels and drive cam. As the operator continues rotating the dial, the drive cam pulls the bolt lever to retract the bolt. When the dial will no longer rotate, the bolt is fully retracted, and the lock is open.

The security afforded by combination mechanisms varies widely. The critical elements are the number of tumblers used in the lock, the number of positions on the tumbler where the gate can be located, and the tolerances in the width of the gate

and fence. Wide tolerances allow the fence to enter the gates even when they are not quite completely aligned, so that, although the proper combination may be 10–35–75, the lock may also operate at 11–37–77.

Until the 1940s it was often possible to open many combination locks by using the sound of the movement of the tumblers and feeling the friction of the fence moving over the tumblers as indicators of tumbler position. (Tumblers in combination locks do not click despite Hollywood's contentions to the contrary.) Skilled operators were often able to use sound and feel to determine when each tumbler came into alignment. Modern technology has all but eliminated these possibilities, however, through the introduction of sound baffling devices, nylon tumblers, improved lubricants to eliminate friction, false fences, and cams which suspend the fence over the tumblers so that they do not make contact until after the gates are already aligned (see Figure 8-14).

Another manipulation technique of recent vintage utilizes the fact that tumbler wheels with gates cut into them are unbalanced: more weight is on the uncut side than on the cut side. By oscillating the dial, these cut and uncut sides are determined, and the location of the gates estimated. The introduction of counterbalanced tumblers has virtually eliminated this approach to the better mechanisms.

Radiology has also been used to defeat combination locks. A piece of radioactive material placed near the lock can produce ghost images of the tumblers on sensitive plates, showing the location of the

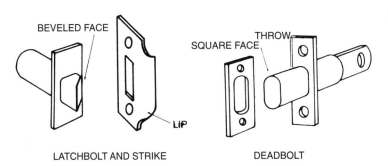

Figure 8-15. Basic types of bolts.

gates. Nylon and Teflon tumblers and shielding material that are opaque to radiation are used to defeat this technique.

Lock Bodies

Most lever tumbler and warded mechanisms contain an integrated bolt as a part of the mechanism. The key operates directly to throw the bolt, thereby opening and locking the lock. This is not true of pin and disc tumbler locks. These consist of two major components. The cylinder plug, the shell, the tumblers, and springs are contained in an assembly known as the *cylinder*. The other major component is the *lock body* that consists of the *bolt assembly* and case or housing. The bolt assembly consists of the bolt itself, a *rollback*, and a *refractor*. This assembly translates the rotating motion of the cylinder plug to the back-and-forth motion that actually operates the bolt. When the cylinder is inserted into the lock body, it is typically connected to the bolt assembly by a *tail piece* or *cam*. A cylinder is used in a number of different lock bodies. Here we will be primarily concerned with the types of bodies used on standard residential and light commercial doors. The pin tumbler is the usual mechanism used in these locks, although some manufacturers offer door locks using disc tumbler cylinders (such as the Schlage Cylindrical Lock introduced earlier).

Bolts

There are two types of bolts used for most door applications: the *latch bolt* and the *deadbolt*. Examples of these are illustrated in Figure 8-15. They are easily distinguished from each other. A latch bolt always has a beveled face, while the face on a standard deadbolt is square.

Latch Bolt

This bolt, which is sometimes called simply a latch, a locking latch (to distinguish it from nonlocking latches), or a spring bolt is always spring-loaded. When the door on which it is mounted is in the process of closing, the latch bolt is designed to automatically retract when its beveled face contacts the lip of the strike. Once the door is fully closed, the latch springs back to extend into the hole of the strike, securing the door.

A latch bolt has the single advantage of convenience. A door equipped with a locking latch with automatically lock when it is closed. No additional effort with a key is required. It does not, however, provide very much security.

The throw on a latch bolt is usually $3/8$ inch but seldom more than $5/8$ inch. Because it must be able to retract into the door on contact with the lip of the strike, it is difficult to make the throw much longer. But, because there is always some space between the door and the frame, this means that a latch may project into the strike no more than $1/4$ inch (often as little as $1/8$ inch on poorly hung doors). Most door jambs can be spread at least $1/2$ inch with little effort, permitting an intruder to quickly circumvent the lock.

Another undesirable feature of the latch bolt is that it can easily be forced back by any thin shim (such as a plastic credit card or thin knife) inserted between the face plate of the lock and the strike. Antishim devices have been added to the basic latch bolt to defeat this type of attack. They are designed to prevent the latch bolt from being depressed once the door is closed. Figure 8-16 shows a latch bolt with antishim device. These are often called *deadlocking latches*; a term that is mildly deceptive since these latches do not actually deadlock and they are not nearly as resistant to jimmying as deadlocks. Often a thin screwdriver blade can be inserted between the

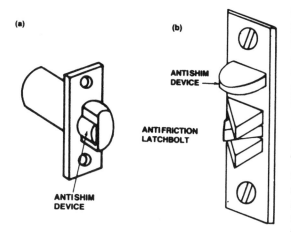

Figure 8-16. Modified latchbolts. (a) Latch bolt with antishim device. (b) Antifriction latchbolt with antishim device.

face plate and the strike, and pressure applied to break the antishim mechanism and force the latch to retract.

Another type of latch bolt is shown in Figure 8-16. This is an *antifriction latch bolt*. The antifriction device is designed to reduce the closing pressure required to force the latch bolt to retract. This permits a heavier spring to be used in the mechanism. Most modern antifriction latches also incorporate an antishim device. Without it, the antifriction latch is extremely simple to shim.

Deadbolt

The deadbolt is a square-faced solid bolt that is not spring-loaded and must be turned by hand into either the locked or unlocked position. When a deadbolt is incorporated into a locking mechanism, the result is usually known as *deadlock*. The throw on a standard deadbolt is also about ½ inch, which provides only minimal protection against jamb spreading. A *long-throw deadbolt*, however, has a throw of 1 inch or longer. One inch is considered the minimum for adequate protection. Properly installed in a good door using a secure strike, this bolt provides reasonably good protection against efforts to spread or peel the jamb.

The ordinary deadbolt is thrown horizontally. On some narrow-stile doors, such as aluminum-framed glass doors, the space provided for the lock is too narrow to permit a long horizontal throw. The *pivoting deadbolt* is used in this situation to get

the needed longer throw (Figure 8-17a). The pivoting movement of the bolt allows it to project deeply into the frame—at least 1 inch, usually more. A minimum of 1 inch is recommended. When used with a reinforced strike, this bolt can provide good protection against efforts to spread or peel the frame.

Increased security against jamb spreading is provided by a number of different types of deadbolts that collectively are known as *interlocking deadbolts*. These are specifically designed to interlock the door and the strike so that the door jamb cannot be spread. The most common of these is the *vertical-throw deadbolt* shown in Figure 8-17b. This is usually a rim-mounted device. The other two devices shown in Figure 8-17 (the *expanding bolt deadbolt* and the *rotating deadbolt*) are meant to be mounted inside the door. These locks require a securely mounted strike or they are rendered ineffective.

Door Lock Types

Five basic lock types are used on most doors in the United States: mortise, rim-mounted, tubular, cylindrical, and unit. Each of these has a number of advantages and disadvantages from the point of view of the protection offered. Each, however, with the single exception of the cylindrical lockset, offers sound security when a good lock is properly installed.

Mortise

It was but a few years ago that almost all residential and light commercial locks were mortise locks. A mortise lock, or lockset, is installed by hollowing out a portion of the door along the front or leading edge and inserting the mechanism into this cavity. Suitable holes are then drilled into the side of the door in the appropriate spot for the cylinders and door knob spindle (where the door knob is part of the unit, as is usually the case). Figure 8-18 shows a typical mortise lockset. These mechanisms require a door that is thick enough to be hollowed out without losing a great deal of its strength in the process. One of the major weaknesses of mortise locks is that the cylinder is usually held in the lock with a set screw which provides very little defense against pulling or twisting the cylinder out of the lock with a suitable tool. Cylinder guard plates can be used to strengthen the lock's resistance to this threat. On

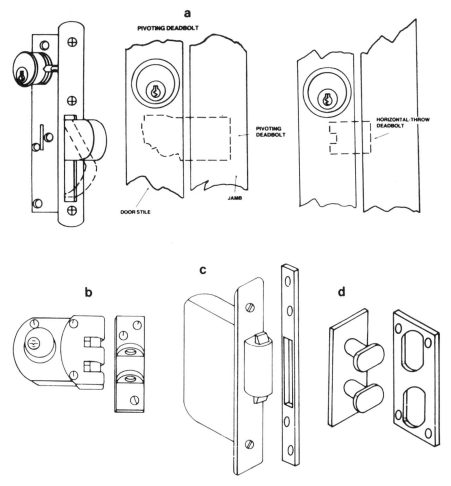

Figure 8-17. Modified deadbolts. Note the difference in penetration into the jamb. The deeper penetration afforded by the pivoting bolt increases protection against jamb spreading.

some mortise locks, the trim plate acts as a cylinder guard.

Rim-Mounted

A rim-mounted mechanism is very simply a lock that is installed on the surface (rim) of the door (Figure 8-18). Most are used on the inside surface, since outside installation requires a lock that is reinforced against direct attacks on the case itself. Commonly these are supplementary locks installed where the primary lock is not considered enough protection. These may or may not be designed for key operation from the outside. If they are, a cylinder extends through the door to the outside where it can be reached by a key.

Tubular

This lock (sometimes called a bore-in) is installed by drilling a hole through the door to accommodate the cylinder (or cylinders) and a hole drilled from the front edge of the door to the cylinder for the bolt assembly (Figure 8-18). This type of installation has virtually replaced the mortise lock in most residential and light commercial applications because it can be installed quickly and by persons of limited skill.

Cylindrical Lockset

The cylindrical lockset ordinarily uses a locking latch as its sole fastening element (Figure 8-18). It is

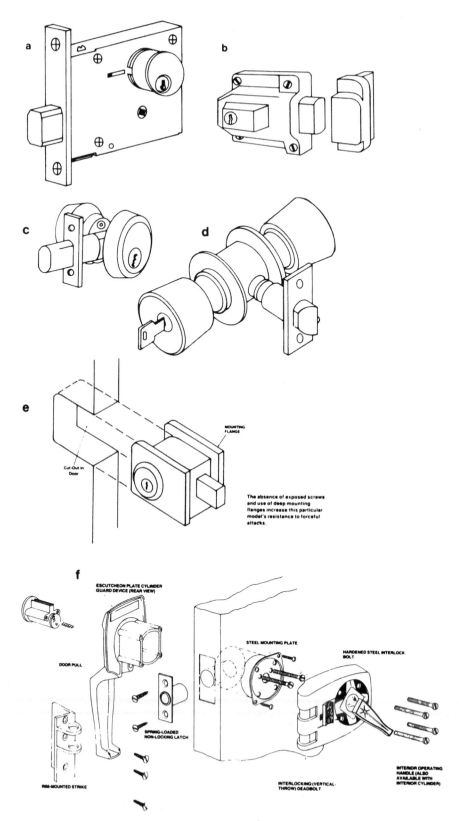

Figure 8-18. Lock types. (a) Mortise deadlock. (b) Rim deadlock with rim strike. (c) Tubular deadlock. (d) Cylindrical (lock-in-knob) lockset. (e) Unit lock. (f) Ideal Superguard Lock II—Note washers must be used for additional protection against cylinder pulling. These are not supplied with the lock.

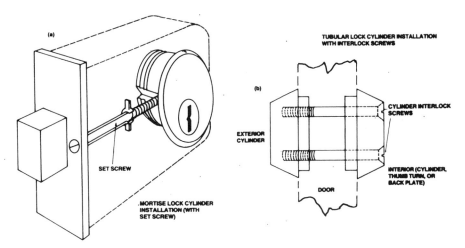

Figure 8-19. Mortise lock cylinder installation. (a) With set screw. (b) With interlock screws.

installed like the tubular lock by drilling two holes in the door. The cylinders are mounted in the door knobs, rather than in a case or inside the door, which makes them vulnerable to just about any attack (hammering, wrenching, etc.) which can knock or twist the knob off the door. Unfortunately, because it is inexpensive and simple to install, about 85% of all residential locks currently being used in new construction in the United States are of this type. It provides virtually no security whatsoever. There is perhaps no harder or faster rule in lock security than the rule that all cylindrical locks should be supplemented by a secure, long-throw deadbolt. Or, better yet, they should be replaced. A number of more secure locks designed to replace the cylindrical lock are now on the market. One of these is illustrated in Figure 8-18.

Unit Locks

A unit lock is installed by making a U-shaped cutout in the front edge of the door and slipping the lock into this cutout. This type of lock usually has the advantage of having no exposed screws or bolts. It is ordinarily used in place of mortise locks where the door is too narrow to mortise without considerable loss of strength. A good unit lock properly installed on a solid door provides excellent protection against attempts to remove the cylinder, or pry or twist the lock off the doors.

Cylinders

Cylinders are mounted in the lock body in a number of ways. Most mortise cylinders are threaded into the

lock and secured with a small set screw (Figure 8-19). Tubular and rim locks use cylinder interlock screws inserted from the back of the lock. Better mechanisms use $1/4$ inch or larger diameter hardened steel screws for maximum resistance to pulling and wrenching attacks (Figure 8-19). Better cylinders incorporate hardened inserts to resist drilling.

Two basic cylinder configurations are available. *Single cylinder* locks use a key-operated cylinder on the outside, and a thumb-turn or blank plate on the inside (Figure 8-20). *Double cylinder* locks use a key-operated cylinder on both sides of the door (Figure 8-20). This prevents an intruder from breaking a window near the door, or punching a hole through the door, reaching in, and turning the lock from the inside. The disadvantage of double cylinders is that rapid exit is made difficult since the key must first be located to operate the inside cylinder. If a fire or other emergency makes rapid evacuation necessary, a double cylinder lock could pose a considerable hazard.

Padlocks

The distinguishing feature of padlocks is that they use a shackle rather than a bolt as the device which fastens two or more objects together (Figure 8-21). The shackle is placed through a hasp that is permanently affixed to the items to be fastened. Three methods are commonly used to secure the shackle inside the lock body. The simplest and least secure method is to press a piece of flat spring steel against an indentation in the shackle. When the key is inserted, it rotates to spread the spring releasing the shackle (Figure 8-22). This is a locking method com-

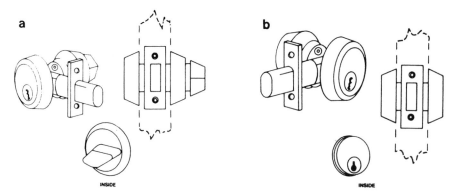

Figure 8-20. (a) Single cylinder deadlock with interior thumb turn. (b) Double cylinder deadlock with interior key cylinder.

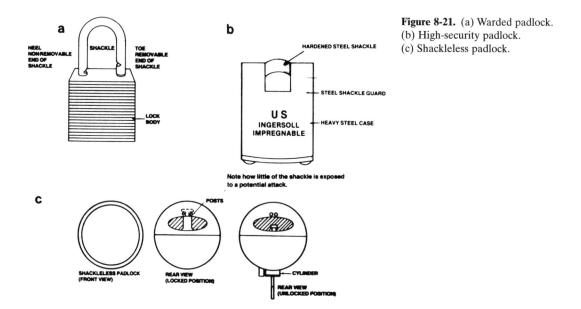

Figure 8-21. (a) Warded padlock. (b) High-security padlock. (c) Shackleless padlock.

monly found on warded padlocks. It is found more rarely on tumbler-type locks, but it is found occasionally on the less expensive models.

A slightly more secure method uses a locking dog. The dog is spring-loaded and fits into a notch cut into the shackle (Figure 8-22). The key is used to retract the dog, permitting the shackle to be withdrawn. Both of these spring-loaded mechanisms are vulnerable to attacks that take advantage of the fact that the locking device can be forced back against the spring by a suitable tool. Shimming and rapping are common techniques used to open them. Often a stiff wire can be pushed down the shackle hole to engage and force back the spring or locking dog. Spring-

loaded padlocks should not be used where reasonable security is required.

Positive locking techniques do much to reduce the vulnerability of padlocks to these types of attacks. The most common positive locking method uses steel balls inserted between the cylinder and the shackle. In the locked position, the ball rests half in a groove in the cylinder, and half in a notch cut into the shackle. In this position the shackle cannot be forced past the steel ball. When the cylinder is turned to the unlocked position, the groove deepens, permitting the ball to retract into the cylinder when pressure is put on the shackle. This releases the shackle and opens the lock. These locks are designed

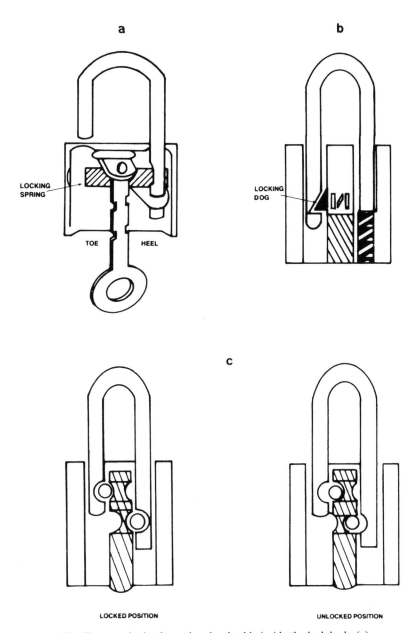

Figure 8-22. Three methods of securing the shackle inside the lock body. (a) Warded padlock with locking spring (heel locking). (b) Padlock with locking dog (toe locking). (c) Positive locking padlock (heel and toe locking).

so that the key cannot be removed unless the lock is in the locked position.

Padlocks are vulnerable to attacks at several points. The shackle can be pried out of the lock by a crowbar or jimmy, or it can be sawed or cut by bolt cutters. The casing can be crushed or distorted by hammering. Modifications have been incorporated into better padlocks to reduce their vulnerability to

these approaches. Heavy, hardened steel cases and shackles are used to defeat cutting and crushing. Rotating inserts and special hardened materials are used to prevent the sawing of shackles. Toe and heel locking is used to prevent prying (Figure 8-22).

High-security padlocks are large and heavy, using hardened metals in the case, and a thick, hardened, and protected shackle. Positive locking methods are

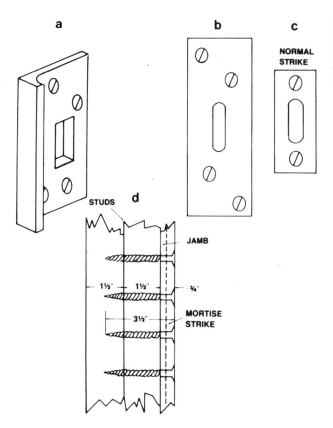

Figure 8-23. High-security strikes. (a) Security strike with reinforced lip to prevent jimmying and shimming. (b) Security strike for wood frames with offset screws. (c) Normal strike. (d) Proper installation of a strike on a wood frame.

always used. As little of the shackle is exposed to attack as possible in the locked position. A typical high-security padlock is shown in Figure 8-21. This is the shackleless padlock, which is designed so that a locking bar, which is contained entirely inside the case, is used in the place of an exposed shackle. This is sometimes called a hasp lock rather than a padlock.

A padlock is, however, no better than the hasp it engages. Hasps offering reasonable security are themselves made of hardened metals. They must be properly mounted on solid materials so that they cannot be pried off. In the locked position, no mounting screw or bolt should be accessible. Padlocks and hasps should always be considered as a unit. There is no point in mounting a high-security padlock on an inferior hasp. The hasp and lock should always be of approximately the same quality. Where they are not, the complete device is only as good as its weakest member.

Strikes

Strikes are an often overlooked but essential part of a good lock. A deadbolt must engage a solid, cor-

rectly installed strike, or its effectiveness is significantly reduced. The ordinary strike for residential use is mounted with two or three short (usually less than 1 inch) wood screws on a soft wood door frame. It can be easily pried off with a screwdriver. High security strikes are wider, longer, and often incorporate a lip that wraps around the door for added protection against jimmying and shimming (Figure 8-23). Three or more offset wood screws at least $3\frac{1}{2}$ inches long are used to mount the strike. These screws must extend through the jamb and into the studs of the door frame. This provides added protection against prying attacks. Additionally, none of the fastening screws should be in line. Inline screws tend to split soft wood when they are screwed in. Strikes designed for installation on wood frames should always use offset screws as fasteners.

Reinforced steel should be used on metal-framed doors, especially aluminum frames. Aluminum is extremely soft metal and, unless a reinforced strike is used, the jamb can be peeled away from the strike area exposing the bolt to a number of attacks, or allowing it to clear the jamb thereby freeing the door to open. Bolts should be used to mount strikes in metal frames. If the bolt does not penetrate a substantial steel framing member, then a steel plate is used to back the bolt (very large steel washers may be an acceptable substitute). This presents the strike from being pried out of aluminum or thin steel frames.

Attacks and Countermeasures

There are two basic methods of attacking locks themselves: surreptitious techniques and force. There are also a number of ways of circumventing a lock by assaulting the objects to which it is fastened. This chapter will be concerned only with techniques used to defeat locks themselves and the measures that can be used to forestall those techniques.

No lock is completely invulnerable to attack. A lock's effectiveness is determined by how long it will resist the best effort of an intruder. An expert can pick an average pin tumbler cylinder in seconds, and no lock can survive strong force applied for a sufficient length of time. The sole object of using any lock at all is to *delay* an intruder. A good lock makes entry riskier or more trouble than it is worth, and that is the objective. Fortunately, most potential intruders are not experts; thus most moderately secure locks can survive for a reasonable amount of time against common attack techniques.

The proper use of countermeasures will significantly reduce a locking system's vulnerability to breaching by an unauthorized person. Not all of the countermeasures suggested in the following sections will be appropriate for every application, however. There is always the necessity of striking a suitable compromise between the expense and inconvenience of a locking system and the value of the items it is designed to protect. Complex and expensive very high-security systems are simply not appropriate for most residential applications. On the other hand, a cheap padlock on a warehouse containing valuable merchandise is an open invitation for someone to break in and steal it. The objective should always be to ensure reasonable protection in the circumstances surrounding a particular application. With locks, overprotection is often more harmful than insufficient protection. If the user is faced with a more complex security system than really necessary, she or he simply will not use it. A great many unlawful entries are still made through *unlocked* doors and windows. The temptation to avoid the inconvenience of constantly locking and unlocking barriers seems to be insurmountable in some people. Contributing to this temptation by insisting on more protection

than the user actually needs simply aggravates the problem.

Surreptitious Attacks

Four basic surreptitious approaches are used to breach locking devices: illicit keys, circumvention of the internal barriers of the lock, manipulation of the internal barriers, and shimming. The susceptibility of any locking device to these approaches cannot be eliminated but can be minimized through the use of commonsense countermeasures.

Illicit Keys

The easiest way of gaining entry through any lock is by using the proper key for that lock. Thousands of keys are lost and stolen every year. A potential intruder who can determine which lock a lost or stolen key fits has a simple and quick means of illicit entry. If an intruder cannot get hold of the owner's key, quite often he or she can make a duplicate. The casual habit of leaving house keys on the key-ring when a car is left in a commercial parking lot or for servicing provides a potential intruder with a golden opportunity to duplicate the house keys for later use. One can also find out the owner's address very quickly by examining the repair bill or tracing the automobile license number.

The risk of lost, stolen, or duplicated keys cannot be eliminated entirely, but certain steps can be taken to minimize it.

Maintain Reasonable Key Security

- Under some circumstances, it is almost impossible to avoid leaving at least the ignition key with a parked car, or one to be serviced. But all other keys should be removed.
- When keys are being duplicated, the owner should ensure that no extra duplicates are made.
- Many locks, particularly older locks, have their key code stamped on the front of the case or cylinder. This permits anyone to look up the code in a locksmith's manual and find the proper combination for that lock (or for that combination lock). Codebooks are readily available for most makes of lock, so if the code appears anywhere on the lock where it can be read after the lock is installed and locked, it should be removed by grinding or overstamping. If removal is not possible, the lock or its combination should be changed.

- Managers and owners of commercial enterprises should maintain strict control over master keys and control keys for removable-core cylinders. The loss of these keys can compromise the entire system, necessitating an extensive and expensive, system-wide recombination. Too often in large institutions, just about everyone can justify a need for a master key. This is nothing more than a demand for convenience that subverts the requirements of good security. The distribution of master keys should be restricted to those who literally cannot function without them.

Since it is impossible to prevent people from losing keys no matter how careful they are, the next precaution is to *ensure that the lost key cannot be linked to the lock it operates.*

- The owner's name, address, telephone number, or car license number should never appear anywhere on a key ring. This has become common practice to ensure the return of lost keys, but if they fall into the wrong hands, the address provides a quick link between the keys and the locks they fit. The proper protection against lost keys is to always have a duplicate set in a secure place.
- For the same reasons, keys, which are stamped with information that identifies the location of the lock, should not be carried around. This used to be a common practice on locker keys, safety deposit box keys, and some apartment building keys. It is no longer as common as it once was, but it still exists. If the keys must be carried, all identifying information should be obliterated, or they should be duplicated on a clean, unmarked key blank.

Recombinate or Replace Compromised Locks. If all these precautions fail and the owner reasonably believes that someone has obtained keys to her or his locks, the combinations of these locks should be changed immediately. Where this is not possible, the locks may have to be replaced. When only a few locks are involved, recombinating cylinders is a fairly quick and inexpensive operation well within the competence of any qualified locksmith.

Another common attack method using a key against which there is less direct protection is the *try-out key*. Try-out key sets are a common locksmith's tool and can be purchased through locksmith supply houses, often by mail. These sets replicate the common variations used in the combination of a particular lock series. In operation, they are inserted into the lock one at a time until one is found that will operate the lock.

Try-out keys are commercially available only for automotive locks. There is nothing, however, to prevent a would-be intruder from building a set for other locks. In areas where one contractor has built extensive residential and commercial developments, most of the buildings will often be fitted with the same lock series. If it is an inexpensive series with a limited number of useful combinations, a homemade try-out key set which replicates the common variations of this particular lock series could be very useful to the potential intruder.

The defense against try-out keys is simply to use a lock with a moderate to high number of available combinations. Any lock worth using has at least several thousand useful combinations. No intruder can carry that many try-out keys, so the risk that he or she will have the proper key is minimal.

Circumvention of the Internal Barriers of the Lock

This is a technique used to directly operate the bolt *completely bypassing* the locking mechanism which, generally, remains in the locked position throughout this operation. A long, thin, stiff tool is inserted into the keyway to bypass the internal barriers and reach the bolt assembly. The tool (often a piece of stiff wire) is then used to maneuver the bolt into the retracted, unlocked position. Warded locks are particularly vulnerable to this method (as was indicated earlier), but some tumbler mechanisms, which have an open passageway from the keyway to the bolt assembly, are also susceptible. Some older padlocks and cylindrical mechanisms have an open passageway of this sort. Few of these are manufactured anymore, but some of the older models are still in use. Any lock, which has such an opening, should be replaced with a better device if reasonable security is a requirement.

Manipulation

The term manipulation covers a large number of types of attacks. At least 50 discrete techniques of manipulating the mechanism of a lock without the proper key have been identified. Fortunately, however, they all fall rather neatly into four general categories: *picking, impressioning, decoding,* and *rapping.* Regardless of the specific technique used, its purpose is to maneuver the internal barriers of a tumbler mechanism into a position where they will permit the bolt to be retracted. In a disc or pin tumbler mechanism, this means that the cylinder plug must be freed to rotate; in a lever lock, the levers must be aligned with the fence.

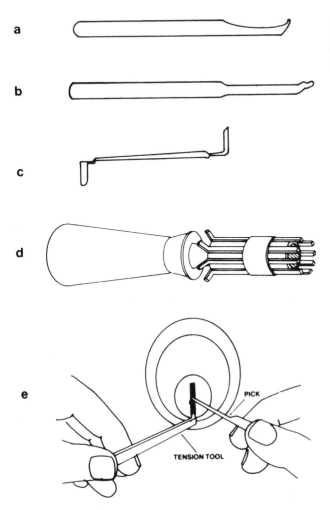

Figure 8-24. Lock picks. (a) Standard pick. (b) Rake pick. (c) Tension tool. (d) Special pick for tubular mechanisms. (e) Pick and tension tool in use.

The basic countermeasures against all forms of manipulation are the use of close tolerances in the manufacture of the mechanism, and increasing the number of pins, discs, or levers. Close tolerances and a large number of tumblers make manipulation a time-consuming process. A number of specific defenses to the various forms of manipulation have also been developed. These will be presented in some detail below.

Picking. Lock picking is undoubtedly the best known method of manipulation. It requires skill developed by dedicated practice, the proper tools, time, and often a small dose of good luck. No lock is proof against picking, but the high-security locks are so difficult to pick that it takes even an expert a long time to open them. One definition of a high-security mechanism, in fact, is one that cannot be picked by an expert in less than half a minute.

The techniques involved in picking the three basic types of tumbler mechanisms are very similar—so similar, in fact, that an example using the pin tumbler cylinder will serve to illustrate the rest.

All picking techniques depend on the slight clearances that must necessarily exist in a mechanism for it to function. The basic technique requires slight tension to be placed on the part of the mechanism that retracts the bolt (which is the cylinder plug in pin tumbler mechanisms) by a special tension tool designed for that purpose (Figure 8-24). The result of this tension is shown in Figure 8-25. The pin chamber in the plug has moved slightly out of alignment with the pin chamber in the cylinder shell, creating two *lips* at points A and B. When the key pin is pushed up by the pick, it tends to catch at the shear line because the lip at point A permits it to go no farther. This pushes the driver above the shear line where the lip at point B prevents it from falling down into the

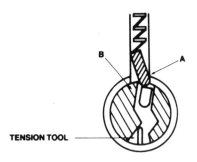

Figure 8-25. Illustration of the misalignment caused in a pin tumble cylinder when tension is applied.

Figure 8-27. Increased misalignment occurs as each pin is picked.

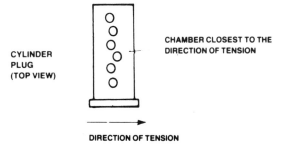

Figure 8-26. Pin chamber misalignment. Pine chambers on even the best cylinders are not in a perfectly straight line. The misalignment in this illustration is highly exaggerated for clarity.

cylinder plug once more. As long as tension is maintained, it will stay above the shear line.

This operation is facilitated by the fact that, as shown in Figure 8-26, the pin chambers in a cylinder plug are seldom in a perfectly straight line. Consequently, the pin closest to the direction of tension will be more tightly bound than the rest of the pins when tension is applied. It can easily be located because it will offer the most resistance to being maneuvered by the pick. Each pin is tested by lifting it with the pick. The pin that is most resistant is picked first. When this pin reaches the shear line, often the cylinder plug will move slightly. The picker receives two important benefits from this very small movement: first it indicates that the pin has indeed been lifted to the shear line, and second, the movement of the cylinder increases the misalignment between the pin chamber in the plug and the one in the shell, making it even less likely that the driver will drop down into the plug (Figure 8-27). Once this pin has been picked, the pin next nearest the direction of tension will be the most tightly bound. It is located and picked next. The cylinder plug will again move a very small amount. This operation continues until all of the pins

are picked above the shear line, and the cylinder plug is free to rotate.

There are endless variations of this basic picking technique. One of the most common is the use of a *rake pick*. When this pick is used, very slight tension is applied to the plug, then the rake is run along the tumblers lifting them slightly each time until all of them reach the shear line. Raking increases the chance that one or more key pins will inadvertently be pushed up into the cylinder shell, which will not allow the plug to rotate. It is often necessary to release the tension applied to the plug, and start over again several times. Nevertheless, it is a very fast technique, and very popular. With luck, an expert using a rake can pick an average pin tumbler in a few seconds.

Most of the improvements in lock technology made over the last few thousand years have been devoted to increasing the resistance of locks to picking. The major defense is the use of very close tolerances in the mechanism during manufacture. This makes the forced misalignment between the plug and shell necessary for successful picking more difficult to achieve. The addition of more tumblers is also some protection against picking, since it takes the operator more time to pick all of the tumblers in the mechanism. The Sargent Keso mechanism and the Duo disc tumbler use this basic approach. The 12 pins in the former, and 14 (soon to be 17) discs in the high-security (Underwriters' Laboratories listed) Duo take a reasonably long time to pick successfully. In addition, the unusual configurations of these tumblers makes picking even more difficult.

The unusual arrangement of tumblers is also a basic security feature of Ace (tubular) mechanisms. These cannot be picked using ordinary picks. But there are special tools available that facilitate picking this lock. The Ace lock also requires special skills, but these are not too difficult to achieve once basic picking techniques have been mastered.

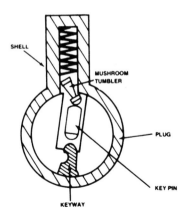

Figure 8-28. Mushroom and spool tumblers tend to bind in the pin hole when manipulation is attempted.

Modifications of pin design for increased resistance to picking (and other forms of manipulation) are becoming increasingly important as a basic means of precluding this form of attack. As shown in Figure 8-28, mushroom, spool, and huck pins tend to bind in the pin chamber when tension is applied to the cylinder plug, preventing the key pin from reaching the shear line. The use of these pins does not provide an absolute defense against picking attempts, but a steady hand and a great deal of skill are required to pick them successfully.

Pins that must be rotated provide what is perhaps the maximum currently available protection against picking. The Medeco and the new Emhart interlocking mechanism both require pins to be lifted to the shear line *and* rotated to a certain position before the lock will operate. It is very difficult to consistently rotate these pins into the correct position. The interlocking pins on the Emhart also make it extremely difficult to pick the key pin to the shear line, since, when interlocked, the two pins act as if they were one solid pin. The key pin and driver will not split at the shear line unless the pins are first rotated to the correct position.

Fewer such embellishments are possible with discs and levers. Most high-security lever locks, however, do use levers that have a front edge cut in a saw-tooth design (serrated). These serrations tend to catch on the fence as it is pushed back to provide pressure on the levers. This often makes it necessary for the operator to release tension and start over again, increasing the time spent picking the lock. The use of two sets of levers with two corresponding fences also increases a lever mechanism's resistance to picking attempts.

Impressioning. Impressioning is a technique used to make a key that will operate the lock. It cannot ordinarily be used against high-security mechanisms, but against the average lock it can be very successful.

To make a key by impressioning, a correct key blank is inserted into the lock. It is then securely gripped by a wrench or pliers (there are also special tools available for this purpose) and a strong rotational tension is applied to the plug. While this tension is applied, the key is moved up and down in the keyway. Since the tumblers are tightly bound in the lock by the tension applied to the plug, they will leave marks on the blank. The longest key pin will leave the strongest impression. The key is then removed and slight cut is filed in the blank at this point. The top of the key is smoothed down with a file or abrasive paper, and the key is again inserted to pick up the impression of the next longest pin. As long as the pin leaves an impression, the cut is deepened. When the pin will no longer leave a mark, the cut is at the right depth. When all of the cuts are to the right depth, the key will operate the lock and permit entry.

Certain types of lock mechanisms are more susceptible to impressioning than others. Warded locks are easily defeated by this method since the fixed wards can be made to leave strong impressions, and, as previously stated, the depth of the cut on a warded key is not critical. Lever locks are probably the most immune to this technique, since it is difficult to bind the levers in such a manner that they will leave true impressions on the key blank. The use of serrated levers greatly increases this difficulty.

The average pin and disc tumbler mechanism is vulnerable to this approach, but some of the better high-security mechanisms, because of their unusual keys, are not. The Medeco and Emhart interlocking mechanisms are highly resistant. The correct angles of the slant cuts necessary on these keys cannot be determined by impressioning. The special design of the pins in the BHI Huck-Pin cylinder makes the pins bind almost anywhere in the pin hole except at the shear line. All the impressions which appear on the key blank are, therefore, likely to be false impressions. So, although this mechanism uses a fairly standard paracentric key, it is still very difficult to defeat by impressioning. Modified spool and mushroom tumblers in any pin tumbler mechanism also tend to increase the difficulty of getting good impression marks.

Decoding. Another method of making a key for a particular lock is through decoding. It was mentioned earlier that most disc tumbler mechanisms

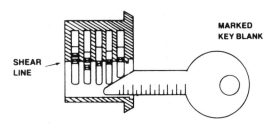

SHEAR LINE

MARKED KEY BLANK

Figure 8-29. Decoding using a marked key blank.

can be sight read fairly easily. Sight reading involves the manipulation of the tumblers with a thin wire while noting their relative positions in the keyway. Since each mechanism has only a limited number of possible tumbler increments, the correct alignment of these increments can be estimated with fair accuracy, permitting a key to be filed or cut on the spot to rotate the lock. This is one method of decoding.

A more common method is to insert a decoding tool or a specially marked key blank for a short distance into the keyway of a pin or disc tumbler mechanism. Using the key, rotational tension is applied to the plug that causes misalignment between the pin chambers in the plug and shell. The key is then slowly inserted into the keyway until it has forced the first tumbler to the shear line (Figure 8-29). The length of this first key pin is determined by the distance the blank (or special tool) enters the keyway. The blank is then moved to the second tumbler, and so on until the length of all of the tumblers is determined and a key can be cut.

Pin tumbler cylinders having wide tolerances are the mechanisms that are most susceptible to this particular decoding method. Disc tumblers are less so, although most can easily be sight read. (The Duo, however, is very resistant to sight reading.) Lever locks require special equipment to decode.

The special features offered on some high-security pin tumbler systems dramatically increase their resistance to this technique. Some are almost immune. The Ace can be decoded, but it usually requires special tools. The use of mushroom or spool tumblers in almost any mechanism increases its resistance to decoding. And, of course, the close tolerances of any of the better mechanisms are a basic defense against decoding as well as impressioning and picking.

Rapping. This approach relies on the fact that pins in a tumbler mechanism can move freely in the pin chambers. Tension is applied to the plug, resulting in the usual misalignment between the core and shell pin bores. The lock is then struck with a sharp tap

just above the tumblers. This causes the pins to jump in their bores. As each key pin reaches its shear line, it pushes the driver before it into the shell where it tends to bind, unable to drop back down into the plug because of the lip caused by the misalignment. Not all of the drivers will be pushed over the shear line by one rap. Several may be required.

Theoretically, almost any lock may be defeated by rapping, but in practice it is a method that is used primarily on padlocks. Since padlocks are not encased in a door, they respond more freely to rapping. Modified, manipulation-resistant pins make rapping very difficult, but not impossible; it is, nevertheless, not a practical approach to high-security padlocks that use close tolerances and modified pins.

Shimming

Any part of a locking mechanism that relies on spring pressure to hold it in place is vulnerable to shimming unless it is protected. Spring-loaded latch bolts can be shimmed by a thin plastic or metal tool unless they are protected by antishim devices. The locking dogs in padlocks are susceptible to a shim inserted into the shackle hole. The shim acts to force the dog back against the spring pressure releasing the shackle. Padlocks that use heel and toe locking are more difficult to shim, but the safest course to use is a nonsprung, positive locking system that cannot be threatened by shimming at all.

Forceful Attacks

If a potential intruder does not have the skills necessary to decode, impression, or pick a lock, the only course is to either find a key or use force against the lock to disable and breach it. Comparatively few intruders have developed manipulative skills, so it is not surprising that the large majority of attacks on locks employ force of one kind or another. Locks can be punched, hammered, wrenched, twisted, burned, pulled, cut, exploded, and pried. Given the right tools and a sufficient amount of time, any lock can be defeated by force. But the nature of forceful attacks entails a number of real disadvantages to an intruder who is trying to gain entry without being discovered in the process. Large and cumbersome tools that are difficult to carry and conceal are often required. This is especially true if one of the better-protected locks is being attacked. Secondly, forceful attacks usually make a considerable amount of noise. Noise, especially unusual noise, tends to prompt people to investigate. Third, it is always immediately evident to even a causal observer that the lock has been attacked. When surreptitious techniques are used, the lock can be opened without damage, and relocked, and no one will be able to tell that an unlawful entry has taken place. This often permits the intruder to thoroughly cover tracks even before an investigation is started.

The object of countermeasures against forceful attacks is to increase these hazards. Generally more force will have to be applied to stronger, better-protected locks, requiring larger and more sophisticated tools, taking more time, making more noise, and leaving more evidence that the lock has been defeated.

While it is sometimes possible to wrench, pry, or pull an entire lock out of a door, most attacks are directed at either the bolt or the cylinder. If the bolt can be defeated, the door is open. If the cylinder can be defeated, the bolt can be maneuvered into an unlocked position. The more common of these attacks will be presented below, along with measures that can be taken to strengthen a lock against them. It bears repeating that no lock is absolutely immune to forceful attacks. The object is to make its defeat more difficult, noisier, and more time consuming, thereby increasing the chances that an intruder will be detected or simply give up before successfully breaching the lock.

Attacks on Bolts

Bolts can be pried, punched, and sawed. The object of these attacks is to disengage the bolt from the strike.

Jimmying and Prying. A jimmy is by definition a short prying tool used by burglars. It is a traditional and well-known burglary tool, but other, more lawful, prying tools will work just as well if not better. These include prybars, crowbars, nail pullers, and large screwdrivers.

The easiest prying attack is against latch bolts with antishim devices. A screwdriver or similar tool with a flat blade is inserted between the strike and latch bolt. Pressure is applied until the antishim mechanism inside the lock breaks. The latch is then easily pushed into the retracted position, and the door is open. A supplementary long-throw or interlocking deadbolt is the best defense against this attack. Noninterlocking, long-throw deadbolts are theoretically vulnerable to jimmying, but it takes a much larger tool, more time, and the destruction or spreading of part of the door jamb so that the end of the dead bolt can be reached with the prying tool.

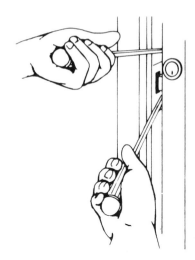

Figure 8-30. Jamb spreading by prying with two large screwdrivers.

Even then, a great deal of force is required to push the bolt back into the lock and free the door. These combined disadvantages make direct jimmying attacks against long-throw deadbolts very impractical. They are even more impractical against interlocking deadbolts. If the lock and strike are properly installed, the whole strike would have to be pried loose. This would ordinarily entail the destruction of a considerable portion of the jamb around the strike.

A deadbolt also can be attacked indirectly by prying. An attempt is made to spread the door frame so that the bolt is no longer engaging the strike (Figure 8-30). An average man can apply about 600 inch-pounds of force using a pry bar 30 inches long. This is usually more than enough to spread a door jamb to clear the normal $\frac{1}{2}$-inch bolt, but a 1-inch (or longer) bolt is more difficult to clear. Interlocking bolts are almost impossible to defeat with this method since they, in effect, anchor the door to the door frame. In order to spread the frame, the entire strike would have to be pried out. A properly installed security strike is very difficult to remove. Interlocking deadbolts were designed to resist just this type of attack. By and large, they are successful. When properly installed they are, as a practical matter, virtually immune.

Automobile bumper jacks (or similar tools) can also be used to spread a door jamb and release the bolt (Figure 8-31). Most American jacks are rated at 1 ton. It is probably safe to say that most wooden door frames will succumb to that much force. Reinforced metal frames are more resistant. Long-throw and interlocking deadbolts provide some protection.

Figure 8-31. Use of an automobile bumper jack to spread the door frame. Standard bumper jacks are rated to 2000 pounds. The force of the jack can be applied between the two jambs of a door to spread them and overcome, by deflection, the length of the latch throw.

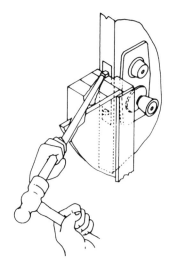

Figure 8-32. Forcing the deadbolt with a drift punch and hammer.

They may even provide enough protection in most circumstances, since a jamb can only be spread so far by the jack before it buckles outward releasing the jack. The best defense against jamb spreading, however, is a properly constructed and reinforced door frame.

Fortunately, this type of attack is fairly rare. An automobile jack is an awkward tool, hard to carry and conceal, and it requires some time to set up and operate.

Punching. The California Crime Technological Research Foundation (CCTRF) identified punching as a possible direct attack on a deadbolt (Figure 8-32). The attacker would have to punch through the wall and framing members to reach the bolt. It would be fairly easy to miss the bolt on the first few tries, so several attempts may be necessary. In essence, the punch and hammer are used to force the bolt back into the body of the lock, allowing it to clear the strike. CCTRF determined that an average man could apply a force of 125 inch-pounds with a 1-pound hammer.

Most bolts will probably succumb to a determined punching attack. But it is a noisy approach, and rather hit or miss since it is somewhat difficult to tell if the punch is actually engaging the bolt, and the punch has a tendency to be a serious disadvantage to an intruder, making this an attack of last resort.

Sawing. Bolts can be sawed by inserting a hacksaw or hacksaw blade between the face plate and the

strike. (A portion of the jamb will usually be removed or the jamb spread to allow easy access.) Better locks now use hardened bolts or hardened inserts inside the bolt to resist sawing. An even better defense are free-wheeling rollers placed inside the bolt. When the saw reaches these rollers, the sawing action rolls them back and forth but will not cut them. Modified bolts are present in almost all relatively secure locks. They are virtually immune to sawing attacks.

Peeling. Another way to expose the bolt in metal-framed doors is by peeling. Thin sheet steel and aluminum can be easily peeled. The normal countermeasure against this attack is to use a reinforced strike. Peeling may also be used with prying in an attempt to force the bolt back into the lock.

Attacks on Cylinders

Like bolts, cylinders can be pried and punched. They also can be drilled, pulled, wrenched, or twisted. The usual objective of such attacks is to completely remove the cylinder from the lock. Once it has been removed, a tool can be inserted into the lock to quickly retract the bolt.

Cylinder Pulling. The tool usually used for cylinder pulling is a slam hammer or dent puller—a common automobile body shop tool ordinarily used to remove dents from car bodies. The hardened self-tapping screw at the end of the puller is screwed into

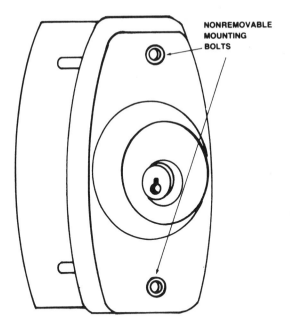

NONREMOVABLE
MOUNTING
BOLTS

Figure 8-33. Bolt-on cylinder guard with backplate. This commercially available plate is of heavy aluminum and is mounted from the inside of the door with hardened steel bolts that enter threaded holes in the guard. It combines good protection with good appearance.

the keyway as far as it will go. The hammer is then slammed back against the handle. More often than not, an unprotected cylinder will be yanked entirely out of the lock with one or two slams. CCTRF determined that 200 inch-pounds of force could be applied to a cylinder by a dent puller using a $2\frac{1}{2}$-pound hammer having an 8-inch throw.

Many cylinders are vulnerable to this kind of attack because they are poorly anchored in the lock. Mortise cylinders, for example, are ordinarily threaded into the housing and held in place with a small set screw. The threads are usually soft brass or cast iron. A good yank shears both these threads and the set screw.

Most tubular and rim cylinders are held in place by two (or more) bolts inserted from the rear of the lock. This is a much more secure method of retaining the cylinder and one which resists pulling. Retaining bolts of at least $\frac{1}{4}$ inch in diameter made of hardened steel is good protection against most pulling attempts.

The threat of pulling can be significantly reduced by the addition of a cylinder guard. Some better lock assemblies are offered with built-in guards. Locks that do not have a built-in guard can be protected with a bolt-on guard. These are bolted over the cylin-

der using carriage bolts that extend completely through the door (Figure 8-33). They offer the maximum available resistance to pulling. The cylinder guard when correctly mounted cannot be pried off without virtually destroying the entire door.

Cylindrical (lock-in-knob) locksets are extremely vulnerable to pulling. Often the door knob will be pulled off with the cylinder, exposing the entire internal mechanism to manipulation. There is no method of reinforcing a cylindrical lockset against the threat of pulling. The best measure is to replace it or add a good supplementary deadlock with a cylinder guard.

Lug Pulling. If the cylinder itself is protected against pulling, an attacker may turn to the cylinder plug. The plug is much harder to pull, and requires a special tool that looks something like a gear puller. A hardened self-tapping screw is engaged in the keyway and pressure is slowly exerted on the plug until the tumblers snap and the plug can be pulled from the cylinder shell. The bolt mechanism can then be operated by a tool inserted through the shell. The ordinary cylinder guard is no protection against this attack. A special guard is available, however, which is designed to prevent the plug from being pulled (see Figure 8-34).

Wrenching, Twisting, and Nipping. Most cylinders project from the surface of the door sufficiently to be gripped by a pipe wrench or pliers. Twisting force is applied to the cylinder by the wrench that is often sufficient to snap or shear the set-screws or bolts that hold the cylinder in the lock. If the cylinder does not project enough for a wrench to be used, a ground-down screwdriver can be inserted in the keyway and twisting force applied to the screwdriver with a wrench. CCTRF found that an 18-inch long pipe wrench could apply a maximum torque of 3300 inch-pounds to a protruding cylinder housing, and a screwdriver turned with a wrench could produce 600 inch-pounds.

The proper protection against this threat once again is a cylinder guard. Some of the built-in guards are free-wheeling, which prevents a twisting force from being successfully applied. Those that are not free-wheeling are still made of hardened steel that does not allow the wrench to get a good bite, but more importantly, prevents the wrench from reaching the actual cylinder. If a screwdriver and wrench are used, the cylinder might be twisted loose, but it cannot be pulled out. So, although the lock might be damaged, it will not be defeated.

Bolt nippers also can be used to remove protruding cylinders by prying and pulling. Cylinder guards also forestall this type of attack.

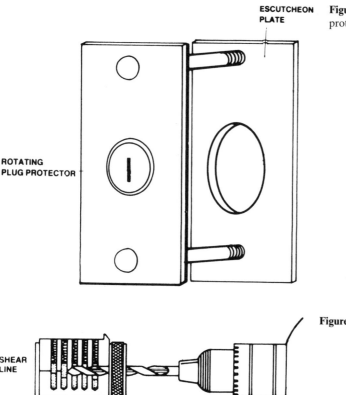

Figure 8-34. Cylinder guard with rotating plug protector.

ESCUTCHEON PLATE

ROTATING PLUG PROTECTOR

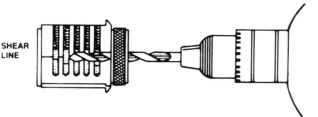

Figure 8-35. Drilling.

SHEAR LINE

Cylindrical locksets are very susceptible to wrenching, twisting, and nipping attacks. Some of the better cylindrical devices have free-wheeling door knobs that provide some protection against wrenching and twisting. Some incorporate breakaway knobs that do not expose the internal mechanism of the lock when the knob is twisted off. Nevertheless, combinations of twisting, pulling, and hammering attacks usually quickly defeat these devices. The best remedy is to replace cylindrical mechanisms or supplement them with guarded deadlocks.

Drilling. Cylinder plugs can be drilled out using a fairly large drill bit, but the most common drilling attack is centered on the shear line between the plug and shell (Figure 8-35). A smaller bit is used to drill through the pins, creating a new shear line and releasing the plug that can then be rotated using a screwdriver or key blank in the keyway. Most of the better locks incorporate hardened inserts to frustrate drilling. Any lock receiving Underwriters' Laboratories approval incorporates these features. Hardened materials do not prevent drilling, but drilling through

tempered steel is a long and slow process that greatly increases the chances of detection.

BHI's Huck-Pin cylinder has an added protection against drilling. When most cylinders are drilled at the shear line, the drivers will fall out of the shell into the plug, releasing the plug to rotate. BHI's drivers are flanged, which prevents them from falling out, so they still effectively lock the mechanism after it is drilled. This does not prevent the entire cylinder from being drilled out, but this is an even longer and slower process than drilling along the shear line.

Punching. Rim-mounted deadlocks are particularly vulnerable to punching. These are ordinarily mounted on the back of a door with wood screws. But, since most of the currently available doors are made with particle board cores under a thin veneer overlay, screws are seldom able to take much pressure. Several good blows with a hammer and punch on the face of the cylinder will often drive it through the door, pulling the screws out, so the entire lock body is dislodged.

Correctly mounting the lock using bolts that extend through the door and engage an escutcheon plate (or even large washers) on the front side generally frustrates punching attacks.

Cylindrical locksets are vulnerable to combination punching and hammering attacks. The knob is first broken off, then the spindle is punched through the lock, exposing the latch bolt assembly to manipulation.

Hammering. Hammering, as well as pulling, wrenching, and twisting, is a quick and very effective way of disabling cylindrical locksets. It is not as effective against cylinders, particularly those that are protected by cylinder guards. Ordinarily the knob on a cylindrical mechanism can be quickly broken off by one or two strong blows. There is no direct defense against this type of attack. Again, the only viable solution is a supplementary guarded deadlock, or replacement of the cylindrical lockset with a more secure lock.

Locks and the Systems Approach to Security

Locks are an essential part of most security systems. They are, however, only one part. The effectiveness of a lock cannot be considered apart from the effectiveness of the entire system. A lock is no better than the door it is on, or the frame in which the door is mounted. The strongest lock available on a substandard door does not prevent the door from being defeated, even though the lock cannot be.

The degree of protection required from any security system reflects the value of the items to be protected. Most residences require only a modest degree of security—sufficient to thwart the casual or opportunistic intruder. Jewelry stores, banks, and other establishments, which must necessarily keep valuable items on the premises, attract a more determined attacker. The degree of protection for these places must, therefore, necessarily be greater. But whatever the degree of protection required, the actual protection offered by any system is no greater than the vulnerability of its weakest member. A good lock on a poor door provides no more protection than the strength of the door. A good lock on a solid door in a substandard wall is as vulnerable as the wall is weak.

The locks employed in any protection system must complement the system. If a moderate degree of security is required (as in a residential application), a good cylinder properly installed in a secure lock body must be correctly mounted on a good, solid door. The door itself must be correctly hung, using good hardware, on a properly constructed door frame. The frame must be strongly braced, and secured to the wall. The wall itself must be at least as strong as the door system installed in it. If the lock, door, frame, or wall is significantly weaker than the rest of the system, it is the point most likely to be successfully attacked.

A good lock is essential to a good security system. It is often the point at which an intruder will focus an attack. But good locks are not synonymous with good security. Always examine the system as a whole.

Key Control*

EUGENE D. FINNERAN

Before an effective key control system can be established, every key to every lock that is being used in the protection of the facility and property must be accounted for. Chances are good that it will not even

be possible to account for the most critical keys or to be certain that they have not been copied or compromised. If this is the case, there is but one alternative—to rekey the entire facility.

Once an effective locking system has been installed, positive control of all keys must be gained and maintained. This can be accomplished only if an effective key record is kept. When not issued or used,

*From *Security Supervision: A Handbook for Supervisors and Managers*, by Eugene D. Finneran (Stoneham, MA: Butterworths, 1981).

keys must be adequately secured. A good, effective key control system is simple to initiate, particularly if it is established in conjunction with the installation of new locking devices. One of the methods that can be used to gain and maintain effective key control follows:

1. *Key cabinet*—a well-constructed cabinet will have to be procured. The cabinet will have to be of sufficient size to hold the original key to every lock in the system. It should also be capable of holding any additional keys which are in use in the facility but which are not a part of the security locking system. The cabinet should be installed in such a manner so as to be difficult, if not impossible, to remove from the property. It should be secured at all times when the person designated to control the keys is not actually issuing or replacing a key. The key to the key cabinet must receive special handling, and when not in use it should be maintained in a locked compartment inside a combination-type safe.

2. *Key record*—some administrative means must be set up to record key code numbers and indicate to whom keys to specific locks have been issued. This record may take the form of a ledger book or a card file.

3. *Key blanks*—blanks which are to be used to cut keys for issue to authorized personnel must be distinctively marked for identification to insure that no employees have cut their own keys. Blanks will be kept within a combination-type safe and issued only to the person authorized to cut keys and then only in the amount that has been authorized by the person responsible for key control. Such authorization should always be in writing, and records should be maintained on each issue that will be matched with the returned key. Keys that are damaged in the cutting process must be returned for accountability.

4. *Inventories*—periodic inventories will have to be made of all key blanks, original keys, and all duplicate keys in the hands of the employees to whom they have been issued. This cannot be permitted to take the form of a phone call to an employee, supervisor, or executive asking if they still have their key. It must be a personal inspection of each key made by the person who has been assigned responsibility for key control.

5. *Audits*—in addition to the periodic inventory, an unannounced audit should be made of all key control records and procedures by a member of management. During the course of these audits a joint inventory of all keys should be conducted.

6. *Daily report*—a daily report should be made to the person responsible for key control from the personnel department, indicating all persons who have left or will be leaving the employment of the company in the near future. A check should be made, upon receipt of this report, to determine whether the person named has been issued a key to any lock in the system. In the event a key has been issued, steps should be initiated to insure that the key is recovered.

Security force personnel will normally be issued master keys, when such a system is in effect, or they will be issued a ring of keys permitting them to enter any part of the guarded facility. Keys issued to the security force should never be permitted to leave the facility. They should be passed from shift to shift and must be receipted for each time they change hands. The supervisor must insure that all security personnel understand the importance of not permitting keys to be compromised.

A lost master key compromises the entire system and results in the breakdown of the security screen. Such compromise will necessitate the rekeying of the entire complex, sometimes at a cost of thousands of dollars.

If rekeying becomes necessary, it can most economically be accomplished by installing new locking devices in the most critical points of the locking system and moving the locks removed from these points to less sensitive areas. Of course, it will be necessary to eventually replace all the locks in the system, but by using the procedure just described the cost can be spread over several budgeting periods.

New Standard Set for Exit Devices, Locks, and Alarms[1]

The Builders Hardware Manufacturer's Association (BHMA) has announced a new American National Standard for exit locks and exit alarms for the safety and security of building occupants.

Developed by BHMA, the new standard was recently approved by the American National Standards Institute (ANSI).

In effect, the new standard recognizes the increased importance of locks, alarms, and other devices that control egress from a building. The standard establishes general requirements as well as operational tests and finish tests for these products. In addition, it gives descriptions and type numbers of exit locks and exit alarms.

Revisions include increased performance requirements with respect to the recommended tests and a slam test not part of the earlier standards has been added. Testing of products in accordance with this standard allows for certification to the ANSI/BHMA standard to be established by third party testing laboratories.

For more information, or to purchase copies of the ANSI/BHMA A156.29 Standard, please visit http://www.buildershardware.com.

Reference

1. *Security Beat* (weekly newsletter by publisher of *Access Control & Security Systems*). 2, no. 7 (February 19, 2002).

Appendix 8.A
Key Control and Lock Security Checklist*

JOHN E. HUNTER

1. Has a key control officer been appointed?
2. Are locks and keys to all buildings and entrances supervised and controlled by the key control officer?
3. Does the key control officer have overall authority and responsibility for issuance and replacement of locks and keys?
4. What is the basis for the issuance of keys, especially master keys?
5. Are keys issued only to authorized personnel? Who determines who is authorized? Is the authorization in writing?
6. Are keys issued to other than installation personnel? If so, on what basis? Is it out of necessity or merely for convenience?
7. Are keys not in use secured in a locked, fireproof cabinet? Are these keys tagged and accounted for?
8. Is the cabinet for duplicate keys regarded as an area of high security?
9. Is the key or combination to this cabinet maintained under appropriate security or secrecy? If the combination is recorded, is it secured?
10. Are the key locker and record files in order and current?

11. Are issued keys cross-referenced?
12. Are current records maintained indicating:
    a. Buildings or entrances for which keys are issued?
    b. Number and identification of keys issued?
    c. Location and number of duplicate keys?
    d. Issue and turn-in of key?
    e. Location of locks and keys held in reserve?
13. Is an audit ever made, asking holders to actually produce keys, to ensure that they have not been loaned or lost?
14. Who is responsible for ascertaining the possession of key?
15. Is a current key control directive in effect?
16. Are inventories and inspections conducted by the key control officer to ensure compliance with directives? How often?
17. Are keys turned in during vacation periods?
18. Are keys turned in when employees resign, are transferred, or are fired?
19. Is the removal of keys from the premises prohibited when they are not needed elsewhere?
20. Are locks and combinations changed immediately upon loss or theft of keys or transfer or resignation of employees?
21. Are locks changed or rotated within the installation at least annually regardless of transfers or known violations of key security?

*Prepared by John E. Hunter, U.S. National Park Service.

22. Are current records kept of combinations to safes and the dates when these combinations are changed? Are these records adequately protected?
23. Has a system been set up to provide submasters to supervisors and officials on a need basis, with facilities divided into different zones or areas?
24. If master keys are used, are they devoid of marking identifying them as master keys?
25. Are master keys controlled more closely than change keys?
26. Must all requests for reproduction or duplication of keys be approved by the key control officer?
27. Are key holders ever allowed to duplicate keys? If so, under what circumstances?
28. Where the manufacturer's serial number on combination locks and padlocks might be visible to unauthorized persons, has this number been recorded and then obliterated?
29. Are locks on inactive gates and storage facilities under seal? Are seals checked regularly by supervisory or key control personnel?
30. Are measures in effect to prevent the unauthorized removal of locks on open cabinets, gates, or buildings?
31. Are losses or thefts of keys and padlocks promptly reported by personnel and promptly investigated by key control personnel?
32. If the building was recently constructed, did the contractor retain keys during the period when construction was being completed? Were locks changed since that time? Did the contractor relinquish all keys after the building was completed?
33. If removable-core locks are in use, are unused cores and core change keys given maximum security against theft, loss, or inspection?
34. Are combination lock, key, and key control records safeguarded separately (i.e., in a separate safe or file) from keys, locks, cores, and other such hardware?
35. Are all locks of a type which offer adequate protection for the purpose for which they are used?

Appendix 8.B

Terms and Definitions for Door and Window Security*

Access Control. A method of providing security by restricting the movement of persons into or within a protected area.

Accessible Window. (1) Residential—any window located within 3.7 meters (12 feet) of grade or a building projection. (2) Commercial—any window located within 4.6 meters (18 feet) of grade or within 3 meters (10 feet) of any fire escape or other structure accessible from public or semipublic areas.

Accordion Gate. See **Sliding Metal Gate**.

Ace Lock. A type of pin tumbler lock in which the pins are installed in a circle around the axis of the cylinder, and move perpendicularly to the face of the cylinder. The shear line of the driver and bottom tumblers is a plane parallel to the face of the cylinder. This type of lock is operated with a push key.

*Reprinted courtesy of United States Department of Commerce, National Bureau of Standards.

Active Door (or **Leaf**). The leaf of a double door that must be opened first and which is used in normal pedestrian traffic. This leaf is usually the one in which a lock is installed.

Anchor. A device used to secure a buildings part or component to adjoining construction or to a supporting member. See also **Floor Anchor, Jamb Anchor**, and **Stud Anchor**.

Antifriction Latch. A latch bolt that incorporates any device which reduces the closing friction between the latch and the strike.

Applied Trim. A separately applied molding used as the finishing face trim of a frame.

Apron. The flat member of a window trim placed against the wall immediately beneath the windowsill.

Architectural Hardware. See **Finish Builders' Hardware**.

Areaway. An open subsurface space adjacent to a building that is used to admit light or to provide a means of access to the building.

Armored Front. A plate or plates secured to the lock front of a mortised lock by machine screws in order to provide protection against tampering with the cylinder set screws. Also called *armored face plate*.

Astragal. A member fixed to, or a projection of, an edge of a door or window to cover the joint between the meeting of stiles; usually fixed to one of a pair of swinging doors to provide a seal against the passage of weather, light, noise, or smoke.

Auxiliary Lock. A lock installed on a door or window to supplement a previously installed primary lock. Also called a *secondary lock*. It can be a mortised, bored, or rim lock.

Back Plate. A metal plate on the inside of a door that is used to clamp a pin or disc tumbler rim lock cylinder to the door by means of retaining screws. The tail piece of the cylinder extends through a hole in the back plate.

Backset, Flush Bolt. The distance from the vertical centerline of the lock edge of a door to the centerline of the bolt.

Backset, Hinge. On a door, the distance from the stop face to the edge of the hinge cutout. On a frame, the distance from the stop to the edge of the hinge cutout.

Backset, Lock. The horizontal distance from the vertical centerline of the face plate to the center of the lock cylinder keyway or knob spindle.

Backset, Strike. The distance from the door stop to the edge of the strike cutout.

Baffle. See **Guard Plate**.

Balanced Door. A door equipped with double-pivoted hardware so designed as to cause a semicounter-balanced swing action when it is opened.

Barrel Key. A key with a bit projecting from a round, hollow key shank which fits on a post in the lock.

Barricade Bolt. A massive metal bar that engages large strikes on both sides of a door. Barricade bolts are available with locking devices, and are completely removed from the door when not in use.

Bead. See **Glazing Bead**.

Bevel (of a door). The angle of the lock edge of the door in relation to its face. The standard bevel is 0.32 cm in 5.1 cm ($\frac{1}{8}''$ in 2″).

Bevel (of a latch bolt). A term used to indicate the direction in which a latch bolt is inclined: regular bevel for doors opening in, reverse bevel for doors opening out.

Bevel (of lock front). The angle of a lock front when not at a right angle to the lock case, allowing the front to be applied flush with the edge of a beveled door.

Bicentric Pin Tumbler Cylinder. A cylinder having two cores and two sets of pins, each having different combinations. This cylinder requires two separate keys, used simultaneously, to operate it. The cam or tail piece is gear operated.

Bit. A blade projecting from a key shank which engages with and actuates the bolt or level tumblers of a lock.

Bit Key. A key with a bit projecting from a round shank. Similar to the barrel key but with a solid rather than hollow shank.

Bitting. See **Cut**.

Blank. An uncut key or an unfinished key as it comes from the manufacturer, before any cuts have been made on it.

Blind Stop. A rectangular molding, located between the outside trim and outside sashes, used in the assembly of a window frame. Serves as a stop for storm, screen, or combination windows and to resist air infiltration.

Bolt. That part of a lock which, when actuated, is projected (or "thrown") from the lock into a retaining member, such as a strike plate, to prevent a door or window from moving or opening. See also **Deadbolt, Flush Bolt**, and **Latch**.

Bolt Attack. A category of burglary attack in which force, with or without the aid of tools, is directed against the bolt in an attempt to disengage it from the strike or to break it.

Bolt Projection (Bolt Throw). The distance from the edge of the door, at the bolt centerline, to the furthest point on the bolt in the projected position.

Bored Lock (or Latch). A lock or latch whose parts are intended for installation in holes bored in a door. See also **Key-in-Knob Lock**.

Bottom Pin. One of pin tumblers that determines the combination of a pin tumbler cylinder and is directly contacted by the key. These are varied in length and usually tapered at one end, enabling them to fit into the "V" cuts made in a key. When the proper key is inserted, the bottom pins level off at the cylinder core shear line, allowing the core to turn and actuate the lock.

Bottom Rail. The horizontal rail at the bottom of a door or window connecting the vertical edge members (stiles).

Box Strike. A strike plate that has a metal box or housing to fully enclose the projected bolt or latch.

Breakaway Strike. See **Electric Strike**.

Buck. See **Rough Buck**.

Builders' Hardware. All hardware used in building construction, but particularly that used on or in connection with doors, windows, cabinets, and other moving members.

Bumping. A method of opening a pin tumbler lock by means of vibration produced by a wooden or rubber mallet.

Burglar-Resistant Glazing. Any glazing that is more difficult to break through than the common window or plate glass, designed to resist burglary attacks of the hit-and-run type.

Butt Hinge. A type of hinge that has matching rectangular leaves and multiple bearing contacts, and is designed to be mounted in mortises in the door edge and in the frame.

Buttress Lock. A lock which secures a door by wedging a bar between the door and the floor. Some incorporate a movable steel rod that fits into metal receiving slots on the door and in the floor. Also called *police bolt/brace*.

Cabinet Jamb. A door frame in three or more pieces, usually shipped knocked down for field assembly over a rough buck.

Cam. The part of a lock or cylinder that rotates to actuate the bolt or latch as the key is turned. The cam may also act as the bolt.

Cam, Lazy. A cam that moves less than the rotation of the cylinder core.

Cam Lock. See **Crescent Sash Lock**.

Cane Bolt. A heavy cane-shaped bolt with the top bent at right angles; used on the bottom of doors.

Case. The housing in which a lock mechanism is mounted and enclosed.

Casement Hinge. A hinge for swinging a casement window.

Casement Window. A type of window which is hinged on the vertical edge.

Casing. Molding of various widths and thicknesses used to trim door and window openings at the jambs.

Center-Hung Door. A door hung on center pivots.

Center Rail. The horizontal rail in a door, usually located at lock height to separate the upper and lower panels of a recessed panel type door.

Chain Bolt. A vertical spring-loaded bolt mounted at the top of door. It is manually actuated by a chain.

Chain Door Interviewer. An auxiliary locking device that allows a door to be opened slightly, but restrains it from being fully opened. It consists of chain with one end attached to the door jamb and the other attached to a keyed metal piece that slides in a slotted metal plate attached to the door. Some chain door interviewers incorporate a keyed lock operated from the inside.

Change Key. A key that will operate only one lock or a group of keyed-alike locks, as distinguished from a master key. See also **Keyed-Alike Cylinders** and **Master Key System**.

Changes. The number of possible key changes or combination changes to a lock cylinder.

Checkrails. The meeting rails of double-hung windows. They are usually beveled, and thick enough to fill the space between the top and bottom sash due to the parting stop in the window frame.

Clearance. A space intentionally provided between components, either to facilitate operation or installation, to insure proper separation, to accommodate dimensional variations, or for other reasons. See also **Door Clearance**.

Clevis. A metal link used to attach a chain to a padlock.

Code. An arrangement of numbers or letters which is used to specify a combination for the bitting of a key or the pins of a cylinder core.

Combination. (1) The sequence and depth of cuts on a key. (2) The sequence of numbers to which a combination lock is set.

Combination Doors or **Windows**. Storm doors or windows permanently installed over the primary doors or windows. They provide insulation and summer ventilation and often have self-storing or removable glass and screen inserts.

Common Entry Door (of a multiple dwelling). Any door in a multiple dwelling which provides access between the semipublic, interior areas of the building and the out-of-doors areas surrounding the building.

Communicating Frame. A double rabbeted frame with both rabbets prepared for single-swing doors that open in opposite directions. Doors may be of the same or opposite hand.

Component. A subassembly which is combined with other components to make an entire system. Door assembly components include the door, lock hinges, jamb/strike, and jamb/wall.

Composite Door. A door constructed of a solid core material with facing and edges of different materials.

Connecting Bar. A flat metal bar attached to the core of a cylinder lock to operate the bolt mechanism.

Construction Master Keying. A keying system used to allow the use of a single key for all locks during the construction of large housing projects. In one such system, the cylinder cores of all locks contain an insert that permits the use of a special master key. When the dwelling unit is completed, the insert is removed and the lock then accepts its own change key and no longer accepts the construction master key.

Continuous Hinge. A hinge designed to be the same length as the edge of the moving part to which it is applied. Also called a *piano hinge*.

Coordinator. A mechanism which controls the order of closing of a pair of swing doors, used with overlapping astragals and certain panic hardware which require that one door close ahead of the other.

Core. See **Cylinder Core**.

Crash Bar. The cross bar or level of a panic exit device which serves as push bar to actuate the lock. See also **Panic Hardware**.

Cremone Bolt. A surface-mounted device that locks a door or sash into the frame at both the top and bottom when a knob or lever is turned.

Crescent Sash Lock. A simple camshaped latch, not requiring a key for its operation, usually used to secure double-hung windows. Also called a *cam lock*.

Cut. An indentation made in a key to make it fit a pin tumbler of a lock. Any notch made in a key is known as a cut, whether it is square, round, or V-shaped. Also called *bitting*.

Cylinder. The cylindrical subassembly of a lock, including the cylinder housing, the cylinder core, the tumbler mechanism, and the keyway.

Cylinder Collar. See **Cylinder Guard Ring**.

Cylinder Core (or **Plug**). The central part of a cylinder, containing the keyway, which is rotated to operate the lock bolt.

Cylinder Guard Ring. A hardened metal ring, surrounding the exposed portion of a lock cylinder, which protects the cylinder from being wrenched, turned, pried, cut, or pulled with attack tools.

Cylinder Housing. The external case of a lock cylinder. Also called the *cylinder shell*.

Cylinder Lock. A lock in which the locking mechanism is controlled by a cylinder. A double cylinder lock has a cylinder on both the interior and exterior of the door.

Cylinder, Mortise Type. A lock cylinder that has a threaded housing which screws directly into the lock case, with a cam or other mechanism engaging the locking mechanism.

Cylinder, Removable Core. A cylinder whose core may be removed by the use of a special key.

Cylinder, Rim Type. A lock cylinder that is held in place by tension against its rim, applied by screws from the interior face of the door.

Cylinder Ring. See **Cylinder Guard Ring**.

Cylinder Screw. A set screw that holds a mortise cylinder in place and prevents it from being turned after installation.

Cylindrical Lock (or **Latch**). See **Bored Lock**.

Deadbolt. A lock bolt which does not have an automatic spring action and a beveled end as opposed to a latch bolt, which does. The bolt must be actuated to a projected position by a key or thumb turn and when projected is locked against return by end pressure.

Deadlatch. A spring-actuated latch bolt having a beveled end and incorporating a feature that automatically locks the projected latch bolt against return by end pressure.

Deadlock. A lock equipped with a deadbolt.

Deadlocking Latch Bolt. See **Deadlatch**.

Disc Tumbler. A spring-loaded, flat plate that slides in a slot which runs through the diameter of the cylinder. Inserting the proper key lines up the disc tumblers with the lock's shear line and enables the core to be turned.

Dogging Device. A mechanism which fastens the cross bar of a panic exit device in the fully depressed position, and retains the latch bolt or bolts in the retracted position to permit free operation of the door from either side.

Dogging Key. A key-type wrench used to lock down, in the open position, the cross bar of a panic exit device.

Door Assembly. A unit composed of parts or components that make up a closure for a passageway through a wall. It consists of the door, hinges, locking device or devices, operational contacts (such as handles, knobs, and push plates), miscellaneous hardware and closure, the frame including the head and jambs, the anchorage devices to the surrounding wall, and the surrounding wall.

Door Bolt. A rod or bar manually operated without a key, attached to a door to provide a means of securing it.

Door Check/Closer. A device used to control the closing of a door by means of a spring and either hydraulic or air pressure, or by electrical means.

Door Clearance. The space between a door and either its frame or the finished floor or threshold, or between the two doors of a double door. See also **Clearance**.

Door Frame. An assembly of members surrounding and supporting a door or doors, and perhaps also one or more transom lights and/or sidelights. See also **Integral Frame**.

Door Jambs. The two vertical components of a door frame called the hinge jamb and the lock jamb.

Door Light. See **Light**.

Door Opening. The size of a doorway, measured from jamb to jamb and from floor line or still to head of frame. The opening size is usually the nominal door size, and is equal to the actual door size plus clearances and threshold height.

Door Stop. The projections along the top and sides of a door frame against which a one-way swinging door closes. See also **Rabbeted Jamb**.

Double-Acting Door. A swinging door equipped with hardware that permits it to open in either direction.

Double-Bitted Key. A key having cuts on two sides.

Double Cylinder Lock. See **Cylinder Lock**.

Double Door. A pair of doors mounted together in a single opening. See also **Active Door** and **Inactive Door**.

Double Egress Frame. A door frame prepared to receive two single-acting doors swinging in opposite directions, both doors being of the same hand.

Double Glazing. Two thicknesses of glass, separated by an air space and framed in an opening, designed to reduce heat transfer or sound transmission. In factory-made double glazing units, referred to as insulating glass, the air space between the glass sheets is desiccated and sealed airtight.

Double-Hung Window. A type of window, composed of upper and lower sashes, which slide vertically.

Double-Throw Bolt. A bolt that can be projected beyond its first position, into a second, or fully extended one.

Double-Throw Lock. A lock incorporating a double-throw bolt.

Driver Pin. One of the pin tumblers in pin tumbler cylinder lock, usually flat on both ends, which are in line with and push against the flat ends of the bottom pins. They are projected by individual coil springs into the cylinder core until they are forced from the core by the bottom pins when the proper key is inserted into the keyway.

Drop Ring. A ring handle attached to the spindle that operates a lock or latch. The ring is pivoted to remain in a dropped position when not in use.

Dry Glazing. A method of securing glass in a frame by use of a performed resilient gasket.

Drywall Frame. A knocked down (KD) door frame for installation in a wall constructed with studs and gypsum board or other drywall facing material after the wall is erected.

Dummy Cylinder. A mock cylinder without an operating mechanism, used for appearance only.

Dummy Trim. Trim only, without lock; usually used on the inactive door in a double door.

Dutch Door. A door consisting of two separate leaves, one above the other, which may be operated either independently or together. The lower leaf usually has a service shelf.

Dutch Door Bolt. A device for locking together the upper and lower leaves of a Dutch door.

Dwelling Unit Entry Door. Any door giving access to a private dwelling unit.

Electric Strike. An electrically operated device that replaces a conventional strike plate and allows a door to be opened by using electric switches at remote locations.

Escutcheon Plate. A surface-mounted cover plate, either protective or ornamental, containing openings for any or all of the controlling members of a lock such as the knob, handle, cylinder, or keyhole.

Exit Device. See **Panic Hardware**.

Expanded Metal. An open mesh formed by slitting and drawing metal sheet. It is made in various patterns and metal thicknesses, with either a flat or an irregular surface.

Exterior Private Area. The ground area outside a single family house, or a ground floor apartment in the case of a multiple dwelling, which is fenced off by a real barrier, which is available for the use of one family and is accessible only from the interior of that family's unit.

Exterior Public Area. The ground area outside a multiple dwelling which is not defined as being associated with the building or building entry in any real or symbolic fashion.

Exterior Semiprivate Area. The ground area outside a multiple dwelling which is fenced off by a real barrier, and is accessible only from the private or semiprivate zones within the building.

Exterior Semipublic Area. The ground area outside a single family house or multiple dwelling, which is accessible from public zones, but is defined as belonging to the house or building by symbolic barriers only.

Face (of a lock). See **Face Plate**.

Face Glazing. A method of glazing in which the glass is set in an L-shaped or rabbeted frame, the glazing compound is finished off in the form of a triangular bead, and no lose stops are employed.

Face Plate. The part of a mortise lock through which the bolt protrudes and by which the lock is fastened to the door.

Fast Pin Hinge. A hinge in which the pin is fastened permanently in place.

Fatigue. Structural failure of a material caused by repeated or fluctuating application of stresses, none of which is individually sufficient to cause failure.

Fence. A metal pin that extends from the bolt of a lever lock and prevents retraction of the bolt unless it is aligned with the gates of the lever tumblers.

Fidelity Loss. A property loss resulting from a theft in which the thief leaves no evidence of entry.

Filler Plate. A metal plate used to fill unwanted mortise cutouts in a door or frame.

Finish Builders' Hardware. Hardware that has a finished appearance as well as a functional purpose and which may be considered as part of the decorative treatment of a room or building. Also called *finish hardware* and *builders' finish hardware*.

Fire Stair. Any enclosed stairway which is part of a fire-resistant exitway.

Fire Stair Door. A door forming part of the fire-resistant fire stair enclosure, and providing access from common corridors to fire stair landings within an exitway.

Floor Anchor. A metal device attached to the wall side of a jamb at its base to secure the frame to the floor.

Floor Clearance. The width of the space between the bottom of a door and the rough or finished floor or threshold.

Flush Bolt. A door bolt so designed that, when installed, the operating handle is flush with the face or edge of the door. Usually installed at the top and bottom of the inactive door of a double door.

Flush Door. A smooth-surface door having faces which are plane and which conceal its rails and stiles or other structure.

Foot Bolt. A type of bolt applied at the bottom of a door and arranged for foot operation. Generally the bolt head is held up by a spring when the door is unbolted.

Forced Entry. An unauthorized entry accomplished by the use of force upon the physical components of the premises.

Frame. The component that forms the opening of and provides support for a door, windows, skylight, or hatchway. See also **Door Frame**.

Frame Gasket. Resilient material in strip form attached to frame stops to provide tight closure of a door or window.

Front (of a lock). See **Face Plate**.

Gate. A notch in the end of a lever tumbler, which when aligned with the fence of the lock bolt allows the bolt to be withdrawn from the strike.

General Circulation Stair. An interior stairway in a building without elevators which provides access to upper floors.

Glass Door. A door made from thick glass, usually heat tempered, and having no structural metal stiles.

Glass Stop. See **Glazing Bead**.

Glazing. Any transparent or translucent material used in windows or doors to admit light.

Glazing Bead. A strip of trim or a sealant such as caulking or glazing compound, which is placed around the perimeter of a pane of glass or other glazing to secure it to a frame.

Glazing Compound. A soft, dough-like material used for filling and sealing the spaces between a pane of glass and its surrounding frame and/or stops.

Grand Master Key. A key designed to operate all locks under several master keys in a system.

Grating, Bar Type. An open grip assembly of metal bars in which the bearing bars, running in one direction, are spaced by rigid attachment to cross bars running perpendicular to them or by bent connecting bars extending between them.

Grout. Mortar of such consistency that it will just flow into the joints and cavities of masonry work and fill them solid.

Grouted Frame. A frame in which all voids between it and the surrounding wall are completely filled with the cement or plaster used in the wall construction.

Guard Bar. A series of two or more cross bars, generally fastened to a common back plate, to protect the glass or screen in a door.

Guard Plate. A piece of metal attached to a door frame, door edge, or over the lock cylinder for the purpose of reinforcing the locking system against burglary attacks.

Hand (of a door). The opening direction of the door. A right-handed (RH) door is hinged on the right and swings inward when viewed from the outside. A left-handed (LH) door is hinged on the left and swings inward when viewed from the outside. If either of these doors swings outward, it is referred to as a right-hand reverse (RHR) door or a left-hand reverse (LHR) door, respectively.

Handle. Any grip-type door pull. See also **Lever Handle**.

Hasp. A fastening device that consists of a hinged plate with a slot in it that fits over a fixed D-shaped ring, or eye.

Hatchway. An opening in a ceiling, roof, or floor of a building which is large enough to allow human access.

Head. Top horizontal member of a door or window frame.

Head Stiffener. A heavy-gauge metal angle or channel section placed inside, and attached to, the head of a wide door frame to maintain its alignment; not a load-carrying member.

Heel of a Padlock. That end of the shackle on a padlock that is not removable from the case.

Hinge. A device generally consisting of two metal plates having loops formed along one edge of each to engage and rotate about a common pivot rod or "pin," used to suspend a swinging door or window in its frame.

Hinge Backset. The distance from the edge of a hinge to the stop at the side of a door or window.

Hinge Edge or **Hinge Stile.** The vertical edge or stile of a door or window to which hinges or pivots are attached.

Hinge Reinforcement. A metal plate attached to a door or frame to receive a hinge.

Hold-Back Feature. A mechanism on a latch that serves to hold the latch bolt in the retracted position.

Hollow Core Door. A door constructed so that the space (core) between the two facing sheets is not completely filled. Various spacing and reinforcing material are used to separate the facing sheets; some interior hollow-core doors have nothing except perimeter stiles and rails separating the facing sheets.

Hollow Metal. Hollow items such as doors, frames, partitions, and enclosures that are usually fabricated from cold-formed metal sheet, usually carbon steel.

Horizontal Sliding Window. A type of window composed of two sections, one or both of which slide horizontally past the other.

Impression System. A technique to produce keys for certain types of locks without taking the lock apart.

Inactive Door (or **Leaf**). The lead of a double door that is bolted when closed; the strike plate is attached to this leaf to receive the latch and bolt of the active leaf.

Integral Frame. A metal door frame in which the jambs and head have stops, trim, and backbends all formed from one piece of material.

Integral Lock (or **Latch**). See **Preassembled Lock**.

Interior Common-Circulation Area. An area within a multiple dwelling which is outside the private zones of individual units and is used in common by all residents and the maintenance staff of the building.

Interior Private Area. The interior of a single family house; the interior of an apartment in a multiple dwelling; or the interior of a separate unit within commercial, public, or institutional building.

Interior Public Area. An interior common-circulation area or common resident-use room within a multiple dwelling to which access is unrestricted.

Interior Semipublic Area. An interior common-circulation area or common resident-use room within a multiple dwelling to which access is possible only with a key or on the approval of a resident via an intercom, buzzer-reply system.

Invisible Hinge. A hinge so constructed that no parts are exposed when the door is closed.

Jalousie Window. See **Louvered Window**.

Jamb. The exposed vertical member of either side of a door or window opening. See also **Door Jambs**.

Jamb Anchor. A metal device inserted in or attached to the wall side of a jamb to secure the frame to the wall. A masonry jamb anchor secures a jamb to a masonry wall.

Jamb Depth. The width of the jamb, measured perpendicular to the door or wall face at the edge of the opening.

Jamb Extension. The section of a jamb which extends below the level of the flush floor for attachment to the rough door.

Jamb Peeling. A technique used in forced entry to deform or remove portions of the jamb to disengage the bolt from the strike. See **Jimmying**.

Jamb/Strike. That component of a door assembly which receives and holds the extended lock bolt. The strike and jamb are considered a unit.

Jamb/Wall. That component of a door assembly to which a door is attached and secured by means of the hinges. The wall and jamb are considered a unit.

Jimmying. A technique used in forced entry to pry the jamb away from the lock edge of the door a sufficient distance to disengage the bolt from the strike.

Jimmy-Pin. A sturdy projecting screw, which is installed in the hinge edge of a door near a hinge, fits into a hole in the door jamb, and prevents removal of the door if the hinge pins are removed.

Keeper. See **Strike**.

Key. An implement used to actuate a lock both or latch into the locked or unlocked position.

Key Changes. The different combinations that are available or that can be used in a specific cylinder.

Keyed-Alike Cylinders. Cylinders which are designed to be operated by the same key. (Not to be confused with master-keyed cylinders.)

Keyed-Different Cylinders. Cylinders requiring different keys for their operation.

Keyhole. The opening in a lock designed to receive the key.

Key-in-Knob Lock. A lock having the key cylinder and the other lock mechanism, such as a push or turn button, contained in the knobs.

Key Plate. A plate or escutcheon having only a keyhole.

Keyway. The longitudinal cut in the cylinder core, being an opening or space with millings in the sides identical to those on the proper key, thus allowing the key to enter the full distance of the blade. See also **Warded Lock**.

Knifing. See **Loiding**.

Knob. An ornamental or functional round handle on a door; may be designed to actuate a lock or latch.

Knob Latch. A securing device having a spring bolt operated by a knob only.

Knob Shank. The projecting stem of a knob into which the spindle is fastened.

Knocked Down (KD). Disassembled; designed for assembly at the point of use.

Knuckle. The enlarged part of a hinge into which the pin is inserted.

Laminate. A product made by bonding together two or more layers of material.

Laminated Glass. A type of glass fabricated from two layers of glass with a transparent bonding layer between them. Also called *safety glass*.

Laminated Padlock. A padlock, the body of which consists of a number of flat plates, all or most of which are of the same contour, superimposed and riveted or brazed together. Holes in the plates provide spaces for the lock mechanism and the ends of the shackle.

Latch (or **Latch Bolt**). A beveled, spring-actuated bolt which may or may not include a deadlocking feature.

Leading Edge. See **Lock Edge**.

Leaf, Door. An individual door, used either singly or in multiples.

Leaf Hinge. The most common type of hinge, characterized by two flat metal plates or leaves, which pivot about a metal hinge pin. A leaf hinge can be surface mounted, or installed in a mortise. See also **Butt Hinge** and **Surface Hinge**.

Lever Handle. A bar-like grip that is rotated in a vertical plane about a horizontal axis at one of its ends, designed to operate a latch.

Lever Lock. A key operated lock that incorporates one or more lever tumblers, which must be raised to a specific level so that the fence of the bolt is aligned with the gate of the tumbler in order to withdraw the bolt. Lever locks are commonly used in storage lockers and safety deposit boxes.

Lever Tumbler. A flat metal arm, pivoted on one end with a gate in the opposite end. The top edge is spring-loaded. The bitting of the key rotates against the bottom edge, raising the lever tumbler to align the gate with the bolt fence. Both the position of the gate and the curvature of the bottom edge of the lever tumbler can be varied to establish the key code.

Light. A space in a window or door for a single pane of glazing. Also, a pane of glass or other glazing material.

Lintel. A horizontal structural member that supports the load over an opening such as a door or window.

Lip (of a strike). The curved projecting part of a strike plate which guides the spring bolt to the latch point.

Lobby. That portion of the interior common area of a building which is reached from an entry door and which provides access to the general circulation areas, elevators, and fire stairs and from these to other areas of the building.

Lock. A fastener which secures a door or window assembly against unauthorized entry. A door lock is usually key-operated and includes the keyed device (cylinder or combination), bolt, strike plate, knobs or levers, trim items, etc. A window lock is usually hand-operated rather than key-operated.

Lock Clip. A flexible metal part attached to the inside of a door face to position a mortise lock.

Lock Edge. The vertical edge or stile of a door in which a lock may be installed. Also called the *leading edge*, the *lock stile*, and *strike edge*.

Lock Edge Door (or **Lock Seam Door**). A door that has its face sheets secured in place by an exposed mechanical interlock seam on each of its two vertical edges. See also **Lock Seam**.

Lock Faceplate. See **Face Plate**.

Locking Dog (of a padlock). The part of a padlock mechanism which engages the shackle and holds it in the locked position.

Lock-in-Knob. See **Key-in-Knob Lock**.

Lockpick. A tool or instrument, other than the specifically designed key, made for the purpose of manipulating a lock into a locked or unlocked condition.

Lock Rail. The horizontal member of a door intended to receive the lock case.

Lock Reinforcement. A reinforcing plate attached inside of the lock stile of a door to receive a lock.

Lock Seam. A joint in sheet metal work, formed by doubly folding the edges of adjoining sheets in such a manner that they interlock.

Lock Set. See **Lock**.

Lock Stile. See **Lock Edge**.

Loiding. A burglary attack method in which a thin, flat, flexible object such as a stiff piece of plastic is inserted between the strike and latch bolt to depress the latch bolt and release it from the strike. The loiding of windows is accomplished by inserting a thin stiff object between the meeting rails or stiles to move the latch to the open position, or by inserting a thin stiff wire through openings between the stile or rail and the frame to manipulate the sash operator of pivoting windows. Derived from the word "celluloid." Also called *knifing* and *slip-knifing*.

Loose Joint Hinge. A hinge with two knuckles. The pin is fastened permanently to one and the other contains the pinhole. The two parts of the hinge can be disengaged by lifting.

Loose Pin Hinge. A hinge having a removable pin to permit the two leaves of the hinge to be separated.

Louver. An opening with a series of horizontal slats so arranged as to permit ventilation but to exclude rain, sunlight, or vision.

Louvered Window. A type of window in which the glazing consists of parallel, horizontal, movable glass slats. Also called a *jalousie window*.

Main Entry Door. The most important common entry door in a building, which provides access to the building's lobby.

Maison Keying. A specialized keying system, used in apartment houses and other large complexes, that enables all individual unit keys to operate common-use locks such as main entry, laundry room, etc.

Masonry. Stone, brick, concrete, hollow tiles, concrete blocks, or other similar materials, bonded together with mortar to form a wall, pier, buttress, or similar member.

Master Disc Tumbler. A disc tumbler that will operate with a master key in addition to its own change key.

Master Key System. A method of keying locks which allows a single key to operate multiple locks, each of which will also operate with an individual change key. Several levels of master keying are possible: a single master key is one which will operate all locks of a group of locks with individual change keys, a grand master key will operate all locks of two or more master key systems, a great grand master key will operate all locks of two or more grand master key systems. Master key systems are used primarily with pin and disc tumbler locks, and to a limited extent with lever or warded locks.

Master Pin. A segmented pin, used to enable a pin tumbler to be operated by more than one key cut.

Meeting Stile. The vertical edge member of a door or horizontal sliding window, in a pair of doors or windows, which meets with adjacent edge member when closed. See also **Checkrails**.

Metal-Mesh Grille. A grille of expanded metal or welded metal wires permanently installed across a window or other opening in order to prevent entry through the opening.

Mill Finish. The original surface finish produced on a metal mill product by cold rolling, extruding, or drawing.

Millwork. Generally, all building components made of finished wood and manufactured in millwork plants and planing mills. It includes such items as inside and outside doors, window and doorframes, cabinets, porch-work, mantels, panelwork, stairways, moldings, and interior trim. It normally does not include flooring, ceiling, or siding.

Molding. A wood strip used for decorative purposes.

Mono Lock. See **Preassembled Lock**.

Mortise. A rectangular cavity made to receive a lock or other hardware; also, the act of making such a cavity.

Mortise Bolt. A bolt designed to be installed in a mortise rather than on the surface. The bolt is operated by a knob, lever, or equivalent.

Mortise Cylinder. See **Cylinder, Mortise Type**.

Mortise Lock. A lock designed for installation in a mortise, as distinguished from a bored lock and a rim lock.

Mullion. (1) A movable or fixed center post used on double door openings, usually for locking purposes. (2) A vertical or horizontal bar or divider in a frame between windows, doors, or other openings.

Multiple Dwelling. A building or portion of a building designed or used for occupancy by three or more tenants or families living independently of each other (includes hotels and motels).

Muntin. A small member which divides the glass or openings of sash or doors.

Mushroom Tumbler. A type of tumbler used in pin tumbler locks to add security against picking. The diameter of the driver pin behind the end in contact with the bottom pin is reduced so that the mushroom head will catch the edge of the cylinder body at the shear line when it is at a slight angle to its cavity. See also **Spool Tumbler**.

Night Latch. An auxiliary lock having a spring latch bolt and functioning independently of the regular lock of the door.

Nonremovable Hinge Pin. A type of hinge pin that has been constructed or modified to make its removal from the hinge difficult or impossible.

Offset Pivot (or Hinge). A pin-and-socket hardware device with a single bearing contact, by means of which a door is suspended in its frame and allowed to swing about an axis which normally is located about 1.9 cm ($^3/_4$ in.) out from the door face.

One-Way Screw. A screw specifically designed to resist being removed once installed. See also **Tamper-Resistant Hardware**.

Opening Size. See **Door Opening**.

Operator (of a window sash). The mechanism, including a crank handle and gear box, attached to an operating arm or arms for the purpose of opening and closing a window. Usually found on casement and awning type windows.

Overhead Door. A door that is stored overhead when in the open position.

Padlock. A detachable and portable lock with a hinged or sliding shackle or bolt, normally used with a hasp and eye or staple system.

Panel Door. A door fabricated from one or more panels surrounded by and held in position by rails and stiles.

Panic Bar. See **Crash Bar**.

Panic Hardware. An exterior locking mechanism which is always operable from inside the building by pressure on a crash bar or lever.

Patio-Type Sliding Door. A sliding door that is essentially a single, large transparent panel in a frame (a type commonly used to give access to patios or yards of private dwellings); "single" doors have one fixed and one movable panel; "double" doors have two movable panels.

Peeling. See **Jamb Peeling**.

Picking. See **Lockpick**.

Pin (of a hinge). The metal rod that serves as the axis of a hinge and thereby allows the hinge (and attached door or window) to rotate between the open and closed positions.

Pin Tumbler. One of the essential, distinguishing components of a pin tumbler lock cylinder, more precisely called a bottom pin, master pin, or driver pin. The pin tumblers, used in varying lengths and arrangements, determine the combination of the cylinder. See also **Bottom Pin, Driver Pin**, and **Master Pin**.

Pin Tumbler Lock Cylinder. A lock cylinder employing metal pins (tumblers) to prevent the rotation of the core until the correct key is inserted into the keyway. Small coil compression springs hold the pins in the locked position until the key is inserted.

Pivoted Door. A door hung on pivots rather than hinges.

Pivoted Window. A window which opens by pivoting about a horizontal or vertical axis.

Plug Retainer. The part often fixed to the rear of the core in a lock cylinder to retain or hold the core firmly in the cylinder.

Preassembled Lock. A lock that has all the parts assembled into a unit at the factory and, when installed in a rectangular section cut out of the door at the lock edge, requires little or no assembly. Also called *integral* lock, *mono* lock, and *unit* lock.

Pressed Padlock. A padlock whose outer case is pressed into shape from sheet metal and then riveted together.

Pressure-Locked Grating. A grating in which the cross bars are mechanically locked to the bearing bars at their intersections by deforming or swaging the metal.

Privacy Lock. A lock, usually for an interior door, secured by a button, thumb-turn, etc., and not designed for key operation.

Projection. See **Bolt Projection**.

Push Key. A key which operates the Ace type of lock.

Quadrant. See **Dutch Door Bolt**.

Rabbet. A cut, slot, or groove made on the edge or surface of a board to receive the end or edge of another piece of wood made to fit it.

Rabbeted Jamb. A door jamb in which the projection portion of the jamb which forms the door stop is either part of the same piece as the rest of the jamb or securely set into a deep groove in the jamb.

Rail. A horizontal framing member of a door or window sash which extends the full width between the sites.

Removable Mullion. A mullion separating two adjacent door openings which is required for the normal operation of the doors but is designed to permit its temporary removal.

Restricted Keyway. A special keyway and key blank for high-security locks, with a configuration which is not freely available and which must be specifically requested from the manufacturer.

Reversible Local. A lock which may be used for either hand of a door.

Rim Cylinder. A pin or disc tumbler cylinder used with a rim lock.

Rim Hardware. Hardware designed to be installed on the surface of a door or window.

Rim Latch. A latch installed on the surface of a door.

Rim Lock. A lock designed to be mounted on the surface of a door.

Rose. The part of a lock which functions as an ornament or bearing surface for a knob, and is normally placed against the surface of the door.

Rotary Interlocking Deadbolt Lock. A type of rim lock in which the extended dead bolt is rotated to engage with the strike.

Rough Buck. A subframe, usually made of wood or steel, which is set in a wall opening and to which the frame is attached.

Rough Opening. The wall opening into which a frame is to be installed. Usually, the rough opening is measured inside the rough buck.

Sash. A frame containing one or more lights.

Sash Fast. A fastener attached to the meeting rails of a window.

Sash Lock. A sash fast with a locking device controlled by a key.

Screwless Knob. A knob attached to a spindle by means of a special wrench, as distinguished from the more commonly used side-screw knob.

Screwless Rose. A rose with a concealed method of attachment.

Seamless Door. A door having no visible seams on its faces or edges.

Secondary Lock. See **Auxiliary Lock**.

Security Glass (or **Glazing**). See **Burglar-Resistant Glazing**.

Setback. See **Backset**.

Shackle. The hinged or sliding part of a padlock that does the fastening.

Shear Line. The joint between the shell and the core of a lock cylinder; the line at which the pins or discs of a lock cylinder must be aligned in order to permit rotation of the core.

Sheathing. The structural exterior covering, usually wood boards or plywood, used over the framing studs and rafters of a structure.

Shell. A lock cylinder, exclusive of the core. Also called *housing*.

Shutter. A movable screen or cover used to protect an opening, especially a window.

Side Light. A fixed light located adjacent to a door within the same frame assembly.

Signal Sash Fastener. A sash-fastening device designed to lock windows that are beyond reach from the floor. It has a ring for a sash pole hook. When locked, the ring lever is down; when the ring lever is up, it signals by its upright position that the window is unlocked.

Sill. The lower horizontal member of a door or window opening.

Single-Acting Door. A door mounted to swing to only one side of the plane of its frame.

Skylight. A glazed opening located in the roof of a building.

Slide Bolt. A simple lock that is operated directly by hand without using a key, turnpiece, or other actuating mechanism. Slide bolts can normally only be operated from the inside.

Sliding Door. Any door that slides open sideways.

Sliding Metal Gate. An assembly of metal bars, jointed so that it can be moved to and locked in position across a window or other opening, in order to prevent unauthorized entry through the opening.

Slip-Knifing. See **Loiding**.

Solid-Core Door. A door constructed so that the space (core) between the two facing sheets is completely filled with wood blocks of other rigid material.

Spindle. The shaft that fits into the shank of a door knob or handle, and that serves as its axis of rotation.

Split Astragal. A two-piece astragal, one piece of which is surface mounted on each door of a double door and is provided with a means of adjustment to mate with the other piece and provide a seal. See also **Astragal**.

Spool Tumbler. A type of tumbler used in pin tumbler locks to add security against picking. Operates on the same principle as the mushroom tumbler.

Spring Bolt. See **Latch**.

Spring Bolt with Antiloiding Device. See **Deadlatch**.

Stile. One of the vertical edge members of a paneled door or window sash.

Stool. A flat molding fitted over the window sill between the jambs and contacting the bottom rail of the lower sash.

Stop (of a door or window frame). The projecting part of a door or window frame against which a swinging door or window closes, or in which a sliding door or window moves.

Stop (of a lock). A button or other device that serves to lock and unlock a latch bolt against actuation by the outside knob or thumb piece. Another type holds the bolt retracted.

Stop Side. That face of a door that contacts the door stop.

Store Front Sash. An assembly of light metal members forming a continuous frame for a fixed glass store front.

Storm Sash, Window, or **Door.** An extra window or door, usually placed on the outside of an existing one as additional protection against cold or hot weather.

Strap Hinge. A surface hinge of which one or both leaves are of considerable length.

Strike. A metal plate attached to or mortised into a door jamb to receive and hold a projected latch bolt or dead bolt in order to secure the door to the jamb.

Strike, Box. See **Box Strikes**.

Strike, Dustproof. A strike which is placed in the threshold or sill of an opening, or in the floor, to receive a flush bolt, and is equipped with a spring-loaded follower to cover the recess and keep out dirt.

Strike, Interlocking. A strike which receives and holds a vertical, rotary, or hook deadbolt.

Strike Plate. See **Strike**.

Strike Reinforcement. A metal plate attached to a door or frame to receive a strike.

Strike, Roller. A strike for latch bolts, having a roller mounted on the lip to reduce friction.

Stud. A slender wood or metal post used as a supporting element in a wall or partition.

Stud Anchor. A device used to secure a stud to the floor.

Subbuck (or Subframe). See **Rough Buck**.

Surface Hinge. A hinge having both leaves attached to the surface and thus fully visible.

Swing. See **Hand**.

Swinging Bolt. A bolt that is hinged to a lock front and is projected and retracted with a swinging rather than a sliding action. Also called *hinged* or *pivot bolt*.

Tail Piece. The unit on the core of a cylinder lock which actuates the bolt or latch.

Tamper-Resistant Hardware. Builders' hardware with screws or nut-and-bolt connections that are hidden or cannot be removed with conventional tools.

Template. A precise detailed pattern used as a guide in the mortising, drilling, etc., of a door or frame to receive hardware.

Template Hardware. Hardware manufactured within template tolerances.

Tension Wrench. An instrument used in picking a lock. It is used to apply torsion to the cylinder core.

Three-Point Lock. A locking device required on "A-label" fire double doors to lock the active door at three points—the normal position plus top and bottom.

Threshold. A wood or metal plate forming the bottom of a doorway.

Throw. See **Bolt Projection**.

Thumb Piece (of a door handle). The small pivoted part above the grip of a door handle, which is pressed by the thumb to operate a latch bolt.

Thumb Turn. A unit which is gripped between the thumb and forefinger, and turned to project or retract a bolt.

Tolerance. The permissible deviation from a nominal or specified dimension or value.

Transom. An opening window immediately above a door

Transom Bar. The horizontal frame member that separates the door opening from the transom.

Transom Catch. A latch bolt fastener on a transom, having a ring by which the latch bolt is retracted.

Transom Chain. A short chain used to limit the opening of a transom; usually provided with a plate at each end for attachment.

Transom Lift. A device attached to a door frame and transom by means of which the transom may be opened or closed.

Trim Hardware. See **Finish Builders' Hardware**.

Tryout Keys. A set of keys that includes many commonly used bittings. They are used one at a time in an attempt to unlock a door.

Tumbler. A movable obstruction in a lock that must be adjusted to a particular position, as by a key, before the bolt can be thrown.

Turn Piece. See **Thumb Turn**.

Unit Lock. See **Preassembled Lock**.

Vertical Bolt Lock. A lock having two deadbolts that move vertically into two circular receivers in the strike portion of the lock attached to the door jamb.

Vision Panel. A fixed transparent panel of glazing material set into an otherwise opaque wall, partition, or door; a nonopening window. See also **Light**.

Ward. An obstruction which prevents the wrong key from entering or turning in a lock.

Warded Lock. A lock containing internal obstacles which block the entrance or rotation of all but the correct key.

Weatherstripping. Narrow or jamb-width sections of flexible material which prevent the passage of air and moisture around windows and doors. Compression weather-stripping also acts as frictional counterbalance in double-hung windows.

Wet Glazing. The sealing of glass or other transparent material in a frame by the use of a glazing compound or sealant.

Window Frame. See **Frame**.

Window Guard. A strong metal gridlike assembly which can be installed on a window or other opening; types of window guards include metal bars, metal-mesh grilles, and sliding metal gates.

Wire Glass. Glass manufactured with a layer of wire mesh approximately in the center of the sheet.

Chapter 9
Security Containers and Storage Areas

CARL ROPER

Corporate, sensitive, or classified government material or information should be used, held, or stored only where there are appropriate protective measures in place or under other conditions that are adequate to prevent unauthorized persons from gaining access to it. The exact nature of the security requirements depends on a thorough security evaluation of local conditions and circumstances. These conditions permit the facility to accomplish its essential functions, while still affording selected items of information a reasonable degree of security protection with a minimum degree of calculated risk that these items are exposed to unauthorized personnel.

Material and information must be stored in approved security containers, vaults, or rooms.

Items having only a monetary value, such as cash, precious metals, jewelry, narcotics, and the like should be stored separately from classified information or other sensitive corporate data. Store these types of items in containers or rooms specifically designated for them. They are *never* intermingled with unlike items.

The most sensitive materials and information are stored in locations that are augmented by the facility security procedures to prevent unauthorized persons from gaining access to the container, vault, or room. The location of the storage equipment within a building or an individual room (which is locked, guarded, or alarmed during nonoperating hours) will have to satisfy any minimum security protection requirements determined by a government contract, commercial contract, insurance requirements, and common sense security practices and procedures.

Storage Equipment Standards

Storage equipment standards (to include rooms and vaults) are based on established and published uniform standards, specifications, and schedules for such containers, vaults, alarm systems, and other associated security devices that are suitable for the storage and protection of classified information and material.

For government and government contractor organizations, the General Services Administration (GSA) issues the appropriate standards. Individual government departments or agencies also have their own security policies and procedural requirements. Here, we will use the most commonly held standard security requirements, that of the Department of Defense (DoD) and the DoD Regulation 5200.1-R.

Facility heads can also establish additional controls to prevent unauthorized access. Such controls are usually developed and coordinated by or through the facility security office and disseminated under the direction of the facility head.

Government security storage containers will bear a "Test Certification Label" on the locking drawer, attesting to the security capabilities of the container and the lock. On some older cabinets, the label is affixed on the inside of the locking drawer compartment. Cabinets manufactured after February 1962 indicate "General Services Administration Approved Security Container" on the outside of the top drawer.

Substandard storage equipment of facility areas (for example, power shelf files, rooms for open storage, or containers not listed on the approved

GSA schedules) may be authorized only for the temporary storage of material, but they are subject to inspection and approval by the site security office prior to their temporary use. The requirement for additional corrective security measures, namely, access controls, alarm systems, special locks, vault-type doors, special construction, as well as the imposition of certain storage limitations upon the user, are not uncommon.

The GSA-approved changeable combination padlock is intended for use only as an indoor or sheltered area protective measure. It is not intended for use either outdoors or to protect against a determined forced entry. This is the only padlock approved for use with locking bar containers. Because of their vulnerability to force, locking bar containers must be limited to the storage of low-level information (confidential for government areas) unless they are situated in a vault or alarmed area. The padlock used is the Sargent and Greenleaf Model 8077 series.

Site security offices should, on request, inspect and evaluate any proposed storage area to determine the type, amount, and degree of security required to afford physical protection equal to or greater than that authorized for classified materials. This will include the various authorities with regard to regulatory requirements for the protection of special access materials.

Storage of Government Classified Material and Information

Classified material and information that is *not* under the personal control and observation of an authorized person must be guarded and stored in an appropriately locked security container.

Top secret information will be stored in a security container having a three-position dial combination lock that is GSA-approved or else stored in a Class A vault or a vault-type room that meets the standards established by the head of an agency or department.

When such containers are maintained in buildings not under U.S. government control, structural enclosures, or other areas, the storage equipment, vault, or vault-type room must also be protected by an alarm system or guarded during nonoperating hours.

An alarmed area—provided that the area can afford protection equal to or better than that indicated above—is used for storage of classified material. This ensures that the protecting physical barrier is adequate to prevent the surreptitious removal of the material and also to prevent observation that would result in the material being compromised. The barrier must be such that a forcible entry attempt will give evidence of the attempted entry into the area. Further, the alarm system must provide an immediate notice of alarm to the security force that an attempted entry is being perpetrated.

The security guard force must respond within a time limit of 5 minutes at most; the typical response time should be 2–3 minutes. Actual response time will vary depending on location of the alarm and location of the responding guard. Note that if at least one individual of the security guard force is a "rover" (on patrol throughout the facility), the response time may vary. Some organizations maintain two personnel at the security alarm system so that one of them can respond immediately. Thus, one person maintains the alarm monitor panel continuously while the second responds to the alarm within the allotted time frame. This also ensures that the panel is never left unattended. If such conditions cannot be met, then top secret storage should neither be permitted nor authorized.

Supplementing the vault with a security container within, assuming the vault is within a substantially constructed and secured building or room and either guarded or alarmed, will satisfy the minimal requirements for the protection of top secret storage.

Guard force personnel need not be cleared for top secret if they are positioned external to the building, vault, or room and are not expected to ever have access. They should, if possible, or by contract guidelines, have at least a secret level security clearance. Inability to meet these standards will mean that the use of augmented security personnel in the area will be required continually to respond to situations that may arise.

Secret and confidential information should be stored in the manner as authorized top secret, a Class B vault, a vault-type room, or secure storage room meeting appropriate standards; until phased out, in a steel filing cabinet having a built-in three-position dial combination lock; or, as a last resort, an existing steel filing cabinet equipped with a steel lock bar, provided it is secured by an approved, changeable combination lock. In this latter instance, the keepers and staples for the locking bar must be secured to the cabinet by welding, rivets, or peeved bolts. Other supplementary controls may also be required.

The actual combination lock used for various types of security containers and vaults must be one that meets GSA standards for government and contractor personnel. The GSA standard is an excellent choice for private concerns also. Specifically, the item of concern becomes: What are the interior tumbler wheels made of—metal or a plastic-like material? If the wheels are metal, the security of the container has just been lowered. Metal wheels are subject to x-ray and the combination can be determined within 30 minutes. Nonmetallic wheels cannot be x-rayed and thus provide a higher level of security against attempted entry. Government security containers that hold classified material cannot have metal wheels. This is also a good argument for private industry to upgrade its containers to protect against possible x-ray of the locking mechanism as a means to determine the combination.

Other storage equipment and requirements include:

1. Field safes and one-drawer containers (able to be carried or easily moved by one individual) can be used for the storage of classified information in situations outside the facility and for the transport of classified information. These containers must be securely fastened or guarded to prevent theft.
2. Map and plan file containers are for the storage of odd-sized items such as computer cards, maps, and charts.
3. Storage areas for bulky materials, other than top secret, must have access openings secured by either changeable combination padlock or a key-operated padlock with a high-security cylinder. The key-operated padlock should have either an exposed or shrouded shackle to protect against forced entry attack on the lock itself.

When combination padlocks are used, their keys are controlled as classified information with classification equal to that of the information being protected

- the keys do not circulate and are not retained by individuals on their person, but are maintained within a security container or other continuous level of protection;
- a key and lock custodian must be appointed to ensure the proper custody and handling of keys and locks;
- a key and lock register must be maintained to identify keys for each lock, their current location, and custody;
- all locks and keys must be audited each month;
- an inventory of keys with the change of custodian responsible for container and applicable keys;
- keys cannot be removed from the premises;
- keys and spare locks must be protected in a secure container;
- no master keying is authorized; and

- locks shall be changed or rotated annually and must be replaced on the loss or compromise of a key.

Hasps that enclose the padlock should be used in high-security applications because they will enhance security by providing the lock a greater level of protection against forcible attack. A chain, when required, should be used with an exposed shackle padlock. Use $3/8$-inch tool-resistant, case-hardened security chain or $3/8$-inch trade size, grade 80 alloy steel chain.

Additional security safeguards to be applied under these types of storage conditions are detailed in this chapter.

Please remember that perfect or absolute security is always a formidable goal, but a state of absolute security can never be attained. No object is so well protected that it cannot be stolen, damaged, destroyed, or observed, given time and expertise. The purpose, therefore, of physical security standards and requirements is to make access so difficult that an intruder will hesitate to attempt penetration or to provide for the intruder's apprehension should the intruder continue to attempt unauthorized entry.

Procurement and Phase-in of Equipment

Any time a security container is requested, facility security personnel must survey current on hand security containers to determine if it is (or is not) feasible to use available equipment or to retire, return, declassify, or destroy it by the security office. Individuals should not change any combinations themselves.

Container Repair

Repair of security containers usually calls for the neutralization of lockouts or the repair of any damage that may affect the security integrity of a container. Such neutralization and repair will be accomplished only by those individuals so authorized, who are cleared or continuously escorted while so engaged. In many instances, the actual repair of the container will be effected by a contracted company. At such times, the damaged container or container drawer may be removed from the premises by the contractor for repair and then returned to the facility.

A container is considered restored to its original state of security integrity when all damaged or altered parts are replaced. It is also considered restored when a container has been drilled immediately adjacent to or through the container dial ring to neutralize the lockout, the replacement lock is equal to the original container equipment, and the drilled hole is repaired with a tapered, hardened steel pin or a steel dowel, drill bit, or bearing with a diameter slightly larger than the hole. This pin or rod is of such a length that when driven into the hole, there remains at each end a recess greater than $\frac{1}{2}$ inch and less than $\frac{3}{16}$ inch deep to permit the acceptance of substantial welds, and the rod is welded both on the inside and outside surfaces. The outside of the drawer head must then be puttied, sanded, and repainted so that no visible evidence of the hole or its repair remains on the outer surface.

Containers that have been drilled in a location or repaired in the manner described above are acceptable. Those that have had a hole drilled in another location, cut, burned, or sliced to gain entry, or repaired in a manner *other* than as specified is not considered restored to their original integrity. The test certification label on the locking drawer and the "GSA-approved security container" label, if any, must be removed immediately from such containers.

If a damaged security container is repaired with welds, rivets, or bolts that cannot be removed and is replaced without leaving evidence of entry, the security container is limited to the storage of secret and confidential classified information.

When any damage is repaired using methods other than those described, the use of the security container will be limited to unclassified information. A notice to this effect should be affixed to or marked on the front of the security container in such a manner that its removal would be difficult and noticeable. If any combination to the container is maintained in the security office files, this must be indicated on it. Also, the facility listing of security containers should indicate that the container is not authorized for classified storage.

Security containers are usually serviceable for approximately 25 years if they have been properly serviced and maintained. Lock or locking bolt linkage malfunctions requiring the neutralization of the container will shorten their life span.

Signs of trouble that indicate a security container may or does have problems.

1. A dial that is unusually loose (to include in and out play) or is difficult to turn.
2. Any movement of the dial ring (determined by applying a twist to the dial ring to detect this).

3. Difficulty in dialing the combination or opening of the container. Some examples include:
   - The need to dial the combination more than once when human error is not at fault.
   - The need to dial numbers slightly above or below the correct number of the combination.
4. Difficulty with the control drawer or other drawers, in such areas as:
   - Drawers rubbing against the container walls. The container may not be level or the tracks (or cradles) may not be aligned properly.
   - Problems with opening or closing drawers because the tracks (or cradles) need lubricant, material is jammed behind the drawer, or the internal locking mechanism is tripped.
5. Difficulties in locking the control drawer, such as:
   - The drawer handle or latch will not return to the locking position when the drawer is closed.
   - On Sargent and Greenleaf locking devices, the butterfly in the center of the dial will not turn after the control drawer is shut and the dial has been turned to "0."
   - The locking bolts move roughly, slip, or drag, or the linkage is burred or deformed.

Users should be alert for early warning symptoms; when they are detected, the appropriate support offices should be contacted. Personnel should never use force to try to correct a problem. Critically needed material should not be stored in containers that exhibit any of these symptoms, because they are not dependable and the user may be "locked out."

Container Classifications and Lock Group Types

For the government, Executive Order 10101, as amended, established the requirement that whenever new security container equipment is procured it should, to the maximum extent feasible and practicable, also be of the type designated as approved for storage of classified material.

Each approved container, including vault doors, will have a label attached to the front. Before 1993, the lettering for the identification label was in black, after that date the lettering was changed to red.

In addition to the label, the control drawer of security containers and the inside of safe and vault doors will bear a test certification label. This label will indicate the class of the container and how long the container will resist forced and surreptitious entry, radiological attack, and manipulation of the locking device.

GSA-approved security containers also have an identification label.

Containers that are used for the storage of government classified information should have all three of these labels. The test certification and identification labels are always located on the side of the control drawer.

Contractor facilities, and others throughout private industry, can also use the GSA standards for the protection of company grade materials and are required to use such standards when working on U.S. government contracts with various departments and agencies of the government. The standards set by safe manufacturers and coordinated with the National Fire Protection Association (NFPA) are also recognized as being adequate to protect other types of materials and information.

Classes of Containers

- **Class I**—An approved insulated container that will resist 20 man-minutes against forced entry, 20 man-minutes against surreptitious entry, 20 man-hours against manipulation of the lock, and 20 man-hours against radiological attack. Must have nonmetallic wheels.
- **Class II**—An approved insulated security container that will resist 5 man-minutes against forced entry, 20 man-minutes against surreptitious entry, 20 man-hours against manipulation of the lock, and 20 man-hours against radiological attack. This type normally has metal wheels.
- **Class III**—An approved noninsulated security container that will resist zero man-minutes against forced entry, 20 man-minutes against manipulation of the lock, and 20 man-hours against radiological attack. Class III containers have been removed from the Federal Supply Schedule and replaced by Class V and VI containers. Class III containers already in use or on hand may be used in lieu of Class V and VI containers until replacement is needed.
- **Class IV**—An approved noninsulated security container that will resist 5 man-minutes against forced entry, 30 man-minutes against surreptitious entry, 2 man-hours against manipulation of the lock, and 20 man-hours against radiological attack. Class IV containers have been deleted from the supply schedule and replaced by Class V and VI containers.

- **Class V**—An approved noninsulated security container that will resist 10 man-minutes against forced entry, 30 man-minutes against surreptitious entry, 20 man-hours against manipulation of the lock, and 20 man-hours against radiological attack.
- **Class VI**—An approved noninsulated security container that will afford zero man-minutes against forced entry, 30 man-minutes against surreptitious entry, 20 man-hours against manipulation of the lock, and 20 man-hours against radiological attack.

Vault Doors

The above protection applies only to the door assembly and not the entire vault.

Note that only Classes V and VI are in use today. The previous classes of containers should not be used. The exception to this rule within government is that any of the previously approved GSA containers that have been in *continuous use* may continue to be used until they are taken out of service. This means that even if a container is emptied and turned in to the organization supply room for only one day, it cannot be reissued to another office for certain types of storage.

Combination Lock Groups

- **Group 1 Lock**—A UL classification for combination locks having a possibility of at least 1,000,000 combinations and will resist manipulation for at least 20 man-hours. A Group 1-R combination lock will also resist radiological attack for at least 20 man-hours. The group marking on combination locks is found on the rear faceplate or cover of the lock.
- **Group 2 Lock**—A UL classification for a combination lock that has a possibility of at least 1,000,000 combinations but is susceptible to manipulation by skilled personnel. The lock, with metallic wheels, will not be used for the storage of government classified information.
- **Combination Padlocks**—There are only a few models that fall in the category of changeable combination padlocks that are currently in use and were manufactured and procured under federal specifications by GSA. All four models are manufactured by Sargent and Greenleaf. It is possible that with improving state-of-the-art

technology in locking devices, others will soon become available.

- **Model 8088**—This model has been replaced by Model 8077A, which is described below. There are several models of the 8088, but none are approved for use on security containers.
- **Model 8077**—This is similar in physical appearance to the 8088 but has a chromed lock case. Most of the dial is concealed, except the portion near the number being dialed. The combination change hole is in the rear of the lock, concealed by a sliding back-plate. This lock is serially numbered both on the shackle and on the rear of the lock to prevent lock substitution. This model is no longer approved for use on security containers, but other authorized 8077 models still maintain the serial numbering system.
- **Model 8077A, A8,** or **AC**—This lock is similar to the 8077 model except for the modification of the sliding back cover. The back cover is manufactured in heavy steel plate, which provides additional security not provided by the 8077 model. This lock is approved for use on security containers.
- **Model 8077AD**—In mid-1995, the S&G 8077AD was approved. This most recent combination padlock has dialing tolerances tighter than any previous models. Because of this, the dial must be viewed straight on rather than from the side or even from a slight angle to ensure accuracy. This becomes more critical when changing the lock's combination.
- **Model 8065**—This is a special padlock without an external shackle. It looks somewhat like models 8077 and 8077A without a shackle. This lock is designed for use in situations where the lock can be placed flat against the locked surface over a suitable locking staple.
- **Moss-Hamilton X-07**—This is a somewhat recent combination lock (1993) that operates on a principle not used in any other locking device currently on the market. It has an interior computer chip and operates on battery power that is generated when the dial is first rotated. It is a unique combination lock and, as of 1993, is the only authorized lock for new containers or lock replacement. The cost is several times more than the S&G model. As of this writing, the X-07 is the only lock that meets government combination lock standards.
- **Model 6120**—In 1994, the Sargent & Greenleaf Company developed this motorized, electronic combination lock. This is a tamper-proof, electronic-controlled lock that has proven to be 100%

resistant to vibration attacks, unlike some solenoid or mechanical locks. It provides the security normally reserved for a UL Group 1 lock.

As of 1995, S&G have developed a competitor to the Moss-Hamilton X-07. Similar to the X-07, it is unique, full of computer electronics, and is now in the testing phase. It is expected to be priced somewhat lower than the X-07. Using the "hands on" technique to compare it to the X-07, the S&G competitor was determined to be easier to use, easier to set or reset, and less complicated to figure out.

Storage Vaults and Rooms

Storage vaults for use in the storage of classified information are used in all types of facilities. Acceptable vault construction standards are shown in Table 9-1.

When considering purchasing and installing—or converting a room to—a storage vault, consider facility insurance requirements. Insurance companies will

Table 9-1. Minimum Construction Standards for Class A, B, and C Vaults

Vault Classification	Approved Storage Level	Thickness		
		Floor	Walls	Ceiling
A	Top Secret	8″ RC[1]	8″ RC	8″ RC
B	Secret	4″ RC	8″[2]	4″ RC
C	Confidential	4″ C[1]	8″[3]	4″ RC

RC = Reinforced concrete; C = Concrete without reinforcement and C vaults

NOTES:
1. All concrete used in vault construction will be monolithic cast in place, conforming to a minimum compressive strength of 3000 psi after 28 days of aging. Reinforcing will be by a minimum $\frac{5}{8}$-inch diameter steel reinforcing bars (rebar) laid to a maximum of 6 inches on centers, creating a cross-hatched steel curtain, to be sandwiched at half thickness of the concrete, parallel to the longest surface. Rebar will be anchored or embedded in all contiguous walls/surfaces.
2. Class B vault walls will be constructed of masonry at least 8 inches thick, such as brick or concrete block employing adequate bond. Hollow masonry, only of the vertical cell (load-bearing) type, can also be used, but if used, each cell will have from ceiling to floor 1/2-inch diameter or larger rebar inserted, and then be filled with pea gravel and Portland cement grout. Rebar will be anchored in both floor and ceiling to a depth of at least 4 inches. In seismic areas, 6 inches or thicker RC will be required.
3. Class C vaults will be constructed of thick-shell concrete block or vertical cell clad tile and be not less than 8 inches thick. In areas of somewhat frequent seismic activity, 6 inches or thicker RC should be used.

set certain construction and protection standards commensurate with those of banking institutions for the protection of certain types of valuable documents or other information, to say nothing of monetary instruments.

Storage rooms or areas converted to storage must meet several acceptable minimum standards. Such rooms are usually within security-controlled access areas, thus they do not follow the standard storage vault criteria. Such rooms, with some exceptions, are not used for open storage of classified material.

Rooms or open areas within a facility controlled area that are converted to storage rooms for classified material will have the following standards applied:

1. True floor to true ceiling walls, appropriately covered so that an attempted penetration can be easily discovered.
2. A solid wood or metal-clad door.
3. A three-position dial-type approved combination lock mounted on the door.
4. An interior intrusion detection alarm system sensor(s).

Areas that have been authorized for the temporary open storage of classified material will also meet the above standards. All such areas should be visually checked at least once every 90 days by a security office representative. A continuing need for open storage will be resubmitted and rejustified every 12 months for approval or disapproval by facility security office personnel.

Within the subject area of security containers, vaults, and classified storage rooms, physical security personnel must also evaluate the responsibilities and precautions with regard to the custodian/supervisor. For the protection of information and other material, it is important to consider the custodial responsibilities, care during and after normal working hours, and the designation of security container combinations.

Custodian Responsibilities

Custodians are responsible for providing protection and accountability of information at all times and for ensuring that such information is locked in appropriate security containers whenever it is not in use or under the direct supervision of an authorized individual. The custodian must follow prescribed regulatory guidance, including facility policy and procedures, to ensure that unauthorized persons do not gain access to such information.

In government areas, only the activity or facility head (or the assigned designee) may authorize the removal of classified information from designated working areas. Check appropriate regulations to ensure maximum protection of the material; the removal is permitted only if operational requirements exist for its removal. Personal convenience on the part of an employee is not justification for approval of a request to remove information from the facility. Each authorization request for removal must be handled individually. Finally, authorization will only be granted when the materials can be protected under adequate security safeguards.

At government installations, the responsibility for protecting sensitive, unclassified, or classified material is the responsibility of each and every individual. Security regulations and policy do not guarantee protection and cannot be written to cover all situations. Thus, a logical interpretation of the regulations must be applied using common sense and security principles. Recently, government regulations have changed such that an agency head must authorize the removal of classified information; this is under much more stringent rules than before.

Care During Working Hours

All personnel shall take appropriate precautions to prevent unauthorized access to classified or unclassified sensitive material. Classified material removed from a security container shall be kept under constant surveillance and should be face down or covered when it is not in use. Appropriately designed classified document cover sheets shall be used. These are attached to the face of a classified document whenever it is removed from a security container.

Preliminary drafts, carbon sheets, plates, stencils, stenographic notes, worksheets, typewriter ribbons, and other items containing classified or other sensitive information shall either be destroyed immediately after having served their purpose or shall be handled and protected equivalently to the information they contain.

Destruction of typewriter ribbons, printer ribbons, personal computer diskettes, and the like, from which classified or sensitive information can be obtained, shall be protected in the same manner as the information they contain, or else they shall be destroyed by burning.

Although we are in the computer age, many people keep old typewriters. Keep in mind that after the upper and lower sections of a fabric ribbon have been cycled through and overprinted five times, they may be treated as unclassified, regardless of their classified use thereafter. Carbon and plastic ribbons and carbon paper that has been used in the production of material should be destroyed, but further considerations of future technology must be considered also.

Currently, any ribbon that uses a technology that enables a ribbon to be struck several times in the same area before it moves to the next position may be treated as unclassified/nonsensitive. However, in the not-too-distant future, a technology will emerge that allows such ribbons to be read or deciphered, thus rendering this policy unworkable. Whenever possible, therefore, typewriter ribbons that fall into this category should be considered classified and handled as such. Destruction of the ribbon by burning, shredding, or some other means will ensure that information cannot be reconstituted.

End-of-Day Security Checks

A system of security checks must be established for each facility at the end of the work day. This ensures that the physical protection of all classified or sensitive classified material is taken into consideration and appropriate protective measures are applied:

- All classified material must be stored in approved security containers.
- Burn bags are properly stored or destroyed.
- Wastebaskets do not contain classified material.
- Desks, tables, or other work areas are free of classified and other extraneous, but related, materials. (A "clean desk" policy is always best.)
- All security containers have been locked by one individual and checked by *another* individual.
- The entire office area for each portion of a facility has been given a complete visual examination to ensure that no classified or sensitive unclassified material has been left out.

Security Container Combinations and Designations

Security containers should be individually numbered for control purposes. There should be nothing on the outside of the container that indicates what types or levels of information are stored in the container.

Only the individuals who have the responsibility and appropriate level security clearance must change security container combinations. Combinations shall be changed:

1. When placed in use.
2. When an individual knowing the combination no longer requires access.
3. When the combination or container has been subject to possible compromise.
4. At least annually, unless other procedures or regulatory guidance dictate otherwise.
5. When the container is taken out of service. At such times, built-in combination locks shall be reset to a standard combination of 50–25–50, while combination padlocks shall be reset to a standard combination of 10–20–30.

Security container combinations, including vaults and storage rooms, shall be assigned a security classification level equal to the highest level of material authorized to be stored in them. A record must be maintained of the combination for each vault, secure room, or container. The record will have the location of the container; the name(s), home address(es), and telephone number(s) of the individual(s) authorized access; and the date the container combination was last changed. The dissemination of the container combination will be restricted to those individuals with a valid need to know. A master combination storage area within a security container that belongs to the facility security office is a true necessity—it ensures proper control of the combinations that allow access to all other security containers within the facility.

Custodians, not to mention the facility security personnel and personnel of affected offices, must realize that electrically actuated locks (cipher and magnetic strip card locks) do not afford any reasonable measure of true security protection. These type devices should never be used as a substitute for a proper locking device or for securing company-sensitive or government classified information. Cipher locks and the like are only *a temporary delay device*, never a true lock. This way of thinking must apply even to short periods of time when the office may be vacant and individuals are "just down the hall a moment."

Chapter 10
Security Lighting*

PHILIP P. PURPURA,
LAWRENCE J. FENNELLY, and
GERARD HONEY

From a business perspective, lighting can be justified because it improves sales by making a business and merchandise more attractive, promotes safety and prevents lawsuits, improves employee morale and productivity, and enhances the value of real estate. From a security perspective, two major purposes of lighting are *to create a psychological deterrent to intrusion* and *to enable detection*. Good lighting is considered such an effective crime control method that the law, in many locales, requires buildings to maintain adequate lighting.

On way to analyze lighting deficiencies is to go to the building at night and study the possible methods of entry and areas where inadequate lighting will aid a burglar. Before the visit, one should contact local police as a precaution against mistaken identity and recruit their assistance in spotting weak points in lighting.

What lighting level aids an intruder? Most people believe that, under conditions of darkness, a criminal can safely commit a crime. But this view may be faulty, in that one generally cannot work in the dark. Three possible levels of light are bright light, darkness, and dim light. *Bright light* affords an offender plenty of light to work but enables easy observation by others; it deters crime. Without light, in *darkness*, a burglar finds that he or she cannot see to jimmy a good lock, release a latch, or do whatever work is necessary to gain access. However, *dim light* provides just enough light to break and enter while hindering observation by authorities. Support for this view was

shown in a study of crimes during full-moon phases, when dim light was produced.

This study examined the records of 972 police shifts at 3 police agencies, for a 2-year period, to compare 9 different crimes during full moon and nonfull-moon phases. Only one crime, breaking and entering, was greater during full-moon phases.[1]

Although much case law supports lighting as an indicator of efforts to provide a safe environment, security specialists are questioning conventional wisdom about lighting.[2] Because so much nighttime lighting goes unused, should it be reduced or turned off? Does an offender look more suspicious under a light or in the dark with a flashlight? Should greater use be made of motion-activated lighting? How would these approaches affect safety and cost-effectiveness? These questions are ripe for research.

Illumination[3]

Lumens (of light output) per watt (of power input) is a measure of lamp efficiency. Initial lumens-per-watt data are based on the light output of lamps when new; however, light output declines with use. *Illuminance* is the intensity of light falling on a surface, measure in foot-candles (English units) or lux (metric units). The *foot-candle* (FC) is a measure of how bright the light is when it reaches 1 foot from the source. One lux equals 0.0929 FC. The light provided by direct sunlight on clear days is about 10,000 FC, an overcast day would yield about 100 FC, and a full moon about 0.01 FC. A sample of outdoor lighting illuminances recommended by the Illuminating Engineering Society of North America are as follows: self-parking area, 1 FC; attendant parking area, 2 FC; covered parking area, 5 FC; active pedestrian entrance, 5 FC; building surroundings, 1 FC. It generally is recommended that gates and doors,

*Purpura, *Security and Loss Prevention, Fourth Edition,* pp. 212–216, Butterworth Heinemann, 2002
Tyska and Fennelly, *Physical Security: 150 Things You Should Know*, Butterworth Heinemann, 2000
Honey, *Emergency and Security Lighting*, pp. 190–191, Newnes, 2001

where identification of persons and things takes place, should have at least 2 FC. An office should have a light level of about 50 FC.

Care should be exercised when studying FC. Are they horizontal or vertical? Horizontal Illuminance many not aid in the visibility of vertical objects such as signs and keyholes. (The preceding FC are horizontal.) The FC vary depending on the distance from the lamp and the angle. If you hold a light meter horizontally, it often gives a different reading that if you hold it vertically. Are the FC initial or maintained?

Maintenance and bulb replacement ensures high-quality lighting.

Lamps[4]

The following lamps are applied outdoors:

- *Incandescent* lamps are commonly found at residences. Passing electrical current through a tungsten wire that becomes white-hot produces light. These lamps produce 10–20 lumens per watt, are the least efficient and most expensive to operate, and have a short lifetime of from 1000–2000 hours.
- *Halogen* and *quart halogen* lamps are incandescent bulbs filled with halogen gas (like sealed-beam auto headlights) and provide about 25% better efficiency and life than ordinary incandescent bulbs.
- *Fluorescent* lamps pass electricity through a gas enclosed in a glass tube to produce light, yielding 40–80 lumens per watt. They create twice the light and less than half the heat of an incandescent bulb of equal wattage and cost 5–10 times as much. Fluorescent lamps do not provide high levels of light output. The lifetime is 10,000–15,000 hours. They are not used extensively outdoors, except for signage.
- *Mercury vapor* lamps also pass electricity through a gas. The yield is 30–60 lumens per watt and the life is about 20,000 hours.
- *Metal halide* lamps are also of the gaseous type. The yield is 80–100 lumens per watt, and the life is about 10,000 hours. They often are used at sports stadiums because they imitate daylight conditions and colors appear natural. Consequently, these lamps complement CCTV systems, but they are the most expensive light to install and maintain.
- *High-pressure sodium* lamps are gaseous, yield about 100 lumens per watt, have a life of about 20,000 hours, and are energy efficient. These lamps are often applied on streets and parking lots and are designed to allow the eyes to see more detail at greater distances (for example, through fog).
- *Low-pressure sodium* lamps are gaseous, produce 150 lumens per watt, have a life of about 15,000 hours, and are even more efficient than high-pressure sodium. These lamps are expensive to maintain.

Each type of lamp has a different *color rendition*, which is the way a lamp's output affects human perceptions of color. Incandescent, fluorescent, and certain types of metal halide lamps provide excellent color rendition. Mercury vapor lamps provide good color rendition but are heavy on the blue. High-pressure sodium lamps, which are used extensively outdoors, provide poor color rendition, making things look yellow. Low-pressure sodium lamps make color unrecognizable and produce a yellow-gray color on objects. People find they produce a strange yellow haze. Claims are made that this lighting conflicts with aesthetic values and affects sleeping habits. In many instances, when people park their vehicles in a parking lot during the day and return to find their vehicle at night, they are often unable to locate it because of poor color rendition from sodium lamps; some report their vehicles as being stolen. Another problem is the inability of witnesses to describe offenders accurately.

Mercury vapor, metal halide, and high-pressure sodium take several minutes to produce full light output. If they are turned off, even more time is required to reach full output because they first have to cool down. This may not be acceptable for certain security applications. Incandescent, halogen, and quartz halogen have the advantage of instant light once electricity is turned on. Manufacturers can provide information on a host of lamp characteristics including the "strike" and "restrike" time.

The following three sources provide additional information on lighting:

- National Lighting Bureau (*http://www.nlb.org?*): Publications.
- Illuminating Engineering Society of North America (*http://www.iesna.org/*): Technical materials and services; recommended practices and standards; many members are engineers.
- International Association of Lighting Management Companies (*http://www.nalmco.org/*): Seminars, training, and certification programs.

Lighting Equipment

Incandescent or gaseous discharge lamps are used in streetlights. Fresnel lights have a wide flat beam that is directed outward to protect a perimeter, glaring in the faces of those approaching. A floodlight "floods" an area with a beam of light, resulting in considerable glare. Floodlights are stationary, although the light beams can be aimed to select positions. The following strategies reinforce good lighting:

1. Locate perimeter lighting to allow illumination of both sides of the barrier.
2. Direct lights down and away from a facility to create glare for an intruder. Make sure the directed lighting does not hinder observation by patrolling officer.
3. Do not leave dark spaces between lighted areas for burglars to move in. Design lighting to permit overlapping illumination.
4. Protect the lighting system: Locate lighting inside the barrier, install protective covers over lamps, mount lamps on high poles, bury power lines, and protect switch boxes.
5. Photoelectric cells will enable light to go on and off automatically in response to natural light. Manual operation is helpful as a backup.
6. Consider motion-activated lighting for external and internal areas.
7. If lighting is required in the vicinity of navigable waters, contact the U.S. Coast Guard.
8. Try not to disturb neighbors by intense lighting.
9. Maintain a supply of portable, emergency lights and auxiliary power in the event of a power failure.
10. Good interior lighting also deters burglars. Locating lights over safes, expensive merchandise, and other valuables and having large clear windows (especially in retail establishments) lets passing patrol officers see in.
11. If necessary, join other business owners to petition local government to install improved street lighting.

Twenty-Five Things You Need to Know about Lighting[5]

1. *Foot-candle* is out. Lux is in.
2. *Foot-candle* is a measure of light on a surface 1 square foot in area on which one unit of light (lumen) is distributed.
3. *Lumen* is a unit of light output from a lamp.
4. *Lamp* is a term that refers to light sources that are called *bulbs*.
5. *Lux* is the measurement of illumination.
6. *Illuminare* is the intensity of light that falls on an object.
7. *Brightness* is the intensity of the sensation from which light is seen by the eye.
8. *Foot-lambert* is a measure of brightness.
9. *Glare* is excessive brightness.
10. *Luminare* is a complete lighting unit. Consists of one or more lamps joined with other parts that distributes light, protects the lamp, positions or directs it, and connects it to a power source.
11. *Ballast* is a device used with fluorescent and high intensity discharge lamps to obtain voltage and current to operate the lamps.
12. *High intensity discharge* (HID) is the term used to identify four types of lamps: mercury vapor, metal halide, and high- and low-pressure sodium.
13. *Coefficient of utilization* is the ratio of the light delivered from a luminare to a surface compared to the total light output from a lamp.
14. *Contrast* is the relationship between the brightness of an object and its immediate background.
15. *Diffuser* is a device on the bottom or sides of a luminare to redirect or spread light from a source.
16. *Fixture* is a luminare.
17. *Lens* is a glass or plastic shield that covers the bottom of a luminare to control the direction and brightness of the light as it comes out of the fixture or luminare.
18. *Louvers* are a series of baffles arranged in a geometric pattern. They shield a lamp from direct view to avoid glare.
19. *Uniform lighting* refers to a system of lighting that directs the lighting specifically on the work or job rather than on the surrounding areas.
20. *Reflector* is a device used to redirect light from a lamp.
21. *Task* or *work lighting* is the amount of light that falls on an object of work.
22. *Veiling reflection* is the reflection of light from an object that obscures the detail to be observed by reducing the contrast between the object and its background.
23. *Incandescent lamps* produce light by the passing an electric current through a tungsten filament in a glass bulb. They are the least efficient type of bulb.
24. *Fluorescent lamps* are the second most common source of light. They draw an electric arc along the length of a tube. The ultraviolet light pro-

duced by the arc activates a phosphor coating on the walls of the tube, which causes light.

25. Of all of the HID lamps (mercury vapor, metal halide, high- and low-pressure sodium), the low-pressure sodium is the most efficient.

Energy Management

The efficiency and management of lighting is becoming a high-priority in commissioning new buildings and upgrading existing systems. Indeed, the subject of energy management is expected to become one of the most important considerations within the building regulation documents and will have a tremendous impact on the way that the construction industry looks at energy. It is apparent that serious measures must now be taken to reduce energy use and waste. This will have an impact on security lighting and the way that it is applied. Lighting experts show an increasing urge to work alongside electrical contractors and installers to help them increase their business opportunities by identifying the roles and applications in which energy-efficient lighting should be installed. Electrical contractors are being better educated in lighting design that is effective and energy efficient.

The needs are therefore to equip personnel to:

- Recognize inefficient installations.
- Appreciate the environmental, cost, and associated benefits of energy-efficient lighting schemes.
- Estimate energy cost savings and calculate the payback period.
- Recognize the situations in which expert and specialist knowledge is needed in the design of management systems.
- Think in terms of increasing business but while accepting the need to save the environment.

At certain points in time, it was said that lighting any system proved an advantage. However, we are now seeing a trend away from large floodlights illuminating the night sky with a strong white glare, as exterior lighting is becoming much more focused on the minimum lux levels required. We are also seeing a move toward directional beams.

The lighting industry wants to remove itself from a proliferation of public and private external lighting schemes to counter the light pollution problem and become more energy and cost conscious in its makeup. There must be a mechanism to tackle the problem of countless floodlights, up lighters, spotlights, and decorative installations. An array of security lighting forms that are badly installed and specified, create light pollution and use high energy levels.

Lighting pollution is now at the forefront of debates for two main reasons:

- Light pollution spoils the natural effect of the night skies.
- The greater the light pollution, the greater the power consumption.

Unfortunately, a certain degree of light pollution is needed to satisfy safety and security applications. Equally, there is always the desire to have purely decorative lighting installations, so the answer lies in a compromise. Systems must be designed with a degree of thought given to the avoidance of light pollution and energy waste. External lighting must provide minimal light pollution, a safe environment, and an attractive feature. For attractive features, we can see a greater use of fiber optic solutions with color changing effects lighting engineered to direct the illumination downwards. Bollards or recessed ground luminaries can be set into walkways so there is no spill into the night sky. Intelligently designed schemes can ensure that lighting is reflected only in a downward direction, so that pedestrians are better guided and the lighting has a pleasing effect with little overspill.

Therefore, within the lighting industry, the need is recognized to raise standards in all aspects associated with light and lighting, in particular when it comes to energy management and light pollution. We need to define and harness the pleasures of lighting but at the same time promote the benefits of well-designed energy efficient schemes among the public at large. There must also be miniaturization and increased lamp life. Energy management must therefore be a part of security lighting.

We can look at a number of ways in which we can recognize waste and exploit the opportunity to a benefit. These all have security lighting involvement.

By improving energy management we can make greater use of security lighting, so it becomes apparent that a part of security lighting must be energy management. Demand-switched lighting has long been known as cost saving because using this technique ensures that luminaries are only energized when lighting is needed. Low energy extended period lighting can equally exploit the opportunity of replacing lighting that is wasting energy.[6]

Lighting Checklist

1. Is the entire perimeter lighted?
2. Is there a strip of light on both sides of the fence?

3. Is the illumination sufficient to detect man movement easily at 100 yards?
4. Are lights checked for operation daily prior to darkness?
5. Is extra lighting available at entry points and points of possible intrusion?
6. Are lighting repairs made promptly?
7. Is the power supply for lights easily accessible (for tampering)?
8. Are lighting circuit drawings available to facilitate quick repairs?
9. Switches and controls—are they
   a. Protected?
   b. Weatherproof and tamper resistant?
   c. Accessible to security personnel?
   d. Inaccessible from outside the perimeter barrier?
   e. Equipped with centrally located master switch(es)?
10. Is the illumination for guards on all routes inside the perimeter?
11. Are the materials and equipment in receiving, shipping, and storage areas adequately lighted?
12. Are bodies of water on perimeter adequately lighted?
13. Is an auxiliary source of power available for protective lighting?

16. Is there an auxiliary power source available?
17. Is the interior of buildings adequately lighted?
18. Are top secret and secret activities adequately lighted?
19. Are guards equipped with powerful flashlights?
20. How many more and what type of lights are needed to provide adequate illumination? In what locations?
21. Do security personnel report light outages?
22. How soon are burned-out lights replaced?
23. Are open areas of the campus sufficiently lighted to discourage illegal or criminal acts against pedestrians?
24. Are there any areas with high-growing shrubs or woods where the light is not sufficient?
25. Are the outsides of buildings holding valuable or critical activities or materials lighted?
26. Are interiors of hallways and entrances lighted when buildings are open at night?
27. Are areas surrounding women's dormitories well lighted?
28. Are campus parking lots lighted sufficiently to discourage tampering with parked cars or other illegal activities?
29. Are areas where materials of high value are stored well lighted? Safes, libraries, bookstores, food storage areas, etc.?

Protective Lighting Checklist

1. Is protective lighting adequate on perimeter?
2. What type of lighting is it?
3. Is lighting of open areas within perimeter adequate?
4. Do shadowed areas exist?
5. Are outside storage areas adequately lighted?
6. Are inside areas adequately lighted?
7. Is the guard protected or exposed by the lighting?
8. Are gates adequately lighted?
9. Do lights at gate illuminate interior of vehicles?
10. Are critical and vulnerable areas well illuminated?
11. Is protective lighting operated manually or automatically?
12. Do cones of light on perimeter overlap?
13. Are perimeter lights wired in series?
14. Is the lighting at shipping and receiving docks or piers adequate?
15. Is lighting in the parking lots adequate?

References

1. Philip Purpura. "Police Activity and the Full Moon," *Journal of Police Science and Administration 7*, no. 3 (September 1979), p. 350.
2. Henri Berube. "New Notions of Night Light," *Security Management* (December 1994), pp. 29–33.
3. National Lighting Bureau. *Lighting for Safety and Security* (Washington, DC: National Lighting Bureau, n.d.), pp. 1–36; Mary S. Smith. *Crime Prevention through Environmental Design in Parking Facilities* (Washington, DC: National Institute of Justice, April 1996), pp. 1–4; Dan M. Bowers. "Let There Be Light," *Security Management* (September 1995), pp. 103–111; Douglas R. Kunze and John Schiefer. "An Illuminating Look at Light," *Security Management* (September 1995), pp. 113–116.
4. Dan M. Bowers. "Let There Be Light," *Security Management* (September 1995), pp. 103–111.
5. Louis A. Tyska and Lawrence J. Fennelly. *Physical Security, 150 Things You Should Know.* Boston: Butterworth–Heinemann, 2000, pp. 155–156.
6. Gerard Honey. *Emergency & Security Lighting*, Boston: Neunes, Butterworth–Heinemann, 2001, pp. 190–191.

Chapter 11

Alarms: Intrusion Detection Systems

MIKE ROLF and JAMES CULLITY

Burglary is a big business. Moreover, crime figures show a staggering rate of increase for burglaries involving private homes. It is no wonder then that many homeowners and businesspeople are giving serious consideration to electronic alarm protection. These operators are in the market to make a fast dollar and the unwary customer who buys what seems to be a bargain too often ends up being cheated.

The selection of a proper alarm system is not a simple matter, because the needs of each individual homeowner or businessperson are different, like a set of fingerprints. Some factors that determine the requirements of an individual alarm system and the questions, which must be answered when selecting a system, include:

- The threat or risk—what is the system to protect against?
- The type of sensors needed—what will be protected?
- What methods are available to provide the level of protection needed?
- The method of alarm signal transmission—how is the signal to be sent and who will respond?

Most of the confusion regarding intrusion detection systems is a result of the variety of methods available to accomplish the proper protection needed. The combination of detection methods ranges into the thousands. An intrusion detection system may serve to deter a would be intruder. However, the primary function of the alarm system is to signal the presence of an intruder. An intrusion detection system can be just a portion of the overall protection needed. Many large businesses supple-

ment them with security guards and other security personnel. The successful operation of any type of an alarm system depends upon its proper installation and maintenance by the alarm installing company and the proper use of the system by the customer.

Components of Alarm Systems

Sensing devices are used in the actual detection of an intruder (see Figures 11-1 and 11-2). They each have a specific purpose and can be divided into three categories: perimeter protection, area/space protection, and object/spot protection.

Perimeter Protection

Perimeter protection is the first in the defense to detect an intruder. The most common points equipped with sensing devices for premise perimeter protection are doors, windows, vents, skylights, or any opening to a business or home. Since over 80% of all break-ins occur through these openings, most alarm systems provide this type of protection. The major advantage of perimeter protection is its simple design. The major disadvantage is that is protects only the openings. If the burglar bursts through a wall, comes through the ventilation system, or stays behind after closing, perimeter protection is useless.

1. *Door switches*. These are installed on a door or window in a way that opening the door or window causes a magnet to move away a contact switch that activates the alarm. They can be surface-

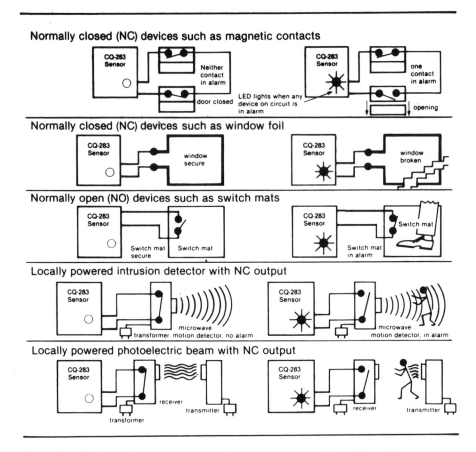

Figure 11-1. Typical application of the use of magnetic contacts, window foil, switch mats, motion detection, and photoelectric beam. (Courtesy of Aritech Corporation.)

mounted or recessed into the door and frame. A variety of switches are manufactured for all types of doors and windows.

2. *Metallic foil (window tape)*. Although it is rarely used today, this method is used to detect glass breakage in show windows, doors, and transoms. When the glass cracks and breaks the foil, it interrupts the low-voltage electrical circuit and activates the alarm.

3. *Glass break detectors*. These detectors are attached to the glass and sense the breakage of the glass by shock or sound.

4. *Wooden screens*. These devices are made of wooden dowel sticks assembled in a cagelike fashion no more than 4 inches from each other. A very fine, brittle wire runs in the wooden dowels and frame. The burglar must break the doweling to gain entry, which breaks the low voltage electrical circuit, causing the alarm. These devices are primarily used in commercial applications.

5. *Window screens*. These devices are similar to regular wire window screens in a home except that a fine, coated wire is a part of the screen, and when the burglar cuts the screen to gain entry, the flow of low-voltage electricity is interrupted activating the alarm. These devices are used primarily in residential applications.

6. *Lace and paneling*. The surfaces of door panels and safes are protected against entry by installing a close lacelike pattern of metallic foil or a fine brittle wire on the surface. Entry cannot be made without first breaking the foil or wire, thus activating the alarm. A panel of wood is placed over the lacing to protect it.

Area/Space Protection (Table 11-1)

These devices protect interior spaces in a business or home. They protect against intrusion whether or not

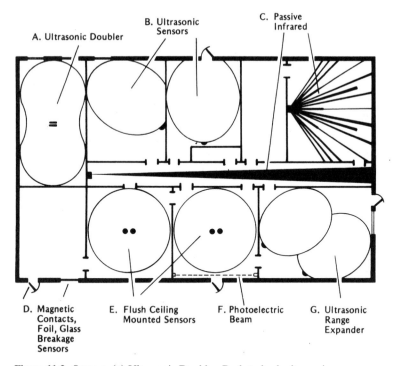

Figure 11-2. Sensors. (a) Ultrasonic Doubler. Back-to-back ultrasonic transceivers provide virtually double the coverage of single detectors at almost the same wiring and equipment cost. With more than 50×25 feet of coverage, the doubler is your best value in space protection. (b) Ultrasonic Sensors. Easy to install, no brackets needed. Mount it horizontally or vertically or in a corner, surface or flush, or with mounting feet on a shelf. Each UL listed sensor protects a three-dimensional volume up to 30 feet wide and high. (c) Passive Infrared. For those zones where the lower cost ultrasonic sensor is inappropriate, there is no need to buy a complete passive infrared system. Both ultrasonic and passive infrared can be used in the same system. (d) Magnetic Contacts, Foil, Glass Breakage Sensors. The building's perimeter protection detectors can be wired into the system via universal interface sensor. There is no need for running a separate perimeter loop. (e) Flush Ceiling Mounted Sensors. Only the two small 2-inch diameter transducer caps are visible below the ceiling tiles. Designed for where minimum visibility is needed for aesthetic or security purposes. (f) Photoelectric Beam. The universal interface sensor allows the connection of any NO or NC alarm device into the system for zoned annunciation. It can be used with photoelectric beams, switch matting, microwave motion detectors, and many other intrusion detectors. (g) Ultrasonic Range Expander. Adding an ultrasonic range expander can increase the coverage of an ultrasonic sensor by 50 to 90%, depending on where it is positioned and the surrounding environment. (Courtesy of Aritech Corporation.)

the perimeter protection was violated. It is particularly effective for a stay-behind intruder or the burglar who cuts through the roof or breaks through a block wall. Space protection devices are only a part of the complete alarm system. They should always be supplemented with perimeter protection. The major advantage of space protection devices is that they provide a highly sensitive, invisible means of detection. The major disadvantage is that improper application and installation by the alarm company can result in frequent false alarms.

The types of area/space protection are photoelectric eyes, ultrasonics, microwave, infrared detectors, pressure mats, sound sensors, and dual-techs.

Table 11-1. Area/Space Protection

	Environmental and Other Factors Affecting Sensor Usage	(Circle one)	Effect on Sensor			Recommendation and Notes
			Ultrasonics	**Microwave**	**Passive I/R**	
1	If the areas to be protected is enclosed by thin walls, or contains windows, will there be movement close by the outside of this area?	Yes No	None	Major	None	Avoid using a microwave sensor unless it can be aimed away from thin walls, glass, etc., which can pass an amount of microwave energy.
2	Will protection pattern see sun, moving headlamps, or other sources of infrared energy passing through windows?	Yes No	None	None	Major	Avoid using a passive I/R sensor unless pattern can be positioned to avoid rapidly changing levels of infrared energy.
3	Does area to be protected contain HVAC ducts?	Yes No	None	Moderate	None	Ducts can channel microwave energy to other areas. If using a microwave sensor, aim it away from duct openings
4	Will two or more sensors of the same type be used to protect a common area?	Yes No	None	None (see Note)	None	Note: Adjacent units must operate on different frequencies.
5	Does area to be protected contain fluorescent of neon lights that will be on during protection-on period?	Yes No	None	Major	None	Microwave sensor, if used, must be aimed away from any fluorescent or neon light within 20′.
6	Are incandescent lamps that are cycled on-and-off during protection-on period included in the protection pattern?	Yes No	None	None	Major	If considering use of passive I/R sensor, make a trial installation and, if necessary, redirect protection pattern away from incandescent lamps.
7	Must protection pattern be projected from a ceiling?	Yes No	None, but only for ceiling heights up to 15′	Major	Major	Only ultrasonic sensors can be used on a ceiling, but height is limited to 15′. At greater ceiling heights, either (1) use rigid ceiling brackets to suspend sensor so as to maintain 15′ limitation, or (2) in large open areas try using a microwave sensor mounted high on a wall and aimed downward.
8	Is the overall structure of flimsy construction (corrugated metal, thin plywood, etc.)?	Yes No	Minor	Major	Minor	Do not use a microwave sensor! Where considerable structural movement can be expected, use a rigid mounting surface for ultrasonic or passive infrared sensor.
9	Will protection pattern include large metal objects or wall surfaces?	Yes No	Minor	Major	Minor (major if polished)	1. Use ultrasonic sensor. metal is highly 2. Use passive I/R sensor.

Table 11-1. *Continued*

Environmental and Other Factors Affecting Sensor Usage		(Circle one)	Effect on Sensor			Recommendation and Notes
			Ultrasonics	Microwave	Passive I/R	
10	Are there any nearby radar installations?	Yes No	Minor	Major when radar is close and sensor is aimed at it	Minor	Avoid using a microwave sensor.
11	Will protection pattern include heaters, radiators, air conditioners, etc.?	Yes No	Moderate	None	Major when rapid changes in air temperature are involved	1. Use ultrasonic sensor. But aim it away from sources of air turbulence (desirable to have heaters, etc., turned off during protection-on period). 2. Use microwave sensor.
12	Will area to be protected be subjected to ultrasonic noise (bells, hissing sounds, etc.)?	Yes No	Moderate, can cause problems in severe cases	None	None	1. Try muffling noise source and use an ultrasonic sensor. 2. Use a microwave sensor. 3. Use passive infrared sensor.
13	Will protection pattern include drapes, carpet, racks of clothing, etc.?	Yes No	Moderate, reduction in range	None	Minor	1. Use ultrasonic sensor if some reduction in range can be tolerated. 2. Use microwave sensor.
14	Is the area to be protected subject to changes in temperature and humidity?	Yes No	Moderate	None	Major	1. Use an ultrasonic sensor unless changes in temperature and humidity are severe. 2. Use a microwave sensor.
15	Is there water noise from faulty valves in the area to be protected?	Yes No	Moderate, can be a problem	None	None	1. If noise is substantial, try correcting faulty valves and use an ultrasonic sensor. 2. Use a microwave sensor. 3. Use a passive I/R sensor.
16	Will protection pattern see moving machinery, fan blades, etc.?	Yes No	Major	Major	Minor	1. Have machinery, fans, etc. turned off during protection-on period. 2. Use careful placement of ultrasonic sensor. 3. Use passive infrared sensor.
17	Will drafts or other types of air movement pass through protection pattern?	Yes No	Major	None	None, unless rapid temperature changes are involved	1. If protection pattern can be aimed away from air movement, or if air movement can be stopped during protection-on period, use an ultrasonic sensor. 2. Use a microwave sensor. 3. Use a passive I/R sensor.
18	Will protection pattern see overhead doors that can be rattled by wind?	Yes No	Major	Major	Minor	1. If protection pattern can be aimed away from such doors, use an ultrasonic sensor. 2. Use a passive I/R sensor.
19	Are there hanging signs, calendar pages, etc. which can be moved by air currents during protection-on period?	Yes No	Major	Major	Moderate, can be a problem	1. Use ultrasonic sensor, but aim pattern away from objects that can move or remove such objects. 2. Use passive infrared sensor.

Table 11-1. *Continued*

	Environmental and Other Factors Affecting Sensor Usage	(Circle one)	Effect on Sensor			Recommendation and Notes
			Ultrasonics	Microwave	Passive I/R	
20	Are there adjacent railroad tracks that will be used during protection-on period?	Yes No	Major	Minor	Minor	A trial installation is required if using an ultrasonic sensor.
21	Can small animals (or birds) enter protection pattern?	Yes No	Major	Major	Major (particularly rodents)	Install a physical barrier to prevent intrusion by animals or birds.
22	Does area to be protected contain a corrosive atmosphere?	Yes No	Major	Major	Major	None of these sensors can be used.
	Approximate ADT cost per square foot of coverage:		0.3	0.4	0.6	

Photoelectric Eyes (Beams)

These devices transmit a beam across a protected area. When an intruder interrupts the beam, the beam circuit is disrupted and the alarm is initiated. Photoelectric devices use a pulsed infrared beam that is invisible to the naked eye. Some units have a range of over 1000 feet and can be used outdoors although it is rarely used today.

Ultrasonics

Although it is rarely used today, it works on a low-frequency sound wave that is projected from the unit. The frequency is in kilohertz (23–26) and its area of coverage can be anywhere from 5 to 40 feet in length. The pattern is volumetric and cannot be aimed, although the pattern may be directed by the use of deflectors. Deflectors will come in 90 or 45° angles. You can also find a doubler type that uses two 45° angles back to back. Ultrasonics work on a change in frequency. This is called the Doppler effect. A motion detector has two transducers; the transmitter sends out a signal that is bounced back to the receiver by immobile objects in the protected area. If an intruder moves toward, or away from the unit, there is a change in its reflected frequency, signaling an alarm. Ultrasonics may be found as stand-alone units or as part of what is called a master system. The stand-alone units compare the reflected signal within the unit itself and trip the control panel by opening or closing a relay contact. Master systems work slightly differently by sending the signal back to a main processing unit. The main processing unit compares the signal and trips the relay contacts of the processor. False alarms are caused by three types of sources:

- *Motion.* Objects that can move in the path of protection, or air turbulence, will be seen as motion because of the frequency of the unit.
- *Noise.* Ultrasonic noise is present when audible noises are heard; hissing such as from high-pressure air leaking, or steam radiators, or bells ringing can be a source of these noises.
- *Radio or electrical interference.* Induced electrical signals or radio frequency (RF) interference from radio transmitters can cause false alarms.

Grounding and shielding are both very important in a master system. If an earth ground is required, it should be a cold water pipe. The length of the ground wire should be as short as possible and with a minimum number of bends.

Potential Problems

- Turbulence and draft, hanging displays, moving draperies, small pets
- Noise caused by air hissing, bells, telephones
- Temperature or humidity can affect range of the ultrasonic

Carpets, furniture, and draperies may absorb some of the signal, decreasing the unit's sensitivity. Ultrasonic energy will not penetrate most objects. The signal may be reflected off some smooth surfaces.

Microwave

Microwave detectors are a volumetric type of space protection. They detect intruders by the use of a radiated radio frequency (RF) electromagnetic field. The unit operates by sensing a disturbance in the generated RF field—the Doppler effect. The frequency range will be between 0.3 and 300 Gigahertz (1 Gigahertz = 1,000,000,000 cps). Any type of motion in the protected area will create a change in frequency, causing an alarm condition. Because the power output from the unit is relatively low, the field radiated is harmless. Microwave energy will penetrate most objects except for metal: it is totally reflected off metal. One of the most important considerations in placement of these units is vibration. The microwave must be mounted on a firm surface: cinder block, brick, or main support beams are ideal mounting locations. You should never mount two microwave units with identical frequencies in the same room or area where the patterns may overlap. This could cause crosstalk between the units, causing false alarm problems. Microwave units draw excessive current, so the proper gauge of wire should be used and the length of the wire run should also be taken into consideration. Current reading should be taken at the end of an installation or while troubleshooting units to ensure that the maximum current of the control panel has not been exceeded. Fluorescent lights may also be a problem because the radiated ionization from the lights may be looked at as motion by the detector.

Potential Problems

- Vibrations or movement of mounting surface can be a major problem
- Reflection of pattern or movement of metal objects in protected area, such as moving fan blades or movement or overhead doors
- Penetration of thin walls or glass if motion or large metal objects, such as trains or cars, are present
- Radio frequency interference (RFI), radar, or AC line transients in severe cases
- Water movement in plastic storm drains or PVC can be a potential interference if located close to the unit. Most microwave units will provide a test point where the amplifier output voltage can be read. By following the manufacturer's recommended voltage settings the microwave can be set up properly and the unit environment can be examined.

Infrared Detectors

These detectors are passive sensors, because they do not transmit a signal for an intruder to disturb. Rather, a source of moving infrared radiation (the intruder) is detected against the normal radiation/temperature environment of the room. Passive infrared detectors (PIRs) sense the radiation from a human body moving through the optical field of view of the detector. The field of view of an infrared unit must terminate on an object to ensure its proper operation and stability. An infrared unit should never be set up to look out into mid-air.

Potential Problems

- Turbulence and drafts, if the air is blowing directly on the unit or causes a rapid change in temperature of objects in the path of protection
- Forms of stray motion (i.e., drapes blowing, hanging objects or displays, small animals)
- Changing temperatures may cause false alarms (i.e., hot spots in machinery, sunlight). The temperature of the background IR level may also affect the unit's sensitivity: PIRs become less sensitive as the temperature increases
- Lightning or bright lights, such as halogen headlights, can also trip PIRs. The IR radiation pattern will be blocked by solid objects as it is unable to penetrate most objects. The pattern of protection may also be affected by reflection off smooth surfaces.

Pressure Mats

These mats are basically mechanical switches. Pressure mats are most frequently used as a backup system to perimeter protection. When used as traps they can be hidden under the carpet in front of a likely target or in hallways where an intruder would travel.

Sound Sensors

Sound sensors detect intrusion by picking up the noise created by a burglar during an attempt to break into a protected area. These sensors consist of a microphone and electronic amplifier/processor. When the sound level increases beyond the limit normally encountered, the unit signals an alarm. Some units have a pulse-counting and time-interval feature. Other types have the capacity for actually listening to the protected premises from a central monitoring station.

Dual-Techs

Dual-technology units, commonly referred to as dual-techs, are made up as a combination of two types of space protection devices. The principle of the unit is that both sections of the detectors must be tripped at the same time in order to cause an alarm condition. A dual-tech unit could be a combination passive/microwave or a combination passive/ultrasonic. By using a dual-technology device an installer is now able to provide space protection in areas that may have presented potential false alarm problems if a single-technology unit was used. Service people are able to replace units that are falsing because of environment or placement. Dual-techs are not the solution to all false alarm problems and unless careful consideration is used in installing or replacing a device the false alarm problems may persist. Since you are now not installing just one but two different types of devices, there is much more to consider. Dual-techs will draw much more current than a conventional type of detector. Current readings are essential and additional power supplies may be necessary in order to provide enough operating current and stand-by power. Until recently if one section of the unit stopped working, or was blocked off in some way by the end user, the unit was rendered inoperable. Manufacturers are now working on supervising the microwave section of these units. If the unit is located or adjusted so that one section of the unit is continuously in an alarm condition, the dual-technology principle is worthless.

Application

For all practical purposes the reason we use space protection is as a backup to the perimeter system. It is not necessary to cover every inch of the premises being protected. The best placement is as a trap in a high-traffic area or to provide spot protection for high-value areas. The worst thing an installer can do is to overextend the area being protected by an individual unit (e.g., trying to cover more than one room with a detector or trying to compensate for placement or environment by over-adjusting sensitivity). By using a little common sense and checking for all possible hazards, you can insure a trouble-free installation. Make sure that the units have adequate power going to each head and that the stand-by batteries are working and charging properly. Be sure to adjust for pets and to brief customers on any potential problems they may create—such as leaving fans or machinery on—and not to open windows that are in the path of protection. Before leaving an installation, make sure that all units have been walk-tested and areas in question have been masked out.

One of the most important considerations in setting up a number of space protection devices is *zoning*. Never put more than two interior devices on one zone if it is at all possible. The majority of false alarms are caused by interior devices. Breaking up the interior protective circuits as much as possible gives the service person a better chance of solving a false alarm problem (even with two heads on one zone you have a 50/50 chance of finding the trouble unit). Zoning a system correctly will help in troubleshooting, make the police department feel better about the company, the company feel better about the installer, and insure good relations with the customer.

Object/Spot Detection

Object/spot detection is used to detect the activity or presence of an intruder at a single location. It provides direct security for things. Such a detection method is the final stage of an in-depth system for protection. The objects that are most frequently protected include safes, filing cabinets, desks, art objects, models, statues, and expensive equipment.

The types of object/spot protection are:

1. *Capacitance/proximity detectors.* The object being protected becomes an antenna, electronically linked to the alarm control. When an intruder approaches or touches the object-antenna, an electrostatic field is unbalanced and the alarm is initiated. Only metal objects can be protected in this manner.
2. *Vibration detectors.* These devices utilize a highly sensitive and specialized microphone called an electronic vibration detector (EVD). The EVD is attached directly to the object to be protected. They can be adjusted to detect a sledge hammer attack on a concrete wall or a delicate penetration of a glass surface. They will alarm only when the object is moved, whereas capacitance devices will detect when the intruder is close to the protected object. Other types of vibration detectors are similar to tilt switches used in pinball machines.

Alarm Control

All sensing devices are wired into the alarm control panel that receives their signals and processes them.

Some of the most severe burglary losses are caused not by a failure in equipment but simply by someone turning off the alarm system. The type of control panel needed is dependent upon the sophistication of the overall intrusion alarm system. Some control panels provide zoning capabilities for separate annunciation of the sensing devices. It may also provide the low voltage electrical power for the sensing devices.

Included in the control panel is the backup or standby power in the event of an electrical power failure. Batteries are used for standby power. Some equipment uses rechargeable batteries; the control has a low-power charging unit—a trickle charger—and maintains the batteries in a fully charged condition.

Modern control panels use one or more microprocessors. This allows the control panel to send and receive digital information to the alarm station. An alphanumeric pad can display zone information as well as supervisory conditions. Each user can also have their own unique code, allowing restriction during specified times or limiting access into certain areas. By using individual code numbers the alarm control panel can provide an audit track of activity as well as having the ability to transmit this information off-site.

If the alarm control panel is connected to a central monitoring station, the times that the system is turned on and off are recorded and logged. When the owner enters the building in the morning, a signal is sent. If this happens at a time that has been prearranged with the central station, it is considered a normal opening. If it happens at any other time, the police are dispatched.

It is possible for the owner or other authorized persons to enter the building during the closed times. The person entering must first call the central station company and identify himself by a special coding procedure. Records are kept at the central station company for these irregular openings and closings.

Tamper protection is a feature that provides for an alarm signal to be generated when the system is compromised in any way. Tamper protection can be designed into any or all portions of the alarm system (control panel, sensing devices, loop wiring, alarm transmission facilities).

Alarm Transmission/Signaling

The type of alarm transmission/signaling system used in a particular application depends upon the location of the business or residence, the frequency of police patrols, and the ability of the customer to afford the cost. Remember that, after deterrence, the purpose of an alarm is to summon the proper authorities to stop a crime during the act of commission or lead to the apprehension of the intruder. It is very important that the response by proper authorities to the alarm comes in the shortest possible time. There are two types of alarm signaling systems in general use.

Local Alarm

A bell or light indicates that an attempted or successful intrusion has taken place. The success of the system relies on someone hearing or seeing the signal and calling the responsible authorities. The local alarm also serves to notify burglars that they have been detected. This may be advantageous in frightening off the less experienced intruder.

Central Station System

The alarm signal is transmitted over telephone lines to a specially constructed building called the central station. Here, trained operators are on duty 24 hours a day to supervise, record, and maintain alarms. Upon receipt of an alarm, the police are dispatched, and, in some cases, the alarm company guard or runner. The record keeping function and guard response assure thorough documentation of any alarm signal. Alarm transmissions to the central station are of the seven types discussed below. Each type of transmission has certain advantages and disadvantages which must be considered in determining the risk. Transmission of an alarm signal to the Underwriters' Laboratories-listed central station is generally regarded as the most reliable method for reducing the burglary losses.

Direct Wire Systems

High-risk locations (banks, jewelers, and furriers) are generally protected with a direct wire system. A single dedicated telephone line is run from the protected premises to the central station or police station where a separate receiver supervises only that alarm. A fixed DC current is sent from the central station to the protected premises and read on a meter at the central station.

The advantage of a direct wire system is that problems can be very quickly traced to a specific alarm system. This makes compromising the alarm signal by a professional burglar more difficult. The disadvantage of such a system is the higher cost of leased telephone lines. This becomes a more serious economic factor as the distance from the central station to the protected premises increases. Proper transmission of the alarm signal to the central station is essential. Problems can result on these telephone lines from shorts and broken wires. Most central stations expect these problems and are well equipped to rapidly make repairs.

Some of today's burglars are more sophisticated. They know they can prevent the transmission of the alarm signal to the central system by shunting or jumpering out the leased telephone line. Special methods are used by the alarm company to protect against jumpering of the alarm signal. Alarm systems having this special line security are classified as AA Grade Central Station alarms by Underwriters' Laboratories.

Circuit (Party Line) Systems

Alarm signals transmitted over circuit transmission systems can be compared to a party line where several alarm customers defray the cost of the telephone line by sharing it. With a circuit transmission system, as many as 15 alarm transmitters may send alarm signals to a single receiving panel at the central station over the same line, or loop. The alarm signals at the central station are received on strips of paper. Each alarm has a distinct code to identify it from others. The advantage of a circuit-loop alarm transmission system is the lower telephone line cost. Thus, a central station can make its services available to more customers by subdividing the cost of the telephone line among different users. The disadvantage of circuit-loop alarm transmission systems is that problems on a leased telephone line are more difficult to locate than with a direct wire system.

Multiplex Systems

The multiplex system is designed to reduce leased telephone line charges while at the same time providing a higher degree of line security than circuit-loop alarms. Multiplex systems introduced data processing—computer based techniques—to the alarm industry.

Digital Communicators

This computer-based type of alarm transmission equipment sends its signal through the regular switch line telephone network. The alarm signal transmitted is a series of coded electronic pulses that can only be received on a computer-type terminal at the central station.

Telephone Dialer

The dialer delivers a prerecorded verbal message to a central station, answering service, or police department when an alarm is activated. Many of the earlier tape dialers were a source of constant problems to police departments, because of their lack of sophistication. Basically, they were relabeled tape recorders. It was not uncommon for the tape dialer to play most of the message before the police could answer the phone. The police knew that an alarm signal had been sent, but did not know its location. The newer, modern tape dialers have solved these problems.

Radio Signal Transmission

This method takes the alarm signal from the protected premises and sends it via radio or cellular phone to either a central station or police dispatch center. Additionally, the alarm signal can be received in a police patrol car.

Video Verification

Along with standard alarm transmissions, video images are sent to the central station. This provides for a higher level of protection while helping to eliminate false alarms by allowing central station operators to see what is happening inside the protected area. With the increase of the false police dispatches, video verification is playing a major role in the battle against false alarms.

Alarms Deter Crime

False alarms waste police resources. They also waste alarm company resources. The police and alarm industry are acutely aware of this, and both have initiated efforts across the country to relieve the dilemma.

The National Crime Prevention Institute has long endorsed alarm systems as the best available crime deterrent. This education institution realizes that most criminals fear alarm systems. They prefer to break into an unprotected building rather than risk capture by a hidden sensor.

Problem deterrence is the alarm business, a field that extends far beyond protecting premises from burglary. The crisis prevention duties of alarm firms range from monitoring sprinkler systems and fire sensors, and watching temperature levels in buildings, to supervising industrial processes such as nuclear fission and the manufacturing of dangerous chemicals.

To alarm companies, deterrence becomes a sophisticated and specialized art. In the area of crime prevention, companies take pride in spotting potential weaknesses in a building and designing an alarm system that will confound the most intelligent criminals.

Crime prevention is the area where police need the most help. The rise in burglary and other crimes has often put police officers in a response posture.

False Alarms

The full crime prevention potential in alarm systems has yet to be realized. Relatively speaking, the number of premises not protected by alarms is great, although those businesses and residences holding the most valuable goods are thoroughly guarded by the most sophisticated sensor systems.

The main drag on the potential of alarms, as industry leaders and police are aware, remains the false alarm problem. A modern instance of the boy who cried "wolf," false alarms erode alarm systems' effectiveness. They are costly to alarm companies and police agencies.

It is a fact that alarm systems prevent crime. These electronic and electrical systems deter burglars, arsonists, vandals, and other criminals. They are both the most effective and most economical crime prevention tool available.

Police budgets have been reduced in most locales and frozen in others, while private investment in alarm security is growing yearly.

The National Burglary and Fire Alarm Association (NBFAA) has asked its members to rate their priorities on association activities. The outstanding response asked for a comprehensive program to help member companies reduce false alarms. Moreover, while researching possible programs the NBFAA learned that many members had already embarked on significant reduction efforts.

Some of the police departments have initiated a written letter program from the police chief to those who have an excessive number of alarm runs. Others have the crime prevention officer do a follow-up visit

to the business or residence; after the other steps have failed, many police departments are assessing false alarm fines.

By protecting such places as hospitals, office buildings, and schools, alarm systems free up police resources and enable patrol officers to spend more time in areas with high crime rates and with fewer premises protected by alarm systems. Police may also dedicate more officers to apprehending criminals. In this manner, police and alarm companies can work together, complementing one another and waging a mutual war on crime.

Alarm Equipment Overhaul

A California alarm station undertook a major overhaul. The effort began with a false alarm inventory, in which subscribers whose systems produced four or more false alarms per week were weeded out. Service workers then replaced, virtually reinstalled, the alarm systems for those subscribers. New sensors, new batteries, new wiring, and new soldering jobs were required in many instances. The process was costly, but it paid off in the long run. The office then had fewer service calls and a relationship with the local police has improved and increased business.

Many NBFAA member companies have instituted training programs for their sales, installation, and service personnel. Also, subscribers are being educated on the operation of their systems three times, by salespeople, installers, and supervisors when they inspect newly installed systems.

One member company weeded out and entirely rebuilt its problem systems. This approach is the most feasible way for smaller firms to attach the problem. Lacking sufficient capital to initiate a comprehensive program, such companies can nevertheless cut down the number of false alarms by renovating the relatively few systems that cause the majority of problems.

Police chiefs and crime prevention officers working in areas troubled by false alarms should meet with the heads of the firms in their areas and discuss reduction programs like those mentioned above.

Additional Resources

Now NBFAA members have a guide in the form of a comprehensive quality control manual outlining measures they can undertake and alleviate false alarms.

To provide an idea of how this *False Alarm Handbook* looks, a list of the sections contained in the handbook are presented here:

1. Determine false alarm rate and causes.
2. Form an alarm equipment evaluation committee.
3. Institute equipment testing procedures.
4. Develop equipment training facilities.
5. Know how to plan and make alarm installations.
6. Be familiar with sensor zoning procedures.
7. Inspect installations.
8. Educate the subscriber.
9. Cooperate with local law enforcement officers.

The theory behind the handbook is evident in the section titles. Companies are encouraged to begin with a series of statistical studies—from the general false alarm rate per total alarms and systems, to causes distinguishing among equipment, user, telephone line, and environmental problems. A separate study helps companies determine how much money false alarms are costing them.

The results of these studies should be reviewed by the company's alarm equipment evaluation committee. That committee, made up of the chief engineer and plant, sales, and general managers, next decides which systems to keep, to drop, and to research further.

Sections 3 and 4 are self-explanatory, both aimed at eliminating equipment-related problems through further testing and by education of all personnel on equipment operations. It should be noted that salespeople will be particularly urged to go through the training process.

The next two sections cover installation procedures. Service workers are warned about environmental hazards that can affect different sensors. Such hazards include heat, static electricity, vibration, and electromagnetic interference from radio waves. The zoning section tells companies how they may set up their installations to isolate faults in different sensors and pieces of equipment.

Under subscriber education, firms are urged to inundate their customers with training films, brochures, seminars, and whatever else it takes to teach them how to operate their alarm systems properly.

The NBFAA has also developed a separate booklet to help educate alarm subscribers. It incorporates a discussion of alarm system fundamentals along with procedures that customers may undertake to reduce mistakes by their employees who operate the systems.

Lastly, the *False Alarm Handbook* asks alarm companies to work closely with the local police on this problem. Here, the NBFAA endorses company-wide research efforts, and the forming of a local private security advisory council to oversee efforts.

Each must recognize that they need the other. Like surgeons and other medical specialists who need sophisticated drugs and instruments to prevent diseases, the law enforcement community needs the alarm industry. Prevention, the reason for alarm protection, must lead the war on crime.

At the same time, the alarm industry must remove from its ranks the flimflam person selling placebos and faulty systems. Users must be taught to care for their security.

Police should take action against such companies and customers when they aggravate the false alarm problem. If some friendly arm-twisting fails to stop such practices, then police should meet with responsible alarm firms, and together they should develop programs and, if necessary, ordinances to penalize negligent subscribers and deceitful companies.

Conclusion

As we begin the 21st century and look back we have seen a lot of changes occur, many for the better. Passive infrared units (PIR) are widely used and ultrasonic motion detectors are rarely used. Foil is no longer placed on glass windows and has been replaced by the proper placement of a PIR. Home and commercial applications of PIR's units come in all shapes and sizes as well as all necessary patterns for proper coverage. Smoke detectors come with remote maintenance reporting to reduce false alarms (2 wire detectors only). Keypads are now hardware, two way voice module and wireless and control panels (UL listed) are in single and multizone panels.

The growth in technology will continue as will the need for updated technology.

Appendix 11.A
Smoke Detectors

The following was extracted on March 6, 2002: GE Interlogix eCommunity message addresses a common question regarding smoke sensors. For information on ESL fire and safety products, visit *http://www.sentrol.com/products/firesafety.asp.*

Q. I have heard a lot of controversial comments about the use of ionization-type smoke detectors versus photoelectric-type smoke detectors. Where would one specifically choose to use ionization-type smoke detectors?

A. Proper selection of a type of detector begins with an understanding of the operating principles of each type of detector. NFPA72-1999, *National Fire Alarm Code,* describes the operating principles of both ionization and photoelectric light scattering spot-type detectors in Chapters 1–4, "Definitions." These definitions are further expanded in Appendix A to give more information to the user.

In an ionization smoke detector, "a small amount of radioactive material is used to ionize the air between two differently charged electrodes to sense the presence of particles. Smoke particles entering the ionization volume decrease the conductance of the air by reducing ion mobility. The reduced conductance signal is processed and used to convey an alarm condition when it meets present criteria."

In a photoelectric light-scattering detector, "a light source and photosensitive sensor arranged so that the rays from the light source do not normally fall onto the photosensitive sensor. Then smoke particles enter the light path; some of the light is scattered reflection and refraction onto the sensor. The light signal is processed and used to convey an alarm condition when it meets preset criteria."

The Appendix further explains that photoelectric light-scattering detectors respond more to visible particles, larger than one micron in size, produced by most smoldering fires. They respond somewhat less to the smaller particles typically produced by flaming fires. They also respond less to fires yielding black or darker smoke, such as fires involving plastics and rubber tires.

Ionization detectors tend to exhibit somewhat opposite characteristics. In a fire yielding "invisible" particles of a size less than one micron, an ionization detector will more likely respond than will a photoelectric light-scattering detector. Particles of this size tend to more readily result from flaming fires. Fuel in flaming fires burners "cleaner," producing smaller particles.

The answer to whether you should use one type of detector over another lies in understanding the burning characteristics of the particular fuel. An ionization-type smoke detector will likely detect a fire more quickly that produces flaming combustion. A photoelectric-type detector will likely detect a low energy fire more quickly that produces larger particles during combustion.

Finally, keep in mind that both types of smoke detectors successfully pass the same battery of tests at the nationally recognized testing laboratories. For example, UL Listed ionization smoke detectors and UL listed photoelectric smoke detectors pass the same tests under UL 268, *Standard for Safety for Smoke Detectors for Fire Protection Signaling Systems.*

This Q&A is provided courtesy of the *Moore-Wilson Signaling Report* (Vol. 9, No. 5), a publication of Hughes Associates, Inc. For subscription information, e-mail tm-wsr@haifire.com.

Chapter 12
Entry Control*

JOHN FAY and MARY LYNN GARCIA

Every exit is an entry somewhere.

—Tom Stoppard

Introduction

A facility that requires even a minor level of protection exercises access controls. Indeed, a legitimate argument can be made that a facility without access controls is an unprotected facility. Access controls regulate movement into, from, and within a designated building or area. The controls are placed on people, forms of transportation, and materials. The people typically affected are employees, visitors, customers, contractors, vendors, repair and salespersons, and deliverers. Transport includes automobiles, trucks, motorcycles and bicycles, trains, buses, watercraft, and aircraft. Materials that are under control when entering can include raw materials, supplies, and equipment; inside the protected area controls can be placed on cash, valuables, and sensitive documents; and when leaving the protected area controls can be applied to finished products, scrap, and refuse, as well as to property hand-carried by employees.

Employee Badges and Visitor Passes

A basic and time-honored access control tool is the employee identification card or badge. A workplace with few employees and low security needs may

*Fay, *Contemporary Security Management,* pp. 161–164, Butterworth Heinemann, 2002
Garcia, *Design and Evaluation of Physical Protection Systems,* pp. 178–184, Butterworth Heinemann, 2001

choose to rely on personal recognition as an alternative to the identification badge, but a workplace with many employees and moderate to high security needs will find the identification badge useful, especially in restricted areas.

The control of visitors works differently. Visitor passes issued at an entry control point substitute for identification cards. The visitor passes are typically constructed of paper and may have a feature that causes self-destruction after one or two days. The pass is (1) dated and issued for a set period, usually one day; (2) applied for at a reception or security desk adjacent to the entry point; and (3) requires that the visitor present a form of photo identification such as a driver's license. A condition of issuance may be approval by an employee. In some situations, only certain employees may approve visitor access, and the day and time of visit must be prearranged. In many situations, the visitor is escorted while inside the facility.

In a safety-sensitive workplace, a visitor may have to undergo a briefing, view a film, sign a release, and put on protective apparel such as a hard hat, safety glasses, and steel-toed boots. Keeping a record of the visit is prudent.

Types of Identification Cards

Control of access at a protected facility is assisted by a card identification system designed to verify each entering person's authority to enter. As one can expect, the efficiency and effectiveness of the system are affected by the reliability of the card identification equipment, number of entry points, size of the workforce, operating hours, and, above all else, human competence. A well designed and skillfully managed identification system controls access without impeding the flow of work.

Many different types of identification cards are available. The type of card purchased corresponds to the system's hardware. A few types carry just the owner's name, affiliation, and signature, but most incorporate a head and shoulders photograph laminated to the card, a tamper-detecting feature, and a post office box number for mailing found cards back to the issuing organization. Nearly all access cards are of the same general size and shape, and in overall appearance look somewhat like a credit card. The common types are Hollerith, magnetic stripe, barium ferrite, bar code, Wiegand, proximity, and smart card.

Hollerith

This early form of access card has small holes that can be read by a light source or contact brushes. Today's use of Hollerith cards is limited to hotel security. The guest slides the card into a slot above the door handle. The lock disengages when reading the card matches a guest's registration at the lobby desk. This simple technology is not suitable for higher-level security.

Magnetic Stripe

This type of card has a data-encoded stripe on one face. When the card is withdrawn from, or swiped through a reader, the stripe passes over a magnetic head not unlike that of a tape player. The code on the stripe is compared to access criteria that were entered into the system earlier. Access criteria reflect the cardholder's identity, the areas the cardholder is authorized to enter, and time frames for entry (e.g., normal operating hours, evenings, weekends, or holidays). Compared to other card types, the magnetic stripe costs less and can hold a large amount of data; however, the magnetic stripe can wear out or become damaged over time, and the vinyl plastic construction of the card can lead to chipping and breaking.

Barium Ferrite

This type of card is sometimes called a *magnetic spot card* or *magnetic sandwich card*. It is cut from three-layer plastic stock. The middle layer, or core, is barium ferrite that has been magnetized with a pattern of dots arranged in a readable pattern. The pattern is a code fixed by the magnetic polarity of the spots. The barium ferrite card is more expensive than the magnetic stripe card. It is also subject to problems resulting from wear and tear and is vulnerable to deciphering.

Bar Code

This card bears a series of lines forming a code readable by an optical scanner on one side (usually the front). The pattern of lines (i.e., the bar code) look like the pattern of lines found on the outside of supermarket items. Because a bar code is easy to duplicate, it is not suitable for high-security practice. This card, however, can be used for tracking inventory; for example, a late-shift security guard with a handheld reader can determine the locations of desktop assets. A processor at the security control center conducts an analysis and prints out findings such as when an asset moved, the asset's current location, and assets that are missing.

Wiegand

The Wiegand card is also called an *embedded-wire card*. The technology is based on the Wiegand Effect, a phenomenon observed when specially prepared ferromagnetic wires suddenly reverse themselves on exposure to an external magnetic field. Wires inside the Wiegand card are formed in a permanently tensioned helical twist. The order and spacing of the wires establish a unique code for each card. The magnetic reversals in the wires are converted into distinct, consistent electrical pulses that are read and processed. The card's thickness and stock composition make it resistant to pocket damage; however, it is susceptible to malfunction arising from wear after many passes through reader slots. The card is moderately priced but capable of storing a moderate amount of data.

Proximity

The proximity card has an embedded microcircuit that emits frequencies detectable by a reader. The reader reacts to the frequencies when the card is placed in close proximity (2 to 4 inches).[1] Sturdy composition makes the card resistant to tampering and the interfering effects of weather and shock. Two other features of the card make it attractive: (1) the emitted frequencies are sufficiently powerful for the reader to be concealed behind a thin wall or mounted inconspicuously (possibly for aesthetic reasons), and (2) the card can work through clothing or a handbag.

Smart Card

Regarded as the card of the future, the smart card contains its own processor, making it capable of running its own internal programs. The large amount of data that can be contained in a smart card allows it to serve purposes beyond access control; for example, the cardholder's medical history can be stored for quick retrieval in a medical emergency, and cashless purchases can be recorded.[2] The downside to the smart card is cost. On the other hand, it offers several advantages: (1) the card is durable and tamper resistant, (2) counterfeiting and duplication are difficult, (3) encryption presents an obstacle to compromising the code, (4) the card can be programmed to expire on a certain date, and (5) smart card technology is suitable for many applications.[3]

Biometrics

Personnel identity verification systems corroborate claimed identities on the basis of some unique physical biometric characteristic(s) of the individual. Commercial equipment is available that uses hand or finger geometry, handwriting, fingerprints, eye pattern, voice, face, and various other physical characteristics. All personnel identity verification systems consider the uniqueness of the feature used for identification, the variability of the characteristic, and the difficulty of implementing the system that processes the characteristic.

Biometric devices can differentiate between verification and recognition. In verification mode, a person initiates a claim of identity, presents the specific biometric feature for authorization, and the equipment agrees. In recognition mode, the person does not initiate the claim; the biometric device attempts to identify the person, and if the biometric information agrees with the database, entry is allowed.

Many biometric technologies use error rates as a performance indicator of the system. A Type I error, also called a false reject, is the improper rejection of a valid user. A Type II error, or a false accept, is the improper acceptance of an unauthorized person. Often these error curves are combined and displayed graphically to show the equal error rate. This is the crossover point where Type I errors equal Type II

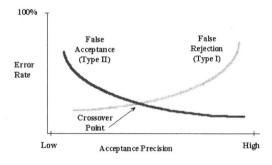

Figure 12-1. Equal error rate graph. The false accept and false reject occurrence at a specific sensitivity of a biometric device can be plotted and their crossover point determined. This point is not where the device should be operated but can be used as a figure of merit when comparing devices.

errors. This point is not necessarily the point at which the device should be operated. The equal error rate does not occur at the point where Type I or Type II errors are both lowest. It is a figure of merit that may be useful when comparing various biometric devices. Figure 12-1 shows an example of the graphical display of error curves and the equal error rate.

When selecting or deploying biometric devices, consideration of the security objectives is required to assure that the device will operate as required. Some systems are set to operate in an area where the device minimizes false rejects, whereas others minimize false accepts. The device cannot minimize both error types simultaneously, so a decision is made as to the balance between false accept and false reject rates. This has a significant implication to system operation. A low false-accept rate compromises system security, but allows all authorized users entry. False rejects, on the other hand, can deny access to authorized users in order to maintain high security. The security manager will undoubtedly hear about the cases of false rejects, particularly if senior managers or other influential employees are denied access. Adversaries, on the other hand, are unlikely to report that entry was obtained due to false acceptance!

Hand/Finger Geometry

Personnel identity verification using the hand geometry system is based on characterizing the shape of the hand. The underlying technique measures three-dimensional features of the hand such as the widths and lengths of fingers and the thickness of the hand (see Figure 12-2).

Figure 12-2. Hand geometry measures. Certain aspects of the hand, such as widths and lengths of fingers and thickness of the hand are measured and used to create a user template.

Figure 12-3. Hand geometry unit. The hand is placed on the platen and a small camera takes a picture. Specific measures are used to create a feature vector, which is compared to the stored user template.

The hand-read sequence is initiated by presenting a coded credential or by entering a personal identification number (PIN). The user then places the hand on a reflective platen; the device has guide pins to help the user properly align fingers. Although the guide-pin arrangement is best suited to the scanning of right hands, the left hand can be enrolled and scanned by placing the left hand on the platen palm up. A solid state camera takes a picture of the hand, which includes a side view for hand thickness. Due to the combination of infrared illumination and the reflective platen, the image of the hand appears as a silhouette to the camera. The system measures the necessary lengths and widths and creates a representation of the hand called a feature vector. Figure 12-3 shows an example of a hand geometry unit.

During verification, the feature vector is compared with previous measurements (the template) obtained during enrollment. If the feature vector and template match within an allowable tolerance, verification is successful. Testing of a hand geometry system at Sandia National Laboratories indicates that Type I and Type II error rates of less than 1% are achievable.[4] A report on the use of a hand geometry unit in an operational environment has also been prepared.[5] A similar system uses two fingers to verify identity. This two-finger geometry system measures finger lengths and widths of the index and middle finger pair. Because only one guide pin is used (between the two fingers), the left or right hand fingers work equally well. The functional concept of this device is similar to the hand geometry system.

Handwriting

Signature verification has been used for many years by the banking industry, although signatures are easily forged. Automatic handwriting verification systems have been developed that use handwriting dynamics, such as displacement, velocity, and acceleration. Statistical evaluation of these data indicates that an individual's signature is unique and reasonably consistent from one signature to the next. Transducers that measure these characteristics can be located in either the writing instrument or tablet. These systems provide low security and are best used in applications where authorizing signatures for a transaction are already in use.

Fingerprints

Fingerprints have been used as a personnel identifier for more than 100 years and are still considered one of the most reliable means of distinguishing one individual from another. The art of processing human

Figure 12-4. Fingerprint identification unit. A PIN is entered into the keypad and the index finger is placed on the center reader. The system then compares the fingerprint to one stored in a file to grant access.

Figure 12-5. Retinal scan device. The user enters a PIN, then looks through the verifier and aligns a target. A scan of the retina is made and compared with the stored image.

fingerprints for identification has been greatly improved in recent years by the development of automated systems. Such systems, which rely on image processing and pattern recognition, have application in personnel entry control. A variety of commercial systems are now available that perform fingerprint verification. Figure 12-4 is an example of a fingerprint verification system. Most fingerprint verification systems use minutia points, the fingerprint ridge endings and bifurcations, as the identifying features of the fingerprint, although some systems use the whole image for comparison purposes. All fingerprint identification systems require care in finger positioning and accurate print analysis and comparison for reliable identification.

Optical methods using a prism and a solid-state camera are most often used to capture the fingerprint image. Dry or worn fingerprints can be difficult to image using optical methods, so special coatings have been applied to the optical platens to enhance the image quality. The purpose of these coatings is to ensure a good optical coupling between the platen and fingerprint.

Ultrasound is another fingerprint imaging method. Because it is able to image below the top skin surface to the lower layers where the fingerprint is not damaged, it is not as susceptible to dry or worn fingerprints. Due to the raster scan required by the ultrasonic transducer, ultrasound imaging is not as fast as optical methods.

Direct imaging sensors that use solid-state devices are also available for acquiring fingerprint images. Capacitive, electric field, and thermal methods have been commercially developed. It is thought that the projected lower cost of these devices, due to the efficient manufacture of silicon chips, will make fingerprint verification devices common on the desktop for secure computer log-on. Overcoming the difficulties of hardening delicate silicon chips for everyday use has delayed their widespread implementation. Electrostatic discharge, finger oil, and sweat are harsh on silicon devices.

Eye Pattern

The retina is the membrane lining the more posterior part of the inside of the eye. It contains light-sensitive cones and rods and nerve cells. A retinal scan identity-verifier is shown in Figure 12-5. The pattern of blood vessels in the body is unique, and the pattern on the retina of the eye can be assessed optically through the lens of the eye. A circular path about the center of vision is scanned with a very low-intensity, nonlaser light from infrared light-emitting diodes (LEDs). The intensity of the reflected light versus beam position during the scan indicates the unique location of the retinal blood vessels. To enroll, the user must look into the verifier and stare at an alignment target while the optical scan is being made. Several such scans are usually taken and algorithmically combined to create the reference profile. If the device is to be used in the verification mode, a PIN number is usually assigned at this time as well.

Verification, which requires only a single scan, is done in a similar manner. The retinal scanner can also operate in recognition mode. In this mode, the

Figure 12-6. Iris scan device. The user aligns the eye with the camera in the center, then waits for a scan to be completed and to be granted access.

entry of a PIN is not required. Because the entire enrollment file must be reviewed, verification processing time increases as the number of enrollees is increased. Data from an operational evaluation in a laboratory environment indicates that Type I and Type II error rates of less than 1.5% are achievable.[6] User acceptance of this unit has been low, due to the unfounded fear of damage to the eye by the LED.

Another technology uses the iris to accomplish identification. The iris is the colored portion of the eye that limits the amount of light allowed into the eye. This system uses a video camera to image the iris structure of the eye (see Figure 12-6). The unique structure of an iris can be used to identify an individual. This system operates in the recognition mode, so entry of a PIN is not required. A distinct advantage for this system is that the camera images the iris at a distance of about 10.12 inches, so no physical contact between the face and the scanner is required. In addition, the eye is externally illuminated with visible light so there is no LED shining in through the lens. Consequently, user acceptance is better than for the retinal scanner.

Data from a laboratory test of a prototype iris scanner indicated some difficulty with glare off glasses. This caused some Type I (false reject) errors. No Type II (false accept) errors were observed in the laboratory test.[7] Later devices incorporated glare detection and compensation features to counteract problems. Transaction times range from 4 or 5 seconds (by practiced users) up to 15 seconds (for those new to the system). Approximately 2% of the population cannot be enrolled due to blindness or other iris damage, people whose eyes are extremely dilated (no iris to work with) or very dark irises, so they require another method of granting secure access. Both retinal scan and iris scan devices offer high levels of security protection in an entry control subsystem.

Voice

Voice is a useful attribute for identity verification and is appropriate for automatic data processing.

Speech measurements useful for speaker discrimination include waveform envelope, voice pitch period, relative amplitude spectrum, and resonant frequencies of the vocal tract. The system may ask the user to speak a specific predetermined word or to repeat a series of words or numbers selected by the system in order to verify access.

While this technology currently offers low security, it is an attractive alternative due to its ease of deployment and acceptance by the public. Voice recognition systems need only be installed on one end of a telephone system, and perhaps centrally located, reducing the number of units required. In addition, most people have experience with using telephones, so training is minimal, and distrust of the technology is low. As a result, several units are currently being marketed for security applications, and further development is active.

Voice systems also have some associated procedural issues. A person's voice can change due to sickness or stress, so a procedure or backup method of access must be provided to accommodate these instances.

Face

Facial verification systems use distinguishing characteristics of the face to verify a person's identity. Most systems capture the image of the face using a video camera, although one system captures a thermal image using an infrared imager. Distinguishing features are extracted from the image and compared with previously stored features. If the two match within a specified tolerance, positive identity verification results.

Although facial systems have been proposed and studied for a number of years, commercial systems have only been available recently. Developers have had to contend with two difficult problems: (1) wide variations in the presentation of the face (head tilt and rotation, presence or absence of glasses, facial hair changes, facial expression changes, etc.); and (2) lighting variations (day versus night, location A versus location B, etc.). Performance of currently available face systems has not yet approached that of more mature biometric technologies, but face technology does have the appeal of noncontact, and the potential to provide face-in-the-crowd identifications, for identifying known or wanted criminals. This latter application could be useful in casinos, shopping malls, or other places where large crowds can gather.

Other Techniques

Keystroke technology (typing patterns) has been developed and marketed for secure computer log-on. Other verifier techniques based on such things as ear shape, gait (walking patterns), fingernail bed, and body odor have been studied, but little development has been attempted.

Because each biometric technology has some limits in terms of inability to enroll certain people, procedures dealing with this event must be developed. Examples include cataract interference with retinal scanners, very dry or heavily damaged skin (scars, etc.) can cause problems with fingerprint devices, some signature and some speech systems have problems handling certain people because their results are not repeatable. In addition, authorized users may occasionally suffer injuries such as broken fingers or hands, eye injuries or surgery, or other medical conditions, which may temporarily affect their ability to use a biometric device. Additional technology or guard intervention may be required to address this problem. For additional information, Jain, Bolle, and Pankanti (1999) have written a thorough review of biometric techniques and their application. Others (Rejman-Greene, 1998) have discussed biometric devices and security considerations.

Personnel Entry Control Bypass

When coded credentials or biometric technologies are used to allow personnel access into rooms, the use of keyed locks as a bypass route should be considered. This bypass will be useful in case of a component or power failure. The possible vulnerability introduced by this alternate access path can be countered through the use of a BMS or other door sensor. In the event that the door is opened, an alarm will be recorded and can be investigated. This will happen whether a key is used or if the lock is picked or broken. For areas or rooms where multiple entry doors exist, only one door need be equipped with a keyed lock.

References

1. Ed San Luis, Louis A. Tyska, and Lawrence J. Fennelly. *Office and Office Building Security*, 2nd ed. (Boston: Butterworth–Heinemann, 1994), p. 216.
2. Lionel Silverman. "End User Demand Spurs Multiple Technology Cards," *Security Technology & Design*, June 1999, p. 28.

3. Gary Funck. "Smart Card Interfacing," *Security*, June 1999, p. 51.

4. J.P. Holmes, L.J. Wright, and R.L. Maxwell. "A performance evaluation of biometric identification devices." SAND91-0276 1991; 1–29.

5. M. Ruehle and J.S. Ahrens. "Hand geometry field application data analysis." SAND97-0614 1997; 1–51.

6. J.P. Holmes, L.J. Wright, and R.L. Maxwell. "A performance evaluation of biometric identification devices." SAND91-0276 1991; 1–29.

7. F. Bouchier, J.S. Ahrens, and G. Wells. "Laboratory evaluation of the IriScan prototype biometric identifier." SAND96-1033 1996; 1–12.

Chapter 13
Contraband Detection*

MARY LYNN GARCIA

Contraband consists of items such as unauthorized weapons, explosives, and tools. Because they can be used to steal or gain access to or damage vital equipment, weapons and explosives are considered contraband. Where these items are a part of the threat definition, all personnel, materials, and vehicles should be examined for contraband before entry is allowed. Vehicles are difficult to search. If possible, it is advantageous to allow only required vehicles into the secured area. Large or high-security sites may not allow vehicles to leave the secured area routinely. Methods of contraband detection include metal detectors, package searches, and explosive detectors.

Metal Detectors

One system employed for the detection of metal is a magnetometer. The magnetometer is a passive device that monitors the earth's magnetic field and detects changes to that field caused by the presence of ferromagnetic materials. This method detects only ferromagnetic materials (those that are attracted by a magnet). Materials such as copper, aluminum, and zinc are not detected. While most firearms are made of steel, some are not and therefore will not be detected by a magnetometer. Although magnetometers have not been used for contraband screening for many years, research and development of a modern magnetometer has been conducted in recent years. Although the term magnetometer is often used to

refer to metal detectors in general, this device differs greatly from modern active metal detectors.

Most metal detectors currently in use to detect contraband carried by personnel actively generate a varying magnetic field over a short period of time. These devices either detect the changes made to the field due to the introduction of metal to the field, or detect the presence of eddy currents that exist in a metallic object caused by a pulsed field. The magnitude of the metal detector's response to metallic objects is determined by several factors including the conductivity of the metal, the magnetic properties of the metal (relative permeability), object shape and size, and the orientation of the object within the magnetic field.

At present two methods are commonly used to actively detect metal: continuous wave and pulsed field. Continuous-wave detectors generate a steady-state magnetic field within the frequency band of 100 Hz to 25 kHz. Pulsed-field detectors generate fixed frequency pulses in the 400 to 500 pulse-per-second range. Due to the complex shape of the waveforms employed, the pulsed fields may have frequency components from zero to several tens of kHz.

A typical coil configuration for continuous wave metal detection is illustrated in Figure 13-1A. A steady-state sinusoidal signal is applied to the transmitter coil located at one side of the detector arch. This coil produces a magnetic field of low strength. The receiver coils are mounted on the opposite side of the arch such that a person being screened passes between the transmitter and the receiver coils. The signal is detected by the receiver coils and then routed to a balanced differential amplifier, which amplifies only the difference between two signals. When there is no metal present within the arch, there is no difference in the signals at the inputs to the dif-

*Garcia, *Design and Evaluation of Physical Protection Systems*, pp. 178–184, Butterworth Heinemann, 2001

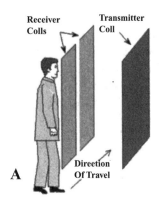

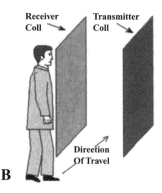

Figure 13-1. Metal detector technologies. (A) Represents a continuous wave device. (B) A pulsed wave device.

ferential amplifier; therefore, there is no output signal from the amplifier. When a metallic object enters the arch, the changes it makes to the magnetic field disturb the balance of the receiver coils. The unbalanced field produces a difference at the differential amplifier resulting in an output signal. This signal is then further amplified and phase-checked. If the signal exceeds a selected threshold, an alarm is generated. The phase detection permits some optimization of detection for either ferromagnetic (high relative permeability) or nonferromagnetic (low relative permeability) metals.

A typical coil configuration for a pulsed-field metal detector is shown in Figure 13-1B. The coil arrangement is similar to that of the continuous-wave metal detector. The greatest difference to the coil configuration is that the balanced receiver coils are not required for pulsed-field operation. The multiple transmitter coils produce magnetic field flux patterns that lessen the effects of object orientation on detector response. The low inductance transmitter coils are driven with a series of pulses that produce short bursts of magnetic field (as short as 50 microseconds), 200 to 400 times per second. During the time that the magnetic field is present, the receiver amplifiers are switched off. Following the end of the transmitted pulse, the receiver amplifiers are switched on for a period of time, typically a few tens of milliseconds. When there is no metal present in the arch, the output of the receiver amplifiers is the low background electromagnetic noise. When there is a metallic object present in the arch, the collapse of the magnetic pulse induces an eddy current in the metal. This eddy current decreases rapidly as a function of the resistivity of the metal but persists long enough to be present when the receiver amplifiers are switched on. The signal is then further amplified and phase detected. If the signal exceeds a selected threshold, an alarm is generated. The phase

detection again allows for optimization for detection of ferromagnetic metals or nonferromagnetic metals. Modern digital technology allows for more analysis of the signal, resulting in better discrimination between different types of metals and real targets and the harmless metallic objects carried by people being screened.

When a portal metal detector is used to detect very small quantities of metal such as gold, detection may be very difficult. In the case of a continuous-wave detector, the use of a higher-than-usual frequency will enhance detection; in all cases very-high-sensitivity operation will be required. Because high-sensitivity operation will sharply increase the nuisance alarm rate, an area for personnel to change out of steel-toed shoes and to remove other metallic items from their body may be required. Handheld metal detectors can detect very small quantities of metals and may be better suited to the task of screening very small items. The disadvantage of handheld metal detectors is the requirement for active guard participation in the screening process and the time required for the search. Handheld metal detectors can also be considered intrusive due to the proximity of the metal detector to the person being screened. This can be especially intrusive when the screener and the person being screened are of opposite sex. Many sites, notably airports, provide same-sex operators to address this unease.

Because the magnetic field is not confined to the area between the coils and metal detectors are sensitive to metal moving outside the physical boundaries of the detector, care must be exercised in determining detector placement. Any movable metallic objects either in front or to the side of the detector, such as doors, forklifts, and carts, can cause nuisance alarms. Electromagnetic transients, such as radio transmitters, power-line fluctuations, and flickering fluorescent lighting, can cause false alarms.

Metal detectors are designed to be tolerant of some nonmoving metal in their immediate area. Reinforcing steel in concrete floors and walls and other metallic building materials can be tolerated to some degree; however, installing a metal detector against a steel support beam is not recommended. Large quantities of metal can cause severe distortions in the magnetic field. In some cases the metal detector will not operate and may generate an error alarm; in other cases the detector may continue to operate but have areas of extremely low or high sensitivity. These distortions may lead to missed targets or unusually high nuisance alarms due to innocuous items. Metallic items, such as safety equipment, metal trash cans, chairs, and other items, may not completely interfere with a metal detector if placed close to the detector but can cause distortions to the detection field. For this reason, some installations institute a no-move rule for these metallic items within the vicinity of the detector following installation testing.

Package Search

Packages may be searched for contraband manually or by active interrogation. Active interrogation methods used to detect various objects considered contraband include single-energy transmission x-ray, multiple-energy x-ray, computer tomography (CT) scan, and backscatter x-ray. In general, these methods are not safe for use on personnel; however, a new x-ray technology for screening personnel will be discussed in the section titled "Bulk Explosives Detection" later in this chapter. In general, simple single-energy transmission x-ray imagers are used to find metallic items and the other techniques are designed to image low-Z materials. Examples of low-Z contraband materials are drugs, explosives, and some foodstuffs. Low-Z materials are materials that are composed of elements that have a low atomic number. Low-Z elements include hydrogen, oxygen, carbon, and all the elements up to aluminum, with Z number 26.

A conventional single-energy-transmission x-ray package search system will not penetrate the heavy materials sometimes used for shipping containers. High-energy x-rays or multiple-energy x-rays can be used to assess the contents of the package being examined. Because most of the development of low-Z screening devices is directed toward the detection of explosives, these technologies are discussed in detail in the section entitled "Bulk Explosives Detection" below. Although discussion of these devices will focus on explosive detection, most of

these technologies can be adjusted to search for drugs as well.

Explosives Detectors

Vapor Detectors

Methods commonly used for inspecting cargo and luggage for explosives, for example, x-ray imaging or neutron activation, are unacceptable for screening personnel because these methods are physically harmful to humans. Passive detection techniques can be used to safely search personnel for explosives by detecting the trace amounts of vapor that are emitted from bulk quantities of concealed explosives. The challenge involved in detecting trace explosives vapors is evident after consideration of the low vapor-phase concentrations of several common high explosives. Concentrations in the parts-per-billion or parts-per-trillion range are typical, with further reductions in vapor pressures encountered when the explosive constituent is packaged in an oil-based gel or solvent (for example, RDX in C-4 plastic explosive). Explosive molecules readily stick to many common materials at room temperature, and decompose upon moderate heating or upon exposure to large doses of energy. Hence, transport and collection of vapor-phase explosive molecules is achieved only at the expense of significant sample loss.

Several approaches have been developed for the vapor-phase detection of explosives. These passive methods of detection include animal olfaction (dogs) and vapor detection instruments. Examples of vapor detection instruments are electron capture detection (ECD), chemiluminescence, ion mobility spectrometry (IMS), and mass spectroscopy.

Canine olfaction is used widely in law enforcement and the military for locating hidden explosives. However, canines require constant retraining to continue to identify synthetic compounds such as explosives. Moreover, the reliability of canine inspection is subject to the health and disposition of the dog and the vigilance and skill of the handler. As a result, the use of canines is very expensive. For these reasons, commercial explosive detectors are gaining greater acceptance as the preferred method for screening personnel for explosives.

Electron capture detectors (ECDs) take advantage of the high electron affinity of nitro compounds to identify trace explosives in a vapor sample. An air sample is drawn into the ECD detection chamber that is plated with a beta particle source such as

Ni-63 that emits low energy electrons (beta radiation). A pulsed positive voltage is applied to the anode, resulting in a measurable standing current, IO. As this positive voltage is switched on and off, the anode current oscillates between zero and IO. In the presence of electrophilic (electron-capturing) materials, such as explosive molecules, this thermal electron population is decreased. When the anode voltage is pulsed, the resulting anode current is reduced from the standing current value IO by an amount proportional to the concentration of high explosives in the detector. This results in a new current I, which is less than IO. Thus, a drop in anode current indicates the presence of electrophilic molecules and signals an alarm. Electron capture technology itself is not specific; that is, it cannot determine the specific explosive detected. By coupling the ECD with another technology such as a gas chromatograph (GC), identification of the type of explosive can be made.

Chemiluminescence detectors use photochemical means to yield detection. The vapor sample is collected and separated into its components using a gas chromatograph. The sample is then heated so that any nitrogen compounds that are present will decompose to form nitrogen oxide (NO). Reaction of NO with ozone forms an excited state of nitrogen dioxide (NO_2), which emits a photon that can be detected using a phototube. The coupling of the photoemission and the chromatograph permits identification of any nitro-based explosive compounds that are present.

Chemiluminescence detectors have excellent sensitivity to common high explosives, including compounds with very low vapor pressures such as RDX and PETN. However, the chemiluminescence instruments are also the most expensive of the commercial detectors, have the longest analysis time, and typically require more maintenance than the ECD units. Because other sources of nitrogen oxide, such as automotive exhaust, may provide potential interferents, chemiluminescent detection is paired with fast gas chromatograph separation to distinguish explosives from other nitrogen containing compounds.

In an ion mobility spectrometer (IMS) the analyte molecules in an air sample are negatively ionized using a beta source (as in the case of ECDs) and then passed into a drift cell through a shutter, which opens periodically over a period of milliseconds. Within the drift region, the ionized species move down an electric field gradient against a counter-flow of an inert gas. The molecules separate by weight, with the lightweight species and their smaller cross-sections progressing more quickly upstream than the massive

species. At the end of the drift region the ions strike a Faraday plate that records the output voltage as a function of molecule drift time. A typical IMS drift cell is 6 to 8 cm in length with an electric field gradient of 200 V/cm. Under these conditions, the drift times of the explosive molecules range from 5 to 20 milliseconds. Coupling with a gas chromatograph is not necessary for identification of the analyte since the time-of-flight separation achieved in the drift region provides specificity.

IMS-based detectors provide high sensitivity to dynamite, military-grade TNT, and plastic explosives compounds, at instrument costs that are considerably lower than those of chemiluminescence detectors. Detection using IMS is highly specific; aside from some compounds used as fragrances in lotions and perfumes, there are few potential interferents. The sensitivity of the IMS-type detector and its relative ease of operation and maintenance account for the rapid development and commercialization of IMS technology for explosive detection applications.

One type of mass spectroscopy is based on the principle that charged particles traveling through a magnetic field will follow a circular path. The radius of the path is determined by the mass of the particle. Because explosive molecules are easy to negatively charge and the mass of each type of explosive is different, this technique allows separation and identification of the explosive materials. Other mass spectroscopy techniques include time-of-flight and quadrapole mass spectroscopy.

From laboratory evaluations of commercial detectors that are currently on the market, it can be stated that the ECD instruments are the simplest to operate, least expensive, and least sensitive of the commercial detectors (Hannum and Parmeter, 1998). ECDs can detect TNT and nitrated dynamite consistently, but they are not reliable for sensing plastic-type explosives. There are some common nonexplosive substances that give rise to potential nuisance alarm signals in ECDs, including chlorofluorocarbons, fertilizers, and some household cleaners. Coated chromatographic columns or membranes are coupled with ECDs to discriminate between true explosives and interferents.

Most commercial explosives detectors achieve greatest sensitivity when used in the surface sampling mode, in which a surface suspected of explosives contamination is swiped with a collector pad made of cloth, sharkskin, or similar material. The collector pad is then placed in a heating unit, which desorbs the particles of explosives that have been gathered and transports them to the detector for analysis. But due to time constraints, this mode of sampling is impractical for screening individuals passing through sensitive high-traffic checkpoints, such as airport boarding areas, for explosive contraband. The development and commercialization of a walk-through portal explosives detector, for screening high throughput areas for concealed explosives contraband, is therefore a high research and development priority.

Commercial explosives vapor detectors must be carefully selected to meet the needs of each facility. The sensitivity, nuisance alarm resistance, response time, and operating and maintenance costs are all factors to consider when selecting a detector.

Bulk Explosives Detection

Bulk explosives detection devices measure some bulk characteristic of materials in an attempt to detect the possible presence of explosives. Some of the bulk characteristics that may be measured are the x-ray absorption coefficient, the x-ray backscatter coefficient, the dielectric constant, the gamma or neutron interaction, and the microwave or infrared emissions. Further analysis of these parameters can result in calculated mass, density, nitrogen content, and effective atomic number (effective Z). While none of these characteristics are unique to explosives, they are sufficiently unique to indicate a high probability of the presence of explosives. Fortunately, many materials that share similar bulk characteristics with explosives are not overly common to everyday items. The nuisance alarm rate for bulk detection devices can be low enough to allow for automatic detection of materials that may be explosives.

Nuclear technologies interrogate a package using gamma rays or neutrons. These devices determine the nitrogen content of a material. Because many explosives are nitrogen rich, these devices can automatically detect their presence. Currently the only two commercially available nuclear technology detectors are the thermal neutron activation (TNA) detector and the pulsed fast neutron absorption (PFNA). The major drawbacks of these devices are the cost (from about \$600,000 to several million), size, and throughput. Some package search systems are based on TNA, and some systems for search of vehicles and large shipping containers are based on PFNA.

In most cases, x-ray technology bulk detectors are modified package search x-ray scanners. These technologies are beginning to provide lower-cost alternatives to nuclear technologies. These devices

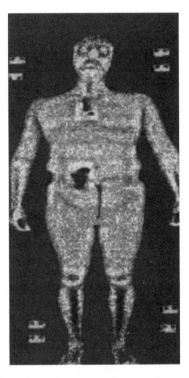

Figure 13-2. Computer-enhanced output of an x-ray personnel scanner. The subject appears to have something around the neck and what looks like a weapon in the belt.

usually serve a dual purpose. The package being searched for guns or other contraband is simultaneously analyzed for the presence of explosives. Simple single-energy-transmission x-ray scanners do not provide enough information to make the explosives search, so a method to extract more information is needed. Dual-energy and dual-axis technologies allow the determination of a material's approximate mass absorption coefficient. CT scanners can extract enough information to calculate the material's mass and density, as well as its mass absorption coefficient. Backscatter technology can determine a material's effective Z by examining the amount of x-ray energy scattered back in the direction of the source.

Fully automating an x-ray backscattering system is not possible at the present time. Certainly the entry and exit of personnel, positioning of personnel to be scanned, and energizing and deenergizing the x-ray system can all be automated. However, the result of a scan is a computer-enhanced image on a display monitor showing the outline of the person and any concealed objects. Recognizing an object as being suspicious and requesting further verification to determine if it is an explosive is the responsibility of the operator or security officer. Figure 13-2 illustrates a typical computer-enhanced image obtained with various materials located on the subject.

Quadrupole resonance (QR) technology is a promising new technology that was recently incorporated into a commercial device. This technology uses pulsed low energy radio waves to determine the presence of nitrogen-rich materials. A QR scanner is compact, relatively low cost (about $100,000), and does not subject the package to ionizing radiation. Until recently, personnel screening for explosives could be done only by an explosive vapor detection portal, a handheld explosive vapor detector, or hand searching. However, low-dose x-ray (also known as soft x-ray and low-energy x-ray) scanning is now available, which can detect contraband concealed on personnel, such as weapons, explosives, and drugs, including gel-type explosives.

In any screening device used on people, safety is of prime importance. The radiation dose received while being scanned needs to be so low that it is virtually indistinguishable from background. Present scanners can scan only one side at a time. A person entering a scanner booth would have to be scanned two times, front and back, to ensure that no explosives are secreted on the person. For general use, the low-dose x-ray system should:

1. Be capable of processing approximately 10 people per minute;
2. Have the demonstrated capability to discern the presence of an explosives mass of 150 g or more on a person; and

3. Demonstrate a radiation output of sufficiently low magnitude that personnel will receive a radiation dose less than the permissible 100 millirem/year, which is required under NRC regulations in 10 CFR Part 20, Section 20.103 (a) (1). Ideally, the radiation dose should be <10 microrem per scan. Other technologies under development involve the use of microwave energy to determine the dielectric constant of a material, millimeter wave devices that image objects under clothing, and passive devices that detect microwave or infrared energy emitted from materials.

It is important to note that the devices described in this section are not explosives detectors but are detectors of materials that have explosive-like characteristics. All have strengths and weaknesses. A successful system based on bulk detection techniques may consist of a combination of two or more of these technologies. If enough information is gathered on a suspect material through this combination, a real determination of the presence of explosives may be made.

Reference

D.W. Hannum and J.E. Parmeter. "Survey of Commercially Available Explosives Detection Technologies and Equipment." National Law Enforcement and Corrections Technology Center. 1998; pp. 9–19. Available at: *http://www. nlectc.org/pdfiles/expsurvey.pdf.*

Chapter 14A
CCTV Surveillance*

HERMAN KRUEGLE

Protection of Assets: An Overview

The application and integration of closed circuit television (CCTV) to safety and security application has come of age. CCTV is a reliable, cost-effective deterrent and a means for the apprehension and prosecution of offenders. Most safety and security applications require several different types of equipment (i.e., alarm, fire, intrusion, access control) with CCTV most often being included as one or more of them.

In today's complex society, security personnel are responsible for the many factors required to produce an effective security and safety system. CCTV plays an important role in these systems. With today's spiraling labor costs, CCTV more than ever before has earned its place as a cost-effective means for expanding security and safety, while reducing security budgets.

Loss of assets and time due to theft is a growing cancer in our society that eats away at the profits of every organization or business, be it government, retail, service, or manufacturing. The size of the organization makes no difference to the thief. The larger the company, the larger the theft, and the greater the opportunity for losses. The more valuable the product is, the easier it is to dispose of, and the greater the temptation to steal it. The implementation of a CCTV system properly designed and applied can be an extremely profitable investment to the institution. The main objective of the CCTV system should not be in the apprehension of thieves but rather in increasing deterrence through security so as to prevent thievery. A successful thief needs privacy in which to operate and it is the function of the television system to prevent this. If an organiza-

tion or company can deter an incident from occurring in the first place, the problem has been solved.

As a security by-product, CCTV has emerged as an effective training tool for management and security personnel. The use of CCTV systems has improved employee efficiency, with a resultant rise in productivity.

The public at large has accepted use of CCTV systems in public and industrial facilities, and resistance by workers to its presence and use is steadily decreasing. With present business economics getting worse, people begin looking for other ways to increase their income and means for paying the bills. CCTV is being applied to counteract these losses, and increase corporate profits.

There are many case histories in which CCTV is installed and shoplifting and employee thefts drop sharply. The number of thefts cannot be counted exactly, but the reduction in shrinkage can be measured, and it has been shown that CCTV is an effective psychological deterrent to crime.

Theft takes the form of removing valuable property from premises, as well as removing information in the form of computer software, magnetic tape and disks, optical disks, microfilm, and data on paper. CCTV surveillance systems provide a means for successfully deterring such thievery or detecting or apprehending offenders. Another form of loss that CCTV prevents is the willful destruction of property. Such crimes include vandalizing buildings, defacing elevator interiors, painting graffiti on priceless art objects and facilities, demolishing furniture or other valuable equipment, and destroying computer rooms.

The greatest potential for CCTV is its integration with other sensing systems (alarms) and its use to view remote areas having potential security and safety problems or fire hazards. CCTV, combined with smoke detectors where the cameras are located

*Kruegle, *CCTV Surveillance*, pp. 1–9, Butterworth Heinemann, 1995

in inaccessible areas, can be used to give advance warning of a fire.

CCTV is an important technology that must comprise a link in the overall security of a facility. It is important that the organization recognize that it needs to develop a complete plan instead of adopting protection measures in bits and pieces and reacting to problems as they occur. The practitioner and end user must understand all aspects of CCTV technology in order to make the best use of the technology. This ranges from the lighting sources needed to illuminate the scene, to the video monitors that display them. The capabilities and limitations of CCTV during daytime and nighttime operation must be understood.

The protection of assets is a management function. Three key factors that govern the planning of an assets protection program are (1) an adequate plan designed to prevent losses from occurring, (2) adequate countermeasures to limit the losses and to limit unpreventable losses, and (3) support of the protection plan by top management.

History

The CCTV industry began in the 1960s, and experienced a rapid growth throughout the 1970s because of the increased reliability and improvements in technology of the tube type camera. In the 1980s the growth continued at a more modest level with further improvements in functions and other accessories required to complete the television security system. During the 1980s, the introduction of the solid-state CCTV camera was the most significant advance; by the early 1990s it had replaced most of the tube cameras used over the past 30 years.

The most significant driving factor causing this CCTV explosion has been the worldwide increase in theft and terrorism and the commensurate need to more adequately protect personnel and assets. The second factor contributing to the proliferation of CCTV security equipment has been the rapid increase in equipment capability at affordable prices.

This is a result of the widespread use of solid-state CCTV for consumer use (made possible through technological breakthroughs) and the resulting availability of low-cost videocassette recorders (VCRs) and associated camera equipment. These two driving functions have been responsible for the accelerated development and implementation of the excellent CCTV equipment available today.

In the past the camera and, in particular, the vidicon sensor tube was the critical item in the system design. The camera determined the overall performance, quantity, and quality of visual intelligence obtainable

from the security system, because the camera's image tube was the weakest link in the system and was subject to degradation with age and usage. The complexity and variability of the image tube and its analog electrical nature made it less reliable than the other, solid-state, components. Performance varied considerably between different camera models and manufacturers, and as a function of temperature and age. Today the situation is considerably different, with the availability of the solid-state charged-coupled device (CCD) and metal oxide semiconductor (MOS) cameras. While the various solid-state cameras from different manufacturers have different features, the cameras are reliable and the performance similar, with modest variations in sensitivity and resolution rather than inherent generic differences as in tube cameras. Systems are more reliable and stable because the remaining wear out mechanism—the vacuum tube—has been displaced by a solid-state device.

This innovation and the widespread consumer use of camcorders have resulted in the widespread use of solid-state monochrome and color cameras in security applications.

Role of CCTV in Asset Protection

CCTV plays an important role in the protection of assets. In one phase, CCTV is used to detect unwanted entry into a facility, beginning at the perimeter location, and continuing by following the intruder throughout the facility (Figure 14-1).

In a perimeter protection role, CCTV is used with intrusion detection devices to alert the guard at the security console that an intrusion has occurred. When an intrusion occurs, multiple CCTV cameras located throughout the facility follow the intruder so that there is a proper response by guard personnel or designated employees. Management determines whether specific guard reaction is required and what the response will be. It is obvious that CCTV is advantageous in that is allows the guard to be more effective, but in addition it improves security by permitting the camera scene to be documented via a VCR or from a hard copy video printer. In the relatively short history of CCTV, there have been great innovations in the permanent recording of video images for later use, brought about primarily by the consumer demand and availability of video camcorders and VCRs. The ability to record video provides CCTV security with a new dimension, going beyond real-time camera surveillance. The specialized time-lapse recorders and video printers as well as magnetic storage of video images on magnetic and optical hard disks now gives management the oppor-

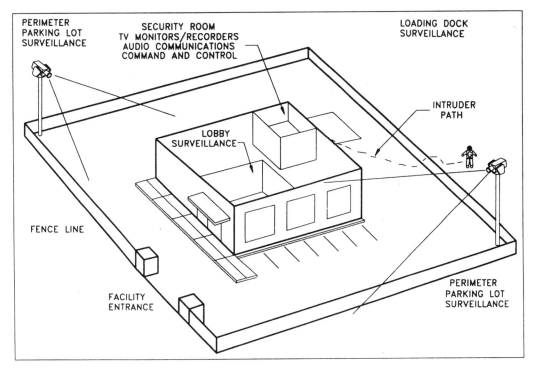

Figure 14-1. CCTV security system.

tunity to present hard evidence for prosecution against criminals. This ability of CCTV is of prime importance to those protecting assets since it permits permanent identification of wrongdoing.

Most CCTV security is accomplished with monochrome equipment, but the solid-state camera has now made color security practical. The tube type color cameras were unreliable, they had short life and high maintenance costs, and their color balance could not be maintained over even short periods of time. The development of color CCD cameras for the consumer VCR market accelerated the availability of these reliable, stable, long-life cameras for the security industry. Likewise, the availability of the VCR technology resulting from consumer demand made possible the excellent time-lapse VCR providing the permanent documentation required for CCTV security applications. While monochrome and not color is the camera specified in major security applications, the trend is toward the use of color in security. As the sensitivity and resolution of the color camera increases and the cost decreases, color cameras will replace most monochrome types.

Along with the introduction of solid-state cameras has come the decrease in size of ancillary equipment (i.e., lenses, housings, pan/tilt mechanisms, and brackets), which decreases cost and pro-

vides more aesthetic installations. Likewise, for covert CCTV applications, the small cameras and lenses are easier to conceal.

The potential importance of color in surveillance applications is illustrated clearly by looking at a color television scene on a television monitor, be it surveillance or other, and then turning off the color to make it a monochrome scene. It becomes quite obvious how much information is lost when the colors in the scene change to shades of gray. Objects easily identified in the color scene become difficult to identify in the monochrome scene. It is much easier to pick out a person with an article of clothing of particular color in the color scene than it is in the monochrome scene. Many other examples of the additional ease of identification when color is available are present in the security application. Part of the reason we can identify better with color than we can with monochrome is that we are used to seeing color, both visually and on our own home television systems. Therefore, when we see a monochrome scene, it takes an additional effort to recognize certain information, in addition to the actual colors being missing from the picture, thereby decreasing the intelligence available. Providing more accurate identification of personnel and objects leads to a higher degree of apprehension and conviction for crimes. The security industry has long recognized the value of color to enhance personnel and article identification in video surveillance and access control.

CCTV as Part of the Emergency and Disaster Plan

Every organization regardless of size should have an emergency and disaster control plan, which should include CCTV as a critical component. Included in this plan should be a procedure for succession of personnel in the event one or more members of top management are unavailable when the disaster strikes. In large organizations the plan should include the designation of alternate headquarters if possible, a safe document storage facility, and remote CCTV operations capability. The plan must include providing for medical aid and assuring the welfare of all employees. Using CCTV as a source of information, there should be a method to alert employees in the event of a dangerous condition and a plan to provide for quick police and emergency response. There should be an emergency shutdown plan and restoration procedures with designated employees acting as leaders. There should be CCTV cameras stationed along evacuation routes and instructions for practice tests. The evacuation plan should be thought out in advance and tested.

A logical and effective disaster control plan includes at least the following aspects:

- It defines emergencies and disasters that could occur as they relate to the particular organization.
- It establishes an organization and specific tasks with personnel designated to carry out the plan immediately before, during, and immediately following a disaster.
- It establishes a method for utilizing the resources, in particular CCTV, to analyze the disaster situation and bring to bear all resources available at the time.
- It recognizes a plan to change from normal operations into and back out of the disaster emergency mode as soon as possible.

CCTV plays a very important role in any emergency and disaster plan:

1. CCTV aids in protecting human life by enabling security or safety officials to see remote locations via CCTV and to view first-hand what is happening, where it is happening, what is most critical, and what areas must be attended to first.
2. CCTV aids in minimizing personal injury by permitting "remote eyes" to get to those people who require the attention first, or send personnel to the area being hit hardest to remove them from the area, or bring in equipment to protect them.
3. CCTV reduces the exposure of physical assets to oncoming disaster (fire, flood, and so forth) or helps to prevent, or at least assess and document, removal (of assets) by intruders or any unauthorized personnel.
4. CCTV documents equipment and assets which were in place prior to the disaster, recording them on VCR, hard disk, and the like, to be compared to the remaining assets after the disaster has occurred and allowing assessment of loss to be made. It documents personnel and their activities prior to, during, and after an incident.
5. CCTV is useful in restoring an organization to normal operation by determining that no additional emergencies are in progress and that normal procedures and traffic flow are occurring in those restored areas.

CCTV, probably more than any other part of a security system, will aid management and the security force in minimizing any disaster or emergency and restoring the organization to normal conditions more effectively.

Protection of Life and Minimization of Injury

Using the intelligence gathered from CCTV, security and disaster control personnel should move all personnel to places of safety and shelter. Personnel assigned to disaster control and remaining in a threatened area should be protected by use of CCTV to monitor access to these locations as well as the safety of the personnel involved. With such monitoring, advance notice is available if a means of support and assistance for those persons is required or if injured personnel must be rescued or relieved.

Reduce Exposure of Physical Assets and Optimize Loss Control

Assets should be stored or secured properly in advance of an emergency so that in an emergency or disaster they will be less vulnerable to theft or loss. CCTV is an important tool, which can be used to continually monitor such areas during and after a disaster to insure that material is not removed. If an emergency or disaster occurs, the well-documented plan will dispatch specific personnel to locations of highly valued assets to secure them and to evacuate personnel.

Restore Normal Operations Quickly

After the emergency situation has been brought under control, CCTV and security personnel provide the functions of monitoring and maintaining security of assets and aiding in determining that employees have returned to normal work and are safe.

Documentation of the Emergency

For future planning purposes, for insurance purposes, and for critique by management and security, CCTV coverage of critical areas and operations during an emergency can save an organization considerable money. Documentation provided by CCTV recordings of assets lost or stolen or personnel injuries or deaths can support the contention that the company was not negligent and that a prudent emergency and disaster plan was in effect prior to the event. While CCTV plays a very important part in the documentation of an event, it is important to supplement it with high-resolution photographs of specific instances or events.

As part of the CCTV documentation, in the event fences and walls are destroyed or damaged in the disaster, it is likely that interested spectators and other outsiders will be attracted to the scene. Looting by employees as well as outsiders is a hazard and must be guarded against, with CCTV playing an important part in preventing and documenting such events.

Emergency Shutdown and Restoration

In the overall disaster threat plan, consideration must be given to the shutdown of equipment such as machinery, utilities, processes, and the like, so that such equipment does not increase the hazards of the situation. Furnaces, gas generators, electrical power equipment, boilers, high-pressure air or oil systems, chemical equipment, or rapidly rotating machinery that could cause damage if left unattended should be shut down as soon as possible. CCTV can aid in determining whether this equipment has been shut down properly, whether personnel must enter the area to do so, or whether other means must be taken to take it offline.

Testing the Plan

While a good emergency disaster plan is essential, it should not be tested for the first time in an actual disaster situation. Regardless of how well the planning has been done, various deficiencies will be discovered during the testing of the plan as well as its serving to train the personnel who will carry it out if it should be necessary. CCTV can play a critical part in evaluation of the plan to identify shortcomings and to illustrate to the personnel carrying out the plan what they did right and wrong. Through such peer review, a practical and efficient plan can be put in place to minimize losses to the organization.

Stand-by Power and Communications

It is likely that during any emergency or disaster, primary power and communications from one location to another will be disrupted. Therefore, a stand-by power generation system should be provided to replace the primary power for emergency monitoring and response equipment. This stand-by power will keep emergency lighting, communications, and strategic CCTV equipment online as needed during the emergency. Most installations use a power-sensing device, which monitors the normal supply of power at various locations to sense when power is lost. When such an alert is received, the various backup equipment automatically switches to the emergency power source comprising a backup gas powered generator or an uninterruptable power supply (UPS), with DC batteries to extend backup operation time. A prudent security plan anticipating an emergency will include a means to power vital CCTV, audio, and other sensor equipment to insure its operation during the event. Since CCTV and audio communications must be maintained over remote distances during such an occurrence, an alternate means of such communication from one location to another should be supplied either in the form of auxiliary hard-wired cable of a wireless (RF, microwave, or infrared) system. Since it is usually impractical to provide a backup path to all CCTV camera locations, only critical cameras will have this auxiliary communication path. It is necessary to properly size the stand-by generator supplying power to the CCTV, safety, and emergency equipment. In the case of batteries supplying the secondary power, if equipment operates from 120 volt AC, inverters are used to convert the low voltage from the DC batteries (typically 12 or 24 volt DC) to the required 120 volt AC.

Security Investigations

CCTV has been used very successfully in security investigations pertaining to company assets and theft, negligence, outside intrusion, and so forth. Using covert CCTV where the camera and lens are hidden from view by any personnel in the area, positive identification and documentation of an event and the person involved is easily made. Many advances in the quality of the video image obtained, the reduction in size of lens and camera, and ease of installation and removal of such equipment has led to this high success. At present, there are many lenses and cameras, which can be hidden in rooms, hallways, and specific objects in the environment. Equipment is available for indoor or outdoor locations operating under bright sunlight or no light conditions to provide such surveillance.

Safety

CCTV equipment is not always installed just for security reasons. Its use and value is often for safety purposes. Many security personnel can observe situations in which unsafe practices are being followed or in which an accident occurs and needs immediate attention. By means of CCTV cameras distributed throughout a facility, in stairwells and loading docks, around machinery, such safety violations or accidents can be observed and documented immediately by an alert guard.

Guard Role

Historically, guards were used primarily for plant protection. Now they are used for protection of assets. Management is now more aware that guards are only one element of an organization's complete security plan. As such, the guard's duties are compared to other security plan functions in terms of ability to protect as well as cost to management. CCTV in this respect contributes much in terms of increased security provided by relatively low capital investment, and low operating cost as compared to a guard. Through the use of CCTV, guards can increase the security coverage or protection of a facility. Alternatively, guard count can be reduced by installing new CCTV equipment. Guards can monitor remote sites, thereby reducing guard and security costs significantly.

Training/Education of Employees

CCTV is a powerful training tool. CCTV is in widespread use in education because it can demonstrate so vividly and conveniently to the trainee what is to be learned, and demonstrate examples of the procedure used to implement a function or desired result.

Examples of all types can be demonstrated conveniently in a short time with instructions during the presentation. Real life situations (not rehearsed or performed) are available to demonstrate to the trainee what can happen when procedures are not followed and the improved results obtained when plans are properly carried out by trained and knowledgeable personnel. Every organization can supplement live training either with professional training videos or by showing actual scenes from their own video system, demonstrating good and poor practices with real situations of intrusion, unacceptable employee behavior, and proper guard reaction to such incidents. Such internal videos can also be used for training a person by having that person takes part in the exercise and later having the video sequence critiqued by his or her supervisor. In this way trainees observe their own actions to determine how they can improve and become more effective. The use of such internal video is very important in carrying out rehearsals or tests of an emergency or disaster plan in which all members of the team observe their response and are critiqued by management or other professionals to improve such performance.

Synergy through Integration

CCTV equipment is most effective when integrated with other security hardware and procedures to form a coherent security system and team that can protect and be responsible for the assets and safety of personnel in an organization. Such an integrated security system is more than a combination or accumulation of sensing security equipment. The hardware used in synergy with CCTV is electronic access control, fire and safety alarms, intrusion detection alarms, communication, and security personnel (Figure 14-2).

Functionally the integrated security system can be regarded as a design coordinated combination of equipment, personnel, and procedures which utilizes each component in such a way as to enhance the use of every other component with an end result that assures optimum achievement of the system's stated objective.

In designing a security system, any element chosen should be analyzed to determine how it will contribute to prevent loss or how it will protect assets and personnel. As an example, if an intrusion occurs, at what point should it be detected, what should the response be? And if there has been violation of some form of barrier or fence, the intrusion detection system should be able to determine that a person has passed through the barrier and not an animal, bird, insect, leaves, or debris (false alarms).

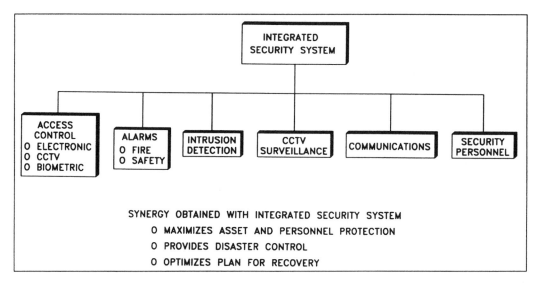

Figure 14-2. Integrated security system.

CCTV proves the most positive means for making this determination. The next step is to have a means for communicating this information to the security personnel reaction force with enough information to permit a guard to initiate a response directed to the intrusion location.

As another example, if materials are being removed from a location by an unauthorized person in an interior area, a CCTV surveillance system activated by a video motion detector alarm should alert the guard and transmit the video information to security personnel for appropriate action. In both cases, there would be a guard response or some other response and the event would be recorded on VCR or printed out on hard copy for efficient response, documentation, and prosecution. In these examples and many others, the combination of different sensors, intelligence communication devices, and the use of guard and documentation equipment provide a synergy that maximizes the security function. The synergistic integration of CCTV, access control, alarms, intrusion detection, and security guards into a system increases the overall security of the facility and maximizes assets protection and employee safety.

It is important for management to recognize that a complete CCTV system may be assembled from components manufactured by different companies, and it is important that all equipment be compatible. CCTV equipment can be specified, installed, and maintained individually by consulting firms, architects/engineers, or small and large security dealers, to complete a security system. The equipment and service should be purchased through a single dealer/installer or general contractor. It is generally advantageous to purchase the CCTV equipment and services from one major supplier who provides a turnkey system including all equipment, training, and maintenance, as opposed to purchasing the system from several sources. This places the responsibility of system operation on one vendor, which is easier to control. Buying from one source permits management to go back to the installer or general contractor if there are any problems. Choosing a single supplier obviously requires that a judicious choice be made after a thorough analysis to determine that the supplier will (1) provide a good system, (2) be available for maintenance when required, and (3) still be in existence 5 to 10 years down the road.

There are presently multiple sources for the pan/tilt mechanisms, lenses, time-lapse recorders, housings, and so forth, required in a sophisticated CCTV system. In the 1970s and mid-1980s there was not this duplication in component manufacturers. While this gives the end user a choice in each component required, it can have the disadvantage that not all the equipment is compatible. The system designer and installer integrating the system must be aware of differences and be capable of interfacing them properly to permit proper use and produce a successful security system. A security plan starting with a simple system with the anticipation of expanding the security equipment at a future time should be designed so that the equipment is built in a modular form and can be expanded in the future to accept new technology as it becomes available. Many of the larger security equipment manufacturing companies anticipate this integration and expansion requirement, and design their equipment accordingly. Many manufacturers now have comparable equipment, but system integrators must take the responsibility of choosing compatible equipment. In a system where equipment is supplied by several manufacturers, someone must take responsibility for system integration and maintenance.

Service is a key ingredient to the successful operation of a security system. If one component fails, it is necessary to have it repaired or replaced quickly so that the system is not shut down and out of service. Near-continuous operation is accomplished by the direct replacement method: (1) immediate maintenance by an in-house service organization, or (2) quick-response service calls from the installer/contractor. An important consideration in any security system is to decide during the planning and initial design stages how service will be accomplished. Most vendors use the replacement technique to maintain and service equipment. If part of the equipment fails, the company replaces the defective equipment and sends it to the factory for repair. This service policy decreases the security system downtime.

If a single vendor supplies the integrated system and there is a problem with the system, there is only one contractor to contend with. When a security system assembled from equipment supplied by several manufacturers has a problem, there is unproductive finger pointing as to whose fault it is, and the customer becomes a negotiator/arbitrator.

The key to a successful security plan is to choose the right or best equipment/service company, one that is customer oriented and acquainted with reliable, technologically superior products that satisfy the customer's needs.

CCTV's Role and Applications

In its broadest sense, the purpose of CCTV in any security plan is to provide remote eyes for a security operator: to provide live action displays from a distance. The CCTV system should have a means of recording—either a VCR or other storage media—to maintain permanent records of what the camera sees, to be used for future training or as evidence in prosecution. Some of the applications for which CCTV provides an effective solution include the following situations:

1. Overt visual observation of a scene or activity is required from a remote location, for security purposes.

2. The scene to be observed is in a hazardous area or presents the potential of life-threatening or injurious action to personnel. These areas may include toxic, radioactive, high fire or explosion potential, x-ray radiation or other nuclear radiations.

3. Visual observation of a scene must be covert (hidden) or clandestine. It is much easier to hide a small camera and lens in a concealable location than to station a person in the area.

4. There is little activity to watch, as in an intrusion detection location or some storage area, but significant events must be recorded when they occur. Integration of CCTV with alarm sensors and a time-lapse/real-time VCR provides an extremely powerful solution for this requirement.

5. Many locations must be observed simultaneously by one person from a central security location. An example of this situation is tracing the entry and path of a person or vehicle through a facility and watching as the person or vehicle progresses from the entry point to final destination in the facility and is then interdicted by the security force. There are many instances when a guard or security officer must only review the activity or inactivity in a scene periodically. The use of CCTV eliminates the guard who would have to make guard rounds to these remote locations, which would result in inefficient use of the guard's time, and unlikely detection of the unauthorized trespasser.

6. When a crime has been committed it is important to have a hard-copy printout of the activity and event. This requires a hard-copy printout from either a television or a photographic system. The proliferation of high-quality printed images from VCR equipment has clearly made the case for using CCTV for a permanent record, be it from VCR or video hard-copy printer.

Problems Solved by CCTV

The most effective way to determine that a theft has occurred, when it occurred, where it occurred, and by whom, is to use CCTV as the means for detection and recording. Using CCTV, the record of the event can be identified, stored, and later reproduced for display or hard copy. Personnel can be identified on monochrome or color CCTV monitors. Most security installations to date use monochrome CCTV cameras that provide sufficient information to document the activity and event or make identifications of personnel or articles. Many newer installations use color CCTV, which permits easier identification of personnel or objects involved.

If there is an emergency or disaster and security personnel must determine the presence or absence of personnel in a particular location, CCTV provides an instantaneous assessment of the personnel location and availability.

There are many examples in which CCTV is used to insure the safety of personnel in facilities and that personnel have not entered them, or that they have exited them at the proper time. These relate to job function, working with dangerous equipment, working in hazardous environments, monitoring dangerous areas, and so forth.

The synergistic combination of audio and CCTV information from a remote site provides an effective source for security. Several camera manufacturers and installers combine video and audio (one-way or duplex) to enhance the intelligence received from the remote site using an external microphone or one installed directly into the camera. The video and audio signals are transmitted over the same coaxial shielded two-wire or fiber optic cable to the security monitoring location where video and audio are monitored live or the video and audio signals are recorded on a VCR. When there is activity in the camera area, the video and audio signal is switched onto the monitor and the guard hears the voice or sound communication from that camera, and initiates the appropriate response.

Choice of Overt or Covert CCTV

Most CCTV installations use both overt and covert CCTV cameras, with more cameras overt than covert. The overt installations are designed to deter crime and provide general surveillance of remote areas such as parking lots, perimeter fence lines, warehouses, entrance lobbies, hallways, production areas. When the CCTV cameras and lenses are exposed and in view, all management, employees, and visitors realize that the premises are under constant television surveillance for the protection of personnel and assets. When the need arises covert installations are used so that clandestine activity can be observed and detected, which would otherwise not be detectable by overt CCTV. Overt video equipment is often large and no effort is made to conceal it; it acts as a deterrent to crime. Covert equipment is usually small and designed to be concealed in various objects in the environment or behind a ceiling or wall, viewing through a small opening in a ceiling tile or wallboard. Overt CCTV is often per-

manently installed, whereas covert is often designed to be put into place quickly, left in place for a few hours, days, or weeks, and then removed. Since minimizing installation time is desirable when installing the covert CCTV, transmission of the video signal is often accomplished using wireless means.

Security Surveillance Applications

CCTV applications can be broadly classified into either indoor or outdoor. This is a logical division since it sets a natural boundary on equipment types: those suitable for controlled environment indoor applications, and those suitable for harsher outdoor environments. The two primary parameters characterizing this division of indoor versus outdoor are environmental factors and lighting factors. The indoor location requires the use of artificial lighting, which can be augmented by daylight entering the viewing area, and subjected to mild indoor temperature and humidity variations, dirt, dust, and smoke. In the outdoor location, precipitation (fog, rain, snow), wind loading, dirt, dust, sand, and smoke must be considered.

Safety Applications

In public, government, industrial, and other facilities, a safety, security, and personnel protection plan must protect personnel from harm whether caused by accident, human error, sabotage, or terrorism. The security forces are expected to have knowledge about the conditions at all locations in the facility through the use of CCTV.

In a hospital room/hallway environment, the television cameras may serve a dual function; they monitor hospital patients while also determining the status and locations of employees, visitors, etc., in the facility. The guard can monitor entrance and exit doors, hallways, operating rooms, drug dispensary, and other vital areas. CCTV is used in safety applications for the evacuation of an area and to determine if all personnel have left the area and are safe. Security personnel can use CCTV for remote traffic monitoring and control and to determine high-traffic locations and how to best control them.

CCTV plays a critical role in public safety in monitoring vehicular traffic on highways and city streets, truck and bus depots, public rail and subway facilities, and airports.

Chapter 14B

Digital Recording Systems*

ALAN R. MATCHETT

With the rapid advancement in computers, a new alternative has become available. By converting the video input from analog to a digital format, digital recording and storage are possible.

Technology advancements have created some major life changes in the last decade. Computer sales and development, as well as computer technology items, have grown exponentially, creating new products to replace others that were new a mere six months earlier. This rapid growth has touched virtually every industry and has created some major improvements in the security industry.

One of the fastest-growing areas of advancement in the security industry is the development of digital and computer-based video systems. In the past, computer systems could not handle the massive memory and processor requirements needed to accurately transmit, record, and store video footage properly. Video would need to be saved in short clips that would often appear jumpy and inconsistent. As the computer industry has grown processors have become much quicker, hard drives have become increasingly larger, memory is larger and faster, and new storage media has been created that make digital video a viable option.

How the video is compressed and transferred has been developed to make data retrieval much more consistent and accurate, to the point that picture quality now exceeds that of the traditional recording methods. The rapid advances in the computer industry have led to faster processors, allowing for an excellent frame rate. Hard drives have grown to allow for the massive storage requirements of a CCTV system.

Digital tape storage space and speed have also grown substantially, and reliable video compression techniques have led to a reduced amount of storage space required for archiving the video.

Digital video systems are utilized for much the same reasons as the traditional camera systems. The concept of a digital system is to eliminate the common problems associated with the traditional recorded video system while increasing functionality and ease of use. There are many wonderful advantages to using a digital recording system as opposed to the traditional recording system. Picture quality, for example, is much higher with digital systems. With a traditional recording system, the recorder is usually the lowest-resolution device used. If color cameras with a resolution of 400 lines are used, but the recorder is only capable of 280 lines for color, the recorded image will only be 280 lines. With the digital system, the recorder is no longer the lowest-resolution device in most cases. This means that users will have the higher resolution they paid for when they bought the higher-resolution cameras.

Another advantage of the digital format is how well the video images hold up over time. Because each picture is digital, it is virtually a new image every time it is viewed and not as likely to degrade over time.

Standard video output is currently always in an analog format. This analog video signal must be converted to digital at some point for a digital system. Some cameras are currently available that perform analog-to-digital conversion inside the camera unit. These cameras are typically connected to a network for transmittal to a remote location either in the same facility or somewhere on the same network. They can also be transmitted for display or access via the Internet or intranets.

*Matchett, *CCTV for Security Professionals*, pp. 118–134, Butterworth Heinemann, 2003

As stated earlier, the video signal must be converted from an analog to a digital signal before it can be digitally recorded. With most systems, the analog-to-digital conversion is done within the digital recording device, but several cameras do the conversion directly at the camera. By doing the conversion at the camera, existing network cabling can be utilized to transmit the images to the security area, where traditional cameras would require dedicated cabling throughout the facility. If the digital cameras are used, however, they must be routed to a device that can accept the digital input. Most digital video recorders still require that the video input be done the traditional way, by direct cabling and an analog video signal. There are currently four common formats for the compression and transmission of the video to a digital format used within the security industry. Each one has distinct advantages and disadvantages, and each has a niche as far as compatibility with system requirements. The four types of compression or formatting in the security industry are JPEG, MPEG, wavelet, and H-263. Each of these will be looked at more closely in the following sections. First, however, it is important to look at the actual conversion of the video signal from analog to digital to understand the differences between these different formats.

File Formats

To make an accurate comparison of the traditional system capabilities and the digital system capabilities, it is important to determine what the actual storage capacity will be for each. Many people choose to go to a digital system because of the perceived advantages and they have heard about how great and advanced the systems are; however, they are often disappointed with the performance, because they thought it would be much more than it is. Some manufacturers may state that you can record continuously for a week, but they fail to mention that it is a very slow frame rate or event recording only.

The first part that is important when determining the overall storage capacity of a system is to determine the size of the files that will be recorded. Many systems allow the file size to be adjusted for better picture quality or higher storage capacity. A larger file size will have better picture quality but lower overall storage capacity as far as number of frames recorded or overall recording time. A smaller file size means that more frames can be recorded, but the picture quality will be less than that of the higher file size. The type of compression used also determines the file size being recorded. Each of the compression and format types will be looked at independently for a good comparison.

JPEG

If the recorder uses JPEG image types, the typical file size is usually around 15 K to 31 K, depending on the resolution of the images and amount of compression. Looking at a file size of 20 K and a frame rate of 20 frames per second, the storage space required would be 400 K per second, 24 M per minute, 1.44 G per hour, and 34.56 G per 24-hour period. As you can see, it is not probable that recording continuously for weeks could be achieved in this situation. If the frame rate were reduced to 10 frames per second, the space required would be 200 K per second, 12 M per minute, 720 M per hour, and 17.28 G per 24-hour period. If 10 cameras were recording, that would produce one frame per second per camera.

MPEG

MPEG technology is slightly different from the JPEG, and it is difficult to determine actual recording capacity. Where the JPEG replaces the entire image with a new image every time, MPEG replaces only those pixels of an image that have changed since the last image was sent. A distinct advantage of this technology is the reduction of the file size for recording. The disadvantage, however, is that the amount of video that can be recorded depends entirely on the amount of activity on the cameras. In other words, if there are few changes to the video images, the file size could be reduced to 10 K or lower. If there is a lot of activity the file size will be substantially larger and vary from one image to the next.

With the calculations of the JPEG technology, it was straightforward to determine how much could be recorded in a 24-hour period. With MPEG the frame rate is established, but the file size for any given image is practically indeterminable. It is possible to establish a range of the file size based on a frame with minimal activity and a frame with maximum activity. Most images are actually somewhere in between.

It seems on the surface that having a varying file size is an advantage if you plan for the maximum file size, and most come in substantially lower than that. Most manufacturer specifications are not written using the maximum file size to determine storage capacity. Most manufacturers using the MPEG technology state a maximum record time that always sounds much longer than the record time of systems using the other technologies. This maximum record time, however, is based on little or no activity in a camera view. Every movement and every increased file size decreases this record time, making the maximum record time virtually unobtainable. Many users are disappointed when they realize that the recording time they were hoping to achieve and the recording time actually received are not close to each other.

The biggest drawback to this scenario, from a security manager's perspective, is the unknown of the actual recording time. If the system is set up to record 24 hours per tape, some days it may achieve half an hour more while other days achieve half an hour less. Although this variance may not seem that important, if no one is available to change to a new tape once the old one is full, there could potentially be an undetermined time period where nothing is being recorded. This potential for missing crucial video footage is something that most security managers cannot tolerate with any system.

If the user understands this problem and bases the frame rate of the cameras and total recording requirements on the minimum record time, as opposed to the maximum, the MPEG recorder is still beneficial to the facility. If you ask manufacturers which technology is better, they will tell you that it is the one they are using, of course. Many manufacturers and users take that a little further, though, when discussing MPEG technology if they do not use it. It is often said that the MPEG technology is less reliable than the JPEG or others. This is not because of the varying file size but because of the nature of how the file size is determined.

Because the MPEG replaces only the pixels that have changed, many JPEG users will tell you that MPEG images are actually altered video and therefore may not be admissible in court. They argue that any given image is not a true depiction of the scene from the camera, because some pixels may be unchanged or changes too minute to warrant an update. Each pixel, however, is actually a numeric value representation of what has been sent by the camera, so if that value has not changed, there is no reason to transmit or record duplicated information.

At the time of writing this book, I am unaware of any court case in which recorded video could not be used because it was recorded with MPEG or any other technology. Although it is possible that it has happened, it has not been a major occurrence noted by the security industry.

Types of MPEG

Digital video recording for the security industry primarily uses three different types of MPEG compression. Each is similar in theory, with differences in the amount of compression and algorithms. To the end user, the only true noticeable difference will be the file size and amount of time that can be recorded.

MPEG-1 was the first MPEG compression type to be introduced. Through continuous improvement and development, MPEG-2 was created. MPEG-2 provided a higher compression rate, meaning smaller average file sizes than MPEG-1 images. The next progression in MPEG technology brought the MPEG-4 compression format, again with a higher compression rate and smaller sizes. Some manufacturers are using MPEG-4 technology for video storage at the time of publication of this book, whereas still more manufacturers are using MPEG-4 for video transmission and viewing, along with a different format for actual video storage. MPEG-4 allows for much easier video transmission either over a network, the Internet, or through a dial-up connection. This allows users to see more frames per second and clearer images in a shorter time frame than if they had used larger files or less compression. Other types of MPEG compression currently under development are MPEG-7 and MPEG-21, but these new formats may or may not ever come to fruition.

Wavelet

Probably the fastest-growing market share of digital recording units belongs to those utilizing wavelet technology. Wavelet technology is difficult to explain in great detail, but basically it looks at the video signal several different times and saves it in little packets of varying resolution. The first show will capture a coarse resolution, then a little finer, and a little finer until the entire image is captured. All of these packets are bundled to create one file that represents that image. Rebuilding the image is much quicker than with JPEG or MPEG, and the file sizes can be much smaller. Because of the nature of the wavelet, it accurately compresses and decompresses the images more than the other technologies.

The name *wavelet* actually gives a good hint at how this technology works, if you think about it. It looks at the entire video waveform and samples a portion of it—thus, wavelet. The use of wavelet for digital video systems adds greatly to the storage capabilities of systems and the use of digital video for remote viewing and storage. Transmitting and viewing with the other technologies require a much higher bandwidth and can be difficult on an existing network because of the load. With wavelet, however, the load is divided up, depending on the amount of network activity, allowing for more even and consistent video transmission and retrieval.

H-263

H-263 video compression is a standard developed for video transmission over a network. It is designed primarily to provide a usable video stream even when the available bandwidth is low. Many manufacturers are using H-263 format for network video servers and remote viewing on network-enabled digital recorders. Some use the H-263 format exclusively on the recorder, whereas others use H-263 strictly for the remote viewing function and one of the other formats, such as JPEG, for the video storage function.

The H-263 video coding standard was created to allow video streaming for lower-bandwidth applications, particularly 56 kbps (kilobytes per second). As with the MPEG standard, H-263 retransmits those portions of the video image that have changed since the previous image. The first image is used as a base image to which the next frames are compared. Those portions of the images that have changed are then transmitted, thus reducing the file sizes.

Although similar to MPEG format, the H-263 standard is not exactly the same. The algorithms that perform the compression vary from MPEG, and a few additional functions are performed with H-263. Two features that reduce file size used in H-263 are motion estimation and compensation. Many items within a video image are the same as previous frames except for their location within those frames. With this being the case, it is not always necessary to retransmit those pixels; it is more efficient to relocate where those pixels are located within the image. Although it is a much more complicated procedure in theory, this is essentially what motion estimation and motion compensation accomplish. They, in essence, predict the location of existing pixels and verify them within multiple frames, thus reducing the number of pixels that must be retransmitted.

Recording Storage Types

Most digital video recording units record the video images to a hard drive or series of hard drives before they are stored to the storage media. In other words,

all of the video images are recorded onto the hard drive(s) temporarily, and then are transferred to whatever type of storage device is being used, such as a CD, DVD, or digital linear tape. Many recorders record primarily to the hard drives and store images elsewhere only when prompted to or under certain conditions.

Recording the information in this manner gives the user several options for recording and storage. The amount of storage that occurs before user intervention depends greatly on several factors. Each frame requires a certain file size, which can vary greatly by the compression type and recording equipment manufacturer. The size of the hard drive is another important factor for the amount of recording that can be done, as is the number of frames per second being recorded.

Whichever technology a system uses, the recording options are usually the same or similar from one manufacturer to the next. As with a computer system, hard drives are utilized to initially record the images before they are sent to another storage medium. This is like doing a tape backup on a home or business computer, but occurring much more frequently.

Hard Drive Recording

Many digital video recorders are designed to store all of the recorded video onto a hard drive or series of hard drives built into the machine. By storing the video images directly to the hard drives, managing the file systems and images are much less complicated than with some systems that immediately transfer the images directly to an external storage device. Uneventful video, for example, can be recorded over on a continuous loop, with the oldest video being overwritten first.

If the recorder is designed to overwrite the oldest video and record in a continuous loop, there is little need for user intervention except when there is suspicion of an incident or an alarm condition occurs. If there is an alarm or an incident that must be retained for future use, the video clip can easily be transferred to an external device so that it can be saved. These external devices can range from a standard recordable compact disc (CD) to a small computer system interface (SCSI) tape backup device, depending on the customer's needs.

In many cases, the programming allows several different options for external storage of video images. Most devices that record to the hard drive allow the user to manually select the image or streams of images, which are transferred to an external device. When this technique is used, the system operator is relied on to transfer the appropriate video clip and verify that the proper information is completely transferred.

Digital Tape Recording

When all of the video images over a predetermined period are recorded to a tape, they are transferred in groups, as the hard drive becomes full. Relatively simple ways to achieve this are through hard drive partitioning and write definitions. With a 20 G hard drive, for example, it could be divided into 20 partitions of 1 G each. Every time 5 or 10 partitions become full, it automatically transfers the images from the hard drive to the tape. Live images continue to record on the next group of partitions so that no activity is missed during the transfer period. In this way, the tape drive is not working all of the time, which means less strain on the unit.

The digital recording tapes are also used for a much longer period than traditional security VHS tapes. T-120 and T-160 tapes are rated by the manufacturer for 35 uses before replacement. DDS tapes, on the other hand, are rated by the manufacturer for 1200 uses before replacement, something that will probably never be achieved. In addition, tapes such as DDS are electronically serial numbered. Many recorders can look at the serial number and last record date directly from the tape. If the recording is too recent, it can stop you from accidentally recording over the wrong tape.

Because the recording times are electronically stamped on each tape, it can be far easier to retrieve and review information with the digital system. With many systems you simply enter your search or review parameters, and the system will let you know which tape is required. If that tape were already loaded, the video footage from your parameters would be sent from the tape back to the hard drive for review. Because the images are digital, there is not the problem common with traditional systems. Each camera can be reviewed easily at real speed, faster, slower, forward, or reverse without the images jumping around and inserting occasional shots from a different camera. This allows the user to play an event backward and forward more quickly and accurately than rewinding and replaying with time-lapse recorders.

This will make reviewing tapes for specific times, as compared with an access control log, for example, more feasible and accurate. If you know that someone went through a particular door at a certain time, you can recall the images from the associated camera 5 minutes before and 5 minutes after that door was opened. Searching through the video archive is much quicker, because it is based on time and not the counter position as with traditional recorders.

The rapid advancements in the computer industry have proven to be both an advantage and disadvantage. The disadvantage is that the advancements in hard drive size, processor speeds, and types of storage media have rapidly made systems already purchased obsolete. Although the older systems are usually still functional and do what the customer wanted at the time, they simply cannot do what a system created 1 year later is capable of.

An important consideration is to establish how long the video is archived for future use. Because the storage media for digital systems are substantially smaller than VHS tapes, less physical storage space is required to archive the video for extended periods, such as 6 months or a year. The digitally archived video holds up better for these extended periods, so many organizations have begun archiving for periods as long as 3 or 5 years. Although this may seem like overkill, for many businesses it proves beneficial later if inventory audits show missing items or in the event of liability suits. One example is slip and fall suits against hotels or casinos. Occasionally, would-be victims decide that these facilities have deep pockets and will settle quickly rather than face the public exposure. If old footage is available to show that the event is either legitimate or not, it can save the organization a lot of grief.

Digital Video (DV) Tape Recording. Many new commercial camcorders record into a digital format that should be mentioned here. DV recording format is commonly used to record digital video images to a standard Super High 8 mm tape. The tape is a standard analog tape that is used in older camcorders as well, but instead of storing an analog video stream onto the tape, the DV recorders send a digital stream to the tape. The tape records approximately the same amount of time as it would with an analog recording, but the resolution and search features are much better with the digital recording format. This recording format is not one of the four main types used within the security industry, but at least one manufacturer is using this type of file format for security-related recorders. Sony has developed DV recording with its consumer product line and has also begun tying it into the security product line.

Combination Storage Systems

Several equipment manufacturers make recorders that combine hard drive and tape backup digital recording within one unit. This allows the user several options regarding video archiving. Archiving of video can be done automatically to the tape storage media, which means that all recorded video is archived. This option is valuable for facilities that require full backup of video images for extended periods. Another option available is to archive video of alarm-triggered events automatically. If this feature is set up properly, it can be a time-saver for tape reviewing.

Many of the larger digital video systems use hard drive and tape storage, with the tape devices saving externally to the recording equipment. This is mainly an issue of physical size restrictions, because larger systems may require many hard drives and tape automation for efficiency. A 600-camera system, for example, requires constant tape changes if automation is not used. Tape machines allow the system to control, manage, and change banks of tapes, allowing for terabytes of video storage relatively easily.

Digital Multiplexing Recorders

Most of the readily available digital recording devices incorporate a multiplexer into the recording unit, although how this can be utilized and set up can vary from manufacturer to manufacturer. Many units write the digital images to the hard drive or storage media in the same manner as traditional multiplexing units—by alternating from one camera to the next for each frame. Some new systems, however, give the user the option of setting the frame rate of each camera individually, giving the user much more control. If only 1 camera in a facility needs to be recorded at 5 frames per second and 10 cameras need to be recorded at 1 frame per second, it would be a waste of space and unfeasible to attempt to record all cameras at the higher frame rate. By selecting each camera individually, a total record rate of only 15 frames per second is required, as opposed to an unachievable 55 frames the other way.

Digital Single-Channel Recorders

A few manufacturers have added a new type of digital recorder that may be easier to implement when upgrading analog systems. A single-channel recorder acts essentially like a digital VCR replace-

ment. It records in the same manner as a time-lapse recorder to the end user, but instead of recording to a VHS tape, it records directly to a hard drive. With the growing size of hard drives, it allows for an increased frame rate for a longer period than traditional recorders. Digital single-channel recorders also allow the user to select the image quality, which affects the file size. Usually the user can choose low, medium, or high resolution images, which equates to different rates of compression. A low-resolution image is compressed much more than a high-resolution image, and the file size is therefore significantly smaller. This allows for more frames in the same amount of hard drive space, extending the overall recording length.

Many single-channel recorders also allow for an external storage device, such as a tape backup system, to store important video clips. This is important for situations where the images must be saved for evidence or future reference. In addition, many units provide a network connection for remote viewing of cameras from authorized computers.

Important Considerations

For longevity of the system, it is beneficial to choose a system that can be easily updated or upgraded to a newer storage medium. For example, if the system has the recording, multiplexing, and storage self-contained in a single unit, the entire unit must be replaced to benefit from technology advancements.

All electronic equipment is rated by the mean time between failure (MTBF). This equates to the life span of the particular components or piece of equipment and is usually measured in hours. With many of the newer components for digital video systems, the MTBF is much longer than with traditional system components, partially because the traditional equipment relies on many more moving parts than its digital counterparts. For most digital components the MTBF is typically 100,00 hours, which equates to 12 years of continuous use. Typically, a traditional recorder can be expected to last somewhere between 3 to 5 years before replacement if it is properly maintained every 10,000 hours and cleaned frequently.

Most digital products will be outdated before they no longer work, but be sure to get the exact MTBF from the manufacturer. It is important to find out the MTBF of each of the major components in the system to help determine the overall life expectancy. If the storage recording and multiplexing are all done in a self-contained unit, there are actually three major components that may fail. Be sure to find out the MTBF of the built-in storage unit or tape drive, the recording portion including the hard drive(s), and the multiplexing portion. The overall MTBF of the unit is the same as the shortest MTBF for any individual component, not the average of all components.

Longer MTBF means less required maintenance and less frequent service replacement. If the final video output to the storage media is a digital image, this can be more easily read in other machines. Many manufacturers make some portion proprietary to ensure that their equipment is used, but this is not always the case. A single JPEG image can be used on practically every computer, which means that an incriminating shot or an image problem can be sent to someone else to analyze—for example, as by e-mail.

Transferring the video to a digital format makes it possible to send the images over a LAN/WAN network. Many units have this option built in to allow for remote system monitoring. The biggest advantage is that a security manager can easily pull up any camera to view at any time, many times with either a Web browser or a custom graphical user interface (GUI). If an organization has multiple facilities all on a network, the security manager can easily access the video images from any camera in any facility. It is even possible to remotely access the images via a dial-up connection to the network or over the Internet.

One common method for transferring video from the hard drive to the storage media is to do so only on alarm. The information can continue to record to the hard drive until an alarm-triggered event occurs. The alarm trigger then causes the information to be automatically sent to the tape drive. By using a hard drive and alarm-triggered events, the hard drive also acts as a video buffer. This allows the user to view the events just before the alarm to see what occurred. With alarm-triggered recording of events on traditional recorders, the recording begins immediately after an event has occurred. With the digital system, that information already exists on the hard drive, so it is simply a matter of recalling the information. Setting a buffer time in seconds or minutes or choosing a number of frames immediately before an incident to record usually does this adequately.

Writing alarm events only to the storage device means that there will be much less time required for reviewing tapes. Instead of sitting through hours of uneventful camera views, as with traditional systems, users only look at those times where actual activity occurred on the screen. They then only have to determine what was an important event and what was normal activity, a much less time-consuming task.

If the system is used with a guard force or other live user, it could be set to record the activity manually based on a user-activated trigger. This would capture events that might otherwise have been missed. An example is shoplifters in a retail environment. It is impossible for a camera to distinguish between a legitimate shopper and a person attempting to conceal merchandise. A loss prevention officer, however, could easily identify the difference and let the camera system know with a trigger, such as a push button, causing the system to record the suspicious activity. The same could be done with a traditional camera system, but again the buffer period of the hard drive would provide a distinct advantage.

Digital Video as Evidence

One concern for many organizations is the use of digital video as evidence. This concern, however, is not specific to the digital systems. Whichever type of system is used, it is important to establish a chain-of-evidence policy before it is actually needed. If a criminal offense is captured in a recording, it is important to establish who will remove the storage medium from the machine, where it is stored and maintained, and has access to it. Consult the corporate counsel or attorney during or before the system installation to determine what is required.

Hundreds of companies are currently making and selling digital video systems or digital video products, and there is no clear-cut standard, partially because it is such a new and growing market. Every manufacturer is trying something a little different in order to gain an advantage over other systems, and few of the products will interface with those of other manufacturers. This makes the user's equipment choice more permanent in addition to the initial cost factor.

Changing from Analog to Digital

When an organization changes from a traditional camera system to a digital one, it is not always a seamless transition. The basic operation of the newer system can be entirely different from what the security staff is used to working with, so training can be a key issue. Many organizations are under the impression that they can simply remove the old multiplexer and recorder, install the new digital unit, and then continue using the system in the same way that they always did. Although a few systems are designed specifically to achieve this goal, it is usually not the case.

If retraining the entire staff is not done adequately from the beginning, the digital system can be more of a hindrance than a help. If the security staff is reluctant to change, they can be quick to complain and find fault with the new system. It must be established initially what the added benefits of the new system are and how they affect each person using it.

The security staff must also sell upper management on the benefit of changing over and should be able to show the return on investment (ROI). One way of achieving this is factoring in long-term costs of repair, replacement, upgrade, and storage media such as VHS tapes and DLT or DDS tapes. The amount of time saved by reduced reviewing time should also be factored in as cost savings.

A disadvantage that was mentioned earlier is the rapid change in technology. As new formatting, compression, and hardware are developed, capabilities increase. This also means that the currently installed systems may be obsolete in a short period. A look at the PC industry shows what this means: Very few people would buy a computer now with a 1 G hard drive and a 60-MHz processor, but a few short years ago that would have been a hot item. The same applies to the digital video products. Most people would not choose a recorder that uses DDS2 tapes and a 2 G hard drive, but a few years ago that would have been an adequate system. High-end equipment being sold today may seem outdated and inadequate in 2 years.

Because the technology is changing so rapidly, many new companies do not survive for long. If a company is not poised financially or with the right product for future development, it will quickly fall by the wayside. Be sure to check the company history and size, as well as customer references, to pick a company that will be around to support you.

For larger systems with 32 cameras or more, it can be quite a task to accurately review the video, regardless of which type of system is used. One of the concepts behind the creation of digital systems is to alleviate this problem, but most end users have been reluctant to set up systems that record only based on alarm activity and video motion detection triggers.

If a digital system is used to record all video, the amount of tapes can be overwhelming, or the frame rate is reduced to a point below what is usually obtainable with a traditional system. Before deciding

to change to a digital system, the minimum performance requirements for the system should be established. These requirements are then used to analyze the feasibility of the digital system as compared with traditional systems. In this way an organization can more easily determine whether a digital system is functional and cost effective compared with existing systems. In many cases, organizations have found that they are better off staying with the traditional recording techniques or just adding a few digital components and keeping the analog system in place.

A digital system can be beneficial if it is used to its fullest potential, which includes remote viewing and monitoring, alarm-activated recording, and video motion detection. If, however, an organization is still set on using the system in the same manner it always has, it will probably be disappointed.

Importance of Enhanced Recording Capabilities

The best way to take advantage of the digital system is to establish alarm triggers and video motion detection to cause certain actions within the system. In this way the recording is set to capture only relevant footage or at least time and date stamp the footage for easier review later. Random video review is no easier than with traditional systems in most cases, but if alarm events are marked for review, the user can go straight to those events and skip the views of an empty room.

If alarm triggers are to be used, it is important to determine what type of occurrence will signify a notable event. For retail facilities, for example, it is not practical to use video motion detection most of the time, because the recorder would constantly be in the alarm state and recording legitimate shoppers as well as suspected shoplifters. An alternative trigger can be an alarm output from an electronic surveillance system. This triggers if someone attempts to walk past a certain area, such as an exit, with tagged merchandise that had not been paid for.

For facilities that are subject to armed robbery, such as banks and convenience stores, a "last bill out" device in the cash drawer would be an excellent way to activate the recording without jeopardizing the safety of the employees. Silent hold-up devices are good also if the system is set up with alarm buffers to capture the events before the alarm. For a bank, for example, it is not recommended to have a device that could jeopardize the safety of the tellers.

If the trigger activates the buffer recording,

however, the tellers are instructed to activate the trigger only after the suspects have left or if they are clearly out of harm's way. Most bank robberies take only a matter of minutes or even seconds, so a buffer is easily established for activation after the event that captures everything at a high frame rate. If the digital system is constantly recording 20 or 30 frames per second and overwriting the data until a trigger occurs, the buffer still has the required camera shots at those high frame rates.

It is important for each facility to decide what type of an event is important enough to record for each individual camera view. For example, it may not be important to record every time someone walks through the front door, but it may be extremely important to record every time someone exits through the rear door. Establishing the parameters for each camera in advance helps ensure that important events are not missed and that there is as little useless recording as possible.

The possibilities of alarm-triggered recording are only limited by the imagination of the installers and system users. Many devices can be utilized to enhance the recording capabilities of the system, from simple door contacts and motion detectors to time-based triggers from access control systems and alarms from other pieces of equipment.

Some Advantages of Digital CCTV

The advantage to all of the advancements in digital technology has been drastically improved functionality for camera systems. In early 1999, the average digital recorder contained a 4 G up to a 12 G hard drive, and many recorded to DDS2 or DDS3 tapes. By the end of 1999, most digital units had a hard drive of 50 G, and several contained a series of 50 G hard drives.

Companies that are most concerned about what happens in their facilities after normal hours of operation are also ideal for digital systems. The system can easily be integrated with the intrusion detection or access control systems to monitor activities in the event of an alarm or suspicious access. Although many facilities may not have such clear-cut choices, most can be readily adapted to the digital environment with creativity and use of technology.

Much of the planning for a digital system is identical to planning for a traditional system. Camera location, field of view, lens type, and extras such as infrared illumination and housings should not change from one system type to the next. If eight cameras are needed to cover the perimeter of a

building with the traditional system, they are still required for the digital system. This may seem like simple common sense, but many users seem to believe that by going to digital they would have a super-system, capable of doing much more with much less equipment.

The digital portion of the system is merely a different type of system control and configuration. Digital systems will not increase the capabilities of the camera or a monitor. Although the digital recorder is usually capable of producing higher-resolution images, if the cameras are only capable of 330 lines of resolution, the recorded images will only look like 330 lines of resolution. Where the difference is noticeable is if high-resolution cameras were installed but were recorded on a traditional recorder that was a much lower resolution. If the digital recorder is used with the same cameras, the images should appear much clearer with the digital system. The resolution produced is only as high as that of the lowest-resolution device.

System design—either for replacement or for a new facility—will start the same way regardless of which system is to be used. The one thing that can cause a change in camera or pan/tilt and zoom choice is system compatibility. Not to say that some cameras are not compatible with some systems, but some features will work only if both components are from the same manufacturer. Tours and patrols, for example, are scripted actions that cause cameras to change to preset positions on a time or triggered event basis. These tours and patrols often will not operate properly if essential components are a mix from various manufacturers. Sometimes this is because of proprietary protocols by the manufacturer, and sometimes it is because one manufacturer may not even offer that possibility. If that is an important feature for the system design, it is important to verify the component compatibility in advance. In this case the manufacturers or a consultant would be the biggest help, because they have probably been asked about this issue on numerous occasions.

There are several major advantages to recording the video in a digital format. One advantage is a much higher picture resolution with no degradation. Resolution with a digital recorder is often higher than with time-lapse and real-time recorders. The resolution can be as high as that of many cameras and monitors, meaning that the recording equipment is no longer the restrictive factor for excellent picture quality.

With digital recording, reviewing previously recorded video is much more efficient. With the traditional multiplexed video, it is not really possible to fast forward or rewind a particular scene while viewing. With digital recording, the video can be set to start playing at a predetermined time, and fast forward or rewind can be used to search for a particular person or incident. Because most digital systems are computer based, video footage can be navigated much more easily than in traditional systems.

An additional benefit of digital storage is the space requirement for archived tapes. To store 60 days of videocassettes would take quite a bit of room, but 60 days of digital tapes is easily put into a desk drawer.

The Bottom Line

The synergy of a CCTV security system implies the following functional scenario:

1. An unauthorized intrusion or entry or attempted removal of equipment will be detected at the time of the event by some alarm sensor.
2. A CCTV camera located somewhere in the alarm area is fixed on the location or pointed manually or automatically (from the guard site) to view the alarm area.
3. The information from the alarm sensor and CCTV camera is transmitted immediately to the security console and monitored by personnel or recorded for permanent documentation.
4. The security operator receiving the alarm information has a plan to dispatch personnel to the location or to take some other appropriate action.
5. After dispatching a security person to the alarm area, the guard resumes normal security duties to view any future event.
6. If after reasonable time the person dispatched does not neutralize the intrusion or other event, the security guard resumes monitoring of that situation to bring it to a successful conclusion.

Use of CCTV plays a crucial role in the overall system plan. During an intrusion or theft, the CCTV system provides information (when signaled by the intrusion alarm) to the guard who must make some identification of the perpetrator, make an assessment of the problem, and provide an appropriate response. An installation containing suitable and sufficient alarm sensors and CCTV cameras permits the guard to follow the progress of the event and assist the response team in countering the attack. The use of CCTV to track the intruder is most effective.

With an intrusion alarm and visual CCTV information, all the elements are in place for a reliable transfer of information to the security offices in a timely fashion. For proper effectiveness, all parts of the security system must work properly and each relies on the other to provide total success. If an intrusion alarm fails, the command post cannot see the CCTV image at the right location and the right time. If the CCTV fails, the guard cannot identify the perpetrator even though he may know that an intrusion occurred. If a security officer is not alert or improperly interprets the alarm and CCTV input, the data from either or both is not processed and acted upon, and the system fails.

In the case of an emergency (for example, fire, flood, machinery out of control, or utility pipeline burst), the operation of CCTV, safety sensors, and human response at the console are all required. The use of CCTV is an inexpensive investment for preventing accidents and minimizing damage when an accident occurs. In the case of a fire, CCTV acts as real-time eyes at the emergency location, permitting security and safety personnel to send the appropriate reaction force with adequate equipment to provide optimum response. Since the reaction time to a fire or other disaster is critical, having various cameras on the location before personnel arrive is very important. In the case of a fire, while a sprinkler may activate or a fire sensor may produce an alarm, a CCTV camera can quickly ascertain whether the event is a false alarm, a minor alarm, or a major event. The automatic sprinkler and fire alarm system might alert the guard to the event, but the CCTVs "eye" viewing the actual scene prior to sending the emergency team often saves lives and reduces asset losses. CCTV permits more effective security personnel use and insures that they are not diverted to false alarms unnecessarily.

In the case of a security violation, if an intrusion sensor detects an intrusion, the guard monitoring the CCTV camera can determine whether or not the intrusion is one that requires the dispatch of personnel or some other response. In the event of a major, well-planned attack on a facility by a terrorist organization or other intruder, a diversionary tactic such as a false alarm of some type can quickly be determined through the use of CCTV, thereby preventing the inappropriate response to the false alarm.

The motivation for an organization to justify expenditures on security and safety equipment is that there must be a positive return on investment; that is, the value of assets not lost must be greater than spent on security, and the security system must adequately protect personnel and visitors at the facility. By utilizing an effective security system the property and asset thefts are reduced and money is saved. Likewise public and employee safety is increased under all conditions. A well-planned security and safety system has the potential to reduce thefts and protect assets, and save lives. In the extreme case of a disaster, the organization will have in place a system well prepared for an emergency or disaster and the ability to recover from it in the best possible way. It has been shown that CCTV does play a crucial role in the success of such a plan.

- Where should the camera be located so that the entire scene to be viewed is covered by the television camera?
- In what direction should the camera be pointed so that the sun, bright lights, or other variable lighting have a minimum effect on picture quality?
- Should the camera have a $\frac{2}{3}$-inch or 1-inch diameter vidicon tube?
- What field of view should the camera cover?
- Should a fixed focus (constant field of view) or zoom lens (variable field of view) be used? What focal length is best?
- Is there sufficient lighting available?
- Is daytime or nighttime operation required?

- Should the camera be mounted with brackets, recessed in the walls or ceiling, or installed in a housing?
- Is a cover (hidden) camera and lens required?
- Should the camera voltage be 117 VAC, 24 VAC, or 12 VDC?
- Should it be powered via the coaxial cable (vidiplexed)?
- What is the distance between the camera and the monitor?
- What coaxial cable type should be used: RG 59 or RG 11?
- Should wireless microwave or other wireless transmission be considered?
- What monitor screen size should be used?
- How should the monitor be connected and terminated?
- Is the monitor to be desktop or rack mounted?
- Should the video recorder use reel-to-reel or tape cassette?
- What is the maximum recording time on the reel or cassette?
- Is time-lapse mode necessary for extending record time?
- Should frames of video be stored on hard disk for later, rapid retrieval?

Chapter 15

Cargo Security: Intermoda/Logistics— The Complete Overview

LOUIS A. TYSKA, CPP

Since September 11, 2001 and with the continuing threats of terrorism to the United States by use of weapons of mass destruction (WMD) and the use of chemical-biological nuclear and environmental (CBNE) agents, concerns for cargo security and the importation of goods have escalated.

The use of border crossings by trucks and containers as well as the seaport entries of containerization cargo have been identified as major concerns of the Office of Homeland Security. The use of technology to track, safeguard, and seal these containers has been emphasized. While the priority is high to implement such technology, the schedule to do so remains questionable. This has been due to two reasons. Technology, such as satellite tracking, is not completely dependable for water borne transportation. There is greater limitation, which is centered on the cost of the hardware and the monitoring-responsive protocols.

Increased involvement by a variety of federal government agencies have been diligently working to form partnerships with industry and public enforcement. There have been suggestions that several major federal departments would be merged. This has not come to finality as of this writing. It has been and shall continue to be that emphasis has been placed upon individual private sector companies and service providers and their commitment to security concerns. Therefore, it is the implementation of the asset protection and security controls outlined in this chapter which are tried and proven to be effective and still recommended for use in the logistics industry.

Finished goods, componentry, and raw materials are most attractive and vulnerable to theft or mis-

appropriation when in storage, in inventory or in transit. This is precisely where they are under the least amount of control.

Manufacturing and marketing departments may go to extremes to plan, produce, and sell goods, but then we frequently turn out the lights and go home once the finished goods are in the inventory or transit system. Industry provides control over these goods, but much more should be done to prevent theft or misappropriation.

The accountability for safeguarding goods in transit or storage lies completely with management for both the manufacturers and transporters of products. As goods pass through various modes of transportation and distribution, legal accountability changes hands and is frequently difficult to identify. It is precisely during these times that the thieves who prey upon the transportation systems will take advantage of the weakness within the network of distribution.

The ultimate consumer pays the cost of transportation and distribution loss. These increased costs are based on the need to file, process, and dispose of claims resulting from loss or damage in transit or storage. In addition, costs are involved in all reorders and reshipments as well as any dollar factors that may be directly charged to inconvenience and loss of timeliness in the marketplace.

Surveys show that the greatest loss a company can suffer is through actions of their own employees (up to 80% according to various governmental reports). Employees who have direct access to and control of goods in transit commit these internal thefts. Adequate physical security is required, but improper employee screening and control lead to significantly greater losses. Effective control is obtained by developing appropriate company procedures and implementing them. The attitude that management assumes concerning security will dictate the success of the loss prevention program and its acceptance.

Transportation and distribution management assumes accountability for goods in transit and responsibility for establishing standards of adequate physical security for the prevention of theft or damage. *The appointment of a security professional does not relieve management from its responsibility.* The role of security is related to the prevention of unauthorized entry, circulation, and exit of personnel and vehicles; perimeter fencing and entrance areas; the protective lighting and alarm systems; pass, badge, and identification systems; and the prevention and detection of crime.

The establishment of physical security controls is difficult. Goods in transit of every type and size move through the intermodal system constantly. Each shipment must be identified and accounted for throughout its entire journey. The size and complexity of the large transportation facilities has made it vital that physical security depend on a comprehensive and continuing evaluation of protective measures and an aggressive program of auditing.

The appropriate degree of protection for any specific facility is based upon two factors: relative criticality and relative vulnerability. If a facility is both highly critical and highly vulnerable, then an extensive physical security program is required.

Every facility is vulnerable in some degree to pilferage and theft. To determine the degree of vulnerability, the volume and value of goods handled and the past history of theft must be evaluated. If these factors rate high then the relative criticality is high.

To determine relative vulnerability, the susceptibility of the facility to theft must be estimated. The degree depends on such variables as the type of facility involved, the value and volume of goods handled, accessibility to the stolen goods market, physical layout and construction, and the loss prevention program in place, if any. If the facility can be easily penetrated and confused by high volumes of rapidly moving goods, and the marketplaces are highly motivated toward illegal practices, then the relative vulnerability is high.

Another complication is the multiplicity of managements using various parts of the specific facility simultaneously, for example, at a large metropolitan airport. Such facilities usually present a high degree of criticality as well as vulnerability. All tenants using a facility of this nature must coordinate and cooperate closely with the specific facility management.

Conditions that greatly influence the scope of the physical and procedural security necessary for a specific facility include:

- Size
- Volume and value of the goods in transit
- Geographic location
- Economic and political conditions in the area
- Ability of public law enforcement agencies to respond
- Sophistication of the criminal element in the local area

The nature of a physical and procedural security program to be implemented in any facility should be no more involved than is called for by an analysis of:

- Criticality
- Vulnerability
- Impact of physical security measures on efficiency of operations
- Limitations imposed by the physical characteristics of the facility
- Cost required to implement a program versus losses

The security professionals at each facility must continually evaluate and analyze, along with management, on a periodic basis. They must devise physical security measures consistent with continuing needs. Criticality and the vulnerability of a specific facility may vary from time to time as circumstances change.

Prevention Plan

Prevention of theft and pilferage demands commitment and determination on the part of all employees and in particular security personnel. Physical security measures and an extensive security awareness program for every employee of the facility are essential. Theft prevention is an ongoing process that must be given dedicated attention, especially to high-value and highly vulnerable goods.

Our prevention plan begins with defining the three types of crimes committed against goods and materials in transit—pilferage, theft, and organized crime—and their influence on cargo loss from the intermodal transportation and distribution systems.

Pilferage

The protection of goods and material while they are in the transportation system is a responsibility of employees at all levels. Pilferage is one of the most annoying and costly causes of cargo theft. Prevention of pilferage is one of the primary functions of the physical and procedural security program. It is difficult to detect, hard to prove, and becomes costly if ignored. Cargo movements are made in all kinds of packaging, some is even moved without packaging, merely tagged and labeled. Small packages are more susceptible to pilferage, since they are more easily concealed and not as readily detected. Actual losses will depend on such variables as volume, accessibility, waiting and loading times, storage areas between carriers or modes of transportation, and a variety of elements which contribute to confusion. Since these factors vary between facilities as well as during different times of day, each must be considered separately in the physical security plan.

A pilferer is one who steals primarily on giving into the temptation of an unexpected, or sometimes arranged, opportunity, and has little fear of being caught. There is usually little or no planning or premeditation involved in pilferage. Pilferers generally act alone. They may take items for which they have no immediate need or use. They may take items for family or friends or for use in the home. The degree of risk involved in pilferage is slight unless very large numbers of persons are engaging in pilferage at the same time. Pilferage will occur whenever an individual feels the need or desire for a certain article and the opportunity to take it is provided by inadequate security measures. Though it involves unsystematic theft of small articles, pilferage is nevertheless very serious, and it may have a great cumulative effect if the stolen items have a high cash or potential resale value. There is always the possibility that casual pilferers, encouraged by successful theft, may turn to systematic theft.

Pilferers are normally an employee of a large transportation facility or employees of other transportation segments whose interface requires them to be in the area. These persons are the most difficult to detect and apprehend.

Pilferage may occur anywhere in the transportation system where goods are being moved within a facility. Goods and materials left unprotected on carts, dollies, or other intraterminal vehicles for any period of time while awaiting the next move are extremely vulnerable. Such situations require adequate physical security measures since cargo accountability may become confused and difficult to determine.

One means of discouraging casual pilferage is to establish a parcel check system at all entry and exit points to a facility. Parcels carried into a facility will have to be logged in at an entry post upon entrance to the facility. Those leaving the facility must submit all parcels for inspection prior to departure. This will bring it to everyone's attention that they may be detected if they attempt the unauthorized removal of merchandise. Care must be taken to insure that personnel are not demoralized and that oppressive physical controls or unethical security practices do not violate their rights.

An aggressive security awareness program can train employees to be diligent and to report pilferage. All employees must understand that pilferage is morally wrong, no matter how insignificant the value of the item taken.

Supervisory personnel should set a proper example and maintain a desirable moral climate for employees by establishing an air of concern for the merchandise in their care and custody.

In establishing any deterrent to pilferage, security personnel must not lose sight of the fact that most employees are honest and disapprove of thievery of any kind. Mutual respect between security personnel and employees of the particular facility must be accomplished if the facility is to be pilferage free. Any security measures that infringe on the human rights or dignity of others will jeopardize, rather than enhance, the overall protection of the facility.

Theft

Theft in the transportation system challenges both management and security personnel. It is the transportation system management's responsibility, working with local law enforcement agencies through its security professionals, to reduce or eliminate cargo theft where possible. It is not an easy task to pinpoint the actual amount of loss that is occurring at any given facility. Cargo accountability records and methods are generally designed to single out thefts by category. Details of such losses may not be disclosed until some time later, usually upon receipt by the ultimate consignee or customer. The specific location may be far removed from the actual point of theft and the management accountable for the delivery may not have been the accountable management at the time of the loss.

Facilities located in and around large metropolitan centers are the most vulnerable for thievery. More goods and materials are being moved, terminals are more crowded, and more people are involved, adding to confusion. Markets for criminal redistribution are more readily available.

Thieves differ from pilferers in that they steal for profit. Thieves steal according to preconceived plans and they steal any and all goods in transit. They are selective only according to their *fence* requests. A thief can work alone but generally has accomplices. It is not unusual to find an accomplice who is an employee of the facility and in a good position to give relevant information to the thief. Some accomplices may even be in an advantageous position to locate or administratively control targeted goods or cause them to be removed from high-security areas. The specific theft may be a one-time occurrence based on inside information pertaining to a particular shipment, or may extend over long periods, even years.

Like pilferage, theft occurs anywhere but, unlike pilferage, theft is planned and organized. It can occur in more unsuspected places, involving switching trailers, misrouting railroad cars, or taking possession of a cargo in the name of a legitimate freight forwarder. The opportunity for theft in the transportation system begins in the shipper's installation and continues throughout the system and into the warehouse of the consignee after receipt. Employees of a shipper or consignee may be working to defraud. They may be part of an organized theft group. Dishonest documentation can result in the transportation system getting blamed for the loss when actually the goods were never sent or were stolen after delivery. One common practice is called *short-loading*. Control of goods in transit is one of the greatest challenges to the transportation industry.

Thieves can infiltrate into transportation ranks as legitimate employees. They can strike at a time of their choosing. Management can do none of these. Management can be ready, however, and can take measures to prevent theft and make it unprofitable and unappealing. Management protects goods by realizing that they are vulnerable and by studying and knowing the opportunities facing thieves and counteracting them.

Thieves' first problem is to identify and locate the cargo to be stolen. Then they must learn the system. They most assuredly will have to check storage areas and documentation. Countermeasures should include the control and movement of personnel and sensitive information through awareness programs. People have a tendency to talk too much and to the wrong people. It losses are occurring in a facility or at a certain place in a facility, management should carefully observe the behavior of employees; unthinking or disloyal employees will give away goods in transit, sometimes unknowingly.

Thieves, after locating the desired goods, must gain access to them and then take possession. To gain possession they may be required to survey such security factors as physical safeguards or guard procedures for weaknesses, attempt to bride guards, alter or forge shipping documents or passes, or create a disturbance to divert the attention of security personnel while the actual theft is taking place.

The next problem is the removal of the cargo. Thieves may have to remove it to a vehicle or vehicles, falsify documents, or alter the vehicle's exterior by painting one for this purpose. The final problem is to dispose of the stolen goods. Thieves need an outlet for stolen goods and must divert them back into the legitimate market for profit. They most probably will sell the goods through fences, pawnbrokers, flea markets, and discount houses. Frequently thieves steal on order and know in advance who will receive the stolen goods.

The knowledge that the thief has the problem of locating, taking possession of, moving, and selling stolen goods offers management the opportunity for constructive preventive measures. Thorough investigation and discovery of the means used to accomplish a theft offers a chance to prevent it from recurring. In addition, thieves must work with other people to disposes of their loot. The primary concern of thieves in selecting a target is its monetary value. Since they steal for profit, thieves will look for items from which they can quickly realize the greatest financial gain. This means that they must already have or be able to quickly find a ready market for the stolen merchandise—such items of high value as pharmaceuticals, metals, or electronic components. A thief may, if the profit is substantial, select a target of great size and weight.

There are many ways by which stolen cargo or items may be removed from transportation facilities:

- Terminal operations are extremely vulnerable to systematic theft. It is here that facility personnel and truck drivers have direct contact with each other and a readily available means of conveyance, which offer opportunity for collusion. Although most truck drivers and employees are honest, some do become victim to temptation presented by poorly controlled goods in transit. For instance, a receiving clerk might certify the receipt of property that the truck driver actually disposed of prior to arrival at the facility or in some instances at the consignee's location. A facility employee, or a thief acting as an employee, can provide a truck driver with cargo and assist in concealing it aboard the truck for unauthorized removal from the facility. Employees can assist a truck driver in removing property by executing a false invoice, which may appear to be legitimate when inspected by security personnel.

The driver's responsibility starts when the truck is loaded and the cargo is receipted for; it ceases when the truck is unloaded at the destination and the receipt is signed. The distribution and security of the load on the truck are also the responsibility of the driver and the management in custody of the cargo.

- Railway employees assigned to switching duties at a facility can operate in a similar manner. Since a railway car normally cannot be directed to a desired location so that stolen cargo can be removed, additional confederates will usually be required to transfer the stolen goods from the railway car, at some point or siding outside the facility, into some other means of transportation for removal to the ultimate destination. This increase in the number of persons involved will reduce profits and increase the chances for discovery and apprehension.

The carrier's responsibility commences when the loaded and sealed railroad car is coupled to the engine. The carrier's responsibility ceases when the railroad car is spotted in the consignee's yard or unloaded at destination.

- Trash disposal and salvage activities offer excellent opportunities to the thief to gain access to valuable material. Property may be hidden in waste material to be removed by a confederate who has the duty to remove trash from the facility.
- There are many other methods which may be employed by a thief to remove cargo from transportation facilities, such as moving items to a wrong location within the facility to be picked up by a confederate, intentionally misrouting cargo to a location where it can be picked up by a confederate, collusion with security personnel, failing to keep goods under surveillance, or removal by custodial or vendor vehicles.
- Thieves do not need to be employees or to be in collusion with employees; they can pose as employees or have false credentials from a nonexistent transportation company. There are many methods for thieves to pass themselves off as legitimate persons employed by legitimate companies in the transportation field. This is particularly true in the overcrowded terminal facilities in the large metropolitan areas.

Organized Crime

Just how much theft of goods from the transportation modes can be attributed to individual thieves and how much to organized crime is not accurately known. The U.S. Department of Justice believes that the vast majority of thefts, both in quantity and in dollar value, are the result of organized crime.

Just as the bookie operates within the framework of organized crime, so does the thief of goods in transit. Since organized crime provides a major network for the disposal of stolen goods, in effect, organized crime has become a theft-to-order operation with the transportation system as the victim. Some complaints have been registered but usually are settled with claims being paid, unhappy consignees, and large shipments of stolen merchandise being offered for sale as unbelievable bargains hundreds of miles from the scene of the actual thefts. Someone must pay for these costs, and it is usually passed on to the public. Legitimate businesses must pay the very large bill for such indirect costs as:

- Spiraling insurance costs or growing deductible coverage that stem from organized crime's unique competitive methods.
- Increased tax burdens resulting from nonexistent records in organized crime enterprises.
- Customer drop-off when legitimate enterprises are forced to raise prices to compensate for theft harassment.

Organized crime is a real and costly hazard to the security of goods in the transportation system. In comparison to the hazards of the pilferer and the unorganized thief, organized crime presents infinitely more complicated problems.

These problems are varied and involve every way that the human mind can conceive of to steal, swindle, defraud, and separate a rightful owner from their property—particularly while it is in the custody of others. Some recommended preventive measures for assisting in reducing the risks associated with organized crime thefts are:

- Engage a trustworthy security professional who works directly for the senior manager of a transportation facility or other levels of management as appropriate.
- Know your supervisors and make them aware of the need for consistent security awareness.
- Investigate all losses promptly and thoroughly and report to the appropriate authorities.

- When losses occur and tend to portray a pattern, maintain extra vigilance of employees and, if the situation dictates, make appropriate personnel changes.
- Provide periodic detailed inspections of the security measures in effect and the transportation operation procedures.

Organized crime activities consist of highly organized, tightly controlled management that will take advantage of any weakness in the transportation system. Can you answer these basic questions?

- What type of organization is required to systematically pinpoint the location of goods and to set them up for theft?
- How is it that a shipment of merchandise is found on the shelves of a retail store thousands of miles from the location where the theft occurred?
- What organizational structure is required to transport and ship stolen goods?
- What organizational patterns are used to effect the sale of such stolen goods in many locations after a theft?

While pondering these questions, remember that when one person is apprehended, the organization continues without interruption.

Dishonest employees, whether working alone or in collusion with other employees or nonemployees, are restricted in their methods of operation only by their own imagination and the existing opportunities to avoid detection. In order to minimize the opportunities to commit thefts while avoiding detection, the following facts concerning thefts, existing opportunities to avoid detection, and elimination of those opportunities within the reasonable cost/risk planning range must be evaluated:

1. Losses experienced (total, including cost of dispositions)
2. Distribution of losses by type:
   a. Pilferage (concealable on person or in vehicle)
   b. Theft (bypassing existing controls)
   c. Damage (accidental, deliberate, elements)
   d. Error (over, short, missing documents)
   e. Unexplained (no evidence to substantiate method causing loss)

Cargo Package and Movement Controls

The responsibilities of the shipper, the carrier, and the consignee must be clearly established if cargo is to be adequately protected in transit. Custody varies according to the size of the shipment and the means of transportation.

For shipments of less than the total capacity of a truck, railroad car, aircraft, or ship, the carrier assumes responsibility when the agent acknowledges receipt at the shipping point and is relieved when delivery is made to the consignee.

The responsibility of the carrier for large shipments depends on the mode of transportation used. If transportation is by truck, the carrier assumes custody when the vehicle is loaded. The truck carrier's responsibility ceases when the truck is unloaded at its destination. The railroad carrier's responsibility begins when the loaded and sealed car is coupled to a locomotive. He or she relinquishes custody when the car is spotted in the consignee's yard or unloaded at its destination.

Air and water carriers assume responsibility when an agent takes possession of the cargo from a shipper. This responsibility ends when the cargo is removed from the vessel or aircraft and is delivered to a freight forwarder, another carrier for transshipment, the consignee, or the agent.

A shipper load and count (SL&C) movement in any of the above modes relieves the carrier of liability for shortages, provided an accurate seal record is maintained.

Trucking Operations

Inclement weather and the possibility of accident are ever-present dangers to cargo in transit. It is incumbent upon the security officer to develop preplanned procedures for real operation, which should be part of the security plan.

The integrity of those responsible for line haul should be unquestionable. Only responsible, screened employees should be assigned as drivers and helpers to transport high-value cargo. The equipment used must be in excellent condition to avoid breakdowns that require emergency security protection. This is often difficult, sometimes impossible, and always expensive to provide. Modifications to equipment are often desirable. They can include additional locking and alarm devices, removal of outside door hardware, and installation of oversize fuel tanks (where permissible).

Employees should receive strict instructions concerning procedures to be followed during rest periods or meal stops while in transit. The vehicle should be locked and parked where it can be observed. The nature of the cargo carried should not be discussed with anyone. The driver should not deviate from the preplanned route. In the event of equipment failure, the driver should notify the nearest terminal immediately. If it is necessary to move high-value cargo over a weekend or on a holiday, it should be delivered to a terminal where maximum security can be provided.

To further protect vehicles on the road, large, brilliant-hued numerals should be painted on the roof and sides. This will help identify the equipment if it is stolen or hijacked and a helicopter search is initiated. The threat or vulnerability to hijacking exists, making the need for rooftop markings a deterrent and prevention tool.

In states where the use of double bottoms is permitted, the most valuable cargo should be loaded in the lead van.

Seals

Seals are invaluable to the protection of cargo in transit, but they are only as effective as the controls maintained over them. The responsibility for seal control must be vested in a specific individual who will maintain a record of all seals issued and to whom. Unissued seals should be stored in a locked container with limited access.

All cargo under seal entering a facility should be checked and the seal numbers recorded. If a seal is found to be broken or removed, or if the number does not agree with the one on the shipping document, an immediate item-by-item inventory of the shipment must be made.

Transfer Points

Transfer points, where cargo is transshipped from one mode of transportation to another or between two carriers of the same mode, are frequently areas where large losses can be expected. Cargo is often left unprotected, particularly in remote parts of the facility or yard.

Shipping documents are apt to be carelessly handled at these points and shipments can be intentionally misrouted into the hands of the criminal.

To reduce loss by theft or misrouting at a transfer point, management must maintain strict accountability of all cargo and demand that a carrier who receives cargo from another would accept custody for it in its original condition. Shipping documents must be examined carefully to guard against falsification or tampering. Employees of carriers using the facility must be able to prove their identity.

In-Transit Storage

While cargo is in the custody of the transportation system, it must frequently be stored for varying periods of time. During these intervals it is highly susceptible to loss, theft, or damage. A few elementary precautions will help reduce the claims filed against the responsible carrier:

- Individual shipments of cargo should be kept intact and stacked as a unit. This will prevent accidental separation and loss of a portion of a shipment.
- Fixed position lights in a storage area should be diffused to eliminate deep shadows. Each guard should be equipped with a strong, high-beam flashlight. Stacks should be arranged in accord with existing lighting to avoid creation of deep shadows.
- Greater emphasis should be placed on personnel control than upon structural or mechanical protection in those areas where cargo is stored for short periods of time. The increased traffic generated in this situation, and consequent increased vulnerability of cargo to pilferage and theft, require more alertness by guard patrols and more careful checking of the credentials of all individuals who are given access to the area. If possible, the storage area should be broken into subareas, with cargo handlers and truckers limited to the one subarea compatible with their credentials and business purpose.

Protected cargo, a term common to shippers of Department of Defense material, consists of items that require special handling because of their value or sensitive nature. The Department of Defense places protected cargo in three categories:

1. *Sensitive.* Small arms, ammunition, and explosives, which have a ready use during civil disturbances, terrorist acts, and other types of domestic unrest and which, if in the hands of militant or revolutionary organizations, present a definite threat to public safety.
2. *Pilferable.* Items vulnerable to theft and having a ready sale potential in illicit markets, such as alcoholic beverages.
3. *Controlled.* Items which require additional control and security in accordance with published regulations and statutes, including money, negotiable instruments, narcotics, registered mail, precious metal alloys, ethyl alcohol, and drug abuse items.

High-value pilferable (protected) cargo should be kept separate from other material and provided a greater degree of security. This material is best stored in a crib or security cage.

High-value, low-volume cargo, such as fissile radioactive materials, jewelry, furs, and securities require special handling and special security measures during storage. Cargo of this nature should pass from accountable officer to accountable officer. It should kept be under close surveillance constantly and always be stored in an exclusion area. When placed in an exclusion area it should be registered, including time, date, accountable party, and witness. The same procedure should be followed when the cargo departs from the facility.

Controlled Areas

A controlled area is any area whose access is governed by special restrictions and controls. In establishing controlled areas, consideration must be given to preserving the facility's cargo-moving goals as well as to its past loss and theft record.

All high-value cargo should be under surveillance or in a controlled area unless it is locked or sealed in the vehicle that transports it. Carrier vehicles, particularly trucks, trailers, and railway cars, containing high-value cargo, must be guarded or protected in a controlled area until they are released to authorized personnel for movement.

To be fully effective a controlled area should be under surveillance by physical or electronic methods and movement within the area controlled. A barricade providing limited access does not, in itself, constitute a controlled area.

The transportation industry provides a public service. As a result, some of its operations must be open to the general public. The general offices, personnel office, and freight receiving offices may need to be outside the controlled area. Where practical, consideration should be given to the installation of convex mirrors in warehouse storage areas so that supervisory and guard personnel can have additional surveillance capability.

A controlled area can extend over many acres and include vehicle marshalling yards, docks, warehouses, and service or supply buildings. Such an area is a first line of defense for the protection of cargo in the transportation system.

Limited Area

A limited area can be established within the controlled area. This will provide a higher degree of security. A different pass, issued to fewer people, should be necessary for entry to a limited area. Sorting, recoopering of crates, and storage may be accomplished here.

Exclusion Area

An exclusion area can be located inside the limited area. Again, a different pass should be required and the number of people granted access strictly limited. The exclusion area is used only for handling high-value, low-volume cargo. The crib, vault, or cargo that comprises the exclusion area should be kept locked or under surveillance at all times.

Access points to any controlled area, regardless of the degree of security involved, should be locked at all times or under physical or electronic surveillance. Strict control of the keys or combinations to locks is essential. Management should make periodic checks to determine the integrity of controlled areas in addition to any checks conducted by security representatives.

Package Control

A good package control system is an invaluable aid in helping to prevent or minimize pilferage and theft. No packages, except those with proper authorization, should be permitted to be brought into controlled areas without inspection or accountability.

A simple system should be established to control movement of packages, materials, and property into and out of the facility. Limitations as to types of property authorized, persons allowed to move authorized property, and approved points of entrance and exit should be included in the facility physical security plan.

A standard package checking system may be used at the entrance pass to a controlled area for the convenience of employees and visitors. When practicable, all outgoing packages should be inspected except those properly authorized for removal. When 100% inspection is impracticable, frequent unannounced checks should be conducted at random times.

Vehicle Control

Strict control of all vehicles entering or leaving a controlled area should be maintained. Parking lots should be located outside of all cargo exchange or controlled areas. The only vehicles entering or leaving a controlled area should be bona fide cargo carrying or handling equipment or emergency vehicles. There are generally three types of vehicles working within the controlled areas: facility vehicles (e.g., primarily small trucks, cargo handling vehicles, cargo loading vehicles); cargo pick-up and delivery and freight forwarder vehicles; and the in-house cargo carrier vehicles. Of primary concern to the security staff are the cargo pick-up and delivery vehicles and freight forwarder vehicles. These vehicles should be both checked in and out, with adequate records being maintained to insure that they are the authorized vehicles for specific cargo movements. The facility vehicles generally remain on the facility but should be properly recorded if they are required to leave the facility. The cargo carrier vehicles should be inspected and documented when arriving or departing. It is essential to maintain accurate records of all cargo carrying vehicles entering or leaving controlled areas.

A close inspection of all trucks entering or leaving a facility should be a general requirement. An orderly system should be established to limit and control the movement of trucks and other conveyances within controlled areas.

All trucks and conveyances entering a controlled area should be required to pass through a control gate manned by security. Truck drivers, helpers, passengers, and vehicle contents should be carefully screened. The security check at truck entrances should cover both incoming and outgoing trucks and should include:

- Appropriate entries on a truck register, including vehicle registration, name of truck firm, description of load, and date and time of entrance and departure.
- Identification of driver and helper, including proof of affiliation with the company owning the truck or conveyance.
- A license check of the vehicle operator.
- Examination of the truck or conveyance.

Passes or some form of documentation should be issued to truck drivers and helpers who have been identified and registered. This documentation should permit only limited access to specific loading and unloading areas.

Incoming traffic should be kept to the minimum essential for the efficient operation of the facility, and escorts should be provided if vehicles are permitted access to controlled or restricted areas.

For trucks with loads that are impractical to examine, door seals may be used at the entrance gate. A designated representative at the receiving end will open these seals. Likewise, the truck doors may be resealed for exit or for other stops within the facility.

Loading and unloading operations should be strictly supervised to assure that unauthorized materials or persons do not enter or leave the facility via trucks or other conveyances. This would also apply to all service or support vehicles that, under most circumstances, have regular access to a given facility.

Warehousing and Storage

Storage is not a normal function of the transportation system for goods in transit. It does, however, become necessary at times to provide at least temporary warehousing. The necessary storage of goods and material is more applicable to the manufacturers or shippers as well as the variety of consignees who receive the goods. It is management's responsibility in all instances to assure adequate protection for goods at all times. This includes terminal storage at either end of the route or, in some instances, en route.

Storage areas may include a warehouse, shed, open areas, or any portion of a facility that is designated for holding purposes. All of the security considerations and principles that apply to the prevention of loss and theft of goods in the transportation system apply equally to warehouse areas.

Open Storage

Open storage is normally used only for those goods not subject to damage by weather conditions, and bulky, nonperishable items that are not sensitive to being easily pilfered. It should never include high-value, low-volume items.

When property is stored in open areas, it should be properly stacked and placed within but not near fenced-in areas. All off-loaded cargos must be properly stacked or stored regardless of the time of receipt.

It is imperative that complete individual shipments of cargo be kept intact. This helps prevent the inadvertent separation and eventual loss of a portion of one shipment in the system of accountability.

Stacks of goods in storage should be a minimum of 50 feet from the perimeter fencing. They should be as symmetrical as possible, and the aisles between stacks or lines should be wide and straight. These arrangements not only provide for visibility by the security staff, but also allow for the proper movement of vehicles and cargo hauling equipment.

Fixed position lights in a storage area should be of a diffused type to eliminate deep shadows.

Covered Storage

The same principles of even stacking and adequate aisle space recommended for use in open storage are applicable to covered storage. Goods in storage should be placed to conform with existing lighting in order to keep deeply shadowed areas to a minimum.

In areas where goods and materials are constantly being moved in and out, or otherwise stored for very short periods, more emphasis should be placed on personnel movement control and security than upon structural or mechanical protection. This is especially so during working hours in order to prevent pilferage or theft by unauthorized personnel or workers.

Highly theft-prone types of goods and material in storage should be kept separate from other cargoes and given a greater degree of security. Sensitive items are those that can be pilfered or stolen and disposed of quickly. They include such items in a separate high-value storage area to provide a much higher degree of physical and procedural security protection. In instances where a separate building is not available or warranted by the requirement for sensitive storage, areas that have previously been described as limited or exclusive areas should be designated and utilized.

High-Value, Low-Volume Storage

All high-value, low-volume items, like jewelry, gems, furs, and securities require special handling and special security measures when in storage. Goods of this nature should pass from one accountable person to another. They should be held under close observation at all times and should always be stored in an exclusion area. All goods placed in the exclusion area should be registered and logged for time, date, and recipient. The goods should also be logged out on removal, with similar notations made. It is essential to maintain accurate records of all persons who enter and leave an exclusion area.

Shipping and Receiving Areas and Personnel

Control of shipping and receiving areas and personnel at a plant, warehouse, or distribution center can do much to prevent cargo theft. A number of practical measures are available to shippers and receivers for improving security of cargo-handling areas and controlling personnel to minimize opportunities for theft. To provide better physical security, shippers and receivers may find it to their advantage to adopt the following precautions in areas where cargo is moved to or from carrier equipment.

1. Maintain perimeter controls. Mark off a perimeter area at a suitable distance, at least 20 feet, from the dock edge and from the wall of the office where carrier personnel report. Place signs reading "Restricted Area—Authorized Personnel Only" along the perimeter line facing the dock and office. Make sure that shipping and receiving areas are well lighted. Use lighting with a foot-candle-power level of 50–60 if possible. Include floodlights to light the interior of railcars and truck vans.
2. Keep all cargo doors closed when not loading or unloading.
3. Do not allow cargo being loaded or unloaded to remain in the operating area between dock front and perimeter line or, generally, in close proximity to railcars or trucks.
4. Provide a secure room in the shipping and receiving area for control of sensitive or high-risk cargo during the shipping or receiving process. Limit access to this room and exercise tight control over movement of such cargo to the carrier or from the carrier to storage.
5. Maintain strict control and accountability for all keys to locked areas, security rooms, and containers.
6. Store seals securely within the office area. Limit issuance of seals to a select few employees. Maintain accurate records of all seals issued.

Strong measures of physical security are essential, and shippers and receivers run serious risk of cargo theft if they neglect them (see Appendix 15.A). Close personnel control and supervision are even more important. They provide the key to high-level security for shipping and receiving operations. Good personnel control begins with preemployment screening. Employers should make the screening process as thorough as possible. It should include a check with previous employers and other available sources. After hiring, employers may find it advisable to take the following precautions:

1. Require identification badges with photographs for every employee.

2. Maintain an up-to-date signature file or other verification system for all employees authorized to sign receipts and other shipping documents.
3. Require employees to enter and leave the premises through a single personnel door or gate. Prohibit access of employees' vehicles to the cargo area.
4. Maintain controls such as special passes for employees who leave the facility during duty hours.
5. Limit to a select few the employees authorized to process receipts for shipments of sensitive and high-value items.
6. Require identification badges for all persons visiting the facility.
7. Indoctrinate all personnel to challenge persons moving about the facility who are not accompanied by an employee.
8. Remind all employees periodically of the penalties for theft, including loss of jobs, and the possible impact of serious theft from the company.

Good supervision will do much to improve cargo security at the shipper's and receiver's premises (see Appendix 15.B). The shipper and receiver may find it useful to instruct company supervisors to observe the following practices:

1. Make their presence conspicuous in the shipping and receiving area, continually overseeing cargo handling operations.
2. Make frequent checks of the quantities of inbound and outbound cargo being handled. Make occasional unannounced spot audits, especially of loading operations.
3. Rotate cargo-handling personnel among different carriers, where feasible.
4. Rotate cargo checkers and handlers on different work cycles, where possible.
5. Prevent nonemployees from assisting in shipping and receiving operations.
6. Report any suspicious activity to the security office.

Documentation

Much cargo loss can be traced to poor documentation practices attributable to the volume of paperwork necessary to control both large and small shipments. Nevertheless, documentation is one of management's most important methods for controlling cargo handling and combating the increasing sophistication of thieves and pilferers. To reduce cargo theft, shippers and receivers should be famil-iar with the security hazards associated with documentation, and the ways in which documentation practices can be improved to increase cargo security.

The purpose of documentation is simple. Documentation gives the characteristics of the cargo, tells how, when, and where a shipment is to move, provides accountability, and forms a basis for carrying out the financing of individual shipments. Documentation, while essential to the movement of cargo, tends by its very nature to expose cargo to risk of theft. It creates serious security hazards, which can be minimized only by stringent control measures.

Accessibility

Many persons have almost unlimited access to the detailed information required to document cargo shipments. The origin, carrier, route, destination, description of commodities, weight cube, value, and time of shipment can be obtained from various shipping documents. The large number of document-processing points associated with each shipment magnifies the problem. Because of easy access to detailed information, shipments can easily be set up for theft and pilferage by company or carrier employees or even by outsiders.

Errors

Errors in documentation constitute a security hazard because they lead to cargo theft. The large number of subsidiary documents with a duplicate date found on source documents repeatedly contain errors in transcription. Consequently, shipments are mis-routed, delayed, or frustrated. The cargo often ends up lying unattended and unaccounted for in terminals, piers, or warehouses, where it becomes a target for thieves because the longer cargo is delayed at any given point along its route the more susceptible it is to theft.

Late Submission

Failure of shippers and receivers to forward documents promptly to the necessary parties delays the processing of cargo, and cargo delayed in transit is extremely vulnerable to theft.

There are a number of practical measures that shippers and receivers may find is advisable to take if they wish to reduce theft and pilferage caused by poor documentation practices:

1. Maintain a continuing review of the company's documentation procedures and change them where necessary to improve cargo security.
2. Analyze records of incidents and losses to determine causes and direct necessary corrective action.
3. Limit access to documentation. Maintain strict controls over the storage and distribution of invoices, shipping orders, manifests, and other vital materials.
4. Avoid wide dissemination of documents. Do not make excess copies of documents. Discourage transmission of information by telephone, telegram, fax, or modem, particularly concerning high-value items.
5. Transcribe information carefully from source documents to subsidiary documents, and check the transcription closely.
6. Forward shipping documents promptly, especially those needed at foreign destinations.
7. Limit the number of persons having knowledge of cargo shipments.
8. Maintain strict control of information on the shipment's routing, time of dispatch, time of arrival, and carrier.
9. Give security personnel advance notice of cargo requiring surveillance and protection. Inform the carrier when special protective services are required on its part.
10. Ensure that documentation procedures provide for a clear audit trail of all cargo shipped and received. Require cargo checkers to use self-inking identification stamps to facilitate audit by overcoming the problem of illegible signatures on receipts. Maintain close control of such stamps.
11. Inspect cargo immediately upon receipt. Note shortages on receipt documents and notify carrier. If theft is suspected, notify the proper law enforcement authorities.
12. Enclose a packing list in each shipping container or package, if practicable, to facilitate prompt and complete survey if pilferage occurs. Do not put the packing list on the outside of the container or package.
13. Select documentation employees carefully; ensure thorough training, including instruction in the security hazards of documentation; and require close supervision.

Receipt of Shipments

The warehouse is particularly vulnerable to theft and pilferage. In addition to security of the physical area and effective control of personnel, however, other safeguards can improve security. An inbound register should be maintained, recording carrier name, commodity, quantity, time of arrival, time of departure, driver's name, the truck, van, or railcar number, and any note of discrepancies. In addition to the inbound register, the receiver may find it advantageous to maintain special control procedures for trucks:

1. Refuse to spot a truck at the dock until receiving personnel are available. A receiving clerk or warehouse worker should meet the driver and request the bills of lading or waybills. He or she should examine these documents against the purchase order to assure legibility, authenticity, and completeness. All discrepancies should be corrected immediately or the cargo refused.
2. Check that driver has a valid gate pass and retain it until ready to sign the release. Note the date and hour of release on the pass so that gate security personnel can ascertain normal time lags in travel from the receiving area to the gate.
3. Examine door seals, if called for by the documentation. If the numbers of the seals are at variance with those on the documents, notify the supervisor immediately so that he or she can notify the shipper and the receiver's security office.
4. Insure that the receiving clerk safeguards the documents through the checking, unloading, and storage process, taking care not to deface or lose them. Require the receiving clerk's signature on the documentation, with date and time information.
5. If a full truckload of the same cargo is moved to a location other than the receiving dock for unloading, do not break the seals until the truck is ready for unloading. Have an employee of the receiver facility accompany the truck while moving from the receiving area to the unloading point.
6. If a truck cannot be fully unloaded before the close of business, close all doors with suitable locking devices until the next workday.
7. Insure that the supervisor checks the interior of the truck after unloading and before the receiving clerk goes to the next vehicle. Then require the driver to depart immediately.

Similarly, the receiver may wish to maintain special control procedures for railcars:

1. Insure that the documents are legible, complete, and authentic before issuing the cargo receipt.

Require immediate correction of any discrepancies.

2. Inspect the seals on loaded railcars and check against the numbers recorded on the documents. Where possible, assign an employee of the traffic section to check the seals as the rail carrier spots the cars. Immediately notify the carrier of discrepancies.

3. Where discrepancies are found in the seals, make a physical check of the contents of the railcar, with a representative of the rail carrier present. Notify the receiver's security office.

4. If a railcar is spotted in a holding area within the facility and later moved to the unloading area by the receiver's equipment, lock the railcar while in the holding area, using the receiver's locking devices.

5. Insure that the supervisor checks the interior of the railcar after unloading and before the receiving clerk goes to the next railcar. Then close the railcar doors immediately.

The security of sensitive or high-value cargo or other goods requiring storage in security rooms calls for additional safeguards. They should be moved directly from truck or railcar to the security room, and the receiving clerk should require a signed receipt from the security room employees who receive the cargo.

Through lack of supervision, control, and checks during the cargo receiving process, the thief or pilferer gains opportunity. A large receiving facility is a complex and active place with much movement of merchandise, personnel, and equipment. Unless the devices of the thief are known and adequate controls are maintained, theft is bound to occur. An informed knowledge of the methods of the thief will help the receiver to adopt and apply more effective controls. Some examples follow.

The Partially Emptied Carton

Opening a carton, removing part of the contents, filling the void with some type of waste material, and resealing the carton hides a theft unless someone handling the carton notices the weight differential. The carton, however, is not always resealed. Therefore, the receiving clerk should immediately check the contents and reseal any open cartons. A strange sound from a carton should also alert the receiving clerk. Substitutes such as rocks and bottles that can create sound have been found. If possible, make frequent spot checks at receiving platforms by opening

a small percentage of cartons not otherwise subject to loss or damage notations. Remember that an open carton quickly becomes an empty carton.

Lunch and Break Periods

Leaving the receiving area unguarded and cargo doors open during lunch and break periods is an invitation to the thief to load checked cargo back on the truck. Cargo doors should be closed and at least one employee should remain on duty in the receiving area during these periods.

Pallet Patterns

After pallet pattern and count have been established, a thief who knows pallet patterns can easily change the pattern by putting one less carton per layer on the pallet. Visible evidence of this change is minimal, and several cartons can be extracted from a full truck or carload. These cartons are difficult to see when slipped into dark confines of the truck, van, or railcar. The receiver should periodically check the pallet load count and inspect the inside of the van or railcar before signing the gate pass or closing the car doors.

The Falsified Document

Large quantities of cargo are lost through theft in receiving activities by employees who falsify the quantity received and leave merchandise in the truck or railcar to be hauled out of the terminal. A receiving clerk in collusion with a driver or a rail employee can steal much cargo simply by leaving the quantity he desires in the truck or railcar and certifying on the documentation that the full quantity was received. Two simple procedures will do much to control this problem:

1. Require each receiving employee to call the supervisor for a final check of the truck or railcar to insure that no merchandise is left in the vehicle. If dock lights are insufficient to illuminate the interior of vans and railcars, the supervisor should use a flashlight or lantern. He or she should insure that merchandise is not concealed under trash or in the cab of the truck. In damage-free railcars the supervisor should check behind the bulkhead doors.

2. Take a 100% inventory periodically of the stored receipt counts of each receiving clerk for one day's receipts.

Trash

Dropping valuable items into trash bins and later retrieving them from the dump is a common practice. In some cases, the employee has an agreement with the dump attendants. Alert observations of employees by supervisors will do much to prevent this type of theft, but also it is desirable to apply trash collection and removal controls, such as establishing timetables for placing trash in bins. Crushing or shredding the contents of trash receptacles prior to removal from the premises will discourage thieves from depositing stolen items in refuse.

Trailers

Unattended trailers and trailers remaining overnight at a receiving point offer an excellent means for the illegal removal of merchandise. Failure of supervisors to make at least one check of each trailer (during unloading and when empty before releasing it) can result in the loss of an entire trailer load. Simply by signing the documents and the cargo receipt, a receiving employee may be able to steal an entire trailer without bringing it to the receiving area. When supervisors insist on checking each carrier vehicle before release, this type of theft can be prevented. When trailers are left unattended by receiving personnel, the driver has a blank check for loading cargo. Lock or seal empty and unattended trailers remaining overnight, weekends, or holidays to prevent them from being filled with stolen goods.

Pallet Exchange

If collusion exists between the receiving employee and the driver, empty pallets can be quickly loaded into the van to conceal cargo. Falsifying the cargo receipt showing that the entire quantity was received will cover up the theft. Close supervision is the only answer.

Serious Oversight

A few cartons used to support the end of an unloading conveyor can be conveniently left on the truck.

If noticed by receiving personnel, the driver claims that it was an oversight. Checking carrier vehicles before release can prevent this type of theft.

Seal Switches

If seals are left in a readily accessible place, carrier personnel can steal them, break the existing seal, and substitute a stolen one after going to another area and loading illicit cargo before going to the perimeter gate. There are cases where a receiving employee has furnished to the driver in collusion a second seal, the number of which has been entered on the gate pass. This seal is placed on the door of the vehicle after illicit cargo has been loaded elsewhere.

Packaging, Pallets, and Containers

Shipping goods in the right kind of container is essential to good cargo security. Good shipping practice requires that packaging be suitable to protect cargo against all hazards of transportation, and theft has become a serious hazard. Not only is inadequate packaging a major reason why shipments arrive damaged, but weak or damaged packaging invites pilferage by making it easy to steal the goods. Most often goods are stolen from broken packing cases in small quantities either in the warehouse or during cargo-handling operations.

There are a number of precautions that shippers and receivers may take to curb losses by increasing difficulty and risk for the thief or pilferer:

1. Select shipping containers strong enough to protect the load from damage and to hold together without breaking open under stress or rough handling.
2. Select shipping containers that are so difficult to breach and close so tightly that the thief must destroy the case to get at its contents.
3. Insure that the shipping container has effective closing devices. Make sure that all flaps of fiberboard containers are fully closed and reinforced with 3-inch paper tape.
4. Reinforce heavy shipments with strap, normally applied girth wise.
5. Examine wooden containers to insure that all nails are driven home and reinforced strapping is used.
6. Avoid using second-hand packaging materials where possible. Marks of previous nails and straps and obliterated addresses make it difficult to

determine on inspection whether pilferage has occurred.

7. Adopt the unitized load principle through use of pallets and van containers to the greatest extent feasible.

The object of the unit load principle is to give greater speed, security, flexibility, and economy to cargo movement by consolidating small packages into unitized loads of optimum size for the use of mechanical cargo-handling equipment. The main applications of the unit load principle are the pallet and the van container.

The pallet affords security to cargo by assembling small packages in units held to the pallet by heavy strapping and various forms of covering. Consolidation into a palletized unit reduces the danger of loss or pilferage of individual packages. To reach a package, the thief ordinarily must cut the strapping or slash the covering or otherwise leave visible evidence of having disturbed the load. There are several variant forms of palletization:

- Consolidation of packages on a standard wood, plastic, or fiberboard pallet, secured by strapping.
- Consolidation of packages into a fiberboard container sealed and strapped to a skid.
- Consolidation of packages onto a standard pallet, with the load secured by transparent shrink wrapping—a heavy plastic coating formed to the shape of the load by application of heat and by consequent shrinkage upon cooling.

The van container normally offers an even greater measure of security to cargo. Its security attributes are substantial because:

- It is usually constructed of steel, aluminum, or plywood; it is difficult to breach without leaving visible marks.
- It can be padlocked and sealed, affording security equal to that of truck trailers and railcars. If seals of good quality and design are used, their removal is difficult without signs of tampering.
- Entire pallets can be accommodated in the van container. This materially increases the degree of protection against pilferage afforded to the goods.
- Containers are adapted to intermodal movement and can be transported door-to-door with a minimum of delay and opening for inspection of the contents. Each opening thus eliminated reduces opportunities for theft.

Experience has shown that theft or pilferage is most likely when containers are open at the shipping and receiving dock. This calls for the same security procedures regarding personnel, documentation, and physical controls as in the case of trucks. Pilferage while containers are en route is most likely if the container has been damaged or is not properly maintained. Proper attention to sealing, with use of reliable, tamper-proof seals, and maintenance of accurate seal records, including noting seal numbers and the reasons for any breaking of seals, will do much to reduce the incidence of pilferage en route. Good maintenance practices are the first line of defense against such pilferage, and the shipper should be careful to reject a damaged or defective container if it is offered for the transportation of cargo.

Liability and Claims

General

In arranging for the movement of cargo, the shipper or receiver must be prepared to accept the fact that on occasion even good security measures may fail, and theft or pilferage may occur. It is at this point, after the harm is done, that liability and claims procedures come into play. Knowledge of the rules of carrier liability and of claim procedures will prove indispensable to the shipper or receiver if he or she is to obtain indemnity. The fact of loss, however, should give shippers and receivers an incentive to go beyond indemnification and consider how to prevent recurrence.

From the standpoint of cargo security, the most important aspect of liability and claims is claims prevention. Every safeguard the shipper or receiver adopts is an act of claims prevention. Moreover, the shipper or receiver can obtain professional help in taking preventive measures on a systematic basis. Many insurance companies have claims prevention specialists who can survey shipper or receiver's operations and recommend ways in which greater security can be attained. Use of consultative services of this kind is a prudent course of action even for the shipper or receiver with relatively good loss experience.

Carrier Liability for Loss to Cargo

When loss occurs through theft or pilferage, liability of the shipper or receiver depends on variable elements. Since there are no uniform rules of carrier liability, the presence and amount of the shipper's indemnity depend in large measure on the mode of transport used to ship cargo. Each mode of transport operates under differing rules, with wide variations in limits of liability and the defenses available to the carrier. For the informed shipper or receiver, these variations among modes of transport determine whether the receiver relies on the carrier's liability or obtains additional protection through cargo insurance.

The present monetary limits of carrier liability should be known by the user and confirmed with the particular carrier or modes of transportation to be used.

Surface transportation in foreign countries usually is subject to local law. Most countries in Western Europe, however, are parties to international conventions that limit the liability of highway carriers.

In air transportation the shipper may obtain an increase in the carrier's limit of liability by paying an additional charge. The same is usually possible in water transportation by agreement between the shipper and carrier.

These monetary limits on carrier liability offer only partial assurance of indemnity to the shipper in view of the numerous defenses available to the carrier. Commonly, the fault of the shipper or owner of the goods is a valid defense. Thus, for example, defective packing frequently exonerates the carrier. The low limits of carrier liability and uncertainty as to recovery have led shippers as a common practice to obtain cargo insurance on goods they ship by air or water carrier. For shipments moving by rail or motor carrier, the need to obtain such insurance may be less compelling, but the shipper may find it prudent to consult an underwriter, especially if the shipment is of high value or would be unduly exposed to theft or pilferage. Additional assistance may be obtained from the carrier's claims prevention section.

Claims Procedures

When loss from theft or pilferage occurs, the shipper or receiver should take care to observe the requisite claims procedures, especially as to notification of loss to the carrier, the formal filing of claims, and, if need be, the institution of suit. As a matter of law or under the contract of carriage, these actions ordinarily must be taken within specified time limits (see Appendix 15.A). Failure to comply may foreclosure the shipper or receiver's right to indemnity, regardless of the merits of his claim (C.F.R. 49 Part 1005 Appendix 21-1a).

Claims Prevention

From a practical standpoint, claims prevention is the most important element of liability and claims. The shipper or receiver must have a reasonable assurance of indemnity if goods are pilfered or stolen, but it is much more beneficial to reduce theft or pilferage to a minimum. The best way is through systematic claims prevention measures. Many of the measures recommended elsewhere in this chapter are in actuality basic claims prevention measures, for they aim to remove opportunities for theft or pilferage and thus reduce the incidence of claims. These recommendations deserve the most serious consideration.

It is desirable to go about a claims prevention program in a systematic way. Even if loss experience is relatively low, the shipper or receiver will usually find it an advantage to make a thorough survey of the operations from beginning to end with the specific objective of locating weak spots. Such a survey should cover all parts of the operation: documentation, communications, procedures, personnel, and physical facilities. One method could be to trace a variety of individual shipments step-by-step. Another might be a concentrated examination of each single element, such as documentation or physical security.

Some shippers or receivers have the capability of making such surveys with their own staff. If a shipper or receiver lacks this capability or wishes to have the objectivity of an outsider, professional help is available through an insurance underwriter or broker.

Many will be able to conduct security surveys with their own staff. Others will prefer to call in specialists from the particular insurance company or association with which they are affiliated.

A single survey, while useful, probably would not suffice in most instances. The prudent course might be to repeat at suitable intervals. In this respect the shipper or receiver could be guided by loss experience. It would be sound practice; however, to order a security survey whenever an important new operation is being set up, for example, when a firm is entering the export business for the first time.

In addition to such surveys, shippers and receivers may find it useful to review their claim files periodically to see if there is a pattern with respect to the number and types of claims resulting from the operations of other shippers and receivers with whom they do business. Examples would be repeated instances of faulty packing or count discrepancies.

Cargo Security Prevention Standards

Buildings

All terminal buildings housing cargo should be constructed of a material that will deter unlawful entry.

Ground floor windows should be steel-barred. Bars should be spaced at intervals of not more than 6 inches and set in a steel frame that is securely affixed to the structure. All windows of buildings that adjoin other structures should also be barred.

Delivery and receiving doors should be constructed of a material that will deter unlawful entry and equipped with a self-locking device that will engage immediately when the door is closed. All delivery and receiving doors should remain closed and locked when not actually in use.

Pedestrian doors should be capable of being locked with a substantial lock. Workforce facilities such as restrooms, locker rooms, and eating or lounging areas should be separated from the area in which cargo is stored.

Maximum security cribs, constructed of a substantial material that deters entry on all four sides, overhead, and from the floor, and provides adequate space for storage of high-value cargo, should be incorporated in each terminal building. They should be constructed in an area that is visible to management or security personnel or under frequent surveillance by the security patrol. (Only designated personnel should be allowed to enter this area; it may be desirable to secure it with a double lock requiring keys held by two different persons.)

The office in which delivery and pick-up orders are processed should be an area to which only authorized personnel have access. Room arrangements should be such that documents being processed are not available to or observable by unauthorized persons.

Fencing and Gates

Whenever possible, perimeter fencing should be provided around terminals in which merchandise is stored. The number of entrances and exits should be held to a minimum.

Fencing should normally be of the chain-link type, maximum 2-inch mesh, at 9 gauge, and not less than 6 feet in height surmounted by an additional 2 feet of barbed wire. Where installed in soft earth, the bottom of the fencing should be anchored below grade and then backfilled. Where installed over concrete, the bottom of the fence should be no more than 2 inches above the surface, but high enough that, when sagging, it does not touch the surface. The top of the fence should be surmounted by at least 3 strands of barbed wire occupying no less than 2 feet vertically, but positioned at a 45° angle to the vertical.

Gates should be constructed of the same chain link fence material, surmounted by an additional 2 feet of barbed wire, within 2 inches of hard ground or paving, and capable of being locked.

The fence line should be maintained in good condition and provisions made to avoid bumping and distortion of the fence by motor vehicles and other equipment. Fence lines should be kept free of shrubbery and other objects impeding the line of sight.

Gatehouses

Gatehouses should be self-contained units, equipped with at least two modes of communications for assured redundancy. These may be commercial telephone, radio, private telephone, or alarms. The exit gatehouse should be set back from the gate so that existing vehicles can be stopped and examined on terminal property without the gate being opened.

Adequate lighting must be provided in the area of the gatehouse so that documents and identifying features, and contents of incoming and outgoing vehicles, can be examined by the guard.

The area around the gatehouse should be free of encumbrances that restrict the guard's line of vision. Procedural signs advising drivers and visitors of the conditions of entry should be prominently displayed on the exterior of all entry gatehouses, preferably where they can be read by drivers before turning off the public street or road into the approach to the gate.

When warranted, photo recorders should be installed in gatehouses to provide a photo record of persons and their documents entering the terminal facility.

Locks and Key Control

All padlocks should be of a single standard type for control purposes. The use of other than the approved type is then easily determined. When possible, the base of the padlock should indicate the company name. These padlocks should have multiple pin tumblers (at least 6), interchangeable cores, a minimum tension pull resistance of 6000 pounds on the shank portion, and shrouded shackle.

The use of nonstandard padlocks should be prohibited. All lockers, gear boxes, and cooper or carpenter shanties should be locked only with padlocks as described above.

No gates or exit areas should be secured by padlocks with the use of chains. All gates and exits should have proper latches that are secured to the surface with nonexposed bolts. The area surrounding the lock, particularly on the exposed side, should have metal backing to prevent accessibility.

The use of electrical switch locks is recommended in gate and exit areas. These permit use of a micro switch to record and indicate the opening of a given lock on a panel or central control indicator.

Key control should be rigid. For every key given out, a signature should be required and a card file maintained that indicates the history of each key. Duplicate keys should be secured under absolute control. The distribution of submaster, master or grandmaster keys should be highly restricted. The key control of all equipment, particularly that which could be used in the commission of a theft, such as hi-los, stackers, and yard tractors, should be very strict. No keys should be left in any equipment overnight or when not assigned. This also should apply to equipment held in the maintenance or repair shops.

Alarm and Communications Systems

All terminal buildings in which merchandise in the transportation scheme is moving should be equipped with an intrusion detection system. However, alarm systems should be considered as an *adjunct* to fencing, lighting, or guard forces, not in lieu of them.

Circuit boards, lines, and control panels for alarm systems should be placed in such locations and constructed in such a manner that they are protected from vandalism or deliberate attempts to disrupt or destroy their usefulness.

There are various recognized alarm systems; a qualified security specialist can best determine the type that meets the needs of a particular facility. The three most popular alarm systems are:

1. The audible alarm, which, when activated, draws attention to the facility or a portion thereof.
2. The silent alarm, which is designed to alert private guard forces or municipal police departments. When considering this system, managers should determine the time required for the guard force to respond to the alert.
3. The visible alarm, which increases light intensity in a given area by utilizing additional lights, by explosive flares, or rockets.

Lighting

Adequate lighting should be provided between dusk and dawn at all entrances and exits, along all boundary lines, around all storage structures, and in all parking areas.

The primary power source at a facility is usually a local public utility. However, to protect against a public power failure, an alternate source of power adequate to provide lights at key control points should be provided.

A gasoline-driven generator that starts automatically upon the failure of outside power is the preferred alternate, although battery power may also be used.

Tables 15-1 and 15-2 provide standards for area coverage and lighting intensity.

Table 15-1. Lighting Area Coverage

Type of Area	Type of Lighting	Width of Lighted Strip (in feet)	
		Inside Fence	Outside Fence
Isolated perimeter	Glare	25	200
Isolated perimeter	Controlled	10	70
Semi-isolated perimeter	Controlled	10	70
Nonisolated perimeter	Controlled	20–30	30–40
Vehicle entrance	Controlled	50	50
Pedestrian entrance	Controlled	25	25
Railroad entrances	Controlled	50	50
Vital structures	Controlled	50	

Table 15-2. Lighting Intensity

Location	Foot-Candles on Horizontal Plane at Ground Level
Vehicular and pedestrian entrances	2.0
Vital structure and other sensitive areas	2.0
Unattended outdoor parking area	1.0

Guard Requirements

Standards for the guard force should include complete background investigations and physical and mental examinations to meet established standards.

The guard should be physically capable of vigorous physical training in self-defense.

Uniforms should be distinctive and complete. Uniforms and equipment should meet high standards of cleanliness and maintenance.

Prior to any duty assignment, basic training must be given to all guards. Training should include such techniques as patrol (both mounted and dismounted), report writing, log and record keeping, use of security equipment, fire and safety regulations, self-defense, crowd and riot control, and firearms instruction.

Under most conditions connected with transportation and distribution systems, guards should not be allowed to remain too long in a given post; they should be rotated periodically. However, under certain conditions, keeping the guard at one post could be an asset, especially when personal recognition of people is desired. Examples are personnel entrances to an office building, trades workers' gates, monitoring stations, areas where recognition and protocol are required, and administrative posts.

Vehicle Control

Movements of all vehicles within the terminal should be strictly controlled. The controls must be a standard operating procedure and prominently posted.

Gate guards should examine all trucks and conveyances entering the facility. Guard checks should include registration of truck, name of driver and helper, and license check of vehicle operator. If possible, a photo record of the driver and documents should be made before entering the terminal. Strict

supervision of loading and unloading operations should be incorporated into procedures. No vehicle should be opened except when actually being loaded, unloaded, or inspected.

Other procedures for vehicle control and operations should include a record of all inbound and outbound trailers and containers and, when not being moved, their storage locations, and a report of any seal discrepancies noted.

Parking lots for personal vehicles of employees and visitors should be located outside and separated from freight handling areas. Only cargo-carrying or handling vehicles should be permitted in controlled areas.

It is advisable to separate entry and exit roadways and gates if the facility permits. Flow of traffic, then, is essentially one-way.

Special Problems—High-Value Cargo

Transportation of merchandise such as fissile radioactive materials, jewelry, furs, optical goods, cameras, electronic articles, whisky, and ammunition presents special security considerations. Precautions include scheduling arrival of goods at hours which permit prompt pick-up, use of secure areas, continuous guards, selection of reliable drivers, delivery in vehicles with two-way radio equipment, a checkpoint system, convoying and *shotgun* guards, use of anti-hijack equipment (looked doors, no steps, high cab), and coordination with federal and local police agencies.

All protective measures for movement of high-value merchandise must be set out in a standard operating procedure.

Only that equipment which is sound should be utilized in transport of high-value cargo.

When regular accounts requiring regular handling of high-value cargo are acquired, modifications to equipment should be made. This could include removal of running boards and addition of extra locking devices, alarm equipment, and oversize gas tanks (where permissible). Routing of vehicles should vary continuously where practicable.

Key control for all equipment undergoing maintenance should be stressed. Often, a breakdown in key control takes place when equipment is turned over to the maintenance department for service. When equipment breaks down while on the road, a preplanned procedure should be effected to safeguard high-value cargo.

The shipper can be advised how to avoid security

pitfalls, whether in packaging or advertising. He or she must carefully control information regarding shipments—destinations, times of arrival and departure, and routes to be traveled—among employees and on labels and packaging. Further, the consignee must plan for immediate pick-up at destinations to avoid high-value cargo being needlessly exposed.

Appendix 15.A
Cargo Security Checklist

The checklist below can be used for many different types of facilities. It permits each facility manager to select those elements pertaining to an establishment and location in making one's own security survey.

Barriers

1. Is the perimeter of the facility or activity defined by a fence or other type of physical barrier?
2. If a fence or gate is used, does it meet the minimum specifications?
   a. Is the top guard strung with barbed wire and angled outward and upward at a 45° angle?
   b. Is it at least 8 feet total height?
3. If building walls, floors, and roofs form a part of the perimeter barrier, do they provide security equivalent at least to that provided by chain link fence? Are all openings properly secured?
4. If a masonry wall or building forms a part of the perimeter barrier, does it meet minimum specifications of perimeter fencing?
5. If a river, lake, or other body of water forms any part of the perimeter barrier, are security measures equal to the deterrence of the 8-foot fence provided?
6. Are openings such as culverts, tunnels, manholes for sewers and utility access, and sidewalk elevators, which permit access to the facility properly, secured?
7. List number, location, and physical characteristics of perimeter entrances.
8. Are all portals in perimeter barriers guarded, secured, or under constant surveillance?
9. Are all perimeter entrances equipped with secure locking devices and are they always locked when not in active use?
10. Are gate or other perimeter entrances that are not in active use frequently inspected by guards or management personnel?
11. Is the security officer responsible for security of keys to perimeter entrances? If not, which individual is responsible?
12. Are keys to perimeter entrances issued to other than facility personnel, such as clearing, trash removal, and vending machine service personnel?
13. Are all normally used pedestrian and vehicle gates effectively and adequately lighted to ensure:
    a. Proper identification of individuals and examination of credentials?
    b. That interiors of vehicles are clearly lighted?
    c. That glare from luminaries is not in the guard's eyes?
14. Are appropriate signs setting forth the provisions for entry conspicuously posted at all principal entrances?
15. Are clear zones maintained for the largest vehicles on both sides of the perimeter barrier? If clear zone requirements cannot be met, what additional security measures have been implemented?
16. Are automobiles permitted to park against or too close to the perimeter barrier?
17. What is the frequency of checks made by maintenance crews of the condition of perimeter barriers?
18. Do guards patrol perimeter areas?
19. Are reports of inadequate perimeter security immediately acted on and the necessary repairs effected?

20. Are perimeters protected by intrusion alarm devices?
21. Does any new construction require installation of additional perimeter barriers or additional perimeter lighting?

Lighting

1. Does adequate lighting protect the perimeter of the installation?
2. Are the cones of illumination from lamps directed downward and away from the facility proper and away from guard personnel?
3. Are lights mounted to provide a strip of light both inside and outside the fence?
4. Are lights checked periodically for proper operations and inoperative lamps replaced immediately?
5. Do light beams overlap to provide coverage in case a bulb burns out?
6. Is additional lighting provided at vulnerable or sensitive areas?
7. Are gate guard boxes provided with proper illumination?
8. Are light finishes or stripes used on lower parts of buildings and structures to aid guard observation?
9. Does the facility have a dependable auxiliary source of power?
10. Is there alternate power for the lighting system independent of the plant lighting or the power system?
11. Is the power supply for lights adequately protected? How?
12. Is the standby or emergency equipment tested periodically?
13. Is emergency equipment designed to go into operation automatically when needed?
14. Is wiring tested and inspected periodically to ensure proper operation?
15. Are multiple circuits used? If so, are proper switching arrangements provided?
16. Is wiring for protective lighting securely mounted?
    a. Is it in tamper-resistant conduits?
    b. Is it mounted underground?
    c. If above ground, is it high enough to reduce possibility of tampering?
17. Are switches and control properly located, controlled, and protected?
    a. Are they weatherproof and tamper-resistant?
    b. Are they readily accessible to security personnel?

c. Are they located so that they are inaccessible from outside the perimeter barrier?
    d. Is there a centrally located switch to control protective lighting? Is it vulnerable?
18. Are the lighting system design and location recorded so that repairs can be made rapidly in an emergency?
19. Is adequate lighting for guard use provided on indoor routes?
20. Are materials and equipment in shipping and storage areas properly arranged to permit adequate lighting?
21. If bodies of water form a part of the perimeter, does the lighting conform to other perimeter lighting standards?

Alarms

1. Is an alarm system used in the facility?
    a. Does the system indicate an alert only within the facility?
    b. Does it signal in a central station outside the facility?
    c. Is it connected to facility guard headquarters?
    d. Is it connected directly to an enforcement headquarters outside the facility proper? Is it a private protection service? Police station? Fire station?
2. Is there any inherent weakness in the system itself?
3. Is the system supported by properly trained, alert guards?
4. Is the alarm system for operating areas turned off during working hours?
5. Is the system tested prior to activating it for nonoperational periods?
6. Is the alarm system inspected regularly?
7. Is the system tamper-resistant? Weatherproof?
8. Is an alternate alarm system provided for use in the event of failure of the primary system?
9. Is an alternate or independent source of power available for use in the event of power failure?
10. Is the emergency power source designed to cut in and operate automatically?
11. Is the alarm system properly maintained by trained personnel?
12. Are periodic tests conducted frequently to determine the adequacy of response to alarm signals?
13. Are records kept of all alarm signals received to include time, date, location, action taken, and cause for alarm?

Communications

1. Is the security communication system adequate?
2. What means of communications are used?
   a. Telephone
      (1) Is it a commercial switchboard system? Independent switchboard?
      (2) Is it restricted for guard use only?
      (3) Are switchboards adequately guarded?
      (4) Are there enough call boxes and are they conveniently located?
      (5) Are open wires, terminal boxes, and cables frequently inspected for damage, wear, sabotage, and wire-tapping?
      (6) Are personnel cautioned about discussing cargo movements over the telephone?
   b. Radio
      (1) Is proper radio procedure practiced?
      (2) Is an effective routine code being used?
      (3) Is proper authentication required?
      (4) Is the equipment maintained properly?
   c. Messenger—Is the messenger always available?
   d. Teletype—Is an operator available at all times?
   e. Public address
      (1) Does it work?
      (2) Can it be seen?
   f. Visual signals
      (1) Do all guards know the signals?
      (2) Can they be seen?
3. Is security communications equipment in use capable of transmitting instructions to all key posts simultaneously?
4. Does the equipment in use allow a guard to communicate with guard headquarters with minimum delay?
5. Is there more than one system of security communications available for exclusive use of security personnel?
6. Does one of these systems have an alternate or independent source of power?
7. Has the communications center been provided with adequate physical security safeguards?

Personnel Identification and Control

1. Is an identification card or badge used to identify all personnel within the confines of the controlled areas?
2. Is the identification medium designed to provide the desired degree of security?

3. Does the identification and control system include arrangements for the following?
   a. Protection of the meaning of coded or printed components of badges and passes
   b. Designation of the various areas requiring special control measures to which the badge holder may be authorized entrance
   c. Strict control of identification data
   d. Clear explanation and description of the identification data used
   e. A clear statement of the authorization and limitations placed on the bearer
   f. Details of where, when, and how badges shall be worn
   g. Procedures to be followed in case of loss or damage to identification media
   h. Procedure for recovery and invalidation
4. If a badge exchange system is used for any restricted area, does the system provide for the following?
   a. Comparison of badge, pass, and personnel
   b. Physical exchange of restricted area badge for general authorization badge at time of entrance and exit
   c. Logging a record of each badge exchanged
   d. Inventory of badges issued by security personnel at the start and completion of tours of duty
   e. Location of personnel who have not checked out of the area at the close of each tour of duty
   f. Security of badges not in use
5. Are messengers who are required to traverse areas of varying degrees of security provided with special identification?
6. Are the prescribed standards for access to exclusion areas supplemented with arrangements for the following:
   a. At least one representative of management or security is in the area at all times when work is in progress.
   b. No other persons are permitted to enter the area until one representative of management or security has entered.
   c. A representative of management or security remains until all others have departed.
7. Are personnel who require infrequent access to a critical area, and who have not been issued regular security identification for the area, treated as visitors, and issued either
   a. A visitor's badge or pass?
   b. A special pass?
8. Are all personnel required to wear the security identification badge while on duty?

9. Do guards at control points compare badges to bearers both upon entry and upon exit?
10. Is supervision of personnel charged with checking identification badges sufficient to ensure continuing effectiveness of identification and control system?
11. Are badges recorded and controlled by rigid accountability procedures?
12. Are lost badges replaced with one bearing a different number or one that is otherwise not identical to the lost one?
13. Are procedures relating to lost, damaged, or forgotten badges adequate?
14. Are temporary badges used?
15. Are lists of lost badges posted at guard control points?
16. Are badges of such design and appearance as to enable guards and other personnel to recognize quickly and positively the authorizations and limitations applicable to the bearers?
17. How long ago were currently used badges originally issued?
18. Do existing procedures ensure the return of identification badges upon termination of employment?
19. Are badges similar or identical to employee badges issued to outside contractor employees working within the installation?
20. Have local regulations governing identification and control been revised in any material respect since first established?
21. Are all phases of the system under supervision and control of a security officer?
22. Is an effective visitor escort procedure established?
23. Are visitors required to conspicuously display identification on outer garments at all times while on installation?
24. When visitors leave the installation, are they required to turn in their identification badges, and is the departure time in each recorded on the visitor's register?
25. What procedures are invoked when visitor identification badges are not turned in prior to departure of the visitor?
26. Is there a central receptionist?
    a. If yes, specify functions.
    b. Are functions performed under the supervision of a security officer?
27. Are receptionists (or guards) stationed at different focal points to maintain visitor control?
28. Are there special procedures applicable to visitors requiring access to cargo handling documents?

29. Are special visitors (e.g., vendors, trades workers, utility workers, or special equipment workers) issued a special distinctive type of visitor badge?
30. What measures are employed, other than the issuance of identification badges, to control the movements of personnel from other transportation companies working within the perimeter of the facility?
31. Does the system used for identification of truck drivers and helpers conform with security regulations?
32. Is the security officer the single responsible official for all aspects of visitor control?

Package and Material Control

1. Are there standard procedures on control of packages and materials?
2. Are all guards conversant with the package control measures?
3. Are notices on restriction and control procedures prominently displayed at each active entrance and exit?
4. Is there a checkroom where employees and visitors can leave their packages?
    a. Is an adequate receipt system in effect?
    b. Are packages inspected in the owner's presence before a receipt is issued?
    c. Is access to the checkroom restricted to authorized personnel only?
    d. Is a policy established for disposition of items left beyond a specified period?
5. Are spot checks of persons and vehicles conducted and, if so, are frequency and scope indicated?
    a. Regular search
    b. Spot search
    c. Special search
6. Are detection devices used?
    a. X-ray or other similar device
    b. Metal detector
    c. Other; evaluate effectiveness
7. Is a property removal slip, signed by an authorizing official, required when property is being removed from the facility?
8. Are removal slips available in the security office for signature by officials authorizing property removals?
9. Are property removal slips surrendered to guards at exit points?
10. Are special rules established for package and material handling?

a. Is a package and material pass used to exempt bearer from search?
  (1) Are time, date, bearer's name, using agency, and description of the contents properly recorded?
  (2) Are preparation and issue rigidly controlled?
  (3) Is the pass serially numbered?
  (4) Does it provide for signature of validating officials?
  (5) Is a signature card readily available to guards for comparison?
  b. Is a trustworthy and identified courier used at all times?
11. Is special clothing issued for wear in the facility to prevent the introduction or removal of unauthorized items?
12. Is an effective procedure used for control and search of special vehicles?
  a. Emergency vehicles
  b. VIP vehicles
  c. Special courier vehicles
  d. Vendor's vehicles
  e. Vehicles with loads that are impracticable to search
13. Is there close coordination between security headquarters and the activities that handle cargo movements?
14. Are new employees given appropriate instructions relating to the handling and safeguarding of cargo?

Vehicle Control

1. Are vehicles that are allowed regular access to the facility registered with the security officer?
2. Have definite procedures been established for the registration of private cars, and are they issued in writing?
3. Do the vehicle registration requirements apply also to motor vehicles owned or operated by employees of any individual, firm, corporation, or contractor whose business activities require frequent use of vehicles on the facility?
4. Is annual or more frequent registration required?
5. What information is incorporated in registration application forms?
6. Do the prescribed prerequisites for registration include a valid state registration for the vehicle and a valid state operator's license?
7. Is mechanical inspection of vehicles or proof of financial responsibility required as a prerequisite of authority to operate a vehicle within the facility?
8. Is decalcomania or metal permit tags affixed to all vehicles authorized to operate within the facility?
9. Do registration permits bear a permanently affixed serial number and numerical designation of year of registration?
10. Do the regulatory control criteria for registration include:
  a. Prohibition against transfer of registration permit tags for use with a vehicle other than the one for which originally issued
  b. Replacement of lost permit tags at the registrant's expense
  c. Return of tags to the security officer when the vehicle is no longer authorized entry into facility
  d. Destruction of invalidated decalcomania or metal tags
11. What is the nature and scope of registration records maintained by the security officer?
12. Do the gate guards make periodic checks to insure that only properly licensed persons operate vehicles on the premises?
13. Is a specified system used to control the movement of commercial trucks and other goods conveyances into and out of the installation area?
14. Are loading and unloading platforms located outside the operating areas, separated one from the other, and controlled by guard-supervised entrances?
15. Are all trucks and other conveyances required to enter through service gates staffed by guards?
16. If trucks are permitted direct access to operating areas, are truck drivers and vehicle contents carefully examined?
17. Does the check at entrances cover both incoming and outgoing vehicles?
18. Are truck registers maintained?
19. Are registers maintained on all company vehicles entering and leaving the facility?
20. Are escorts provided when vehicles are permitted access to operating or controlled areas?
21. Does the supervision of loading and unloading operations insure that unauthorized goods or people do not enter or leave the installation via trucks or other conveyances?
22. Are company trip tickets examined?
23. Is a temporary tag issued to visitor's vehicles?
24. Are automobiles allowed to be parked within operating or controlled areas?

25. Are parking lots provided?
26. Are interior parking areas located away from sensitive points?
27. Are interior parking areas fenced so that occupants of automobiles must pass through a pedestrian gate when entering or leaving the working area?
28. Are separate parking areas provided for visitors' vehicles?
29. What is the extent of guard surveillance over interior parking areas?
30. Are there restrictions against employees entering private vehicle parking areas during duty hours?
31. Are automobiles allowed to park so close to buildings or structures that they would be a fire hazard or obstruct fire fighters?
32. Are automobiles permitted to be parked close to controlled area fences?
33. Are parking facilities adequate?

Lock Security

1. Has a key control officer been appointed?
2. Does a key control officer control the locks and keys to all buildings and entrances?
3. Does the key control officer have overall responsibility for issuance and replacement of locks and keys?
4. Are keys issued only to authorized personnel?
5. Are keys issued to other than facility personnel?
6. Is the removal of keys from the premises prohibited?
7. Are keys not in use secured in a locked, fireproof cabinet?
8. Are current records maintained indicating:
   a. Clear record of person to whom key is issued?
   b. Time of issue and return of keys?
   c. Buildings or entrances for which keys are issued?
   d. Number and identification of keys issued?
   e. Location and number of master keys?
   f. Location and number of duplicate keys?
   g. Location of locks and keys held in reserve?
9. Is a current key control directive in effect and understood?
10. Are locks changed immediately upon loss or theft of keys?
11. Are inventories and inspections conducted by the key control officer to ensure compliance with directives? How often?
12. If master keys are used, are they devoid of markings identifying them as such?
13. Are losses or thefts of keys promptly investigated by the key control personnel?
14. Must all requests for reproduction or duplication of keys be approved by the key control officer?
15. Are locks on inactive gates and storage facilities under seal? Are they checked periodically by guard personnel?
16. Are locks rotated within the installation at least semi-annually?
17. Where applicable, is the manufacturer's serial number on combination locks obliterated?
18. Are measures in effect to prevent the unauthorized removal of locks on open cabinets, gates, or buildings?

Appendix 15.B
Personnel Security Checklist

This checklist has been prepared as an action guide for transportation industry management to use in upgrading personnel security measures. The *Dos* and *Don'ts* contained herein should not be considered to be all-inclusive but should be viewed as steps from which to build a more effective personnel security program.

Management Policy and Response

1. Do recognize that employees are participants in a substantial majority of theft and pilferage losses.
2. Do promulgate company security measures.
   a. Assign authority and responsibility for execution of the personnel security program to official within the organization.
   b. Involve personnel security considerations in the decision-making process of the organization.
   c. Provide support and cooperation of all levels of management of the personnel security program.
3. Do integrate personnel security measures into the existing employment system—including a firm commitment by management to elements of the program.
   a. Identify weaknesses inherent in the present employment process that might allow employment of applicants with questionable backgrounds.
   b. Examine procedures being used by security-conscious employers for screening and investigating their applicants.

c. Implement procedures designed to upgrade employment practices regarding personnel security. Specific managerial prerogatives are discussed later.
   d. Adopt measures to insure periodic review of the personnel security program.
4. Don't evade the problem of employee theft and pilferage.
5. Don't respond to the problem with lip service policy and ineffective procedures.
6. Don't ignore the economic advantages of incorporating effective, but relatively inexpensive, personnel security measures into the existing employment process through the exercise of certain management prerogatives.

Employment Application Forms

1. Do require submission of a detailed employment application by all prospective employees—including applicants for clerical and maintenance positions as well as applicants for cargo-handling positions.
2. Do design the application form to include information that will be helpful in judging the applicant in terms of honesty, integrity, and reliability. The following information should be required by the application forms:
   a. Gaps in employment continuity
   b. Frequent job shifts
   c. Complete employment history, including:
      (1) Reasons for leaving
      (2) Sufficient data with which to make contact with former employers and supervisors

(3) Salary information

(4) Brief statement of duties and responsibilities

d. Educational background, including specific information regarding schools attended and dates

e. All names used by the applicant

f. Type of military discharge

g. Citizenship

h. Present residence and prior residence information for the past 10 years

i. Affiliations and organizations

j. Selective Service classification

k. Personal references

l. Bonding history

m. Criminal history—when permitted by law, indictments, arrest and conviction data should be obtained.

n. Conditions to which applicant agrees by signing the application form including:

(1) Misrepresentations on the form shall be considered acts of dishonesty.

(2) Permission is granted to the employer or agent to investigate the applicant's background, including a credit check.

(3) The application for employment in no way obligates the employer to hire the applicant.

3. Do carefully review the employment application form for accuracy and completeness prior to consideration for processing.

4. Do consider the use of a separate form for obtaining security-related information (e.g., fingerprints, driving record, and criminal history). Such a procedure makes the applicant aware of the organization's interest in employing personnel with a high degree of honesty, integrity, and reliability.

5. Don't employ applicants prior to submission of a detailed employment application form.

6. Don't use a standard type of application form that makes little or no provision for obtaining security-related information.

7. Don't accept applications that are inaccurate or incomplete.

Fingerprinting and Photographing of Applicants

1. Do include the fingerprinting of applicants and the taking of identification photographs in the preemployment process.

2. Do make arrangements with the local police department for fingerprinting and a local photographer for taking applicant ID photos if in-house facilities for such procedures are not feasible.

3. Don't fail to recognize the discouragement to undesirables and the deterrence to thieves or criminals provided by fingerprinting and photographing requirements.

Interviews

1. Do make provisions for a personal interview of all applicants to be conducted by trained interviewers.

2. Do design the interview session to insure that the following security-related elements are completed:

a. Verification of information submitted on the employment applicable form.

b. Clarification of details regarding questionable or derogatory information detected on the application form or during the initial preemployment background investigation.

c. Obtaining additional information not contained in the application.

d. Obtaining information from the applicant that will help to appraise personality, character, motivation, honesty, integrity, and reliability—and judging appearance and personal characteristics face-to-face.

e. Informing the applicant about the company, including security policies and procedures.

3. Don't allow interviews to be conducted solely by department managers or line supervisors.

4. Don't expose the applicant to a brief, noncomprehensive type of interview that is void of security considerations.

Confirmation of Personnel Data

1. Do confirm significant data contained on the employee application form and contact references.

2. Do conduct thorough background investigations—go beyond the basic confirmation of factual data. Include searches for information regarding the applicant's character, integrity, honesty, and reliability. Such information should include, but not be limited to:

a. Any deliberate misrepresentation, falsification, or omission of material facts.

b. Any criminal, infamous, dishonest, immoral, or

notoriously disgraceful conduct, habitual use of intoxicants to excess, or drug addiction.

c. Conviction of crimes of violence, including assault with a deadly weapon.

d. Any facts which furnish reason to believe that the individual may be subjected to coercion, influence, or pressure which may cause her or him to act contrary to the best interests of the company.

e. Any previous dismissal from employment for delinquency or misconduct, theft, or embezzlement.

3. Do select the most effective method of conducting background investigations within the existing capabilities of the organization. Methods available include:

a. Mail verification

b. Telephone interviews

c. Contracts with outside firms, ranging in cost from $10 to $70 each, depending on the service required.

4. Do search applications being processed against local security or trade association indexes to ascertain whether any derogatory information is on file regarding:

a. The applicant

b. The names of applicant's references

c. The name of applicant's spouse

d. The identity of applicant's friends or relatives working in the industry

5. Do organize local trade indexes to minimize the chances of hiring applications already determined to possess undesirable characteristics by another member of the transportation industry.

6. Don't adopt procedures that allow the employment of applicants without completion of a thorough background investigation.

7. Don't let the cost or the time required to conduct background investigations be the sole factor in rejecting such procedures.

8. Don't restrict background investigation to mere verifications of factual data.

9. Don't limit the scope of background investigations by subscribing to only one method. Tailor procedures to the need and to the resources available locally.

Appendix 15.C
Physical Security Checklist

1. Do you have a written security plan that is updated at least once a year?

2. Are the functions of security clearly defined?

3. Do you have a preplanned procedure for internal and external notification in case of theft or emergency?

4. Do you have fixed management responsibility for theft or pilferage?

5. Are your records stored and safeguarded properly?

6. Does your shipping and receiving facility have adequate lighting?

7. Is your entire shipping and receiving area fenced or enclosed?

8. Are your entrance and exit gates secured properly or are they secured only by the use of chains and padlocks?

9. Do you have a sufficient number of competent checkers for your needs?

10. Do you have a sufficient number of supervisors?

11. Do you check your facility during the evening and early morning hours to determine the caliber of supervision during those times?

12. Is there a pass system for logging vehicles in and out?

13. Do you have a security crib for placement of high-value cargo?

14. Where called for, are interior or exterior alarms used?

15. Is the monitoring of your alarms provided on a continual basis?

16. Do you issue padlocks to equipment operators for use when vehicles are left unattended?

17. When assigning keys to individuals, are signatures obtained?

18. Do you issue master keys only where operationally essential?

19. Are periodic checks conducted on key control and locking devices?
20. Are spare keys and locking devices kept under tight controls?
21. Do you check to see if equipment parked or left unattended is left with keys in the ignition?
22. Is there a predesignated, high-value holding area for cargo held in shipping and receiving areas?
23. Do you periodically examine the refuse removal and cleaning service equipment and personnel when they leave your facility?
24. Have you screened the vendor companies with which you are doing business?
25. Are you conducting a preemployment investigation on all prospective applicants?
26. Are you taking fingerprints or photographs of all new employees?
27. Are casual employees included in your preemployment screening process?
28. Is there a probationary period for new employees?
29. Are your personnel records safeguarded?
30. Have you displayed reward posters with proper wording and considerations?
31. Are you engaged in a security education program?
32. Is your total management team security conscious?
33. Are you providing any type of in-service training for dealing with security problems?
34. Is your paper documentation controlled?
35. Are you tallying cargo properly as it goes on and off equipment?
36. Are you using seals and recording the numbers?
37. Are seal numbers being verified at destination?
38. Do you keep your seals under tight security controls?
39. Are seals being affixed by responsible management personnel?
40. Is a report made to security for trailer or container seal discrepancies, if found?
41. Are files maintained which indicate the number of times an employee is involved in a theft or shortage?
42. If dealing with interline activities, are controls maintained on their movements and is equipment checked?
43. Do you restrict your employees, including management, from parking near cargo operations?
44. Are controlled parking areas provided for employees' cars?
45. Do you prevent unauthorized employee access to areas where cargo or paper flow dealing with cargo is being handled?
46. Are unauthorized personnel and unidentified visitors allowed in your shipping and receiving areas?
47. Are employees prohibited from visiting their vehicles during working hours?

Appendix 15.D
Inspection Report Forms

The following form, developed during the Cargo Theft Program at the National Crime Prevention Institute, Louisville, Kentucky, by consultant Sarlan Flinner, is an excellent tool for a complete security plan and training program.

The thoughtful security director needs to constantly monitor all areas of the overall security plan. It means setting up a checklist of possible problem areas that may become troublesome. As a result of this forethought, many security directors have a tendency of developing a form of tunnel vision, and often miss problems developing in so-called safe areas. A checklist of the type we suggest is of great importance to pick up on areas that are too easily overlooked. Setting a regular schedule to cover this checklist is all that is necessary; everything else follows logically. Potential problem areas are routinely covered. If *vigilance* is the watchword of all security, this checklist is an excellent systematic method of maintaining that vigilance.

Terminal Security Inspection Report

————————————————————Terminal

————————————————————Date

————————————————————Inspector

PURPOSE: A periodic security check should be made of each terminal to determine whether or not standard security and operating procedures are being followed to check the handling of freight, the vulnerability of the terminal to theft by outsiders, the condition of the fencing and lighting, and to provide a vehicle for evaluating the overall security of the terminal and make possible specific recommendations.

1. **Terminal Building (Exterior)**
   a. Condition of the building
   b. Outside doors
   c. Windows clean and in good repair?
   d. Lighting
   e. Company identification sign
   f. Condition of parking area
   g. Employee and guard cars parked in proper parking area

2. **Terminal Building (Interior)**
   a. Reception area for visitors?
   b. Condition of offices
   c. Condition of store rooms and supply rooms
   d. Arrangements for janitorial/cleaning services
   e. Condition of restrooms

3. **Terminal Office**
   a. What are bank deposit arrangements and are they satisfactory?
   b. How are paychecks distributed?
   c. Checks and drafts secured at all times?
   d. Petty cash locked up?
   e. Is a safe available? In use?
   f. Are keys assigned?
   g. Are keys redeemed if key personnel leave?
   h. Are locks changed as warranted?
   i. D/R file
   j. Term 64 file
   k. Term 51 file
   l. Pud manifest file
   m. Summary manifest file
   n. Photo file
   o. Fingerprinting equipment
   p. Fingerprinting policy compliance
   q. Polaroid camera
   r. Photographic policy compliance

4. **City Drive Check-in**
   a. Nondelivery report used properly?
   b. Over/damage report being used properly?
   c. Do bills of lading reflect driver's signature and number of pieces picked up?
   d. Tally sheet attached to bills in the morning?
   e. Tally sheet attached to bills when they are turned in?
   f. Exceptions being listed in accordance with company policy?

5. **Over, Short, and Damaged (OS&D) Records**
   a. Shortage files being properly maintained?
   b. "All short" bills filed in pretax file?
   c. "All short" bills reported on control report?
   d. Security reports made to regional security chief?
   e. Over freight processed per policy?
   f. Any bills over 30 days old on the control list? Why?
   g. Refused shipments properly safeguarded?

6. **Dock Area**
   a. What is general appearances of dock?
   b. Is the dock striped?
   c. Are doors and bays clearly identified?
   d. Adequate storage for OS&D freight?
   e. Hot room (or cage) available and in use?
   f. Are any dock lights burning during daylight hours?
   g. Are dock door locks in good condition?
   h. Fire extinguishers available? Inspected?
   i. Recooping equipment available?
   j. Are there any damaged shipments on the dock?
   k. Are OWB shipments written up promptly and placed on OS&D bay?
   l. Seal procedures
      (1) Seal procedures being followed?
      (2) Are seals adequately controlled?
      (3) Discrepancies reported to supervisors?
   m. General condition of trailers and loads during this inspection
   n. Trash receptacles available? In use? Need emptying?
   o. Reward posters displayed on bulletin board?
   p. Are locks assigned to city units? Policy being followed?

7. **Freight Bills Procedures**
   a. Bill boxes available on dock?
   b. Freight bills handled in accordance with established procedures?
   c. Does break-out man account for all bills given him?
   d. Are security shipments (e.g., firearms, clothing) given proper treatment?
   e. Are shortages, overages, and damaged freight brought to foreman's attention?

8. **Guard Service**
   a. Hours of service?
   b. Written reports submitted by guard?
   c. Are there written instructions for the guard?
   d. Is the service adequate? Specific problem areas?
   e. Is the guard performing other than security-related duties?

f. Is supervision by guard company adequate?

g. Are complaints processed to a satisfactory and speedy solution?

h. Are emergency phone numbers available?

9. **Yard Area**

a. Yard fenced?

b. Fence condition?

c. Grass kept cut on either side of fence?

d. Are gates locked at night?

e. Are high-value loads protected?

f. Signs posted on or near gates prohibiting cars from entry?

g. Is employee access controlled?

h. Lighting

(1) Adequate?

(2) Controlled by timer?

(3) Any burned out?

(4) Would additional lights help?

i. General condition of yard

10. **Maintenance Area**

a. Gas pumps locked when the terminal is shut down?

b. Fire extinguishers available? Inspected?

c. Maintenance work orderly?

d. Does it appear well organized?

e. Parts and tools properly secured?

f. Inventory method used?

This report was discussed with _____ by _____ at _____ on _____ 20 _____.

Security Inspection Report

Master Log

Year:
_____

TERMINAL	REGION	DATE OF INSPECTION
_____	_____	_____
_____	_____	_____
_____	_____	_____

Appendix 15.E
Documentation

There are numerous items of documentation that are necessary to move goods in transit and storage from one point to another as well as through the various modes of the modern intermodal transportation systems. Various forms involve financing, transfer of ownership, taxes, export laws, and so forth. The list that follows represents the major portion of the types of documentation one is likely to encounter. It is essential to remember that much of this data is computer driven; however, hardcopy does accompany the movement of goods in transit.

Commercial Documents

1. Forwarder's Invoice
2. Manufacturer's Inspection Certificate
3. Advance Shipping Notice and Insurance Data
4. Certificate of Documents Forwarded
5. Shipping Order
6. Inland Freight Invoice
7. Acknowledgment of Order
8. Letter of Transmittal
9. Shipment Notifications to Consignee
10. Insurance Bordereau
11. Forwarders Acknowledgement
12. Shipment Lineup Sheet
13. Consolidated Car Manifest
14. Overseas Inland Way Bill
15. Cargo On-Board Report
16. Out Port Booking Confirmation
17. Document Master
18. Order Mat
19. Shipping Release

20. Importer's Purchase Order
21. Confirmation of Purchase Order
22. Exporter's Purchase Order
23. Commercial Invoice
24. Packing List
25. Inland Bill of Lading
26. Shipper's Letter of Institutions
27. Certificate of Insurance
28. Ocean Bill of Lading
29. International Air Waybill
30. Delivery Receipts
31. Dock Receipt
32. Arrival Notice to Consignee
33. Warehouse Receipt
34. Commodity Sheet Release—Nonvehicle Material
35. Delivery Instruction for Local Cartage Agent
36. Transportation Agreement
37. Due Bill (International Freight)
38. Pro Forma Invoice
39. Importer's Purchase Order
40. Delivery Instructions to Inland Carrier
41. Shipping Instructions to Plant
42. Importer's Letter of Instruction
43. Import Broker's Invoice
44. Forwarder's Specification Sheet
45. Warehouse Receiving Order
46. Recapitulation of Invoice for Packages Received
47. Forwarder's Space Release Confirmation
48. Freight Bill Release—Import Broker
49. Exporter's Transmittal to Import Broker
50. Receipt for Registered Mail
51. Terminal Charge Bill for Handling
52. Pier Release
53. Exporter's Space Release
54. Ocean Bill of Landing Worksheet
55. Warehouse Invoice
56. Delivery Instruction—Overseas Inland Carrier
57. Application for Letter of Credit Amendments
58. Letter of Confirmation
59. Letter of Credit—Import
60. Application and Special Permit for Immediate Delivery
61. Analysis Delivery
62. Shipper's Export Declaration for Intransit Goods C.F. 7513
63. Invoice Abstract
64. Public Voucher
65. Controller's Letters
66. Invoice Information Commercial Invoice AID-18–24
67. Invoice Information Insurance
68. Certificate Req: Commission and Service Payments

69. Carrier's Certificate
70. Import License
71. Consular Invoice
72. In-Bond Release Certificate
73. Import Document Packet
74. Import Duty Exemption Application
75. Authority for Exemption of Duties
76. Poliza De Consumo
77. Weight List
78. Supplier's Certificate
79. Dangerous Cargo Manifest
80. Certificate and List of Measurement (or Weight)
81. Blacklist Certificate
82. Certificate of Origin

Documents Regularly Used

1. Acknowledgement of Order
2. AID (torch emblem) affixed to each package
3. Application and Special Permit for Immediate Delivery, U.S. Customs—3461
4. Arrival Notice to Consignee
5. Bank Drafts
6. Bank Draft—Letters of Instructions and Transmittal
7. Buyer's Purchase Order
8. Carrier's Certificate of Release Order, U.S. Customs—7529
9. Certificate of Analysis
10. Certificate of Insurance
11. Certificate of Origin
12. Certifications to AID and Request to Opening Bank, AID—283
13. Consumption Entry, U.S. Customs—7501
14. Delivery Instruction to Inland Carrier
15. Delivery Instructions for Local Cartage Agent
16. Delivery Order
17. Export License
18. Forwarder's Acknowledgement
19. Forwarder's Invoice
20. Inland Freight Invoice
21. International Freight Bill
22. Invoice-and-Contract-Abstract, AID 282
23. Invoice Information—Bill of Lading, AID 18–24
24. Invoice Information—Commercial Invoice, AID 18–24
25. Invoice Information—Insurance, AID 18–24
26. Letter of Application for Water of Transportation
27. Letter of Transmittal—Consignee
28. Letter of Transmittal—To Import Broker

29. Letter of Transmittal—Insurance
30. Letter of Transmittal—Sales Agents
31. License Application—O.E.C.
32. Outward Foreign Manifest—U.S. Customs—1374
33. Overseas Representative's Purchase Order
34. Pro Forma Invoice
35. Proof of Consular Fees
36. Shipping Instructions to Plant
37. Shipper's Manifest
38. South African Customs Invoice
39. Special Customs Invoice, U.S. Customs—5515
40. Supplier's Invoice
41. Supplier's Letter of Transmittal to Exporter and Forwarder

Maritime Industry Documents and Reports

1. Shipping Documents
2. Bills of Lading
3. Exception Reports
4. OS&D Report
5. Claims Report
6. Cross-Dock Reports
7. Shipping Report
8. Receiving Report
9. Transfer Report
10. Salvage Report
11. Disposal Report
12. Unexplained Loss Report
13. Waybill

Appendix 15.F
The Role of Private Security[1]

ROBERT J. FISCHER

Since, according to an analysis made by the U.S. Department of Transportation (DOT), 85% of goods and material stolen go out the front gates on persons and vehicles authorized to be in cargo-handling areas of transportation facilities, it would appear that by far the greatest burden falls on the security apparatuses of the private concerns involved.[2] It is true that public law enforcement agencies must make a greater effort to break up organized fencing and hijacking operations, and they must find a way to cut through their jurisdictional confusion and establish more effective means of exchanging information. But the bulk of the problem lies in the systems now employed to secure goods in transit.

There is no universally applicable solution to this problem. Every warehouse, terminal, and means of shipment has its own particular peculiarities. Each has weaknesses somewhere, but certain principles of cargo security, when they are thoughtfully applied and vigorously administered, can substantially reduce the enormous losses so prevalent in today's beleaguered transport industry.

A good loss-prevention manager must recognize that the key to good cargo security is an well-organized cargo-handling system. As Louis Tyska and Lawrence Fennelly note, cargo loss exists whenever the "three Cs of cargo theft" are present.[2] The three Cs are confusion, conspiracy, and the common denominator (the dishonest employee). Confusion is a primary ingredient and represents the loss-prevention specialist's opportunity to reduce theft. Confusion arises when an adequate policy does not exist or, if it does exist, when it is not followed. Tyska and Fennelly identify the following activities as great contributors to the confusion variable:

1. Personnel entering and exiting the specific facility. These people include everyone from repair people to regular employees.
2. Movement of various types of equipment (for example, trucks, rail cars, and lift trucks).
3. The proliferation of various forms of paper (for example, freight bills, bills of lading, manifests, and so on).

Conspiracy builds on confusion. Two or more people take advantage of their positions and the confusion to steal. Many cargo security losses would not occur, however, without the common denominator, the dishonest employee. When the security manager is dealing with more than cargo pilferage, monitoring the employee is essential. The manager must be aware of the preceding variables. By eliminating any one variable, opportunities for theft are reduced.

References

1. Robert Fischer. *Introduction to Security*, 6th ed., Boston: Butterworth–Heinemann, 1998, p. 394.
2. Louis Tyska and Lawrence Fennelly. *Controlling Cargo Theft.* Boston: Butterworth–Heinemann, 1983.

Chapter 16

Electronic Surveillance and Wiretapping*

PHILIP P. PURPURA, CPP

Electronic surveillance utilizes electronic devices to covertly listen to conversations. Whereas *wiretapping* pertains to the interception of telephone communications. The prevalence of these often illegal activities probably is greater than one would expect. (The legality of such acts is supported by court orders.) Because detection is so difficult, the exact extent of electronic surveillance and wiretapping and what this theft of information costs businesses is impossible to gauge.

Electronic eavesdropping technology is highly developed to the point where countermeasures (debugging) have not kept up with the art of bugging. Consequently, only the most expertly trained and experienced specialist can counter this threat.

Surveillance equipment is easy to obtain. An electronically inclined person can simply enter a local electronics store and buy all the materials necessary to make a sophisticated bug. Prebuilt models are available by mail, or certain retailers will sell them if the buyer signs a statement that they will not be used for audio surveillance. Retail electronics stores sell FM transmitters or microphones that transmit sound without wires to an ordinary FM radio. Sound is broadcast over a radio several feet away after tuning to the right frequency. These FM transmitters are advertised to be used by public speakers who walk around as they talk and favor wireless microphones; the voice is transmitted and then broadcast over large speakers. They are also advertised to listen in on a baby from another room.

Miniaturization has greatly aided spying. With the

advance of the microchip, transmitters are apt to be so small that these devices can be enmeshed in thin paper, as in a calendar, under a stamp, or within a nail in a wall. Bugs may be planted as a building is under construction, or a person may receive one hidden in a present or other item. Transmitters are capable of being operated by solar power (i.e., daylight) or local radio broadcast.

Bugging techniques are varied. Information from a microphone can be transmitted via a "wire run" or a radio transmitter. Bugs are concealed in a variety of objects or carried on a person. Transmitting devices can be remotely controlled with a radio signal for turning them on and off. This makes detection difficult. A device known as a carrier current transmitter is placed in wall plugs, light switches, or other electrically operated components. It obtains its power from the AC wire to which it is attached.

Many spies use a dual system. One bug is placed so that it will be found, which in many instances satisfies security and management. A second bug is more cleverly concealed.

Telephones are especially vulnerable. A "tap" occurs when a telephone conversation is intercepted. Telephone lines are available in so many places that taps are difficult to detect. A tap can be direct or wireless. With a direct tap, a pair of wires is spliced to the telephone line and then connected to a tape recorder. An FM transmitter, similar to a room bug, is employed for a wireless tap. The transmitter is connected to the line and then a receiver and tape recorder are concealed nearby. Wireless taps (and room bugs) are spotted by using special equipment. Direct taps are difficult to locate. A check of the entire line is necessary.

Because telephone traffic travels over space radio in several modes (for example, cellular, microwave,

*Purpura, *Security and Loss Prevention, Fourth Edition,* pp. 443–448, Butterworth Heinemann, 2002

and satellite) the spy's job is made much easier and safer since no on-premises tap is required. What is required is the proper equipment for each mode. In one case a Mossad agent in Berne, Switzerland, was arrested after he tried to tap the telephone of a Hezbollah target. His technical system was a cellular telephone device that would be activated when the target telephone was put in use. The device would automatically call a second cellular telephone where the target's telephone would be monitored.[1]

Another technique transforms the telephone into a listening device whether it is in use or not. A technique known as a "hookswitch bypass" short circuits (by changing wires) the telephone hookswitch (the switch that disconnects the microphone in the mouthpiece to the outside when a person hangs up) and transforms the ordinary telephone into a bug. This is easy to detect by hanging up the telephone, placing a radio nearby (for noise), tapping into the telephone line, and listening for the radio.

When guarding against losses of sensitive information, consideration must be given to a host of methods that may be used by a spy. These include infrared transmitters that use light frequencies below the visible frequency spectrum to transmit information. This can be defeated through physical shielding (e.g., closing the drapes). Another method, a laser listening device, "bounces" a laser off of a window to receive audio from the room. Inexpensive noise masking systems can defeat this technique.[2]

Computer, e-mail, facsimile, and other transmissions are also subject to access by spies. A spy may conceal a tape recorder or pinhole-lens camera on the premises, or wear a camera concealed in a jacket or tie. If drawings or designs are on walls or in sight through windows, a spy, for example, stationed in another skyscraper a few blocks away might use a telescope to obtain secret data. Or, a window washer might appear at a window for surveillance. Another method is a spy disguised as a janitor to be assigned to the particular site. All of these methods by no means exhaust the skills of spies as covered earlier under "espionage techniques."

Countermeasures

The physical characteristics of a building have a bearing on opportunities for surveillance. Some of these factors are poor access control designs, inadequate soundproofing, common or shared ducts, and space above false ceilings enabling access. Comprehensive security methods will hinder spies. The in-house security team can begin countermeasures by conducting a physical search for planted devices. If a decision is made to contact a specialist, *only the most expertly trained and experienced consultant should be recruited.*

The Countermeasures Consultant

Organizations often recruit a countermeasures consultant to perform contract work. As a consumer, ask for copies of certificates of Technical Surveillance Countermeasures (TSCM) courses completed and a copy of the insurance policy for errors and omissions for TSCM services. What equipment is used? What techniques are employed for the cost? Are sweeps and meticulous physical inspections conducted for the quoted price? Watch for scare tactics. Is the consultant really a vendor trying to sell audio surveillance detection devices? Will the consultant protect confidentiality? The interviewer should request a review of past reports to clients. Were names deleted to protect confidentiality? These questions help to avoid hiring the unqualified "expert."

One practitioner offered clients debugging services and used an expensive piece of equipment to conduct sweeps. After several years and hundreds of sweeps, he decided to have the equipment serviced. A service person discovered that the device was not working because it had no battery. The surprised "expert" never realized a battery was needed.

For a comprehensive countermeasures program, the competent consultant will be interested in sensitive information flow, storage, and retrieval. Extra cost will result from such an analysis, but it is often cost effective. The employer should use an outside public telephone to contact the consultant in order not to alert a spy to impending countermeasures.

Equipment

Detection equipment is expensive. A firm should purchase its own equipment only if it is cost effective and many sweeps will be conducted. A sample of equipment includes the nonlinear junction detector, costing $15,000, and capable of detecting radio transmitters, microphones, infrared and ultrasonic transmitters, tape recorders, and other devices hidden, even when they are not working. The telephone analyzer is another tool, costing up to $6000 and designed for testing a variety of single and multiline telephones and fax machines. Other types of specialized equipment are on the market.[3]

Some security personnel or executives plant a bug for the sole purpose of determining if the detection specialist and his or her equipment are effective. This "test" can be construed as a criminal offense. An alternative is specially designed test transmitters, commercially available, that have no microphone pickup and therefore can be used without liability. Another technique is to place a tape recorder with a microphone in a drawer.

A tool kit and standard forms are two additional aids for the countermeasures specialist. The tool kit consists of the common tools (e.g., screwdrivers, pliers, electrical tape) used by an electrician. Standard forms facilitate good record keeping and serve as a checklist. What was checked? What tests were performed? What were the readings? Where? When? Who performed the tests? Why were the tests conducted? Over a period of time, records can be used to make comparisons while helping to answer questions.

Who do you think has "the edge," those who seek sensitive information or those who protect it?

Another strategy to thwart listening devices is "shielding," also called *electronic soundproofing*. Basically, copper foil or screening and carbon filament are applied throughout a room to prevent acoustical or electromagnetic emanations from leaving. Although this method is very expensive (costing more than $100,000), several organizations employ it to have at least one secure room or to protect information in computers.

Equipment is available on the market that *may* frustrate telephone taps and listening devices. Scramblers, attached to telephones, alter the voice as it travels through the line. But no device or system is foolproof. Often, simple countermeasures are useful. For instance, an executive can wait until everybody is present for an important meeting, and then relocate it to a previously undisclosed location. Conversants can operate a radio at high volume during sensitive conversations, and exercise caution during telephone and other conversations.

It must be remembered that sensitive information can be collected in many different ways besides through the use of physical devices. Losses can occur through speeches and publications by employees, in company trash, and by unknowingly hiring a spy. Comprehensive, broad-based defenses are necessary.

Counterintelligence

Another avenue to protect sensitive information is *counterintelligence*, which is a broad term referring to activities that identify and counter threats by adversaries. The military and police agencies engage in counterintelligence activities. Examples include investigative and research units that collect and analyze intelligence on adversaries, internal awareness programs, and misinformation directed at adversaries. Although businesses have a different mission than the military and police, certain counterintelligence techniques, within legal guidelines, can be implemented by businesses.

Economic Espionage Act of 1996

Because intellectual property assets are often more valuable to businesses than tangible assets, Congress passed the Economic Espionage Act of 1996. This act makes it a federal crime for any person to convert a trade secret to his or her own benefit or the benefit of others with the intent or knowledge that the conversion will injure the owner of the trade secret. The penalties for any person are up to 10 years of imprisonment and a fine up to $250,000. Corporations can be fined up to $5 million. If a foreign government benefits from such a crime, the penalties are even greater. The act defines *trade secret* broadly as information that the owner has taken "reasonable measures" to keep secret because of the economic value from it. Case law has further defined the act; the greater the protection and value of the information and the fewer people who know about the information, the more likely the courts will recognize its status as a protectable trade secret.[4]

The act raises two major concerns for management:

- *Protecting trade secrets.* This would include a comprehensive SPI program.
- *Hiring employees from competitors.* Employers may violate the act if they hire employees from other firms who may bring with them trade secrets. Prevention includes a thorough interview of applicants, ascertaining whether the applicant signed contracts or agreements with others for the protection of sensitive information, and use of a company form that signifies that the new employee understands the act's legal requirements.[5]

The act also links the economic well-being of the nation to national security interests. And, it allows the FBI to investigate foreign intelligence services bent on acquiring sensitive information of U.S. companies. At some point, a company may have to decide whether to report a violation of the act to law enforcement authorities. The disadvantages are lost time and money, unwanted publicity, and the fact that the defendant's attorney may request secrets that could then be revealed in court. Although the act offers some protection for proprietary information, this protection may depend on how a judge or attorneys in the case interpret the act. Discovery proceedings may result in information loss greater than the original loss. Also, the case may be lost in criminal and civil courts. Therefore, management must carefully weigh decisions on legal action. Another point to consider is that the act requires businesses to protect themselves from losses, which presents liability issues relevant to due diligence.[6] *Prevention is seen here, as with many other vulnerabilities, as the key avenue for protection.*

References

1. Business Espionage Controls and Countermeasures Association. "News of Hostile Activity," http://www.espionbusiness.com (June 6, 2001).
2. Tom Jones. *Surveillance Countermeasures in the Business World* (Cookeville, TN: Research Electronics International, 2000), pp. 1–17.
3. Correspondence (June 2, 2001) with Information Security Associates, Inc., Stanford, CT (isa-tscm.com/).
4. R. Mark Halligan. "Do Your Secrets Pass the Test?" *Security Management* 45 (March 2001), pp. 53–58.
5. *Legal Alert Memo* (May 20, 1997), Childs & Duff, P.A., P.O. Box 11367, Columbia, SC 29211.
6. John A. Nolan. "Economic Espionage, Proprietary Information Protection: Difficult Times Ahead." *Security Technology and Design* (January–February 1997), pp. 54–57.

Chapter 17

Guard Service in the Twenty-First Century

JOSEPH G. WYLLIE

Ever since September 11, 2001, security has had a whole different meaning. Security officers must be more proactive and responsible for the scope of work to which they are assigned.

Liabilities Connected with Guard Force

Various legal aspects of industrial security and plant protection must be fully understood by the security guard. A guard force is not engaged in law enforcement as such; therefore, the guard is not a law enforcement officer, like a police officer or sheriff. Guards are engaged in the protection of goods and services. The plant management makes the rules regarding the conduct of persons engaged in production. The final objective is a smooth flow of production—now law enforcement. Rules and regulations do not have the same force as law. An employee cannot be deprived of freedom to help production because of breaking a rule or regulation. The most that can be done is to dismiss the employee. Violation of law by someone working in the plant brings the same repercussions as breaking the law elsewhere: The case is under the jurisdiction of law enforcement agencies, local, state, or federal. The work performed by a security guard is not related to police work. Execution of the job and training are different. The security guard must leave law enforcement to the responsible agency.

In special situations, a security guard may make arrests. A security guard, peace officer, or any other person may arrest an offender without a warrant if the offense is a felony or an offense against public peace. A felony is ordinarily an offense punishable by confinement in a penitentiary for a period of more than 1 year. Arrests such as these should be made only with the consent of a superior, except in an emergency situation, and only on company property. False arrests and searches can result in civil and criminal suits. A security guard has no authority in a civil case, and if required to testify in any civil case, the security guard should report the facts to the supervisor of the force and in turn demand a subpoena to testify. Before making the arrest, the security guard should know that the law has actually been violated, that the violation is a crime, and that information proves beyond a reasonable doubt that the person committed the crime. No arrest is legal until after the actual violation of the law. No person may be arrested on a charge of suspicion. The arrest is made by actual restraint of the person or by the guard saying, "You are under arrest." Actual touching of the person is unnecessary; it is enough if the person submits to your custody. The guard has no authority beyond the company property line other than that of a private citizen. No person is to be transported as a prisoner off company property by a security guard. The guard must notify the local law enforcement agency and turn the prisoner over to that agency on the company property. Crimes that may occur on company premises include murder, arson, assault, burglary, larceny, intoxication, and violation of sabotage and espionage laws. When a crime is committed on company property, the guard on duty must take prompt measures to afford protection of the crime scene. In the event of a serious crime, the security guard will not investigate the area. The guard should refrain from touching any evidence at the crime scene and should prevent unauthorized persons from handling such evidence. The nature of the crime and the type of evidence in the area require that the security guard be extremely careful in moving about so as not to obliterate or otherwise destroy crime evidence. The security guards rope off or isolate the area and avenue of entry or escape believed to have been used. No one should be allowed to enter or leave the area pending the arrival of representatives of the law enforcement agency having primary investigative jurisdiction. The guard should then obtain the names and addresses of any possible witnesses to be furnished to the law enforcement agency.

Power and Authority of the Security Guard

The accentuation of professionalism in the ranks of law enforcement in the United States has filtered down to the ranks of the contract security guard. Although some of the duties of the security guard are similar to the duties of the police officer, their overall powers are entirely different. Recent court decisions have found the security guard is not encumbered by these so-called Miranda warnings of rights. The security guard is not a law enforcement officer. Some recent State of Missouri Supreme Court decisions have made the arrest powers of a security guard must easier to understand in the current wave of lawlessness. As you can see from the following information, the security guard in today's society must of necessity receive at least basic training.

Training

In view of the demands of industry for fully trained security guards, a new phase of the guard industry has come into being. To provide the training required for the basic guard, who could be working at a one-guard site up to the basic guard at a nuclear power plant, a new look has been given to guard training. Training today must be organized to provide the initial or basic training as well as the follow-up programs necessary to maintain quality standards for the personnel. Most professional security agencies offer at least a basic security officer's program. These programs can run as long as 24 hours and cover subjects ranging from laws of arrest to weapons safety. The present system attempts to package the training in a practical delivery system and keep quality high in terms of testing. Many of the basic training courses are tailored to individual client's needs. In recent years, a number of states have mandated requirements for security officers and most states have mandated requirements for weapons training.

Report Writing

Very few people like paperwork, yet it seems that paperwork is required in all occupations. For the security officer, the paperwork is in the form of reports. There are four basic reasons for completing so many reports.

1. *To inform.* Written communications reduce the chance of misunderstandings or errors. Verbal communications, however, is highly prone to misunderstandings and errors in reproduction and can be easily ignored.
2. *To record.* Never trust memory. No memory is perfect. Exact amounts, costs, dates, times, and similar data are easily forgotten unless recorded.
3. *To demonstrate alertness.* By recording incidents, the security officer makes both supervisor and client aware of the job being done. It is very easy for people to get the impression that security officers do little but stand around. One way of avoiding this type of image is to conscientiously document all incidents.
4. *To protect yourself.* There may come a time when it becomes necessary for a security officer to prove to have witnessed an event, accomplished a certain action, or notified the proper authorities of an incident. Reports accomplish all four of these goals.

The report should be clear and concise. A good report answers five basic questions.

1. *What?* The report must state what happened as accurately as possible.
2. *Where?* The exact location of an occurrence can have great bearing in establishing guilt, innocence, or liability.
3. *Who?* When writing a report, the officer should answer as many whos as possible; for example, who did it and who was notified?
4. *When?* The time of an incident may establish an alibi or help to prevent damage, theft, or injury.
5. *Why?* The why involves judgement and opinion and may not be easily proven, but it may be very important in judgement of guilt or liability.

In addition to answering these questions, there are simple guidelines to follow when preparing a report to ensure that the final result is clearly written and well organized:

1. Use simple language that anyone can understand. When using technical words and phrases, be sure the meaning is clear. Avoid using slang terms or words that have multiple meanings.
2. Be sure that you use the proper spellings and addresses of the individuals involved in the report.
3. Prepare the report in such a manner that the happenings are in logical sequence and, when possible, show the approximate time of the occurrence.
4. Do not ramble. It is preferable to use short paragraphs, with each covering one particular point.
5. Do not use vague descriptions. Write only specific observations.
6. When descriptions of individuals are obtained, list all the usual manners of description, such as height, weight, color of hair, but also include unusual details such as presence of a mustache, sideburns, eyeglasses, tattoos, body piercings, and any peculiarities of walk or speech. Notice and report all information possible on types and color of dress.
7. Avoid contradictory statements that would tend to discredit the overall information.
8. Facts, not opinion, are important. If you include your opinion, label it as your opinion, not as a fact.

Any problem, from a missing light bulb to a major safety hazard, should be reported. The security officer should continue to provide written reports on any incident until appropriate action is taken to correct the situations. In this way, you can demonstrate your importance to the client.

Weapons Safety

No part of the training of a security officer is more critical than firearms training. Your life, as well as the lives of others, depends on your skill with a revolver and knowledge of its proper and safe use. Safety is the basic reason for the existence of security personnel. They are employed to assure the safety of persons and property and should always reflect this concept. Weapons safety, unlike any other aspect of a security officer's job, places a great demand on skills, knowledge, and the judgment necessary to best use both. Judgment can be exercised only when the factual basis for making such judgment is present. In this case, the principles of firearms safety must be well understood by security officers before any judgment can be made. The first principle of weapons safety is control. The officer must control the firearm when wearing, storing, and firing it.

Wearing a Firearm

When the officer is on duty, his or her weapon must be readily available for immediate use. It should be worn in a manner that permits swift access while offering maximum safety. To satisfy this requirement, the weapon should be worn at the belt line and on the same side as the strong shooting hand. The weapon should always be carried in its holster. Any other method, such as tucked in the belt, is hazardous and has contributed to self-inflicted gunshot wounds. The holster strap or flap should be kept securely snapped over the gun. This prevents the weapon from accidentally falling or being jarred out of the holster. It also prevents someone from grabbing the revolver. When the shifts change and the revolver must be transferred from one officer to his relief, the weapon should be empty. Never transfer a loaded weapon. More accidents occur at this time than at any other time of duty. When transferring a weapon, unload the gun and hand it to the person receiving it with the breach open. The cartridges should be transferred separately. An additional benefit is derived from this procedure: the relief officer must check and load the weapon prior to assuming the duties of the post.

Storing a Weapon

Common sense demands that all firearms be kept out of the reach of children and irresponsible adults. Unloaded weapons should be locked up at all times and cartridges should be secured separate from the weapon. Never store a loaded weapon.

Firing a Weapon

The security officer must keep the weapon under control while firing it. This statement may seem obvious, but it is often misunderstood. Control, in this case, refers to the mental discipline required to know when not to fire as well as the physical control necessary to hit the target. Consider these situations:

- An armed intruder is firing at you. There is a crowd of bystanders behind the intruder. Do you return fire?
- A saboteur is on a four-story rooftop in a crowded facility, well silhouetted against the sky. Do you shoot?
- An arsonist is standing in front of a light frame building. You do not know if anyone is inside. Do you shoot?

The answer to all three questions is no. In the first situation, returning fire would most assuredly endanger the bystanders. In the second case, the path of a bullet, after passing the target, could injure or kill a person several blocks away. In the third instance, the bullet could penetrate the frame building and kill an occupant, even after passing through the target. Never underestimate the penetrating power of a gun. Control in firing also means having the mental discipline to never draw a weapon unless there is the intention to kill the target to protect life itself.

The Guard and the Weapon

No publication can describe all the cases in which a guard should and should not use a firearm. It is possible, however, to present some general guidelines and specific examples. The guard who considers these carefully and discusses them with the supervisor and fellow guards should be able to develop good judgment in the use of a firearm. The first thing an armed security officer should keep in mind is that an error in the use of a firearm will probably have a long-lasting, perhaps permanent, effect. It is necessary therefore to give long and careful consideration to the answers to the questions: "Why do I have a firearm?" "When should I use it?" "When should I not use it?" While a private security officer, like a police officer, is armed, do not confuse the guard's rights and responsibilities concerning firearms with those of a public counterpart. Specific and definite laws govern the police officer and the use of a firearm. Laws just as specific and just as definite, are there regarding a private officer's use of a weapon. A firearm is a symbol of a guard's authority and duty to carry out specific tasks as ordered by the employer. The police officer's duties and responsibilities are obviously much broader. The police officer can arrest suspects, a security guard cannot. A police officer can use a gun to stop a speeding automobile, a guard cannot. A police officer can use a weapon to protect property and, again, a guard cannot. To simplify matters a bit, the security officer may use a firearm to protect a life and only to protect a life. That life may be the guards own or that of a bystander. In any case, the guard can use the gun to protect a life. When not to use a firearm? Fortunately, there are many more of these instances. Do not use a weapon

- To prevent a theft
- To stop a fleeing suspect
- To stop a speeding automobile
- To stop someone from bothering or harassing

- On someone who would like to harm you but cannot, for example, a knife wielder or club wielder restrained by a fence or gate, or other people
- To fire warning shots at a fleeing criminal
- To attempt to frighten people

Safety

Accident prevention is said to be everybody's job, but as everybody's job, no one does too much about it. It does, however, fall well within the domain of security personnel. The security officer is responsible for observing all unsafe conditions and warning people of potential hazards. Also, the guard is responsible for reporting any violations of safety rules and setting a good example by his or her own behavior. Far too many accidents happen due to unsafe conditions that were not noted, reported, or corrected. After finding an unsafe condition, the officer must either correct the condition or report it to someone who can make the correction. If a storm blows down a power line, the security officer should report it. If, on the other hand, a guard who finds a bag of oil rags in a corner would simply place them in a metal-covered container and report it later. Safety is purely a matter of common sense. Corrective action should be taken when possible or the proper authority called to handle the situation. It is important that the security officer undertake the sometimes thankless task of safety. It is important both to the client and the people being protected from injuries due to careless safety practices.

Safety Checklist

1. Are the floors kept clean and free of dirt and debris?
2. Are rough, splintered, uneven, or otherwise defective floors repaired or the hazards suitably marked?
3. Are nonskid waxes used to polish floors?
4. During bad weather, are storm mats placed near entrances and floors mopped frequently?
5. Are stairways equipped with handrails?
6. Are steps equipped with handrails?
7. Are stairways well lighted?
8. Are electric fan or heater extension cords tripping hazards?
9. Are cords of electric fans or heaters disconnected from the power source when not in use and at the end of each working day?

10. Are electric fans or heaters adequately grounded?
11. Are cigarette or cigar stubs placed in suitable ashtrays or containers?
12. Are grounds free of debris, and the like?
13. Are sufficient containers provided for trash, ashes, and so forth?
14. Are floors free of oil spills, grease, or other substances that create a slipping hazard?
15. Are windows clean?
16. Is broken glass in evidence?
17. Are the aisles clearly defined and free of obstruction?
18. Is material neatly stacked and readily reached?
19. Does piled material project into aisles or passageways?
20. Are tools left on overhead ledges or platforms?
21. Is the lighting adequate?
22. Are materials stored under or piled against buildings, doors, exits, or stairways?
23. Are walks kept clear of obstruction, slipping and tripping hazards, broken glass, and snow and ice?

Bomb Threats

Bomb threats are a serious concern to all security personnel. Fortunately, most bomb threats turn out to be false alarms, but the next encounter with such a threat may turn out to be real, so none should be taken lightly. All bomb threats should be treated with quick, calm, steady professional action. Normally, local police authorities are notified by client management when a bomb threat occurs. On receiving a bomb threat, a security officer's first duty is to notify the client immediately and take the action ordered. If ordered to call the police, do so, then evacuate anyone in or near the facility. The handling of bombs and bomb disposal are police duties. The security force's job is to assist the police in finding the bomb and evacuation proceedings. The security officer should *not* attempt to examine a bomb, regardless of any previous experience in the world of explosives. Many bombs are extremely complicated and designed to explode when any attempt is made at deactivation. Only trained demolition experts are qualified to safely handle a bomb.

Bomb Search

The locations where a bomb may be hidden are innumerable, and only the most obvious places can be searched in a reasonable amount of time. However, most facilities have areas that are generally more vulnerable than others and should be checked first. The following points should be kept in mind when searching for a bomb:

1. Do not touch anything that need not be disturbed. If lights are off, do not turn them on. If fuse panels are turned off, do not activate them. These may be wired to detonate explosives.
2. Most bombs actually found were of the time-mechanism variety. The timing devices are usually cheap alarm clocks, which can be heard ticking at surprising distances. Be on the alert for ticking sounds.
3. Bombs found in searches were usually found near an exit. Look closely in areas near doorways.
4. Be alert for objects that look out of place or are of unusual size or shape.
5. Thoroughly check any areas accessible to the public. Restrooms and janitor's closets are frequently used as hiding places.
6. A bomb search should be conducted for a period of 20–30 minutes. This should provide ample time for a reasonable search, without creating unnecessary danger to the searchers.
7. A methodical search technique is necessary to ensure that no areas are overlooked. An orderly investigation of all rooms within the facility is mandatory. It is wise to prepare in advance a checklist of places to be searched so that a thorough search can be conducted.
8. As you search, be alert to:
   - Freshly plastered or painted places
   - Disturbed dirt in potted plants
   - Pictures or other hanging objects not straight
   - Ceiling tiles that have been disturbed
   - Torn furniture coverings
   - Broken cabinets or objects recently moved
   - Trash cans, air conditioning ducts, water fountains
   - Elevator shafts, phone booths

Precautions

A security officer can assist police by observing the following precautions. Do not:

- touch a bomb.
- smoke in the immediate vicinity of a suspected bomb.
- expose the bomb to sun. Direct rays of the sun or light of any kind may cause detonation.
- accept identification markup as legitimate. Do not take for granted the identification markings on

packages and boxes, as they may be forged. Keep in mind that bombs are usually camouflaged to throw the recipient off guard. Do not take for granted that the package is bona fide because it's been sent through the mail. Many bombs are forwarded in this manner. Others are sent through express agencies, while some are delivered by individual messengers.

- take for granted that it is a high-explosive bomb. Be prepared in the event that it is of the incendiary type. Have sand and extinguisher on hand.
- use two-way radios, as transmitting could detonate a bomb.
- have unnecessary personnel in the immediate area of the suspected bomb or explosive.

Do

- evacuate the building or area around the suspected bomb, only if the client orders it. In large cities, this function is usually performed by the fire department. Only vital and necessary personnel should be allowed within 100 yards of the package.
- remove all valuable equipment, important files, computer tapes, and the like, at least 100 yards away from the package.
- open all windows and doors in the immediate vicinity of the suspected devices. This allows the blast to escape, reducing pressure on the walls and interiors. It also reduces window breakage and the hazards caused by flying glass and debris.
- shut off all power services to the area immediately. This reduces the possibility of gas explosion or electrical fires.

Types of Explosives

- *Blasting caps or detonators.* These are metallic cylinders approximately 2 inches long, $3/16$ inch in diameter (may be larger or smaller) and closed at one end. They are partially filled with a small amount of relatively easily fired or detonated compound. When they are fired, the resultant shock or blow is sufficient to detonate explosives. They are very dangerous to handle, as they can be detonated by heat, friction, or a relatively slight blow.
- *Nitroglycerin.* This is a colorless to yellow liquid with a heavy, oily consistency. It is highly dangerous: extremely sensitive to heat, flame, shock, or friction.
- *Dynamite.* Dynamite is a high explosive, usually cylindrical in shape, $1\frac{1}{4}$ inches in diameter and approximately 8 inches long (may be up to 12

inches diameter and 30 inches long). The outer wrapper is often covered in paraffin and usually marked "DANGEROUS—HIGH EXPLOSIVE." It is shock sensitive and needs a blasting cap for detonation.

Fire Protection

Of the many jobs a security officer performs, one of the most important is that of fire protection. To do the job effectively, the guard must be familiar with fire fighting equipment and know how and when to use it. Fire is comprised of three elements: heat, fuel, and oxygen. Remove any of these three and the fire goes out. If a fire should break out, the following directions most effectively safeguard persons and property against harm and damage.

1. Call the fire department first.
2. Direct all employees out of the burning building and keep them out after evacuation.
3. Notify and enlist the help of the company fire brigade if one exists.
4. Check and close fire doors.
5. Shut off machinery, power, and gas.
6. Check to see if gate valves are in working condition, if a sprinkler system exists.
7. Now and only now, attempt to control the fire by means of an extinguisher.
8. Post someone to direct the firefighters to the fire.
9. Remove motor vehicles from the area.
10. Once the fire is contained, keep a close watch on the area to see that the fire does not start again.
11. Be sure all extinguishers used are immediately recharged.
12. Complete a written report covering all of the information about the fire.

Fire Prevention

The best way to fight a fire is to prevent a fire from starting. The following is a list of things to be alert for while on patrol to eliminate sources of fire and obstructions that might lead to fire spreading:

1. Look for violations of no-smoking regulations.
2. Investigate any unusual odors, especially smoke and gas. Do not be satisfied until the cause is found and action taken.
3. Check for obstructed passageways and fire doors.
4. Look for obstructions in front of fire-alarm boxes, extinguishers, and fire hydrants.

5. On every patrol, check all gas or electric heaters and coal and kerosene stoves to see that they do not overheat.
6. Check that boxes, rubbish, or hazardous materials are not left close to stoves, boilers, or steam or smoke pipes.
7. Check that all gas or electric appliances not in use are disconnected.
8. Check that all discarded and disposable materials have been placed in their proper containers.

Emergency Medical Assistance

A security officer might be present when someone needs medical assistance. The first reaction should be to summon help. If this is not possible, the officer should be prepared to assist the victim. Guards should be trained in emergency medical assistance (EMA) procedures in the event a severe accident occurs. Someone's life may depend on your knowledge of EMA.

At the Scene

People at the scene of an accident are excited. A security officer must remain calm, dealing with the most serious injury or condition first. The most urgent medical emergencies that require prompt action to save a life are severe bleeding, stoppage of breathing, and poisoning. Shock may accompany any of these conditions, depending on the body functions and keeping the heart, lungs, and other organs from functioning normally.

What to Do after Call for Help and Assistance if First on the Scene

1. Do not move an injured person, unless it is absolutely necessary to save the victim from danger. If victims have been injured internally or the spine is broken, unnecessary movement may kill or cripple the victim.
2. Act fast if the victim is bleeding severely, swallowed poison, or stopped breathing because of drowning, gas poisoning, or electric shock. Every second counts. A person may, for example, die within 3 minutes of the time breathing stops, unless given artificial respiration.
3. Because life-and-death emergencies are rare, in most cases a guard can start EMA with these steps: Keep the patient lying down quietly. If she

or he has vomited and there is no danger that the neck is broken, turn the head to one side to prevent choking. Keep the victim warm with blankets or coats, but do not overheat or apply external heat.
4. Work with medical help. The doctor should be told the nature of the emergency and asked what should be done.
5. Examine the patient gently. Cut clothing, if necessary, to avoid movement or added pain. Do not pull clothing away from burns.
6. Reassure the patient, and try to remain calm. Calmness will convince the patient that everything is under control.
7. Always be prepared to treat shock.
8. Do not force fluids on an unconscious or semiconscious person. Fluids may enter the windpipe and cause asphyxiation. Do not try to arouse an unconscious person by slapping, shaking, or shouting. Do not give alcohol to any victim.
9. Following any incident where EMA would be rendered, a detailed written report should be made covering all of the circumstances. Be sure to include the treatment given.

Controlling Bleeding

The adult human body contains approximately 6 quarts of blood. Although an adult can readily withstand the loss of a pint, the amount usually taken for transfusion purposes, that same loss by a child may have disastrous results. In an adult, lack of consciousness may occur from the rapid loss of as little as a quart of blood. Because a victim can bleed to death in a very short period of time, immediate stoppage of any large, rapid loss of blood is necessary.

Direct Pressure

The preferred method for control of severe bleeding is direct pressure by pressing a hand over a dressing. This method prevents loss of blood from the body without interfering with normal circulation. Apply direct pressure by placing the palm of the hand on a dressing directly over the entire area of an open wound on any surface part of the body. In the absence of compresses, the fingers or bare hand may be used, but only until a compress can be obtained and applied. Do not disturb blood clots after they have formed within the cloth. If blood soaks through the entire compress without clotting, do not remove, but add additional layers of padding and continue direct hand pressure, even more firmly. On most parts of the body, a pressure bandage can be placed to hold pads of cloth over a wound. Properly applied, the bandage frees the hands for other EMA. To apply the bandage, place and hold the center directly over the pad on the wound. Maintain a steady pull on the bandage to keep the pad firmly in place while wrapping the ends around the body part. Finish by tying a knot over the pad.

Elevation

If there is no evidence of a fracture, a severely bleeding hand, arm, or leg should be elevated above the level of the victim's heart. Once elevated, the force of gravity reduces blood pressure at the site of the wound and slows the loss of blood. Elevation is used in addition to direct pressure. The combination of pressure and elevation stops severe bleeding in most cases; however, sometimes additional techniques are required. One additional technique is pressure on the supplying artery.

Pressure on the Supplying Artery

If severe bleeding from an open wound of the arm or leg does not stop after the application of direct pressure plus elevation, the use of pressure points may be required. Use of the pressure point technique temporarily compresses the main artery that supplies blood to the affected limb against the underlying bone and tissues. If the use of a pressure point is necessary, do not substitute its use for direct pressure and elevation, but use the pressure point in addition to those techniques. Do not use a pressure point in conjunction with direct pressure any longer than necessary to stop the bleeding. However, if bleeding recurs, reapply pressure at a pressure point.

Pressure Point: Open Arm Wound. Apply pressure over the brachial artery, forcing it against the arm bone. The pressure point is located on the inside of the arm in the groove between the biceps and the triceps, about midway between the armpit and the elbow. To apply pressure on the brachial artery, grasp the middle of the victim's upper arm, the caregiver's thumb on the outside of the victim's arm and the caregiver's other fingers on the inside. Press your fingers toward your thumb to create an inward force from opposite sides of the arm. The inward pressure holds and closes the artery by compressing it against the arm bone.

Pressure Point: Open Leg Wound. Apply pressure on the femoral artery by forcing the artery against the pelvic bone. The pressure point is located on the front center part of the diagonally slanted hinge of the leg, in the crease of the groin area, where the artery crosses the pelvic bone on its way to the leg. To apply pressure to the femoral artery, position the victim flat on the back, if possible, and place the heel of the caregiver's hand directly over the pressure point. Then lean forward over the straightened arm to apply the small amount of pressure needed to close the artery. To prevent arm tension and muscular strain, keep the arm straight while applying the technique.

Call for Assistance

Whenever possible, get medical assistance as soon as the victim is comfortable and not in immediate danger. Often, someone can do more harm than good by not summoning proper help immediately. If in doubt as to a victim's well-being, keep the person quiet, preferably lying down and covered. Sometimes, a concussion victim appears perfectly normal and insists on returning to work, only to collapse later. In any case, do not allow the victim to move around. Remember, the greatest contribution to a victim's well-being may be to restrain efforts to move the person in a mistaken belief that such efforts are helpful. It is usually best to let the victim remain calm and relaxed before transporting to the medical station. Obtain professional help whenever possible.

Reporting a Medical Case

When reporting a medical case, the following information must be given clearly so that the necessary equipment and medical assistance can reach the victim in the shortest possible time:

- Exact location and phone number from which the report is being made
- Type of injury, if evident
- Seriousness of injury
- Number of persons involved
- Visible symptoms, such as heavy bleeding, poison stains, and so forth
- Cause of injury, if known, so that adequate personnel may be sent to the area to handle such dangerous conditions as leaking gas, flowing chemicals, or the like

Guard Supervision

In every business organization, different management levels are responsible for various tasks. At the top of the structure are people who must decide the organizational goals and policies. At the people end of the operational spectrum are those immediately responsible for the accomplishment of established goals. Between top management and these workers are the people who must explain managements' objectives to all employees. These people give guidance and leadership. They represent top management to the workers by setting standards, developing work schedules, training employees, and exercising necessary controls to insure high-quality performance. A guard supervisor is one of these important people.

The Supervisor

A supervisor, the person in the middle, is the key to success. The greater the ability to carry out your responsibilities, the more efficiently the company operates. In addition to job skills, a modern supervisor must be familiar with up-to-date personnel practices and the legal requirements that affect the jobs of the personnel. He or she must also know how to deal with the day-to-day problems of a security department. One of the most important ways a supervisor can get the best results from the people is to let them know they have his or her full support. The supervisor can reinforce this knowledge by giving employees the necessary authority to do their jobs and seeing that this authority is respected. Step in to share responsibilities and, if things go wrong, help clear up the problem without condemnation. As happens on occasion, a good worker may run into controversy. When this occurs, it is comforting to know that the boss will stand by. This does not mean insisting someone is right when clearly he or she is not, but rather accepting some of the responsibility for a poor plan and helping someone to carry the blame. All these steps demonstrate a supervisor's support of the crew, and people support a leader who supports them.

Another important trait of a good supervisor is willingness to accept suggestions from the workers. In fact, encourage such comments. It is natural for people to offer suggestions. If, as a supervisor, you make it clear that you are not interested in such input, you cut off an important flow of communication between supervisor and staff. Once the employees realize their supervisor is not interested in their ideas, maybe even resent him or her, the supervisor will not take the time to devise a better system of doing things. Making the mistake of ignoring the thoughts and ideas of others hinders working relationships within the company. One person cannot think of everything. Those employees most knowledgeable in a specific area could be of assistance and should not be overlooked. The people who handle the day-to-day situations are in the best position to suggest changes in the organization's policies and operations. The best way to get more suggestions from the staff is to simply ask for them. Whenever a problem arises, the supervisor should discuss the situation with the people involved to further encourage input. By offering them the chance to do some of the thinking, the manager is openly demonstrating interest in their ideas. Most employees would love to do some brainwork.

Keep Communications Open

While not every idea submitted is a workable one, no suggestion deserves the 15-second brush-off. The supervisor appreciates all suggestions, regardless of caliber. Every idea merits consideration. The employee should be thanked for the time and interest and encouraged to keep trying, on the premise that the next idea could be a winner.

Leadership

The guard supervisor sets the example of professional quality for the staff. The subordinates are a mirror of the management. If a guard appears sloppy, unshaven, in need of a haircut and a shoeshine, the supervisor probably needs to take a good look at his or her own appearance. If a guard speaks sharply to the client's customers or employees, it may be a reflection of the person who is in charge. Perhaps the supervisor should pay careful attention to his or her own manner. The guard force reflects the company's image and the supervisor should ensure that the proper appearance is being projected.

Techniques for Setting the Example

1. Be physically fit, well groomed, and correctly dressed.
2. Master your emotions. Erratic behavior, ranging from anger to depression, is ineffective.

3. Maintain an optimistic outlook. Excel in difficult situations by learning to capitalize on your own capabilities.
4. Conduct yourself so that your own personal habits are not open to censure.
5. Exercise initiative and promote the spirit of initiative in your subordinates.
6. Be loyal to those with whom you work and those who work with you. Loyalty is a two-way street.
7. Avoid playing favorites.
8. Be morally courageous. Establish principles and stand by them.
9. Share hardships with your people to demonstrate your willingness to assume your share of the difficulties.

The Professional Security Supervisor

Today's security work requires a person with an exceptionally high degree of skill, training, and information. The person who demonstrates these qualities is recognized by others as a professional. Professionals exude the confidence and skill to enable the rest of the community to have faith in their ability to act in the public's interest. The security officer who meets these standards is a professional in the fullest meaning of the word and respected as such.

Education

By virtue of having completed certain education programs and having passed official examinations, professional people are recognized as possessing distinctive kinds and degrees of knowledge and skill. These are types of knowledge and skill in which the average citizen feels different and therefore turns to professionally trained people for help in the form of advice or other services.

Standards of Performance

Professional people are expected to be dedicated to high ideals. They are assumed to operate under a superior code of ethics. To this end, the professional organizations establish standards of ethical performance as well as standards of competence. Professional people take pride in these standards and expect member of their profession to meet them. Because of the continuous flow of social and economic changes in our world, training and the improvement of standards is a continuing problem for every security authority. The understanding of fundamental principles distinguishes the competent professional person from the mere technician. This is as true in security work as it is in medicine, law, and other professional fields. A security supervisor is personally judged by the general public. The client, as well, looks on him or her as the contact with the organization and measures the company by the supervisor. The security personnel also look to the supervisor to set an example. As in other areas, therefore, the leader must maintain a professional code of ethics. Professionalism is vital to any position of authority, and this is no less true for the security supervisor.

Train Personnel Effectively

The responsibilities of a guard supervisor include providing sound, effective training to the staff. An understanding of every operational requirement of the security officers gives the supervisor more awareness of the difficult facets of their work, areas where he or she may be able to offer assistance when and where it is needed. The supervisor can facilitate this aspect of the job by determining the duties of each security officer and establishing a master training plan to teach new employees their respective tasks. This plan also serves as refresher training for personnel who have been on the force for a long period of time.

Treat Employees Courteously

Mutual respect is essential to an efficient working relationship. Employees should not be treated as natural enemies or made to feel inferior. The supervisor must in turn report to higher level bosses and treat the staff in the same courteous manner expected from his or her superiors. Consideration is a key word. A demand should be accompanied by an explanation. Advance notice of any situations that might alter an employee's plans, such as overtime, post reassignments, or special orders, is a simple courtesy that will prevent unnecessary ill will. Making reprimands or criticisms private, away from the watchful eyes of one's peers, precludes humiliation of a staff member.

Develop Loyalty

An effective supervisor is loyal to the employees, the company, and the client. Constant criticism of the company and management is destructive to employee morale. While criticism is a necessary and unavoidable part of any activity, it must be offered constructively to resolve a problem, improve a system, or lower costs, or for other worthwhile purposes. Criticism for the sake of criticism has no worth and no place in business. A responsible supervisor does not indulge in or pass on gossip or rumors about other employees. A supervisor who is loyal to the personnel is usually repaid with loyalty from the unit.

When Criticism Is Necessary

"To err is mortal; to forgive, divine." The supervisor sits on the semicolon of this statement. Not only must you recognize errors, see that they are corrected, and discourage further mistakes, they are also expected to maintain composure while doing so. Most people resent being told that they have done something wrong, especially if the person criticizing is tactless and forceful. Harsh criticism can hurt a person's morale, damage the ego, and create lasting antagonisms. When faced with the job of criticizing an employee, the supervisor should try to follow these seven simple rules:

1. *Be sure of the facts.* Ask the right people the right questions, and do so objectively. Only when sufficiently satisfied that an error has been made should the supervisor call in the employee. If being criticized for something one did can cause resentment, being criticized for something one did not do really breeds antagonism.
2. If the mistake is important and upsetting; *cool off before talking to the employee.* When angry, a person is more likely to say something personal. Avoid personal criticism, address comments to correcting the mistake, not to punishing the security officer.
3. *Discuss the situation in private.* Nothing embarrasses a person more than being reprimanded before his or her peers or worse yet, subordinates. Take time to move away from inquisitive eyes and ears. The criticism will be better and lasting resentment may be avoided.
4. *Ask questions first—do not accuse.* This fits in neatly with the "Be sure of the facts" rule. Do not come into the discussion with the mind made up. Ask for the employee's side of the story. Everyone appreciates being heard, especially when a mistake has been made.
5. *Before you criticize*, let your worker know that you appreciate some of the good work produced.

Medicine is easier to swallow if you mix it with sugar.
6. When the situation dictates that an oral reprimand is given, *explain to the employee the reasoning behind such actions.* An employee deserves to know why there is criticism and how this will affect the future. For example, if a security officer is being criticized for the first tardiness, the officer should not be made to feel that the job is in jeopardy. However, if the reprimand is for continual absences or lateness and the job is on the line, the employee should know this as well.
7. If at all possible, *leave a good impression* with the employee at the end of the discussion. This does not mean you should make light of mistakes. Rather, it removes some of the tension and embarrassment if, when the employee returns to work, you pat the person on the back or say something like, "At least we know you're human."

These seven rules help a supervisor to deal tactfully with the situation when criticism is needed. Remember that the goal of criticism is to leave the person with the feeling of having been helped.

Personnel Counseling

Every supervisor must be prepared to discuss an employee's personal problems when asked to do so, but only to the extent that the individual desires and within limits carefully set by the supervisor. The biggest problem for the manager, in a counseling situation, is to steer a proper course of giving practical and constructive advice and staying clear of amateur psychiatry in particular. When an employee seeks personal counseling, the supervisor should consider these guidelines:

1. *Watch your general attitude.* Always show a continuing sincere interest in staff members as individuals with homes and families and not simply as subordinates. If there is sickness at home, remember to ask about progress. If someone's daughter is graduating from high school, show some interest in that also.
2. *Be available.* If someone indicates a desire to talk about a matter that has come up, answer by saying that, if it is important to the employee, you will be glad to take whatever time is necessary. The employee will probably agree to have the interview after hours, when nobody else is around. In any case, it is obvious that you should make it possible to have the employee talk in private. Hold the meeting as soon as possible after the request.

3. *The supervisor must initiate meetings.* This can occur, for example, when a usually competent and reliable person shows a marked falling-off in interest or quality of work or is unusually tardy or frequently absent—all indicating some personal situation is interfering with efficiency. Do not keep putting the meeting off—it will never be any easier than at the present moment.

4. *Be as prepared as possible.* If you have initiated the meeting, be sure of your facts, with specific examples of the kinds of behavior that gives you concern. If the employee has asked for the meeting, refresh your memory about any personal situations that may previously have come to light about the employee.

5. *Put the employee at ease.* The supervisor already achieves part of this by arranging for a private meeting. Maybe a cup of coffee or a soft drink is indicated.

6. *Be a good listener.* Whether the problem is real or imagined, give the employee a chance to explain the situation without interruption.

7. *Be wary of advice on personal matters.* On emotional and personal problems, your best contribution is to serve as a sounding board. The supervisor can, of course, give advice on any company policy that may be involved, avenues of financial assistance available through the company, and other matters where you are sure of your ground. But with a personal problem, the main function as a counselor should be to help the individual recognize what the problem is and explore possible alternate solutions, with final decisions left to the individual. Always remember, when dealing with personal and emotional problems, the supervisor rarely is in possession of enough facts to take the responsibility for recommending specific solutions.

8. *Avoid assuming the psychiatrist's function.* If there is reason to believe that the employee has more than the normal kinds of anxiety, suggest professional counsel.

Expanded Security Officer Training Program

Some of the larger guard agencies have developed training institutes to actually train in-house guard forces as well as contract guards for small agencies. The guards can be trained at the site of operation where the in-house force is operating, or the guards can travel to the institute where the training is given away from their regular facility. The following is a break down of a training program.

Section I. General

Training and qualification of security officers is necessary to ensure a thorough knowledge and understanding as to exactly what is expected of each officer. The legal responsibilities and limitations involved in the execution of their duties must be made clear to those employed to protect persons and property of private and public industry. Special emphasis must be placed on the skills necessary to perform this responsibility of protection.

Section II. Objectives

1. To provide the student with a basic understanding of the responsibilities of a security officer.
2. To teach the student those basic skills that will enable that individual to attain an acceptable level of performance.
3. To identify to the student the restrictions placed on a security officer while serving, in a limited capacity, to protect persons and property.
4. To administer to the student a written examination, sampling the material presented during the program and designed to measure the retention of knowledge of basic skills with 70% accuracy.

Section III. Specific Subject Areas and Hours

SUBJECT	HOURS
Ethics and professionalism	1
Legal authority of a security officer	1
Human relations	1
Public relations	$\frac{1}{2}$
Patrol procedures	2
Report writing	1
Field note taking	$\frac{1}{2}$
Ingress and egress control	$\frac{1}{2}$
Emergency medical assistance	2
Firefighting	1
Self defense/security baton	$2\frac{1}{2}$
Firearms safety and range firing	10
Law—criminal and civil	4
Review, final exam and critique	1
Total	28

Section IV. Synopsis

- *Ethics and professionalism* (1 hour). Professional behavior and attitudes, security officer code of ethics, use and care of clothing and equipment
- *Legal authority of a security officer* (1 hour). Legal rules, practices, procedures, and including arrests, self-incrimination, and the concept of deadly force

- *Human relations* (1 hour). Security officers' relationship with client, employees, and visitors to the site
- *Public relations* ($\frac{1}{2}$ hour). Effects of adverse publicity, a policy of responding to press and public
- *Patrol procedures* (2 hours). Characteristics and advantages of the patrol, the concepts of observation and knowledge, the various hazards to life and property, and the various methods and techniques of patrolling
- *Report writing and field note taking* ($1\frac{1}{2}$ hours). The Value of accurate field notes and client/company reports: techniques and methods, with practical application in filling out reports
- *Ingress and egress control* ($\frac{1}{2}$ hour). Personnel, vehicle, and package control while entering and exiting facility, physical security measures
- *Emergency medical assistance* (2 hours). Treatment for shock, respiratory arrest, severe bleeding, open wounds
- *Firefighting* (1 hour). The security officers' responsibilities in preventing and fighting fires, classes of fire and types of extinguishers
- *Self defense/security baton* ($2\frac{1}{2}$ hours). Methods of defending oneself, either armed or unarmed, demonstration and practical application in defensive holds, throws, and come-along holds
- *Firearms safety and range firing* (10 hours). Weapons familiarization, weapons safety and revolver range firing, qualification score for weapon
- *Review, written final examination, and critique* (1 hour). Review of material, final examination, and critique of examination

Conclusion

Over the last fifty years, the security guard industry has grown at a rapid rate, and as we move into the 21st century, it appears that this growth will continue at this astronomical pace. In the early 1990s, as many as 10,000 security firms were in the United States. The rapid growth is duplicated in Canada, Europe, the New East, and the Far East. The guard industry has found its place in the sun. What once was a lower bottom of the scale type of employment is now a good-paying, desirable position that offers a fine future. Many universities in the United States offer a degree in Criminal Justice, and many that graduate find their way into management in the security guard business. As we move further into the 21st century, we find the requirements for the security guard increasing in many areas. Local, state, and federal police departments are reaching out to the security industry to take over many of the responsibilities that unarmed security officers can handle. In the decade of the 1990s, the security industry was involved in building prisons and maintaining the entire facility, including feeding, clothing, and protecting. Security companies work with U.S. Immigration and Naturalization supplying the holding areas of transients with visas at airports and ship ports. Some are involved in setting up training academies for nuclear programs for the United States government. This industry now offers our society a diversified activity that does not end with but actually starts with the security guard.

Chapter 18

Management of Bomb Incidents*

JOHN J. FAY

In every operation there is an above the line and a below the line. Above a line is what you do by the book. Below the line is how you do the job.

—John Le Carré

The organization's security leader is generally considered to be a main player in the management of bomb incidents. Even in the absence of a history of threats and with no reason to believe the organization has become a target, the security leader must anticipate the possibility and have a program in place.

A balanced program for the management of bomb incidents includes proactive steps, for example:

- Coordinate with law enforcement agencies to learn the methods and operating locales of groups known to use bombs. Determine if the organization is a potential target.
- Stay current with new developments in bomb construction and concealment.
- Confer with security counterparts to learn the bomb incident experiences of other organizations. Set up information-sharing agreements.
- Liaise with bomb disposal experts, who can be helpful in conducting training programs for bomb incident respondents, for employees generally, and for certain employees whose duties would bring them into contact with mail bombs.
- Control suspect packages entering the workplace. Control can include examining packages at an off-

site location that poses minimum danger in the event of an explosion; using bomb detection equipment; and training the package examiners in the visual techniques for spotting the indicators of package bombs.
- Maintain a positive means of identifying and channeling people who enter and move within the workplace.
- Educate employees to look for and report strangers in the workplace, and educate employees and visitors alike to not leave personal items, such as briefcases and gym bags, unattended in public areas of the facility.
- Conduct periodic inspections of the workplace to identify areas where a bomb could be planted with a minimal chance of detection and simultaneously cause major property damage or personal injuries (e.g., the facility's power plant, flammable storage rooms, telephone switching center, computer room, and executive offices).
- Educate employees generally, and security and maintenance personnel specifically, to be alert for suspicious persons and activities.
- Require security officers to make random checks of public areas during each tour of duty to look for unauthorized persons who may be hiding in or reconnoitering the facility.
- Ensure physical protection of key assets against bomb damage. Fire-resistant safes and vaults can protect sensitive documents, cash, small valuables, magnetic media, and similar materials.
- Educate fire wardens and other bomb incident respondents to look for and report unusual activities that might signal the early stage of a bombing attempt.

*Fay, *Contemporary Security Management,* pp. 271–286, Butterworth Heinemann, 2002

Planning

Three steps constitute a program to manage bomb incidents: (1) develop the plan, (2) prepare implementing procedures, and (3) train the persons responsible for carrying out the plan. The security leader, who is logically the principal developer of the plan, will identify the following:

- Purpose and objectives
- Major preventive, anticipatory, and response functions
- Responsibilities assigned to particular positions
- Interfaces with outside response agencies, such as police and fire departments
- Equipment required
- An approach for bringing various elements of the plan together to form a synchronous whole

The plan provides an overall framework that allows a variety of response options at the outset and during the course of the incident. Because the plan commits to action several units and persons that operate outside the security group, development of the plan requires the security leader to work through and coordinate with all of the interested inside parties (e.g., the security officer force, building maintenance workers, and fire wardens). If the organization is a tenant, the landlord or building management office will be involved in plan development and execution. Outside parties could include an explosives detection team, a bomb disposal team, fire control units, ambulance services, and postincident investigative units.

Developing a plan is more than just putting pen to paper. The plan is the product of a logical planning process. A model that works well in effectuating the process has the following five sequential steps or phases that occur in a cycle:

1. Decide a general strategy.
2. Prepare a plan that incorporates actions consistent with strategy.
3. Implement the plan.
4. Test the plan.
5. Evaluate results.

Decide the Strategy

A strategy considers the organization's exposure and vulnerability to a bomb attack. The security leader gets the answers to these questions:

- Is the organization a target of a militant adversary?

- Is the organization partnered in any way with an organization or government that is targeted? Partnering includes providing products, materials, technical assistance, and technical training, or operating plants or facilities.
- Has the organization or its leaders contributed money to, provided support for, or been politically affiliated with any charity, aid program, cultural exchange, or educational program that could in any way be construed as affiliated with a terrorist target?
- Does the organization support political or social causes that would make it a likely target for radical "hate" groups?
- Has the organization refused to do business with, withdrawn from, or failed to successfully negotiate business contracts with companies, organizations, or governments within the last two years that are affiliated with current terrorists?
- Does the organization manufacture or produce military arms or equipment?
- Have any of the organization's leaders made public statements, been quoted or interviewed, or written papers on terrorist activity or topics?

The answers to these questions will lead to the following further questions:

- Is the organization a target?
- What is the probability of an attack?
- Who are the likely attackers?
- What are the motives and capabilities of the attackers?
- What will the form and delivery method of the attack be?
- Is the organization vulnerable to an attack?
- What are the organization's specific areas of vulnerability?

Now coming into play is the experience of the security leader and his or her ability to tap into valuable information sources: reports of government intelligence and law enforcement agencies, the expertise of consultants, the experiences of security peers, and the research capabilities of professional associations serving the security industry. Also revealing are the findings of intraorganizational security inspections and surveys, current news media stories, and the application of old-fashioned common sense.

A given in the determination of a strategy is the recognition that a 100% level of security cannot be attained, no matter how much money and effort the organization may be willing to expend. The strategy will reflect a balance between cost and effect. When the homework has been done, the security leader will be able to calculate the increases and decreases of risk associated with proposed increases and decreases in security. For example, the installation of an electronic access control system has dollar costs that can be readily determined and placed into contrast with the reasonably estimated dollar costs of injury, death, property destruction, and loss of business opportunity that would result from a bomb explosion.

Prepare the Plan

Although bomb incident plans vary widely among organizations, they typically contain the following elements:

- A statement reflecting management's concern about bomb incidents, support of the plan, and authority to expend resources needed for plan execution
- The objectives of the plan. At least three objectives apply: (1) provide for the safety of people, (2) protect property against damage or destruction, and (3) restore the organization to normal operations
- A description of the threat and an assessment of risk
- Definitions of terms that are important to understanding the plan and assigning accountability
- A delineation of job positions and units, including external agencies, which have plan responsibilities (The delineation will reflect lines of communication and formal authority.)
- A description of the facility in terms of geography and demography, access routes, physical construction, entry points, utility interfaces, hours of operation, types of work activities, and numbers and types of persons within the facility
- A description of the dedicated resources, such as a security control center and public address system (This description could also mention evacuation routes and assembly areas.)
- An identification of procedures that carry out the plan; for example, procedures used by: maintenance personnel in shutting down utility systems, fire wardens in evacuating the facility, security officers in conducting bomb searches

Implement the Plan

Although it is not possible to predict and plan for every scenario, the security leader can posit a broad scenario that permits adjustment to meet specific needs. The plan will require implementing procedures that may or may not be a part of the plan. The procedures will, however, flow from the plan and provide detailed guidance to the responders. The security leader, for example, would develop procedures for security group responders, such as corporate investigators and security officers, and the property manager would develop procedures for maintenance employees. A full set of procedures may be an integral part of the plan or an appendix to it.

The procedures are in the nature of directives and leave no room for interpretation because the potential for severe consequences affords no allowance for mistakes in judgment.

Test the Plan

A plan can be tested partially or fully. A partial test might be a practical exercise on a certain floor or at a location. It may simulate a bomb threat call that precipitates a search. The responders would react in accordance with the procedures. For the security officers, reaction would consist of responding to the simulated call, making notifications, searching the premises, and communicating search findings. Practice of this type is a form of hands-on training; essential knowledge and skills are applied, and response equipment, such as the public address system and radio communications system, are put into use. Briefings and orientations for familiarizing the responders with the established procedures must precede the exercise, and a critique designed to improve future performance should be held immediately after the exercise. Learning acquired in this manner is powerful and lasting. Without it, plan execution will unquestionably suffer.

Evaluate Results

The exercise is assessed objectively, and a postaction report is prepared. The response procedures, as well as the plan itself, are modified in light of lessons learned through testing. Every test is an evaluation, but testing is only one element in an ongoing process; readiness and ability to respond are assessed continuously. For example, glitches may be uncovered in the course of daily activities and in the operation of equipment and as changes occur in bomb technology and the motives of those who use bombs to achieve their ends.

An intelligent and determined adversary is likely to find a chink in even the finest defensive armor. Without considering elaborate schemes, some of the readily available means to introduce a bomb into a workplace are on the person of an employee, by postal or commercial delivery service, and by motor vehicle into the facility's garage. Once inside, placement of a bomb is mainly a matter of the attacker's nerve and knowledge of the premises. The attacker might choose to place the bomb in a restroom, janitor's closet, stairwell, receiving platform, lobby, or elevator.

The security leader must ensure access control at entry points. Control at the perimeter is the first and most important line of defense in a proactive strategy. Although most bomb threats prove to be hoaxes or are resolved by disarming the bomb before detonation, the security leader cannot rule out the skilled attacker intent on inflicting maximum harm without warning. The best preventive course in such a case is to deny access.

A fertile imagination can easily postulate a comprehensive menu of bomb incidents, but for the sake of making a discussion of the topic less complicated, let's agree that bomb incidents consist of two broad categories—the threat and the execution of the threat.

The Bomb Threat[1]

An elementary observation about bomb threats is that they are rarely made in person by the bomber or an emissary, sometimes conveyed in a written format (such as a handwritten or typed letter, an e-mail message, or a document made of pasted clippings), and almost always made over the telephone. The bomber prefers the telephone, believing that it presents the lowest risk of identification. If the format of threat message has been written or typed, the document should be handled carefully, touched by as few persons as possible, and the envelope or any other accompanying materials preserved as evidence. Observing these simple precautions can be extremely helpful to a postincident investigation.

If one is to assume that a received threat is real, it logically follows that the person communicating the threat has knowledge that a bomb has been or will be placed and wants to minimize injuries by alerting persons at the target area. The tail end of that assumption is that the communicator's intent is to disrupt normal activity and cause inconvenience. One must also consider that a bomber's intent may be to maximally inflict injury, and if so, would not give advance warning.

In the American workplace, a high percentage (more than 95%) of threats are hoaxes, and within that number is a low percentage (less than 2%) involves placement of a simulated bomb. The other side of that reality is that there is no way to be absolutely sure that a threat is a hoax. Every threat demands close examination followed by an action decision heavily biased toward protection of life.

The opportunity of the security leader or other management person to make a close examination of a bomb threat received by telephone can be lost or severely diminished when the person receiving the call fails to capture relevant details. When a caller says, "There's a bomb in your building," panic can be a natural reaction. A good way to keep that from happening is to teach employees how to respond and provide them with a checklist that can be kept handy for use. Those employees most likely to receive bomb threat calls should be specially trained. In this group are switchboard operators, security officers, receptionists, and executive secretaries. The key teaching points are:

- Keep the caller talking for as long as possible.
- Ask the caller to repeat the message.
- Take notes. Write down the exact words used by the caller.
- Ask the caller to specifically state where the bomb is located and when it is set to detonate.
- Ask what part of the facility should be evacuated first.
- Ask for a description of the bomb. What does it look like? How is it packaged? What is it made of and how does it work?
- Ask why the bomb was placed and what group is responsible. Ask the caller if he or she was the person who placed the bomb. Ask where the caller is now.
- Tell the caller that the facility is occupied and that a detonation could result in death and serious injury to many innocent people.
- Listen closely to the caller's voice. Is the caller male or female? Calm or excited? Does he or she have an accent? Speech impediment?
- Pay attention to background noises that may give a clue about the caller's location. Traffic sounds, music, and voices heard in the background may be important.
- Keep the line open after the call has ended. It may be possible to trace the call.
- Notify the security control center immediately after the caller hangs up. Be ready to be interviewed and provide notes made during the call.

Evaluating a Bomb Threat Call

The first task of the security leader who has been informed of a bomb threat call is to evaluate it. Interviewing the person who received the call and examining notes taken during the call are the preliminaries to a judgment. The evaluation considers the details and characteristics of the call itself, prior bomb threat calls, and similar threats that have been made in the community or against counterpart organizations. Evaluation is essentially a process of judging the credibility of the threat; in other words, is the call a hoax or is it the real thing?

The security leader has to recognize that absolutes are never possible and that if an error in judgment is made, it has to be made on the side of caution. For example, in considering the details of a call, the security leader may note that the caller was described as a giggling young girl, hard rock music was heard in the background, and the girl's answer to the question about motive was that "you people are so uncool." In this case, the security leader may conclude that the call is probably a hoax. Another case can have entirely different indicators, such as an adult male who expresses anger against the organization and reveals knowledge of the workplace and bomb construction. This threat could be genuine. In still another case, the indicators may be few or unrevealing, a circumstance that requires the security leader to treat the threat as if it were real.

The security leader's evaluation is not always the only evaluation. The property manager of the facility may be asked by policy or plan to share in making a joint evaluation or make a separate evaluation. The same can apply to the operations manager, the chief executive officer, or the senior executive in the facility at the time the threat is received. Like too many cooks spoiling the broth, too many evaluators can spoil the evaluation and use up time that could be better spent making a response.

Response Options

An evaluation of a bomb threat call falls into one of three categories: (1) we think it is a hoax, (2) we think it might be real, and (3) we don't know. The response taken is influenced by the category. Other influences may also apply. For example, a regulatory standard of a safety-sensitive industry may require immediate and full evacuation irrespective of how management views the threat, or a collective bargaining agreement could require that employees be informed of the receipt of a bomb threat so that those who wish to leave may do so. Another influence may be management's worry about liability arising from injuries sustained by employees as they evacuate the facility.

Three options proceed from a judgment of the threat:

1. *Search without evacuating.* This option is appropriate when the threat is thought to be a hoax. This option also allows upgrading to evacuation when, for example, a suspected bomb is found or when a subsequent, determinative threat call is received.
2. *Evacuate partially or fully and then search.* This option is appropriate when the threat might be real. The caller may have said the bomb is located in a particular area, in which case that area and its surrounding areas would be evacuated and then searched. The caller may have described multiple bomb locations or a bomb that is devastating, in which case the entire facility would be evacuated and then searched.
3. *Fully evacuate and not search.* This option is appropriate when the threat might be real, to a higher degree of concern. The caller may have revealed a knowledge of bomb construction or stated that he or she represents a militant group that opposes the organization. Prior acts may be relevant, such as attempted arson or sabotage. This option reflects the management's belief that it is better to get out of the facility and wait for the detonation to occur.

A habit of automatic evacuation seems to have developed during the relatively short history of bomb threats in the American workplace. Experience has shown that this practice is not good for several reasons. First is the matter of safety. Even the most orderly evacuation can produce injuries from tripping and falling. Second is the risk of moving large numbers of people along designated exit routes or into an assembly area where a bomb might be planted for the purpose of causing mass casualties. Evacuation is also disruptive to work. Although the protection of life certainly outweighs any economic loss, repeated threats and evacuations would soon escalate productivity losses to an unacceptable level.

When a Suspect Bomb Is Found

The size and location of a suspect bomb influences the extent of evacuation. For example, a suspect bomb about the size of a cigarette pack that is found in a nonsafety-sensitive area might not require a total evacuation. As a general rule, at least 300 feet of lateral area around a suspect bomb should be cleared of all nonessential response personnel. The vertical areas above and below a suspect bomb should also be cleared. If a suspect bomb is found on a floor of a multistory building, the floor involved plus the floors immediately above and below it should be cleared.

Total evacuation is mandatory when a discovered bomb is judged capable of inflicting injury. In the absence of that judgment, certain employees, such as security officers and maintenance employees, may remain to perform essential life-protecting and shut-down tasks.

How to Search

Bomb searching is usually conducted by persons familiar with the workplace and almost never by police officers. Public safety policy often discourages the participation of police officers in bomb searches on private property, unless probable cause exists to believe that a bomb is in fact present. Probable cause can be established by the details of the bomb threat call or by the discovery of a suspect bomb. With a belief established, the police are more likely to want to be actively involved in making or directing the search. Although employees at the workplace have a greater familiarity with the possible places of bomb concealment, officers trained in bomb disposal know how to avoid booby traps and mistakes that can lead to detonation.

The following points about searching need to be emphasized:

- *The search has to be thorough.* The searchers should be people familiar with the physical environment (e.g., security officers, maintenance workers, and other employees who know the nooks and crannies).
- *The searchers have to be careful.* They should be trained in how to conduct a search, particularly in respect to spotting booby traps.
- *Anything of a suspicious nature has to be approached with great caution.* The searcher making the discovery should report the finding so that bomb disposal technicians can be summoned.

Thoroughness is affected by the size and configuration of the workplace to be searched. It is fair to say that making a thorough search is not easy in any working environment. Even small environments uncomplicated by multiple workstations, equipment, and labor-intensive activities present problems. Large and complex environments, such as manufacturing plants and high-rise office buildings, are searchable on a genuinely thorough basis only with substantial expenditure of effort and time. A 20-story office building, for example, might require 48 hours of uninterrupted looking with a 20-person team before it can be said with certainty that every conceivable hiding place has been examined.

Conducting a comprehensive search in a large and complex environment is seldom possible because time will not allow looking into false ceilings, examining every file cabinet, and removing panels from equipment. Neither is it acceptable to disrupt or shut down work operations for two full working days while a search is in progress. A practical solution might be to prioritize—as part of the planning process—those places that should and can be thoroughly searched within the time available for searching. What this means is that searching with thoroughness remains firm but that selectivity is introduced with respect to what should be searched.

In deciding what to search, two factors are pertinent: probability and criticality. How probable is it that a bomber would be able to penetrate the organization's security defenses? If the probability is high, how probable is it that a bomb or bombs would be placed in some areas as opposed to others? An evaluation of probability might lead to a search priority that concentrates on areas that are outside the umbrella of high security control, such as lobbies, garages, and other areas easily accessible to the public. Criticality considers a priority for searching in areas where the greatest damage can be done to the organization's most valuable assets.

Probability and criticality need to be balanced. For example, it may not be sensible to set a high priority on searching the computer center when the probability is low that a bomb could be brought into the computer center without detection. On the other hand, the computer center may demand a search because of its criticality to business operations.

Prioritizing a search can be assisted by the use of a card system. Each area to be searched is represented by a card that names and describes the location. The cards are coded according to priority and are handed out to search team members at the briefing that precedes the start of a search. At the end of the search, checkmarks or signatures on the cards provide a quick reference for ensuring that no areas were overlooked.

Nonevacuation Search Method

As the name suggests, this search method is used when a decision has been made not to evacuate. It is performed in a "walk-through," but not cursory, manner. The searchers are usually security officers and maintenance workers who work alone. They move in a steady, unhurried pace looking for objects that seem out of place. Employees engaged in normal work activity can be a source of information in judging if an object is really suspicious. In areas where few or no employees are present, the searcher should give close attention to containers, closets, and places that offer concealment.

Postevacutation Search Method

This method is used when employees are absent, such as after an evacuation or during nonworking hours. The searchers examine workstations, offices, conference rooms, shelves, wastebaskets, storage bins, and the like. Even though searchers can move faster when employees are not in the way, any time gained is expended by searching with greater intensity. Also, if the search is conducted after hours, the search team will not be at full force because the day workers who would normally assist in the search are off duty.

Discovery of a Suspicious Object

The rule to not touch a suspicious object has to be emphasized. On the other hand, searchers cannot thoroughly search without a certain amount of touching, such as to open doors and drawers and poke into wastebaskets. But at the instant a suspicious object is seen, all touching should stop. The searcher alerts people nearby, instructs them to leave, and notifies the search team leader. Actions that follow include:

- Questioning employees who may be able to account for the presence of the suspicious object.
- Ordering a partial or full evacuation.
- Notifying the bomb disposal team.
- Notifying the fire department.
- Readying first-aid supplies and calling for standby medical personnel and equipment.
- Asking the police to assume command of the situation.

The bomb disposal team leader or the fire officer in charge may ask for further information about the location of the suspect device relative to stored fuels, chemicals, flammables, power plant, and fire exits. Because of the possibility that more than one bomb has been planted, orders may be made for the search team to continue examining areas that have not yet been searched.

Bomb Types

Bombs can be constructed in many different ways and easily disguised. They can be placed in bags, cases, or everyday containers, and large bombs can be carried inside motor vehicles. Bombs are often classified by type: high explosive, vehicle, incendiary, and postal. All can be initiated by the use of timing devices, command detonation, disturbance (pull, push, and trip), or pressure pad.

Vehicle and postal bombs can be either high-explosive or incendiary, and all can be hand-carried.

High-Explosive Bombs

These bombs can kill or injure by blast or flying debris, particularly glass shards. Bombs small enough to be hidden in a hand-carried bag can easily cause a powerful and widespread killing and damaging effect. Bombs of this type are typically made with commercial or military explosives in blocks or sticks. Some include an electric detonator, timer, or power source and are contained in some way with the explosive material.

The best protection against a high-explosive bomb is to prevent it from being brought on or close to the property. The preventive measures include stringent access control, inspection of packages, and the use of explosives-detecting devices, supplemented with rules that prohibit parking immediately adjacent to the property and leaving packages, parcels, and bags unattended. Hiding places in areas accessible to the public should also be eliminated and maximum use made of technical surveillance equipment, such as closed-circuit television and intrusion detection sensors. An excellent preventive measure is the collective watchfulness of employees.

Vehicle Bombs

A motor vehicle of any type can be the means for delivering a bomb to the target. The protective measures include controlling access to parking areas, searching vehicles at entry points, and patrolling the parking areas. An excellent deterrent is the appearance (and existence) of high security in adjacent parking areas.

Incendiary Bombs

The purpose of these bombs is to cause fire. They can be small, difficult to spot, and innocuous looking. Once inside the targeted premises, a bomber can assemble the components of an incendiary bomb and detonate it immediately or rig it with a timer as simple as a burning book of matches. Incendiary bombs of the Molotov Cocktail type are designed to be thrown.

Letter and Parcel Bombs

These bombs, which are intended to kill or injure, are usually designed to detonate on opening. They are often delivered by the postal service or a commercial delivery service. The following indicators can signal a letter bomb:

- Foreign mail, airmail, or special delivery markings
- Restrictive markings such as "Confidential" and "Personal"
- Nonmetered postage
- Too many stamps
- Handwritten or poorly typed address
- Incorrect title
- Title but no name
- Misspellings
- Oily stains or discoloration
- A smell like marzipan or machine oil
- No return address
- Excessive weight
- Heavier in some places than others
- Rigid envelope
- Lopsided or uneven envelope
- The outer wrapping is soft but the contents hard
- Protruding wires or tinfoil
- Excessive wrapping materials such as masking tape and string

When a bomb is suspected, the action steps are:

- Alert nearby persons and tell them to leave the area.
- Place the item in a holding or carrying container and take it to the isolation area.
- Without touching the item, examine the visible sides and record in notes the information appearing on it (e.g., name and address of addressee and sender, postmark, cancellation date, post office codes, types of stamps, and any other markings). Describe any peculiarities (e.g., oil stains and overwrapping).
- Make notifications required by procedures.

Upon receiving notification, the security leader follows the established procedures, which may include:

- Dispatch a security officer to the isolation area to take photographs of the item.
- Obtain the notes of the individual who discovered the item.
- Contact the addressee and inquire:
  Is the addressee familiar with the sender?
  Is the addressee expecting correspondence from the sender? If so, what would be the contents of the item and its approximate size?
  If the sender is unknown, is the addressee expecting any other correspondence from the place of origin of the suspect item?
  Is the addressee aware of any friends, relatives, service personnel, or business acquaintances currently on vacation or on business trips in the place of origin?
  Has the addressee purchased or ordered anything from anybody in the place of origin?
- If suspicion cannot be removed, notify the local police department's bomb squad.
- Notify senior management.
- Stand by to offer assistance to the bomb squad.

The Aftermath

The response actions that immediately follow the explosion of a bomb are often delineated in plans and procedures related to building evacuation, emergency medical services, and rescue operations. All of these functions involve participation by the security leader, and when the functions have been discharged, one other important function remains— that is, protection of the scene in order to facilitate a thorough investigation. The objective is to not disturb evidence by demarcating the scene, establishing a temporary perimeter, and controlling access. A bomb scene, despite massive destruction, can yield valuable clues to the identity of the person or persons responsible. A search begins with the premise that everything at the scene at the instant of explosion is still there unless vaporized. The searchers have intertwining objectives: find everything that can be found and identify everything that has been found. The first search occurs at the scene,

Figure 18-1. Photo of bomb destruction at Oklahoma City Federal Building. The bombing of a federal building in Oklahoma City delivered a tragic reminder to Americans of the cruelty of terrorists.

Figure 18-2. A photo of Pan Am 103 bombing. The Pan Am 103 bombing served as a worldwide wakeup call to the threat of terrorism.

whereas the second occurs primarily in forensic laboratories. When the two objectives are achieved, conclusions can be reached about what happened and who made it happen.

A bomb incident is often managed from a single point and conducted in two dimensions: one is the examination of the scene and the other is a general investigation that seeks to identify and take custody of the responsible parties. In major incidents, overall management is by the Federal Bureau of Investigation (FBI); the search is conducted by agents of the Bureau of Alcohol, Tobacco, and Firearms (ATF);

Figure 18-3. Security and police organizations often use trained dogs to search for bombs.

Figure 18-4. Letter bombs are a threat that business organizations must take seriously.

and general investigative work is handled by FBI agents.

Trained specialists operating from a single plan carry out the search. A command post and an evidence collection center are often set up nearby. Many tasks are performed simultaneously: photographing, fingerprint processing, sifting debris, and protecting and tagging physical evidence. Supervisors at the command post oversee the search and coordinate the efforts of the many specialists involved.

Figure 18-5. A photo of bombed Khobar Towers building. A terrorist attack on a peacekeeping force in Dhahran, Saudi Arabia, left 19 dead and hundreds injured.

Safety is a concern. Searchers recognize the possibility of a secondary bomb, a "jammed" bomb, or live explosives in the debris. They also are aware that walls, ceilings, and floors can collapse on them as they work. Bomb remains are examined to identify bomb components such as switches, batteries, blasting caps, tape, wire, timing mechanisms, fabrication techniques, unconsumed explosives, and overall construction of the bomb. Instrumental examination is made of explosives and explosive residues, and bomb components are examined microscopically for tool marks. Timing mechanisms can sometimes be identified regarding type, manufacturer, and model, and determinations are sometimes possible about the time displayed by the mechanism when the explosive detonated and about the relative length of time the mechanism was functioning before the explosion.

Reference

1. John J. Fay. *Model Security Policies, Plans, and Procedures* (Boston: Butterworth–Heinemann, 1999), pp. 163–166.

Chapter 19
Homeland Security

LAWRENCE J. FENNELLY

The White House
President George W. Bush
For Immediate Release
Office of the Secretary
March 12, 2002

Gov. Ridge Announces Homeland Security Advisory System

The Homeland Security Advisory System will provide a comprehensive and effective means to disseminate information regarding the risk of terrorist attacks to Federal, State, and local authorities and to the American people.

As part of a series of initiatives to improve coordination and communication among all levels of government and the American public in the right against terrorism, President Bush signed Homeland Security Presidential Directive 3, creating the Homeland Security Advisory System (HSAS). The advisory system will be the foundation for building a comprehensive and effective structure for the dissemination of information regarding the risk of terrorist attacks to all levels of government and the American people.

The Attorney General will be responsible for developing, implementing, and managing the system. In conjunction with the development of this new system, the Attorney General will open a 45-day comment period in order to seek the views of officials at all levels of government, law enforcement, and the American public. Ninety days after the conclusion of the comment period, the Attorney General, in coordination with the Director of the Office of Homeland Security, will present a final Homeland Security Advisory System to the President for approval. The Homeland Security Advisory System will provide the following:

National Framework for Federal, State, and Local Governments, Private Industry and the Public

There are many federal alert systems in our country—each tailored and unique to different sectors of our society: transportation, defense, agriculture, and weather, for example. These alert systems fill vital and specific requirements for a variety of situations in both the commercial and government sectors. The Homeland Security Advisory System will provide a national framework for these systems, allowing government officials and citizens to communicate the nature and degree of terrorist threats. This advisory system characterizes appropriate levels of vigilance, preparedness, and readiness in a series of graduated Threat Conditions. The Protective Measures that correspond to each Threat Condition will help the government and citizens decide what action they take to help counter and respond to terrorist activity. Based on the threat level, Federal agencies will implement appropriate Protective Measures. States and localities will be encouraged to adopt compatible systems.

Factors for Assignment of Threat Conditions

The Homeland Security Advisory System will provide a framework for the Attorney General, in consultation with the Director of the Office of Homeland Security, to assign Threat Conditions, which can apply nationally, regionally, by sector or to a potential target. Cabinet Secretaries and other members of the Homeland Security Council will be consulted as appropriate. A variety of factors may be used to assess the threat. Among these:

- Is the threat credible?
- Is the threat corroborated?
- Is the threat specific or imminent?
- How grave is the threat?

Unified System for Public Announcements

Public announcements of threat advisories and alerts help deter terrorist activity, notify law enforcement and State and local government officials of threats, inform the public about government preparations, and provide them with the information necessary to respond to the threat. State and local officials will be informed in advance of national threat advisories when possible. The Attorney General will help develop a system for conveying relevant information to Federal, State, and local officials and the private sector expeditiously. Heightened Threat Conditions can be declared for the entire nation, or for a specific geographic area, functional or industrial sector. Changes in assigned Threat Conditions will be made when necessary.

A Tool to Combat Terrorism

Threat Conditions characterize the risk of terrorist attack. Protective Measures are the steps that will be taken by government and the private sector to reduce vulnerabilities. The Homeland Security Advisory System (HSAS) establishes five Threat Conditions with associated suggestive protective measures:

1. Low Condition—Green
   Low risk of terrorist attacks. The following Protective Measures may be applied:
   - Refining and exercising preplanned Protective Measures
   - Ensuring personnel receive training on HSAS, departmental, or agency-specific Protective Measures
   - Regularly assessing facilities for vulnerabilities and taking measures to reduce them
2. Guarded Condition—Blue
   General risk of terrorist attack. In addition to the

previously outlined Protective Measures, the following may be applied:
   - Checking communications with designated emergency response or command locations
   - Reviewing and updating emergency response procedures
   - Providing the public with necessary information
3. Elevated Condition—Yellow
   Significant risk of terrorist attacks. In addition to the previously outlined Protective Measures, the following may be applied:
   - Increasing surveillance of critical locations
   - Coordinating emergency plans with nearby jurisdictions
   - Assessing further refinement of Protective Measures within the context of the current threat information
   - Implementing, as appropriate, contingency and emergency response plans
4. High Condition—Orange
   High risk of terrorist attacks. In addition to the previously outlined Protective Measures, the following may be applied:
   - Coordinating necessary security efforts with armed forces or law enforcement agencies
   - Taking additional precaution at public events
   - Preparing to work at an alternate site or with a dispersed workforce and restricting access to essential personnel only
5. Severe Condition—Red
   Severe risk of terrorist attacks. In addition to the previously outlined Protective Measures, the following may be applied:
   - Assigning emergency response personnel and prepositioning specially trained teams: monitoring, redirecting or constraining transportation systems
   - Closing public and government facilities
   - Increasing or redirecting personnel to address critical emergency needs

Homeland Security in 2002

What is Homeland Security, aside from briefly saying it is the overall protection of the United States? It is a coordinated effort to communicate with bureaucracies in Washington, DC, all forms of State and Governmental agencies like the CIA, FBI, Health and Human Services, FEMA, Aviation Security, ATF, DOT, Coast Guard, U.S. Customs, and INS, and reach into local areas as well.

Some of the objectives of Homeland Security include:

1. Tighten security and increase awareness
2. Training of first responders for police, fire, and medical personnel
3. Obtain the necessary equipment to deal with biological and chemical issues and terrorism
4. Hazmat training
5. To be proactive in our own defense

There is no established blueprint for this huge undertaking. Every security principal and concept will apply. The security sector also is involved as are local law enforcement agencies to develop and coordinate the implementation of a comprehensive national strategy to secure the United States from terrorist threats and attacks.[1]

Final Comments

Homeland Security is complicated. However, it will be a minimum of over 5 years to properly develop net results and to be somewhat effective. Critics will nit-pick. That is Washington politics. Dr. Phil Anderson, Homeland Security Program said, "Ridge has to be a bridge builder."

Whoever is in charge of the private sector will have to be involved. Any time you are proactive it is controversial and requires the involvement of many individuals as well as critics.

Reference

1. Securitymagazine.com, February 13, 2002. "Into the Fire by John Mesenbrienke." *Reference Homeland Security and Defense Newsletter*, January 30, 2002. See *www.aviationnow.com/hsd.*

Web Sites

www.homelandsecurity.org
www.globalsecurity.org
www.domesticpreparedness.com
www.CIAO.gov
www.tsa.gov
www.bookings.edu

Index